CIMA

Paper C01

Fundamentals of Management Accounting

Study Text

CIMA Certificate in Business Accounting

Published by: Kaplan Publishing UK

Unit 2 The Business Centre, Molly Millars Lane, Wokingham, Berkshire RG41 2QZ

Acknowledgements

We are grateful to the CIMA for permission to reproduce past examination questions. The answers to CIMA Exams have been prepared by Kaplan Publishing, except in the case of the CIMA November 2010 and subsequent CIMA Exam answers where the official CIMA answers have been reproduced.

Notice

The text in this material and any others made available by any Kaplan Group company does not amount to advice on a particular matter and should not be taken as such. No reliance should be placed on the content as the basis for any investment or other decision or in connection with any advice given to third parties. Please consult your appropriate professional adviser as necessary. Kaplan Publishing Limited and all other Kaplan group companies expressly disclaim all liability to any person in respect of any losses or other claims, whether direct, indirect, incidental, consequential or otherwise arising in relation to the use of such materials.

British Library Cataloguing in Publication Data

A catalogue record for this book is available from the British Library.

ISBN: 978-1-78415-108-9

Printed and bound in Great Britain.

Contents

Paper Introduction

How to Use the Materials

These official CIMA learning materials brought to you by CIMA Publishing and Kaplan Publishing have been carefully designed to make your learning experience as easy as possible and to give you the best chances of success in your *Fundamentals of Management Accounting* computer based assessment.

The product range contains a number of features to help you in the study process. They include:

- a detailed explanation of all syllabus areas;
- extensive 'practical' materials;
- generous question practice, together with full solutions;
- a computer based assessment preparation section, complete with computer based assessments standard questions and solutions.

This Study Text has been designed with the needs of home study and distance learning candidates in mind. Such students require very full coverage of the syllabus topics, and also the facility to undertake extensive question practice. However, the Study Text is also ideal for fully taught courses.

The main body of the text is divided into a number of chapters, each of which is organised on the following pattern:

- *Detailed learning outcomes*. This is expected after your studies of the chapter are complete. You should assimilate these before beginning detailed work on the chapter, so that you can appreciate where your studies are leading.
- *Step-by-step topic coverage*. This is the heart of each chapter, containing detailed explanatory text supported where appropriate by worked examples and exercises. You should work carefully through this section, ensuring that you understand the material being explained and can tackle the examples and exercises successfully. Remember that in many cases knowledge is cumulative: if you fail to digest earlier material thoroughly, you may struggle to understand later chapters.
- *Activities.* Some chapters contained illustrations and worked examples designed to stimulate discussion.

- *Question practice*. The test of how well you have learned the material is your ability to tackle exam standard questions. Make a serious attempt at producing your own answers, but at this stage do not be too concerned about attempting the questions under computer based assessment conditions. In particular, it is more important to absorb the material thoroughly by completing a full solution than to observe the time limits that would apply in the actual computer based assessment.
- *Solutions.* Avoid the temptation merely to 'audit' the solutions provided. It is an illusion to think that this provides the same benefits as you would gain from a serious attempt of your own.

Having worked through the chapters you are ready to begin your final preparations for the computer based assessment. The final section of this Study Text provides you with the guidance you need. It includes the following features:

- A brief guide to revision technique.
- A note on the format of the computer based assessment. You should know what to expect when you tackle the real computer based assessment and in particular the number of questions to attempt.
- Guidance on how to tackle the computer based assessment itself.
- Revision questions. These are of computer based assessment standard and should be tackled under computer based assessment conditions, especially as regards the time allocation.
- Solutions to the revision questions.
- Two mock computer based assessments.

You should plan to attempt the mock tests just before the date of the real computer based assessment. By this stage your revision should be complete and you should be able to attempt the mock computer based assessments within the time constraints of the real computer based assessment.

If you work conscientiously through this Official CIMA Study Text according to the guidelines above you will be giving yourself an excellent chance of success in your computer based assessment. Good luck with your studies!

Quality and accuracy are of the utmost importance to us so if you spot an error in any of our products, please send an email to mykaplanreporting@kaplan.com with full details, or follow the link to the feedback form in MyKaplan.

Our Quality Co-ordinator will work with our technical team to verify the error and take action to ensure it is corrected in future editions.

Icon Explanations

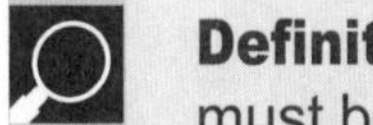

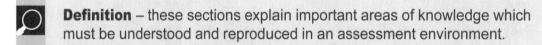

Definition – these sections explain important areas of knowledge which must be understood and reproduced in an assessment environment.

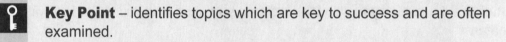

Key Point – identifies topics which are key to success and are often examined.

Supplementary reading – these sections will help to provide a deeper understanding of core areas. The supplementary reading is **NOT** optional reading. It is vital to provide you with the breadth of knowledge you will need to address the wide range of topics within your syllabus that could feature in an assessment question. **Reference to this text is vital when self studying**.

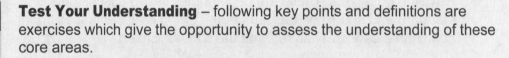

Test Your Understanding – following key points and definitions are exercises which give the opportunity to assess the understanding of these core areas.

Illustration – to help develop an understanding of particular topics. The illustrative examples are useful in preparing for the Test Your Understanding exercises.

Exclamation Mark – this symbol signifies a topic which can be more difficult to understand, when reviewing these areas care should be taken.

Study technique

Passing exams is partly a matter of intellectual ability, but however accomplished you are in that respect you can improve your chances significantly by the use of appropriate study and revision techniques. In this section we briefly outline some tips for effective study during the earlier stages of your approach to the computer based assessment. Later in the text we mention some techniques that you will find useful at the revision stage.

Planning

To begin with, formal planning is essential to get the best return from the time you spend studying. Estimate how much time in total you are going to need for each subject you are studying for the Certificate in Business Accounting. Remember that you need to allow time for revision as well as for initial study of the material. You may find it helpful to read "Pass First Time!" second edition by David R. Harris ISBN: 978-1-85617-798-6. This book will help you develop proven study and examination techniques. Chapter by chapter it covers the building blocks of successful learning and examination techniques. This is the ultimate guide to passing your CIMA exams, written by a CIMA examiner and shows you how to earn all the marks you deserve, and explains how to avoid the most common pitfalls. You may also find "The E Word: Kaplan's Guide to Passing Exams" by Stuart Pedley-Smith ISBN: 978-0-85732-205-0 helpful. Stuart Pedley-Smith is a senior lecturer at Kaplan Financial and a qualified accountant specialising in financial management. His natural curiosity and wider interests have led him to look beyond the technical content of financial management to the processes and journey that we call education. He has become fascinated by the whole process of learning and the exam skills and techniques that contribute towards success in the classroom. This book is for anyone who has to sit an exam and wants to give themselves a better chance of passing. It is easy to read, written in a common sense style and full of anecdotes, facts, and practical tips. It also contains synopses of interviews with people involved in the learning and examining process.

With your study material before you, decide which chapters you are going to study in each week, and which weeks you will devote to revision and final question practice.

Prepare a written schedule summarising the above and stick to it!

It is essential to know your syllabus. As your studies progress you will become more familiar with how long it takes to cover topics in sufficient depth. Your timetable may need to be adapted to allocate enough time for the whole syllabus.

Students are advised to refer to the notice of examinable legislation published regularly in CIMA's magazine (Financial Management), the students e-newsletter (Velocity) and on the CIMA website, to ensure they are up-to-date.

The amount of space allocated to a topic in the Study Text is not a very good guide as to how long it will take you. For example, the material relating to 'Decision making' accounts for 15% of the syllabus but has three chapters in the text to reflect the breadth and complexity of the topics covered. The syllabus weighting is the better guide as to how long you should spend on a syllabus topic.

Tips for effective studying

(1) Aim to find a quiet and undisturbed location for your study, and plan as far as possible to use the same period of time each day. Getting into a routine helps to avoid wasting time. Make sure that you have all the materials you need before you begin so as to minimise interruptions.

(2) Store all your materials in one place, so that you do not waste time searching for items every time you want to begin studying. If you have to pack everything away after each study period, keep your study materials in a box, or even a suitcase, which will not be disturbed until the next time.

(3) Limit distractions. To make the most effective use of your study periods you should be able to apply total concentration, so turn off all entertainment equipment, set your phones to message mode, and put up your 'do not disturb' sign.

(4) Your timetable will tell you which topic to study. However, before diving in and becoming engrossed in the finer points, make sure you have an overall picture of all the areas that need to be covered by the end of that session. After an hour, allow yourself a short break and move away from your Study Text. With experience, you will learn to assess the pace you need to work at.

(5) Work carefully through a chapter, making notes as you go. When you have covered a suitable amount of material, vary the pattern by attempting a practice question. When you have finished your attempt, make notes of any mistakes you made.

(6) Make notes as you study, and discover the techniques that work best for you. Your notes may be in the form of lists, bullet points, diagrams, summaries, 'mind maps', or the written word, but remember that you will need to refer back to them at a later date, so they must be intelligible. If you are on a taught course, make sure you highlight any issues you would like to follow up with your lecturer.

(7) Organise your notes. Make sure that all your notes, calculations etc. can be effectively filed and easily retrieved later.

Computer based assessment

CIMA uses objective test questions in the computer based assessments. The most common types are:

- Multiple choice, where you have to choose the correct answer from a list of four possible answers. This could either be numbers or text.
- Multiple choice with more choices and answers, for example, choosing two correct answers from a list of eight possible answers. This could either be numbers or text.
- Single numeric entry, where you give your numeric answer, for example, profit is $10,000.
- Multiple entry, where you give several numeric answers.
- True/false questions, where you state whether a statement is true or false.
- Matching pairs of text, for example, matching a technical term with the correct definition.
- Other types could be matching text with graphs and labelling graphs/diagrams.

In every chapter of this Study Text we have introduced these types of questions, but obviously we have had to label answers A, B, C etc rather than using click boxes. For convenience we have retained quite a few questions where an initial scenario leads to a number of sub-questions. There will be questions of this type in the CBA but they will rarely have more than three sub-questions.

Guidance re CIMA online calculator

As part of the CIMA Certificate level computer based assessment software, candidates are now provided with a calculator. This calculator is onscreen and is available for the duration of the assessment. The calculator is available in each of the five Certificate level assessments and is accessed by clicking the calculator button in the top left hand corner of the screen at any time during the assessment.

All candidates must complete a 15 minute tutorial before the assessment begins and will have the opportunity to familiarise themselves with the calculator and practice using it.

Candidates may practise using the calculator by downloading and installing the practice exam at http://www.vue.com/athena/ . The calculator can be accessed from the fourth sample question (of 12).

Please note that the practice exam and tutorial provided by Pearson VUE at http://www.vue.com/athena/ is not specific to CIMA and includes the full range of question types the Pearson VUE software supports, some of which CIMA does not currently use.

Fundamentals of Management Accounting Syllabus

The computer based assessments for Fundamentals of Management Accounting are 2 hour assessments comprising 50 compulsory questions, with one or more parts. There will be no choice and all questions should be attempted.

Additional CBA resources, including sample assessment questions are available online at www.cimaglobal.com/cba2011.

Structure of subjects and learning outcomes

Each subject within the syllabus is divided into a number of broad syllabus topics. The topics contain one or more lead learning outcomes, related component learning outcomes and indicative knowledge content.

A learning outcome has two main purposes:

(a) To define the skill or ability that a well prepared candidate should be able to exhibit in the examination

(b) To demonstrate the approach likely to be taken in examination questions

The learning outcomes are part of a hierarchy of learning objectives. The verbs used at the beginning of each learning outcome relate to a specific learning objective e.g.

Calculate the break-even point, profit target, margin of safety and profit/volume ratio for a single product or service

The verb '**calculate**' indicates a level three learning objective. The following table lists the learning objectives and the verbs that appear in the syllabus learning outcomes and examination questions.

Certificate level verbs

CIMA VERB HIERARCHY

CIMA place great importance on the choice of verbs in exam question requirements. It is thus critical that you answer the question according to the definition of the verb used.

In Certificate level exams you will meet verbs from levels 1, 2, and 3. These are as follows:

Level 1: KNOWLEDGE

What you are expected to know

VERBS USED	DEFINITION
List	Make a list of.
State	Express, fully or clearly, the details of/facts of.
Define	Give the exact meaning of.

Level 2: COMPREHENSION

What you are expected to understand

VERBS USED	DEFINITION
Describe	Communicate the key features of.
Distinguish	Highlight the differences between.
Explain	Make clear or intelligible/state the meaning or purpose of.
Identify	Recognise, establish or select after consideration.
Illustrate	Use an example to describe or explain something.

Level 3: APPLICATION

How you are expected to apply your knowledge

VERBS USED	DEFINITION
Apply	Put to practical use.
Calculate	Ascertain or reckon mathematically.
Demonstrate	Prove with certainty or exhibit by practical means.
Prepare	Make or get ready for use.
Reconcile	Make or prove consistent/compatible.
Solve	Find an answer to.
Tabulate	Arrange in a table.

PAPER C01
FUNDAMENTALS OF MANAGEMENT ACCOUNTING

Syllabus overview

This paper deals with the basic techniques for the identification and control of costs and cost management. It introduces the context of management accounting in commercial and public sector bodies and its wider role in society. It identifies the position of the management accountant within organisations and the role of CIMA.

Classification of costs and cost behaviour provides a basis for understanding the various tools available for planning, control and decision making. Budgetary control requires the setting of targets and standards while the analysis of variances demonstrates the levels of performance within organisations. Accounting control mechanisms are identified and applied to provide information to managers to achieve operational efficiency. Investment appraisal, break-even analysis and profit maximising are used to aid both long and short-term decision making.

Syllabus structure

The syllabus comprises the following topics and study weightings:

A	The context of management accounting	10%
B	Cost identification and behaviour	25%
C	Planning within organisations	30%
D	Accounting control systems	20%
E	Decision making	15%

Assessment strategy

There will be a two hour computer based assessment, comprising 50 compulsory questions, each with one or more parts.

A variety of objective test question styles and types will be used within the assessment.

C01 – A. THE CONTEXT OF MANAGEMENT ACCOUNTING (10%)

Learning outcomes On completion of their studies students should be able to:			**Indicative syllabus content**
Lead	**Component**	**Level**	
1. explain the purpose of management accounting	(a) define management accounting; (b) explain the importance of cost control and planning within organisations; (c) describe how information can be used to identify performance within an organisation; (d) explain the differences between financial information requirements for companies, public bodies and society.	1 2 2 2	• The CIMA definition of management accounting. [1] • The IFAC definition of the domain of the professional accountant in business. [1] • Characteristics of financial information for operational, management and strategic levels within organisations. [1] • Cost object, concepts of target setting and responsibility accounting. [1] • Performance measurement and performance management using actual v budget comparisons, profitability and return on capital. [1] • Financial information requirements for companies, public bodies and society, including concepts of shareholder value, meeting society's needs and environmental costing. [1]
2. explain the role of the management accountant.	(a) explain the role of the management accountant and activities undertaken; (b) explain the relationship between the management accountant and the managers being served; (c) explain the difference between placing management accounting within the finance function and a business partnering role within an organisation.	2 2 2	• The CIMA definition of the role of the management accountant. [1] • The IFAC definition of the role of the professional accountant in business. [1] • The nature of relationships between advisers and managers. [1] • The positioning of management accounting within the organisation. [1]
3. explain the role of CIMA as a professional body for management accountants.	(a) explain the background to the formation of CIMA; (b) explain the role of CIMA in developing the practice of management accounting	2 2	• The need for a professional body in management accounting – CIMA. [1] • CIMA's role in relation to its members, students, the profession of management accounting and society. [1]

C01 – B. COST IDENTIFICATION AND BEHAVIOUR (25%)

Learning outcomes On completion of their studies students should be able to:			**Indicative syllabus content**
Lead	**Component**	**Level**	
1. apply methods for identifying cost.	(a) explain the concept of a direct cost and an indirect cost; (b) explain why the concept of 'cost' needs to be defined, in order to be meaningful; (c) distinguish between the historical cost of an asset and the economic value of an asset to an organisation; (d) prepare cost statements for allocation and apportionment of overheads, including reciprocal service departments; (e) calculate direct, variable and full costs of products, services and activities using overhead absorption rates to trace indirect costs to cost units; (f) apply cost information in pricing decisions.	2 2 2 3 3 3	• Classification of costs. [2] • The treatment of direct costs (specifically attributable to a cost object) and indirect costs (not specifically attributable) in ascertaining the cost of a 'cost object' e.g. a product, service, activity, customer. [2] • Cost measurement: historical versus economic costs. [2] • Overhead costs: allocation, apportionment, re-apportionment and absorption of overhead costs. ***Note:*** the repeated distribution method only will be used for reciprocal service department costs. [3] • Direct, variable and full costs of products, services and activities. [3] • Marginal cost pricing and full cost pricing to achieve specified return on sales or return on investment, mark-up and margins. ***Note:*** students are not expected to have a detailed knowledge of activity based costing (ABC). [3]
2. demonstrate cost behaviour.	(a) explain how costs behave as product, service or activity levels increase or decrease; (b) distinguish between fixed, variable and semi-variable costs; (c) explain step costs and the importance of timescales in their treatment as either variable or fixed; (d) calculate the fixed and variable elements of a semi-variable cost.	2 2 2 3	• Cost behaviour and activity levels. [2] • Fixed, variable and semi-variable costs. [2] • Step costs and the importance of timescale in analysing cost behaviour. [2] • High-low and graphical methods to establish fixed and variable elements of a semi-variable cost. ***Note:*** regression analysis is not required. [2]

C01 – C. PLANNING WITHIN ORGANISATIONS (30%)

Learning outcomes **On completion of their studies students should be able to:**			**Indicative syllabus content**
Lead	**Component**	**Level**	
1. prepare budgetary control statements.	(a) explain why organisations set out financial plans in the form of budgets, typically for a financial year; (b) prepare functional budgets and budgets for capital expenditure and depreciation; (c) prepare a master budget based on functional budgets; (d) explain budget statements; (e) identify the impact of budgeted cash surpluses and shortfalls on business operations; (f) prepare a flexible budget; (g) calculate budget variances; (h) distinguish between fixed and flexible budgets; (i) prepare a statement that reconciles budgeted contribution with actual contribution.	2 3 3 2 2 3 3 2 3	• Budgeting for planning and control. [8] • Functional budgets including materials, labour and overheads; capital expenditure and depreciation budgets. [8] • Master budget, including income statement, statement of financial position and statement of cash flow. [8] • Reporting of actual outcomes against budget. [8] • Fixed and flexible budgeting. [8] • Budget variances. [8] • Interpretation and use of budget statements and budget variances. [8]
2. prepare statements of variance analysis.	(a) explain the difference between ascertaining costs after the event and establishing standard costs in advance; (b) explain why planned standard costs, prices and volumes are useful in setting a benchmark; (c) calculate standard costs for the material, labour and variable overhead elements of the cost of a product or service; (d) calculate variances for materials, labour, variable overhead, sales prices and sales volumes; (e) prepare a statement that reconciles budgeted contribution with actual contribution; (f) prepare variance statements.	2 2 3 3 3 3	• Principles of standard costing. [7] • Preparation of standards for the variable elements of cost: material, labour, variable overhead. [7] • Variances: materials – total, price and usage; labour – total, rate and efficiency; variable overhead – total, expenditure and efficiency; sales – sales price and sales volume contribution. ***Note:*** students will be expected to calculate the sales volume contribution variance. [7] • Reconciliation of budget and actual contribution showing: variances for variable costs, sales prices and sales volumes, including possible inter-relations between cost variances, sales price and volume variances, and cost and sales variances. [7]

C01 – D. ACCOUNTING CONTROL SYSTEMS (20%)

Learning outcomes **On completion of their studies students should be able to:**			**Indicative syllabus content**
Lead	**Component**	**Level**	
1. prepare integrated accounts in a costing environment.	(a) explain the principles of manufacturing accounts and the integration of the cost accounts with the financial accounting system; (b) prepare a set of integrated accounts, showing standard cost variances; (c) explain job, batch, and process costing; (d) prepare ledger accounts for job, batch and process costing systems.	2 3 2 3	• Manufacturing accounts including raw material, work in progress, finished goods and manufacturing overhead control accounts. [9] • Integrated ledgers including accounting for over and under absorption of production overhead. [9] • The treatment of variances as period entries in integrated ledger systems. [9] • Job, batch and process costing. ***Note:*** only the average cost method will be examined for process costing but students must be able to deal with differing degrees of completion of opening and closing stocks, normal losses and abnormal gains and losses, and the treatment of scrap value. [10]
2. prepare financial statements for managers.	(a) prepare financial statements that inform management; (b) distinguish between managerial reports in a range of organisations, including commercial enterprises, charities and public sector undertakings.	3 2	• Cost accounting statements for management information in production companies, service companies and not-for-profit organisations. Showing gross revenue, value-added, contribution, gross margin, marketing expense, general and administration expenses. [11]

C01 – E. DECISION MAKING (15%)

Learning outcomes **On completion of their studies students should be able to:**			**Indicative syllabus content**
Lead	**Component**	**Level**	
1. demonstrate the use of break-even analysis in making short-term decisions.	(a) explain the contribution concept and its use in cost-volume-profit (CVP) analysis; (b) calculate the break-even point, profit target, margin of safety and profit/volume ratio for a single product or service; (c) prepare break-even charts and profit/volume graphs for a single product or service;	2 3 3	• Contribution concept and CVP analysis. [4] • Break-even charts, profit volume graphs, break-even point, profit target, margin of safety, contribution/sales ratio. [4]
2. apply basic approaches for use in decision making.	(a) explain relevant costs and cash flows; (b) explain make or buy decisions; (c) calculate the profit maximising product sales mix using limiting factor analysis.	2 2 3	• Relevant costs and cash flows. [5] • Make or buy decisions. [5] • Limiting factor analysis for a multi-product company that has limited demand for each product and one other constraint or limiting factor. [5]
3. demonstrate the use of investment appraisal techniques in making long-term decisions.	(a) explain the process of valuing long-term investments; (b) calculate the net present value, internal rate of return and payback for an investment.	2 3	• Net present value, internal rate of return and payback methods. [6]

Present Value Tables

Present value of 1 unit of currency, that is $(1+r)^{-n}$ where r = interest rate; n = number of periods until payment or receipt.

Periods (n)	Interest rates (r)									
	1%	2%	3%	4%	5%	6%	7%	8%	9%	10%
1	0.990	0.980	0.971	0.962	0.952	0.943	0.935	0.926	0.917	0.909
2	0.980	0.961	0.943	0.925	0.907	0.890	0.873	0.857	0.842	0.826
3	0.971	0.942	0.915	0.889	0.864	0.840	0.816	0.794	0.772	0.751
4	0.961	0.924	0.888	0.855	0.823	0.792	0.763	0.735	0.708	0.683
5	0.951	0.906	0.863	0.822	0.784	0.747	0.713	0.681	0.650	0.621
6	0.942	0.888	0.837	0.790	0.746	0705	0.666	0.630	0.596	0.564
7	0.933	0.871	0.813	0.760	0.711	0.665	0.623	0.583	0.547	0.513
8	0.923	0.853	0.789	0.731	0.677	0.627	0.582	0.540	0.502	0.467
9	0.914	0.837	0.766	0.703	0.645	0.592	0.544	0.500	0.460	0.424
10	0.905	0.820	0.744	0.676	0.614	0.558	0.508	0.463	0.422	0.386
11	0.896	0.804	0.722	0.650	0.585	0.527	0.475	0.429	0.388	0.350
12	0.887	0.788	0.701	0.625	0.557	0.497	0.444	0.397	0.356	0.319
13	0.879	0.773	0.681	0.601	0.530	0.469	0.415	0.368	0.326	0.290
14	0.870	0.758	0.661	0.577	0.505	0.442	0.388	0.340	0.299	0.263
15	0.861	0.743	0.642	0.555	0.481	0.417	0.362	0.315	0.275	0.239
16	0.853	0.728	0.623	0.534	0.458	0.394	0.339	0.292	0.252	0.218
17	0.844	0.714	0.605	0.513	0.436	0.371	0.317	0.270	0.231	0.198
18	0.836	0.700	0.587	0.494	0.416	0.350	0.296	0.250	0.212	0.180
19	0.828	0.686	0.570	0.475	0.396	0.331	0.277	0.232	0.194	0.164
20	0.820	0.673	0.554	0.456	0.377	0.312	0.258	0.215	0.178	0.149

Periods (n)	Interest rates (r)									
	11%	12%	13%	14%	15%	16%	17%	18%	19%	20%
1	0.901	0.893	0.885	0.877	0.870	0.862	0.855	0.847	0.840	0.833
2	0.812	0.797	0.783	0.769	0.756	0.743	0.731	0.718	0.706	0.694
3	0.731	0.712	0.693	0.675	0.658	0.641	0.624	0.609	0.593	0.579
4	0.659	0.636	0.613	0.592	0.572	0.552	0.534	0.516	0.499	0.482
5	0.593	0.567	0.543	0.519	0.497	0.476	0.456	0.437	0.419	0.402
6	0.535	0.507	0.480	0.456	0.432	0.410	0.390	0.370	0.352	0.335
7	0.482	0.452	0.425	0.400	0.376	0.354	0.333	0.314	0.296	0.279
8	0.434	0.404	0.376	0.351	0.327	0.305	0.285	0.266	0.249	0.233
9	0.391	0.361	0.333	0.308	0.284	0.263	0.243	0.225	0.209	0.194
10	0.352	0.322	0.295	0.270	0.247	0.227	0.208	0.191	0.176	0.162
11	0.317	0.287	0.261	0.237	0.215	0.195	0.178	0.162	0.148	0.135
12	0.286	0.257	0.231	0.208	0.187	0.168	0.152	0.137	0.124	0.112
13	0.258	0.229	0.204	0.182	0.163	0.145	0.130	0.116	0.104	0.093
14	0.232	0.205	0.181	0.160	0.141	0.125	0.111	0.099	0.088	0.078
15	0.209	0.183	0.160	0.140	0.123	0.108	0.095	0.084	0.079	0.065
16	0.188	0.163	0.141	0.123	0.107	0.093	0.081	0.071	0.062	0.054
17	0.170	0.146	0.125	0.108	0.093	0.080	0.069	0.060	0.052	0.045
18	0.153	0.130	0.111	0.095	0.081	0.069	0.059	0.051	0.044	0.038
19	0.138	0.116	0.098	0.083	0.070	0.060	0.051	0.043	0.037	0.031
20	0.124	0.104	0.087	0.073	0.061	0.051	0.043	0.037	0.031	0.026

Cumulative present value of 1 unit of currency per annum, Receivable or Payable at the end of each year for n years $\frac{1-(1+r)^{-n}}{r}$

Periods (n)	Interest rates (r)									
	1%	2%	3%	4%	5%	6%	7%	8%	9%	10%
1	0.990	0.980	0.971	0.962	0.952	0.943	0.935	0.926	0.917	0.909
2	1.970	1.942	1.913	1.886	1.859	1.833	1.808	1.783	1.759	1.736
3	2.941	2.884	2.829	2.775	2.723	2.673	2.624	2.577	2.531	2.487
4	3.902	3.808	3.717	3.630	3.546	3.465	3.387	3.312	3.240	3.170
5	4.853	4.713	4.580	4.452	4.329	4.212	4.100	3.993	3.890	3.791
6	5.795	5.601	5.417	5.242	5.076	4.917	4.767	4.623	4.486	4.355
7	6.728	6.472	6.230	6.002	5.786	5.582	5.389	5.206	5.033	4.868
8	7.652	7.325	7.020	6.733	6.463	6.210	5.971	5.747	5.535	5.335
9	8.566	8.162	7.786	7.435	7.108	6.802	6.515	6.247	5.995	5.759
10	9.471	8.983	8.530	8.111	7.722	7.360	7.024	6.710	6.418	6.145
11	10.368	9.787	9.253	8.760	8.306	7.887	7.499	7.139	6.805	6.495
12	11.255	10.575	9.954	9.385	8.863	8.384	7.943	7.536	7.161	6.814
13	12.134	11.348	10.635	9.986	9.394	8.853	8.358	7.904	7.487	7.103
14	13.004	12.106	11.296	10.563	9.899	9.295	8.745	8.244	7.786	7.367
15	13.865	12.849	11.938	11.118	10.380	9.712	9.108	8.559	8.061	7.606
16	14.718	13.578	12.561	11.652	10.838	10.106	9.447	8.851	8.313	7.824
17	15.562	14.292	13.166	12.166	11.274	10.477	9.763	9.122	8.544	8.022
18	16.398	14.992	13.754	12.659	11.690	10.828	10.059	9.372	8.756	8.201
19	17.226	15.679	14.324	13.134	12.085	11.158	10.336	9.604	8.950	8.365
20	18.046	16.351	14.878	13.590	12.462	11.470	10.594	9.818	9.129	8.514

Periods (n)	Interest rates (r)									
	11%	12%	13%	14%	15%	16%	17%	18%	19%	20%
1	0.901	0.893	0.885	0.877	0.870	0.862	0.855	0.847	0.840	0.833
2	1.713	1.690	1.668	1.647	1.626	1.605	1.585	1.566	1.547	1.528
3	2.444	2.402	2.361	2.322	2.283	2.246	2.210	2.174	2.140	2.106
4	3.102	3.037	2.974	2.914	2.855	2.798	2.743	2.690	2.639	2.589
5	3.696	3.605	3.517	3.433	3.352	3.274	3.199	3.127	3.058	2.991
6	4.231	4.111	3.998	3.889	3.784	3.685	3.589	3.498	3.410	3.326
7	4.712	4.564	4.423	4.288	4.160	4.039	3.922	3.812	3.706	3.605
8	5.146	4.968	4.799	4.639	4.487	4.344	4.207	4.078	3.954	3.837
9	5.537	5.328	5.132	4.946	4.772	4.607	4.451	4.303	4.163	4.031
10	5.889	5.650	5.426	5.216	5.019	4.833	4.659	4.494	4.339	4.192
11	6.207	5.938	5.687	5.453	5.234	5.029	4.836	4.656	4.486	4.327
12	6.492	6.194	5.918	5.660	5.421	5.197	4.988	7.793	4.611	4.439
13	6.750	6.424	6.122	5.842	5.583	5.342	5.118	4.910	4.715	4.533
14	6.982	6.628	6.302	6.002	5.724	5.468	5.229	5.008	4.802	4.611
15	7.191	6.811	6.462	6.142	5.847	5.575	5.324	5.092	4.876	4.675
16	7.379	6.974	6.604	6.265	5.954	5.668	5.405	5.162	4.938	4.730
17	7.549	7.120	6.729	6.373	6.047	5.749	5.475	5.222	4.990	4.775
18	7.702	7.250	6.840	6.467	6.128	5.818	5.534	5.273	5.033	4.812
19	7.839	7.366	6.938	6.550	6.198	5.877	5.584	5.316	5.070	4.843
20	7.963	7.469	7.025	6.623	6.259	5.929	5.628	5.353	5.101	4.870

chapter

1

Management accounting

Chapter learning objectives

After completing this chapter, you should be able to:

- define management accounting;
- explain the importance of cost control and planning within organisations;
- describe how information can be used to identify performance within an organisation;
- explain the differences between financial information requirements for companies, public bodies and society;
- explain the role of the management accountant and activities undertaken;
- explain the relationship between the management accountant and the managers being served;
- explain the difference between placing management accounting within the finance function and a business partnering role within an organisation;
- explain the background to the formation of CIMA;
- explain the role of CIMA in developing the practice of management accounting.

1 Session content diagram

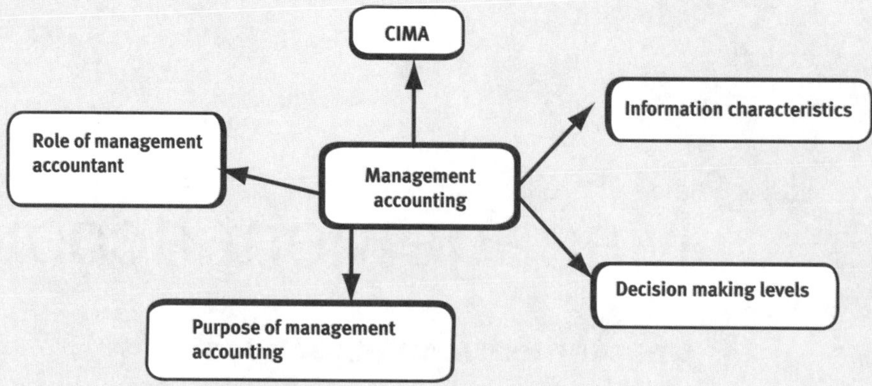

2 Management accounting

Accountancy involves the measurement, analysing and reporting of financial and non-financial information to help managers, shareholders and other interested parties make decisions about organisations.

As a student of CIMA, you have decided to focus on management accounting, although you will also study financial accounting as part of the CIMA qualification. There are a number of differences between these two branches of accountancy.

Financial accounting	Management accounting
Externally focused	Internally focused
Statutory requirement	At the discretion of management
Concerned with the production of statutory accounts for an organisation	Concerned with the provision of information to management to aid decision making
Governed by many rules and regulations	Not governed by rules or regulations, can be provided in any format

The *CIMA Terminology* defines **management accounting** as 'the application of the principles of accounting and financial management to create, protect, preserve and increase value for the stakeholders of for-profit and not-for-profit enterprises in the public and private sectors.'

The following has been produced by CIMA:

Management accounting is an integral part of management. It requires the identification, generation, presentation, interpretation and use of relevant information to:

- Inform strategic decisions and formulate business strategy.
- Plan long-, medium- and short-run operations.
- Determine capital structure and fund that structure.
- Design reward strategies for executives and shareholders.
- Inform operational decisions.
- Control operations and ensure the efficient use of resources.
- Measure and report financial and non-financial performance to management and other stakeholders.
- Safeguard tangible and intangible assets.
- Implement corporate governance procedures, risk management and internal controls.

You can see from CIMA's definition above that the scope of management accounting is wide ranging and makes a very important contribution to the success of any organisation.

Test your understanding 1

State whether the following characteristics relate to management accounting or financial accounting:

(a) Internally focused.

(b) Governed by rules and regulations.

(c) Required by law.

(d) Output is mainly used by external parties.

(e) One of its main purposes is planning.

3 The Chartered Institute of Management Accountants (CIMA)

CIMA was formed in 1919 (originally as the Institute of Cost and Works Accountants (ICWA)). It was granted its Royal Charter in 1975 and became known as the Chartered Institute of Management Accountants in 1986.

CIMA is the world's largest and leading professional body of management accountants. Members and students are located in over 160 countries. CIMA supports organisations in both the private and public sector. It focuses on the needs of businesses, no matter what type of business.

The CIMA qualification

The CIMA qualification is very highly regarded across the world and CIMA members hold many high profile finance positions.

The CIMA qualification is constantly updated to ensure that it continues to meet the needs of business. Before admission to membership, students must demonstrate their experience by completing their professional experience records. This ensures that CIMA members do not just have the technical knowledge, but also practical knowledge of business.

Members are required to undertake continuing professional development (CPD) to ensure that they maintain and develop their knowledge.

All of this ensures that CIMA members and students will enhance any business they join and it gives assurances to potential employers that they are recruiting well-trained and knowledgeable individuals.

Professional standards

In addition to the technical requirements for members, CIMA are committed to upholding the highest **ethical and professional standards**. This ensures that employers and members of the public can have confidence in CIMA and CIMA members.

CIMA has a **code of ethics** which all members and students are required to comply with.

The code of ethics is made up of five fundamental principles:

- **Integrity**: Being straightforward, honest and truthful in all professional and business relationships.
- **Objectivity**: Not allowing bias, conflict of interest or the influence of other people to override your professional judgement.
- **Professional competence and due care**: An ongoing commitment to your level of professional knowledge and skill.
- **Confidentiality**: You should not disclose professional information unless you have specific permission, or a legal or professional duty, to do so.
- **Professional behaviour**: Compliance with relevant laws and regulations. You must also avoid any action that could negatively affect the reputation of the profession.

CIMA also provides students and members with guidance on how to handle situations where their ethics may be compromised. Members and students can contact CIMA for advice on how to handle situations arising in their professional duties. CIMA will also deal with complaints from the general public about CIMA students or members.

The work of CIMA ensures that the public and businesses are protected, and that members are trained to the highest levels and adhere to the highest ethical and professional standards. CIMA continues to work developing management accounting for the benefit of businesses across the world as it has done for more than 90 years.

Chartered Global Management Accountants (CGMA)

In 2012, CIMA undertook a joint venture with the AICPA (American institute of Certified Public Accountants). Together they have created a new designation for management accountants known as CGMA.

When you become a qualified CIMA member you will be entitled to use the CGMA designation.

The purpose of the new designation is to elevate the profession of management accounting around the world. Businesses around the world will recognise the CGMA designation and will be confident that members of CGMA will be able to assist them in making critical business decisions and will contribute to driving strong business performance.

Test your understanding 2

Which of the following are fundamental principles from the CIMA code of ethics? Mark all that apply.

(a) Confidentiality.

(b) Responsibility.

(c) Integrity.

(d) Accountability.

(e) Objectivity.

Governing bodies

The **IFAC (International Federation of Accountants)** is the worldwide organisation for the accounting profession. Its members include the professional accounting bodies across the world, including **CIMA**. It represents more than 2.5 million accountants.

There are many professional accountancy bodies across the world, in addition to CIMA, some of the main ones operating in the UK are:

- ACCA – Association of Chartered Certified Accountants
- ICAS – Institute of Chartered Accountants of Scotland
- ICAEW – Institute of Chartered Accountants in England and Wales
- ICAI – Institute of Chartered Accountants in Ireland
- CIPFA – Chartered Institute of Public Finance and Accountancy

Traditionally, CIMA concentrates on management accounting, while ICAS, ICAEW and ACCA focus more on financial accounting and auditing. CIPFA is dedicated to the accounting requirements of public bodies. However, many accountants who are qualified with these bodies do a variety of accounting roles within the profession. An ACCA member, for example, may work in a management accounting role within an organisation.

4 The management accountant

The changing role of the management accountant

The whole of the accountancy profession is changing, and this is especially true for the management accountant.

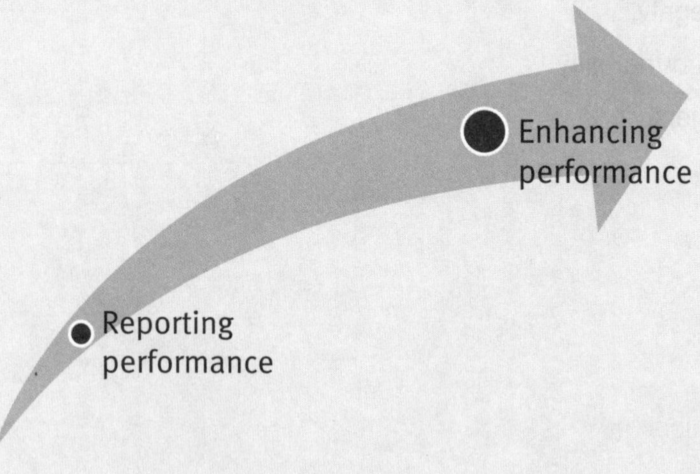

The traditional management accountant was largely involved in reporting business results to management, but this is no longer the case. Management accountants today are seen as **value-adding business partners** and are expected to not only forecast the future of the business, but to assist in delivering this future by identifying opportunities for enhancing organisational performance. Management accountants now work alongside business managers as mentors, advisors and drivers of performance.

Management accountants are an integral part of any business, providing a variety of information to management for the purposes of planning, control and decision making. Management accountants often hold senior positions in the organisation.

The role of the management accountant

The work of the Chartered Management Accountant (produced by CIMA):

Chartered management accountants help organisations establish viable strategies and convert them into profit (in a commercial context) or into value for money (in a not-for-profit context). To achieve this they work as an integral part of multi-skilled management teams in carrying out the:

- formulation of policy and setting of corporate objectives;
- formulation of strategic plans derived from corporate objectives;
- formulation of shorter-term operational plans;
- acquisition and use of finance;
- design of systems, recording of events and transactions and management of information systems;
- generation, communication and interpretation of financial and operating information for management and other stakeholders;
- provision of specific information and analysis on which decisions are based;
- monitoring of outcomes against plans and other benchmarks and the initiation of responsive action for performance improvement;
- derivation of performance measures and benchmarks, financial and non-financial, quantitative and qualitative, for monitoring and control; and
- improvement of business systems and processes through risk management and internal audit review.

Through these forward-looking roles and by application of their expert skills management accountants help organisations improve their performance, security, growth and competitiveness in an ever more demanding environment.

We will start to look at some of these functions in the *Fundamentals of Management Accounting* syllabus, and others will be studied in later papers. It can be seen from this that there is no one clear definition of the role of the management accountant. Their work, experience and responsibilities are extraordinarily varied and continue to change to reflect the changing needs of stakeholders.

IFAC definitions

IFAC definition of the roles and domain of the professional accountant in business

Of the 2.5 million professional accountants who are members of the IFAC, over half of these work in business. This includes those who work in commerce, industry, the public sector, education and the not-for-profit sector.

The roles of the professional accountant in business:

The IFAC state that 'the roles that professional accountants in business perform include:

- implementing and maintaining operational and fiduciary controls;
- providing analytical support for strategic planning and decision making;
- ensuring that effective risk management processes are in place, and
- assisting management in setting the tone for ethical practices.'

The domain of the professional accountant in business:

The IFAC have analysed the main activities of the professional accountant in business as:

- The generation or creation of value through the effective use of resources (financial and otherwise) through the understanding of the drivers of stakeholder value (which may include shareholders, customers, employees, suppliers, communities, and government) and organisational innovation.
- The provision, analysis and interpretation of information to management for formulation of strategy, planning, decision making and control.

- Performance measurement and communication to stakeholders, including the financial recording of transactions and subsequent reporting to stakeholders typically under national or international Generally Accepted Accounting Principles (GAAP).
- Cost determination and financial control, through the use of cost accounting techniques, budgeting and forecasting.
- The reduction of waste in resources used in business processes through the use of process analysis and cost management.
- Risk management and business assurance.

IFAC list of the typical mainstream job titles held by accountants in business

These include:

- chief financial officer (CFO)
- finance director
- financial controller
- financial analyst
- treasurer
- chief information officer
- investor relations officer
- planning manager
- strategy analyst
- chief accountant
- management accountant
- cost accountant
- financial accountant
- consolidation accountant
- internal auditor
- compliance officer
- project manager
- programme manager.

Many professional accountants also move on to have more general management responsibilities such as operations director, chief executive officer (CEO), chairman and non-executive director.

5 The positioning of management accounting within the organisation

It is clear that the breadth of the work carried out by management accountants, and their remit continues to grow. Accountants within business can be part of an internal finance function, or may be part of a business partnering role. When deciding on their structure, it is important for organisations to consider where best to position the management accountant within the organisation. There are three options available:

- Dedicated business partners
- Shared services centres (SSC)
- Business Process Outsourcing centres (BPO)

5.1 Dedicated business partners

With this approach, the management accountant is an integral part of the business area that they support. This brings many benefits to both the accountants and the management of the area.

The relationship between the management accountant and the managers of the business area is an important business relationship. To work in the best interests of the company, they must work as business partners and the relationship must be based on trust, honesty and respect.

From the accountant's point of view, they must:

- *act professionally at all times* – as representatives of the accounting profession, they are expected to show professional care and attention in the way they conduct themselves;
- *demonstrate technical awareness* – can be demonstrated by being a qualified member of CIMA;
- *demonstrate business awareness* – they must be aware of the nature of the business and the needs of the managers;
- *act with integrity* – the work of the management accountant should be done in the best interests of the company and society and they should never put themselves in a position where their personal interests conflict with these interests.

From the manager's point of view, they must:

- *trust* the accountant and the information being provided
- *respect* the accountant's knowledge, experience and professionalism
- be able to discuss all aspects of work *confidentially* with the accountant
- be able to *state clearly what their requirements are.*

It is important to remember that both the management accountant and the managers of the business want the business to succeed and they have to work together to achieve this.

The management accountant as an adviser

The management accountant plays a range of roles within the organisation from their more traditional score-keeping role to a full-fledged, value-adding, business partner. An advisory role falls in between these extremes. As a technical expert, the management accountant is expected to advise management on a range of topics, including financial and non-financial analysis, costing, pricing, Business Process Reengineering and performance management.

As advisers, management accountants no longer simply need financial skills, but increasingly, communication and presentation skills.

The advantages of this approach are:

- The management accounting function is part of the business it serves.
- Increased knowledge of the business area and its needs.
- Strong relationships can be built up between the accountants and the business.

The disadvantages are:

- Duplication of effort across the organisation.
- Lack of knowledge. There is no sharing of knowledge which can happen within a larger, more diverse team.
- The accountants can feel isolated within the business and may develop their own ways of working which may not constitute best practice.
- The accountant can lose sight of the overall goals of the organisation.

5.2 Shared services centre (SSC)

An alternative to having the management accountant as a dedicated business partner is to set up a shared services centre (SSC). This is where the whole finance function is brought together as one centre and this centre provides all the accounting needs of the whole organisation.

The advantages of dedicated business partners listed above may be lost, but the creation of a SSC brings other **advantages**:

- Cost reduction. This comes from reduced headcount, premises and associated costs. The SSC, for example, may be located in a geographic area with favourable labour or property rates.

- Increased quality of service. The central team can become very experienced and adopt best practice.
- Consistency of management information throughout the organisation.

5.3 Business Process Outsourcing centres (BPO)

While setting up SSCs is often thought of as 'internal outsourcing', some organisations decide to outsource the finance function completely. BPO is contracting with a third party (external supplier) to provide all or part of a business process or function. Typically the functions which are outsourced are procurement, ordering and reporting functions, although decision support and other corporate functions may also be outsourced.

The advantages of this approach are:

- Cost reduction. As with a SSC, there will be headcount reduction and reduction in property and associated costs.
- Access to specialist providers. This can bring new expertise into the organisation.
- Release of capacity. If only the more routine functions are outsourced, the retained finance function can concentrate on their role of providing the best information for management decision making.

The disadvantages of this approach are:

- Loss of control. The work is being carried out remotely so management are unable to supervise the function on a day-to-day basis.
- Over-reliance on external providers. Often the systems containing the information are not accessible to the organisation, meaning that they are only able to get the information the outsourcers provide. It can also become very difficult to bring the function back in house.
- Confidentiality risk. Important information could end up getting into the wrong hands.
- Loss of quality. Quality requirements must be specified when the contract is set up and quality control must be put in place to monitor the work of the outsourced function.

Test your understanding 3

Which of the following are advantages of setting up a shared services centre?

(a) Closer to the business needs.

(b) Cost savings.

(c) Consistency of information across the organisation.

(d) Adoption of best practice.

6 The purpose of management accounting

There are three main purposes of management accounting:

- Planning.
- Control.
- Decision making.

6.1 Planning

Planning involves establishing the objectives of an organisation and formulating relevant strategies that can be used to achieve those objectives.

In order to make plans (budgets), it helps to know what has happened in the past so that decisions about what is achievable in the future can be made. For example, if a manager is planning future sales volumes, they need to know what sales volumes have been in the past.

Planning can be done at different levels in an organisation:

- **Strategic** – long-term planning carried out by the highest level of the organisation.
- **Managerial** – short- to medium-term planning, carried out by middle level management.
- **Operational** – short-term planning for day-to-day operations.

Planning is looked at in more detail in the budgeting chapter.

6.2 Control

Once planning has been carried out, targets can be set. This allows for evaluation of performance.

Information relating to the actual results of an organisation must be gathered and compared to the targets. The differences (variances) can be reported to management. This type of information facilitates managers to control their operations.

Many measures can be used to measure performance within an organisation, it is largely dependent on the type of organisation. Some common performance measurements are:

- **Variances** – comparison of actual results against budgeted results.
- **Profitability measures** – absolute measures such as gross profit or net profit, or relative measures such as gross margin %.
- **Return measures** – financial ratio measures such as return on capital.

These measures will be covered in more detail in later chapters.

6.3 Decision making

Decision making involves considering information that has been provided and making informed decisions. In most situations, decision making involves making a choice between two or more alternatives. Managers need reliable information to compare the different courses of action available and understand what the consequences might be of choosing each of them.

You can see from the above that managers require information at various levels and for various purposes.

It is the role of the management accountant to provide that information.

Test your understanding 4

Activities:	**Planning**	**Control**	**Decision making**
Preparation of the annual budget			
Revise budgets for next period			
Implement decisions based on information provided			
Set organisation's objectives for next period			
Compare actual and expected results for a period			

Required:

Complete the table shown above, identifying each activity as either a planning, a decision making or a control function.

7 Management information

Characteristics of good information

The operations of organisations generate a huge quantity of data. Data consist of raw facts and statistics before they have been processed. Once data have been processed into a useful form, they are called information.

Managers need good information in order to make good decisions. A useful way to remember the characteristics of good information is **ACCURATE**:

A. Accurate: The degree of accuracy depends on the reason the information is needed.

For example, reports may show figures to the nearest $1,000, or to the nearest $100,000 for a report on the performance of different divisions. Alternatively, when calculating the cost of a unit of output, managers may want the cost to be accurate to the nearest dollar or even cent.

C. Complete: Managers should be given all the information they need, but information should not be excessive, for example a complete control report on variances should include all standard and actual costs necessary to understand the variance calculations.

C. Cost beneficial: The value of information should not exceed the cost of producing it. Management information is valuable, because it assists decision making. If a decision backed by information is different from what it would have been without the information, the value of information equates the amount of money saved as a result.

U. Understandable: Use of technical language or jargon must be limited. Accountants must always be careful about the way in which they present financial information to non-financial managers.

R. Relevant: The information contained within a report should be relevant to its purpose. Redundant parts should be removed.

A. Authoritative: Information should be trusted and provided from reliable sources so that the users can have confidence in their decision making.

T. Timely: Information should be provided to a manager in time for them make decisions based on that information.

E. Easy to use: We must always think about the person using the information we provide and make sure the information meets their needs.

Information for different levels of management

There are three levels of management: **Strategic**, **Managerial** and **Operational**. Information needs differ at each of these levels.

Strategic level: Management need to know about developments in the markets in which they operate and in the general economic situation. They also need to know about any new technology that emerges, and about the activities of competitors. Decisions made at this level:

- will have a large impact on the whole organisation
- will be long term
- tend to be unstructured.

Managerial level: Management at this level might want to know about issues such as product or service quality, speed of handling customer complaints, customer satisfaction levels, employee skills levels and employee morale. Decisions made at this level:

- will have a medium impact on the whole organisation
- will be medium term
- will act as a bridge between the strategic and operational levels.

Operational level: At this level, management may want to know about the number of rejects per machine, the lead time for delivering materials and the number of labour and machine hours available. Decisions made at this level:

- will have a small impact on the whole organisation; they will normally only affect one business unit or department
- will be short term
- tend to be highly structured.

You can see from the above that the information requirements change at the different levels within the organisation. The nature of the information also changes:

Information characteristics:	Strategic level	Operational level
Source	Historical and forecasts.	Historical.
Timeliness	The timeliness is less crucial at this level as decisions tend to be taken over a period of weeks or months.	Information must be available immediately as decisions are taken daily.

Accuracy	Often highly rounded and will contain many subjective estimates.	Information will be objective and accurate.
Breadth	Wide variety of information in different forms, covering many aspects of the organisation's operations.	Focused on the decision to be made.
Detail	Highly summarised.	Detailed.

Managerial level – Just as managerial decision making forms a link between strategic and operational management, the information it requires has some of the characteristics of each.

Non-financial information

Information provided by management accountants needs to be both financial and non-financial. Financial information is important for management because many objectives of an organisation are financial in nature, such as making profits and avoiding insolvency.

Managers also need information of a non-financial nature, such as the number of complaints or the number of orders processed.

The management accounting systems in many organisations are able to obtain non-financial as well as financial information for reporting to management. The importance of non-financial information within the reporting system should not be forgotten; in fact it is often the information which is most valuable to managers in their decision making.

Test your understanding 5

Which of the following are characteristics of good information? Mark all that apply.

- Cost beneficial
- Detailed
- Understandable
- Accurate
- Complete
- Regular
- Timely
- Accountable

Requirements of different users

Financial information is required by a variety of different users, each with different needs.

Commercial organisations

The main objective of commercial organisations is usually to maximise the wealth of its shareholders (although it can have many other, sometimes conflicting objectives).

The sort of financial information required by this type of business would include:

- Costing of departments, functions or products.
- Profit measurement.
- Calculation of return on capital.

Shareholders of these businesses are interested in the growth of their investment and they will be able to judge the performance of the organisation by examining the statutory accounts. Other information of interest to the shareholders will be the level of dividend payments.

Public bodies

The main objective of public bodies is to provide services to the public in line with government requirements. The information requirement of public bodies will differ from commercial organisations. There will be no profit measurements as these are not-for-profit organisations, therefore the focus will be more on cost management. As these bodies must be run in the public interest, the level of information must be detailed and accurate and allow assessment of the efficiency and effectiveness of the organisation to be assessed by central government and by the public.

Society

Society also has a need for financial information relating to the organisations it deals with. Members of the public may be shareholders, employees or customers of these organisations and they will have an interest in how these organisations are run and are performing. Society will also be interested in the impact organisations have on the local and wider community. Environmental reporting, where organisations measure and report on their impact on the environment, can be of great use to the public.

8 Environmental costing

There is an increasing need for management accountants to provide information relating to environmental issues.

Environmental costs can be split into two categories:

Internal costs

These are costs that directly impact on the statement of profit or loss of a company. There are many different types, for example:

- improved systems and checks in order to avoid penalties/fines
- waste disposal costs
- product take back costs (i.e. in the EU, for example, companies must provide facilities for customers to return items such as batteries, printer cartridges etc. for recycling. The seller of such items must bear the cost of these 'take backs')
- regulatory costs such as taxes (e.g. companies with poor environmental management policies often have to bear a higher tax burden)
- upfront costs such as obtaining permits (e.g. for achieving certain levels of emissions)
- back-end costs such as decommissioning costs on project completion.

External costs

These are costs that are imposed on society at large but not borne by the company that generates the cost in the first instance. For example,

- carbon emissions
- usage of energy and water
- forest degradation
- health care costs
- social welfare costs.

However, governments are becoming increasingly aware of these external costs and are using taxes and regulations to convert them to internal costs. For example, companies might have to have a tree replacement programme if they cause forest degradation, or they receive lower tax allowances on vehicles that cause a high degree of harm to the environment. On top of this, some companies are voluntarily converting external costs to internal costs.

9 Chapter summary

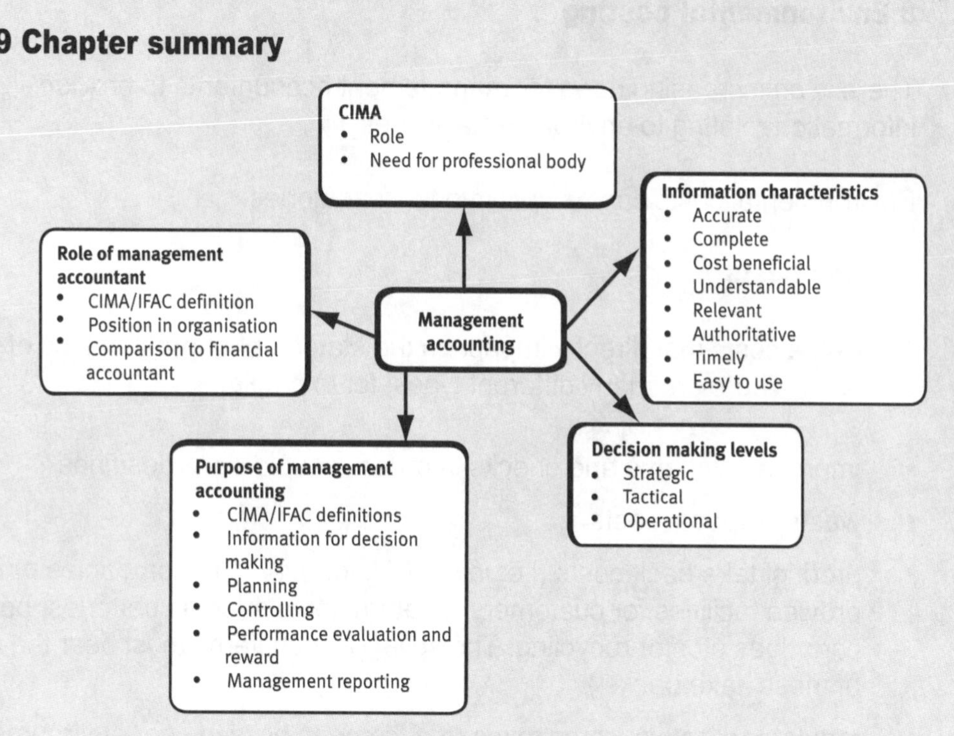
CIMA
• Role
• Need for professional body
Information characteristics
• Accurate
• Complete
• Cost beneficial
• Understandable
• Relevant
• Authoritative
• Timely
• Easy to use
Role of management accountant
• CIMA/IFAC definition
• Position in organisation
• Comparison to financial accountant
Management accounting
Decision making levels
• Strategic
• Tactical
• Operational
Purpose of management accounting
• CIMA/IFAC definitions
• Information for decision making
• Planning
• Controlling
• Performance evaluation and reward
• Management reporting

10 End of chapter questions

Question 1

The following statements relate to financial accounting:

(i) The main purpose of financial accounting statements is to provide a true and fair view of the financial position of an organisation at the end of an accounting period.

(ii) Financial information may be presented in any format deemed suitable by management.

Which of the above statements is/are true?

A (i) and (ii)

B (i) only

C (ii) only

D neither

Question 2

Pairs of information characteristics are given. For each, decide which characteristic is most appropriate at the strategic level and which would be more appropriate at the operational level.

	Strategic	**Operational**
Subjective/Objective		
Detailed/Summarised		
Historical/Future		
Focused/Wide ranging		
Frequent/Infrequent		

Question 3

Which of the following are **disadvantages** of business process outsourcing? Mark all that apply.

(a) Loss of control.

(b) Reduction in quality.

(c) Duplication of effort.

(d) Increased cost.

(e) Confidentiality risk.

Question 4

Which of the following statements about CIMA are true?

(a) CIMA's main focus is financial accounting.

(b) CIMA was established over 90 years ago.

(c) Members of CIMA are known as Chartered Management Accountants.

(d) CIMA only covers organisations based in the UK.

(e) CIMA has a code of ethics which all students and members must adhere to.

Question 5

Which of the following is NOT one of the roles of management accounting as defined by CIMA:

(a) Plan long-, medium- and short-run operations.

(b) Design reward strategies for executives and shareholders.

(c) Prepare statutory accounts consisting of statement of profit or loss, statements of financial position and cash flow statements.

(d) Control operations and ensure the efficient use of resources.

(e) Measure and report financial and non-financial performance to management and other stakeholders.

Question 6

The objective of not-for-profit organisations is often 'value for money'.

True or false?

Test your understanding answers

Test your understanding 1

(a) and (e) relate to management accounting.

(b), (c) and (d) relate to financial accounting.

Management accounting is internally focused and one of its main purposes is planning.

Financial accounting is governed by rules and regulations, required by law and its output is mainly used by external parties.

Test your understanding 2

(a) Confidentiality.

(b) Integrity.

(c) Objectivity.

are all fundamental principles from the CIMA code of ethics.

Test your understanding 3

(b), (c) and (d) are advantages of a SSC.

(a) is an advantage of having the management accountant as a dedicated business partner.

Test your understanding 4

Activity	**Planning**	**Control**	**Decision making**
Preparation of the annual budget	X		X
Revise budgets for next period		X	X
Implement decisions based on information provided			X
Set organisation's objectives for next period	X		X
Compare actual and expected results for a period		X	X

Note that all planning and control functions are part of the decision making process.

Test your understanding 5

- Cost beneficial.
- Understandable.
- Accurate.
- Complete.
- Timely.

Question 1

B is correct. Statement (ii) is incorrect as financial statements must be presented in the prescribed formats.

Question 2

Strategic	**Operational**
Subjective	Objective
Summarised	Detailed
Future	Historical
Wide ranging	Focused
Infrequent	Frequent

Question 3

(a) and (e) are **disadvantages** of business process outsourcing.

Question 4

(b), (c) and (e) are true.

(a) is false. CIMA's main focus is management accounting.

(d) is false. CIMA is a worldwide organisation.

Question 5

(c) is NOT a role of management accounting. It is a financial accounting role.

Question 6

True.

chapter

2

Cost identification and behaviour

Chapter learning objectives

After completing this chapter, you should be able to:

- explain the concept of a direct cost and an indirect cost;
- explain why the concept of 'cost' needs to be defined, in order to be meaningful;
- distinguish between the historical cost of an asset and the economic value of an asset to an organisation;
- explain how costs behave as product, service or activity levels increase or decrease;
- distinguish between fixed, variable and semi-variable costs;
- explain step costs and the importance of time-scales in their treatment as either variable or fixed;
- calculate the fixed and variable elements of a semi-variable cost.

1 Session content diagram

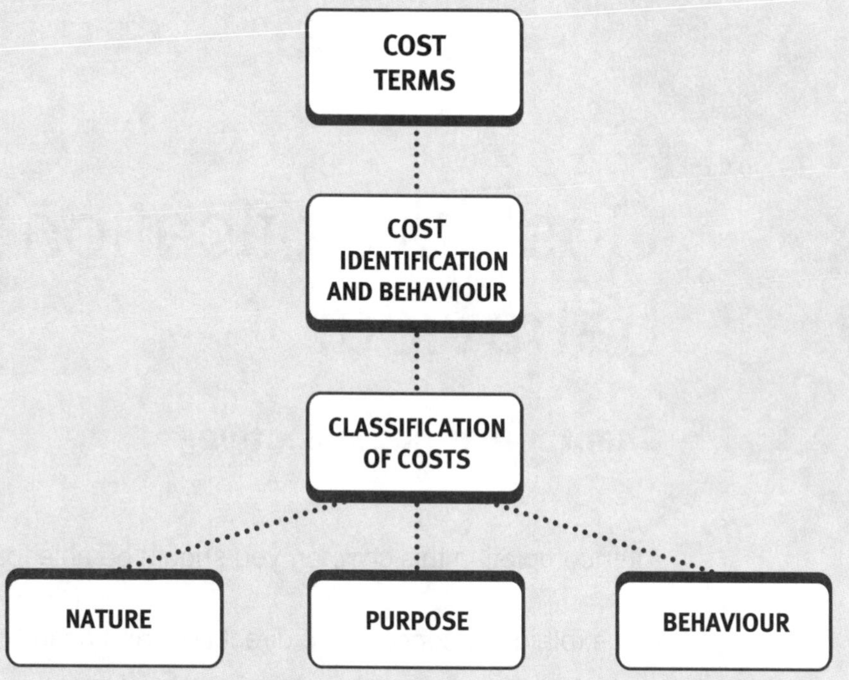

Costing systems

Most organisations will have a **costing system** which is used to gather the cost information for the organisation together. An organisation's costing system is the foundation of the internal financial information system for managers. It provides the **information** that management needs to **plan** and **control** the organisation's activities and to **make decisions** about the future.

Examples of the type of information provided by a costing system and the uses to which it might be put include the following:

- **Actual unit costs** for the latest period; could be used for cost control by comparing with a predetermined unit cost. Could also be used as the basis for decisions about pricing and production levels. For example, a manager cannot make a decision about the price to be charged to a customer without information which tells the manager how much it costs to produce and distribute the product to the customer.

- **Actual costs of operating a department** for the latest period; could be used for cost control by comparing with a predetermined budget for the department. Could also be used as the basis for decisions such as outsourcing. For example, a manager might be considering the closure of the packing department and instead outsourcing the packing operations to another organisation. In order to make this decision the manager needs to know, amongst other things, the actual cost of operating the packing department.
- **The forecast costs to be incurred at different levels of activity**. Could be used for planning, for decision making and as a part of cost control by comparing the actual costs with the forecasts. For example, a manager cannot make a well-informed decision about the appropriate production level for the forthcoming period unless information is available about the costs that will be incurred at various possible output levels.

This is by no means an exhaustive list of the information that is provided by a costing system. However, it should serve to demonstrate that organisations need costing systems that will provide the basic information that management requires for ***planning, control and decision-making***.

2 What is meant by cost

The word 'cost' can be used in two contexts. It can be used as a noun, for example when we are referring to the cost of an item. Alternatively, it can be used as a verb, for example we can say that we are attempting to cost an activity, when we are undertaking the tasks necessary to determine the costs of carrying out the activity.

The word 'cost' can rarely stand alone and should always be qualified as to its nature and limitations. You will see throughout this text that there are many different types of cost and that each has its usefulness and limitations in different circumstances.

Some terms that you will need to understand when studying cost:

- Historical cost.
- Cost unit.
- Composite cost unit.
- Cost centre.
- Cost object.

Historical cost

The term historical cost is normally used when we consider the purchase of an asset. This applies to both non-current assets, such as buildings or vehicles, or current assets such as inventory. Historical cost is the original cost paid for the asset at the time of acquisition.

By their nature, historical costs are out of date and might not reflect the current value of the asset to the organisation.

The economic value of an asset is the value the organisation derives from owning and using the asset. This value can be higher or lower than the historical cost, depending on current circumstances. It can be affected by how the asset is currently being used, the alternative uses for the asset or the current inflation rate.

This area will be covered in more detail in the relevant cost section in Chapter 5.

Cost units

The *CIMA Terminology* defines a **cost unit** as 'a unit of product or service in relation to which costs are ascertained'.

This means that a cost unit can be **anything for which it is possible to ascertain the cost**. The cost unit selected in each situation will depend on a number of factors, including the purpose of the cost ascertainment exercise and the amount of information available.

Cost units can be developed for all kinds of organisations, whether manufacturing, commercial or public-service based. Some examples from the CIMA *Terminology* are as follows:

Industry sector	*Cost unit*
Brick-making	1,000 bricks
Electricity	Megawatt-hour (MwH)
Professional services	Chargeable hour
Education	Enrolled student

Activity	*Cost unit*
Credit control	Account maintained
Selling	Customer call

Direct costs can be clearly identified with the cost object we are trying to cost. For example, suppose that a furniture maker is determining the cost of a wooden table. The manufacture of the table has involved the use of timber, screws and metal drawer handles. These items are classified as *direct materials*. The wages paid to the machine operator, assembler and finisher in actually making the table would be classified as *direct labour*. The designer of the table may be entitled to a royalty payment for each table made, and this would be classified as a *direct expense*.

Indirect costs cannot be directly attributed to a particular cost unit, although it is clear that they have been incurred in the production of the table. These indirect costs are often referred to as **overheads**. Examples of indirect production costs are as follows:

Cost incurred	*Cost classification*
Lubricating oils and cleaning materials	Indirect material
Salaries of supervisory labour	Indirect labour
Factory rent and power	Indirect expense

It is important for you to realise that a particular cost may sometimes be a direct cost and sometimes an indirect cost. It depends on the cost object we are trying to cost.

For example, the salary of the machining department supervisor is a direct cost of that department because it can be specifically identified with the department. However, it is an indirect cost of each of the cost units processed in the machining department because it cannot be specifically identified with any particular cost unit.

Test your understanding 2

Spotless Ltd is an office cleaning business which employs a team of part-time cleaners who are paid an hourly wage. The business provides cleaning services for a number of clients, ranging from small offices to high-street shops and large open-plan offices.

In determining the cost of providing a cleaning service to a particular client, which of the following costs would be a direct cost of cleaning that client's office and which would be an indirect cost?

	Direct cost	Indirect cost
(a) The wages paid to the cleaner who is sent to the client's premises.	□	□
(b) The cost of carpet shampoo used by the cleaner.	□	□
(c) The salaries of Spotless Ltd's accounts clerks.	□	□
(d) Rent of the premises where Spotless Ltd stores its cleaning materials and equipment.	□	□
(e) Travelling expenses paid to the cleaner to reach the client's premises.	□	□
(f) Advertising expenses incurred in attracting more clients to Spotless Ltd's business.	□	□

Elements of cost

Now we have looked at some of the basic cost classifications, we can use these to produce a costing for a cost object. The elements of cost are the constituent parts of cost which make up the total cost of a cost object.

Illustration 1

The outline cost statement for a single cost unit shows how the total or full cost for a unit might be built up.

Notice in particular that a number of subtotals can be highlighted before the total cost figure is determined.

	$	$
Direct material		15
Direct labour		5
Direct expenses		2
Prime cost or total direct cost		22
Production overhead:		
indirect material	4	
indirect labour	6	
indirect expenses	6	
		16
Total production/factory cost		38
Selling, distribution and administration overhead		2
Total (full) cost		40
Profit		10
Selling price		50

Note that the costing is split by both *nature* and *purpose*. The direct costs are shown first, split by nature. The total of the direct costs is known as **prime cost**.

Indirect costs (or overheads) are shown next, again split by nature.

This now gives the **total production (or factory) cost**.

Once the non-production costs (those costs which are incurred after production of the goods) are added, **the total (or full) cost** can be ascertained.

The usefulness of each of these subtotals depends on the management action that is to be taken based on each of the totals.

Detailed cost analysis

Suppose that the cost analysis in Illustration 1 has been provided by the management accountant to help us to decide on the selling price to be charged for a luxury wall-mounted hairdryer: the type that is fixed to the wall for customers' use in hotel bedrooms.

Let us look at the sort of costs that might be incurred in manufacturing and selling a hairdryer, and how each cost would be classified in terms of the above analysis of the elements of cost.

- *Direct materials.* This is the material that actually becomes part of the finished hairdryer. It would include the plastic for the case and the packaging materials. If we make another batch of hairdryers then we will need to purchase another batch of these and other direct materials.
- *Direct labour.* This is the labour cost incurred directly as a result of making one hairdryer. If we make another batch of hairdryers then we will need to pay more direct labour cost.
- *Direct expenses.* These are expenses caused directly as a result of making one more batch of hairdryers. For example, the company might be required to pay the designer of the hairdryer a royalty of $2 for each hairdryer produced.

The three direct costs are summed to derive the **prime cost** of $22. This is one measure of cost but we still have to add production overheads.

Production overheads are basically the same three costs as for direct cost, but they are identified as *indirect* costs because they cannot be specifically identified with any particular hairdryer or batch of hairdryers. Indirect costs must be shared out over all the cost objects using a fair and equitable basis.

- *Indirect materials.* These are those production materials that do not actually become part of the finished product. This might include the cleaning materials and lubricating oils for the machinery. The machines must be clean and lubricated in order to carry out production, but it will probably not be necessary to spend more on these materials in order to manufacture a further batch. This cost is therefore only indirectly related to the production of this batch.
- *Indirect labour.* This is the production labour cost which cannot be directly associated with the production of any particular batch. It would include the salaries of supervisors who are overseeing the production of hairdryers as well as all the other products manufactured in the factory.
- *Indirect expenses.* These are all the other production overheads associated with running the factory, including factory rent and rates, heating and lighting, etc. These indirect costs must be shared out over all of the batches produced in a period.

The share of indirect production costs is added to the prime cost to derive the **total production cost** of $38. This is another measure of cost but we still have to add a share of the other overheads.

- *Selling and distribution overhead.* These include the sales force salaries and commission, the cost of operating delivery vehicles and renting a storage warehouse, etc. These are indirect costs which are not specifically attributable to a particular cost unit.
- *Administration overhead.* These include the rent on the administrative office building, the depreciation of office equipment, postage and stationery costs, etc. These are also indirect costs which are not specifically attributable to a particular cost unit.

In this example, the non-production overheads amount to $2 per unit, this is added to the total production cost to give a **total (or full) cost** of $40.

Now that you understand the nature of each of the cost elements which make up the full cost we can think a bit more about the price to be charged for the hairdryer.

In this example a profit of $10 has been added, suggesting a selling price of $50.

Incremental cost

From Illustration 1, we can also consider which costs would be incurred as a result of making one additional hairdryer.

The direct cost of $22 would definitely be incurred if another hairdryer was produced. This is the extra material that would have to be bought, the extra labour costs that would have to be paid and the extra expenses for royalties that would be incurred.

The $16 production overhead cost would not be incurred additionally if another hairdryer was produced. This is the share of costs that would be incurred anyway, such as the cleaning materials, the factory rent and the supervisors' salaries.

The $2 share of selling, distribution and administration overhead would probably not be incurred if another hairdryer was produced. This includes the office costs, the depreciation on the delivery vehicles and the rent of warehousing facilities. This sort of cost would not increase as a result of producing another hairdryer or batch of hairdryers. However, there may be some incremental or extra selling and distribution costs, for example we would probably need to pay a sales commission to the sales team for all their hard work in winning the sale, and there would be some costs involved in delivering the goods to the hotel chain. For the sake of our analysis let us suppose that this incremental cost amounts to $1 per hairdryer, rather than the full amount of $2 shown in the cost analysis.

You can see from the discussion in this exercise that in fact the only extra or **incremental cost** to be incurred in producing another hairdryer is $23 ($22 direct cost plus assumed $1 incremental selling and distribution costs).

Therefore it may be possible to sell the hairdryer for say $25 per hairdryer, and still be better off than if the sale was not made at all!

The extra $2 per hairdryer ($25 – $23 extra cost) would at least contribute towards the costs which are being incurred anyway – the production overheads, administration overheads, etc.

This discussion has illustrated that the concept of cost needs to be qualified if it is to be meaningful. We need to know to which cost we are referring when we state something like 'The cost is $40'.

The $40 cost quoted is the full cost, which includes a fair share of all costs incurred on behalf of the cost object. In our discussion we derived the **marginal or incremental cost** of $23 which would be incurred as a direct result of making and selling another hairdryer.

Therefore, we have seen that different costs are useful in different circumstances and we must always qualify what we mean by 'cost'. Do we mean direct cost, marginal cost, full cost or some other measure of cost?

Note: This example introduces an important concept in management accounting known as **relevant costs**. This will be covered in more detail in Chapter 5.

Test your understanding 3

Ducker Company is a car manufacturer.

Required:

Write the correct classification for each of the costs below into the box provided, using the following classifications (each cost is intended to belong to only one classification):

(i) direct materials

(ii) direct labour

(iii) indirect production overhead

(iv) administration costs

(v) selling and distribution costs.

1	cost of advertising the car on television	
2	wages of workers moving raw materials from stores	
3	cost of metal used for the bodywork of the car	
4	cost of materials used to clean production equipment	
5	assembly worker's wages	
6	wages of office workers	
7	wages of storekeepers in material store	

4 Cost behaviour

In management accounting, when we talk about cost behaviour we are referring to the way in which costs are affected by **fluctuations in the level of activity**.

The level of activity can be measured in many different ways, including:

- the number of units produced
- miles travelled
- hours worked
- meals served
- percentage of capacity utilised.

An understanding of cost behaviour patterns is essential for many management tasks, particularly in the areas of planning, decision making and control. It would be impossible for managers to forecast and control costs without at least a basic knowledge of the way in which costs behave in relation to the level of activity.

The main cost behaviours are:

- Fixed
- Variable
- Semi-variable.

It is important to be able to identify the cost behaviour and also to be able to represent the cost graphically.

Fixed cost

The *CIMA Terminology* defines a **fixed cost** as a 'cost incurred for an accounting period, that, within certain output or turnover limits, tends to be unaffected by fluctuations in the levels of activity (output or turnover)'.

Another term that can be used to refer to a fixed cost is a **period cost**. This highlights the fact that a fixed cost is incurred according to the time elapsed, rather than according to the level of activity.

Examples of fixed costs are:

- rent
- rates
- insurance
- executive salaries.

A fixed cost can be depicted graphically as shown:

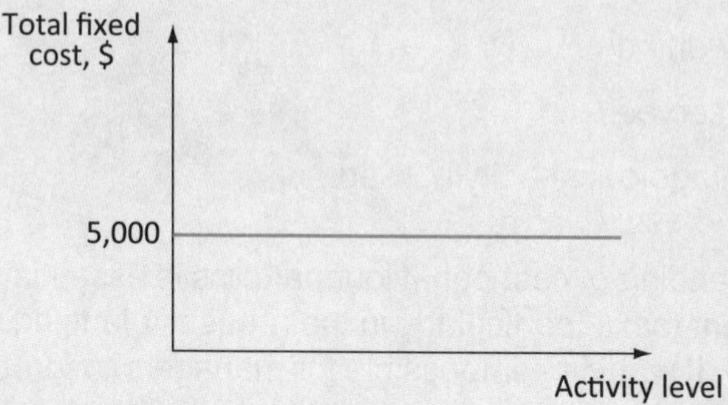

The graph shows that the cost is constant (in this case at $5,000) for all levels of activity. However, it is important to note that this is only true for the **relevant range** of activity. Consider, for example, the behaviour of the rent cost. Within the relevant range it is possible to expand activity without needing extra premises and therefore the rent cost remains constant.

Stepped fixed cost

If activity is expanded beyond the relevant range to the point where further premises are needed, then the rent cost will increase to a new, higher level.

This cost behaviour pattern can be described as a stepped fixed cost or step cost, as shown below:

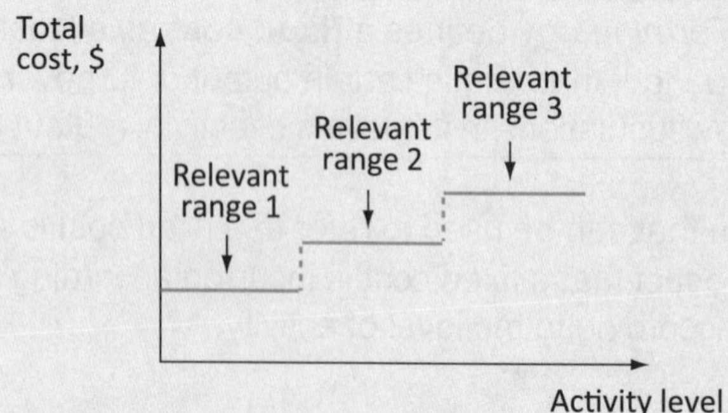

The cost is constant within the relevant range for each activity level but when a critical level of activity is reached, the total cost incurred increases to the next step.

When you are drawing or interpreting graphs of cost behaviour patterns, it is important that you pay great attention to the label on the vertical axis. In the previous examples for fixed cost and stepped fixed cost, the graphs depicted the **total cost** incurred. If the vertical axis had been used to represent the fixed cost **per unit**, then it would look as shown below:

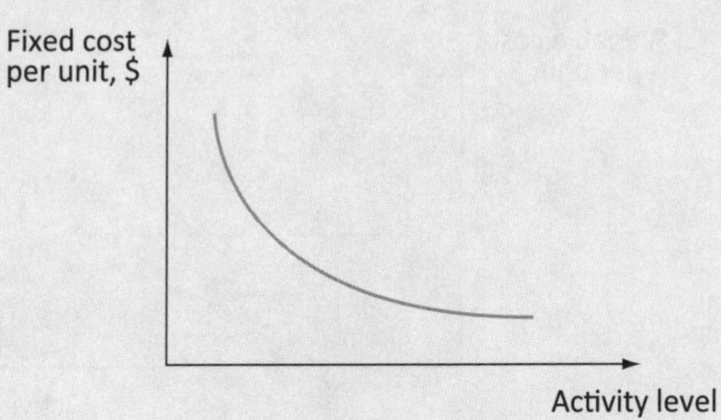

The fixed cost per unit reduces as the activity level is increased. This is because the same amount of fixed cost is being spread over an increasing number of units.

Variable cost

The *CIMA Terminology* defines a **variable cost** as a 'cost that varies with a measure of activity'.

Examples of variable costs are:

- direct material
- direct labour
- variable overheads.

The following graph depicts a linear variable cost. It is a straight line through the origin, which means that the cost is nil at zero activity level. When activity increases, the total variable cost increases in direct proportion. For example, if activity goes up by 10%, then the total variable cost also increases by 10%, as long as the activity level is still within the relevant range.

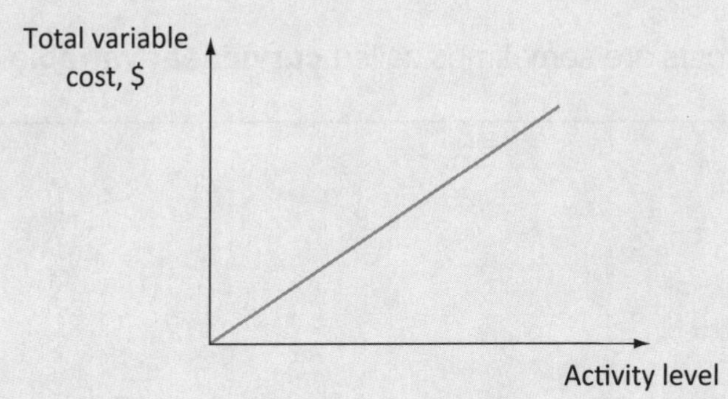

The gradient of the line will depend on the amount of variable cost per unit. A higher variable cost per unit will result in a steeper line.

The above shows the total variable cost, we can also show the variable cost per unit:

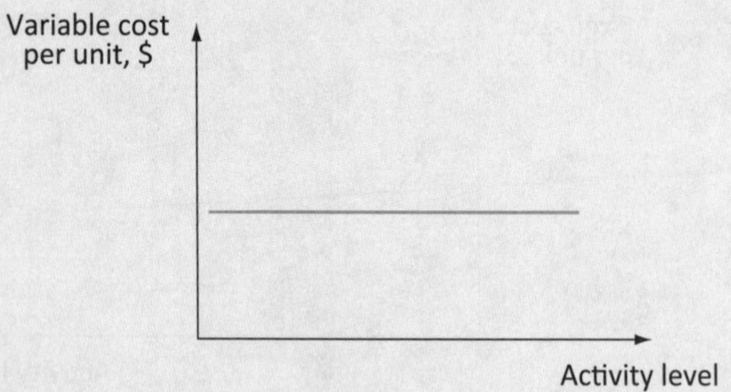

You will notice that this shows a horizontal line as it suggests that the variable cost per unit will not change over the relevant range.

Note: The graph showing the variable cost per unit looks exactly the same as the total fixed cost graph. It is always important to check the vertical axis on the graph as these two are easily confused.

Non-linear variable costs

In most assessment situations, and very often in practice, variable costs are assumed to be linear. Although many variable costs do approximate to a linear function, this assumption may not always be realistic. A variable cost may be non-linear as depicted in the diagrams shown below:

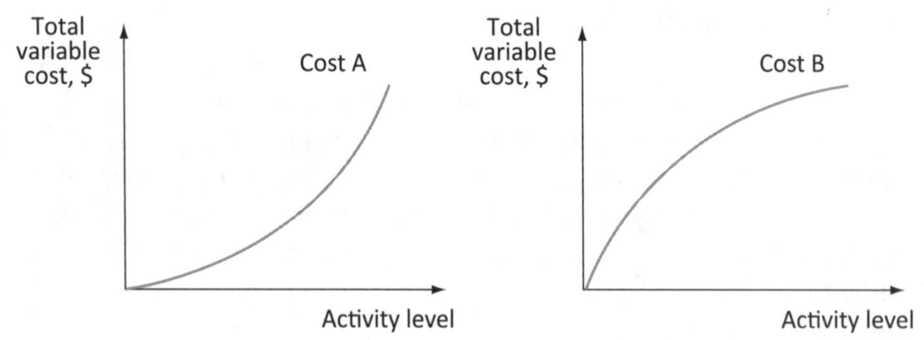

These costs are sometimes called **curvilinear variable costs**.

The graph of cost A becomes steeper as the activity level increases. This indicates that each successive unit of activity is adding more to the total variable cost than the previous unit. An example of a variable cost which follows this pattern could be the cost of direct labour where employees are paid an accelerating bonus for achieving higher levels of output. The graph of cost B becomes less steep as the activity level increases. Each successive unit of activity adds less to total variable cost than the previous unit. An example of a variable cost which follows this pattern could be the cost of direct material where quantity discounts are available.

Semi-variable cost

The *CIMA Terminology* defines a **semi-variable cost** as a 'cost containing both fixed and variable components and thus partly affected by a change in the level of activity'.

A semi-variable cost can also be referred to as a semi-fixed or mixed cost.

Examples of semi-variable costs are:

- gas
- electricity
- telephone

These expenditures consist of a fixed amount payable for the period regardless of the level of use, with a further variable amount which is related to the consumption of gas or electricity, or the number of telephone calls.

A graph of a semi-variable cost might look like the following:

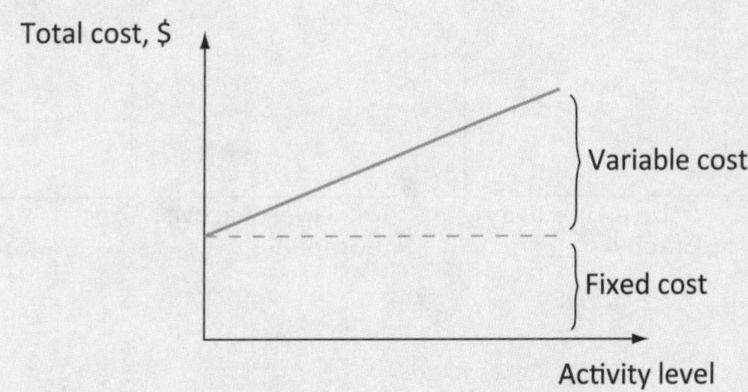

Alternative semi-variable cost behaviour

Alternatively a semi-variable cost behaviour pattern might look like this:

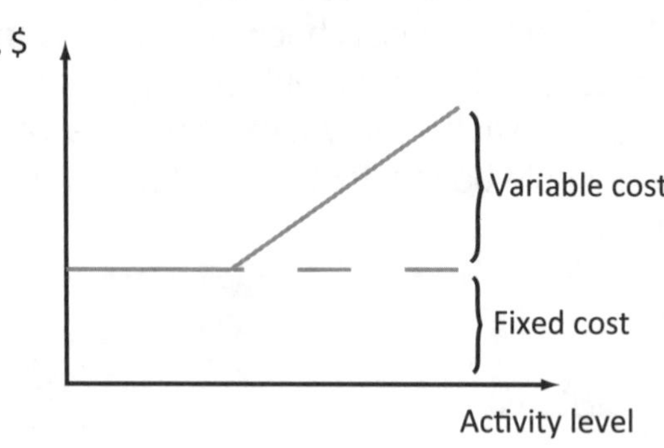

This cost remains constant up to a certain level of activity and then increases as the variable cost element is incurred. An example of such a cost might be the rental cost of a photocopier where a fixed rental is paid and no extra charge is made for copies up to a certain number. Once this number of copies is exceeded, a constant charge is levied for each copy taken.

Test your understanding 4

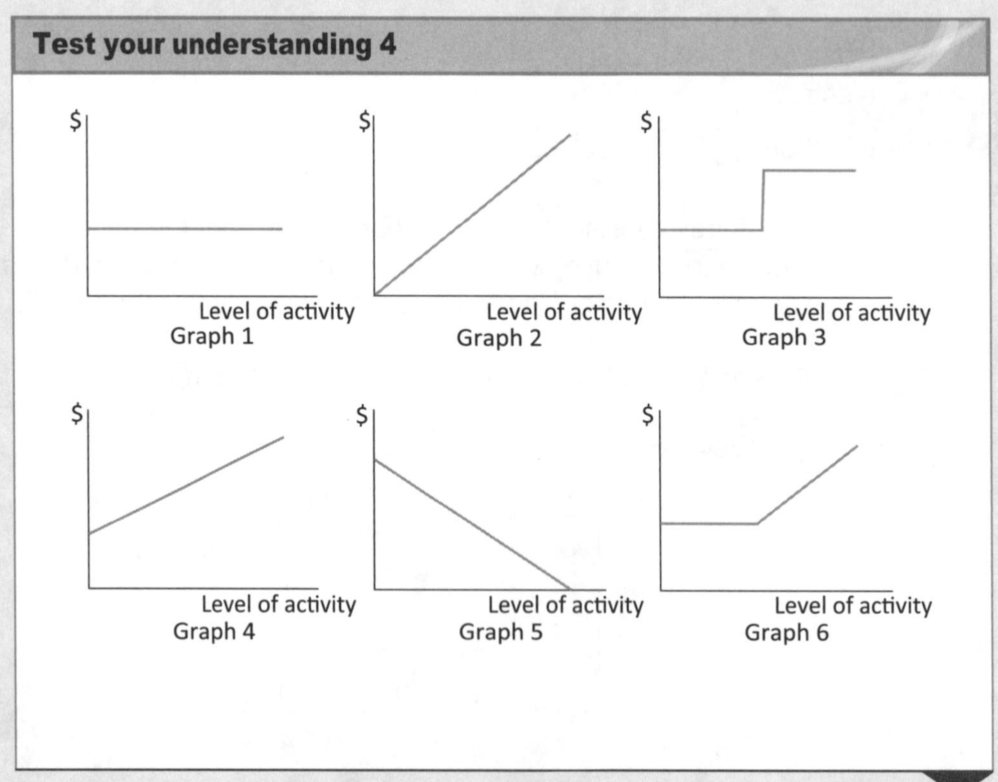

Which one of the above graphs illustrates the costs described below?

(a) A linear variable cost – when the vertical axis represents cost incurred.

A Graph 1

B Graph 2

C Graph 4

D Graph 5

(b) A fixed cost – when the vertical axis represents cost incurred.

A Graph 1

B Graph 2

C Graph 3

D Graph 6

(c) A linear variable cost – when the vertical axis represents cost per unit.

A Graph 1

B Graph 2

C Graph 3

D Graph 6

(d) A semi-variable cost – when the vertical axis represents cost incurred.

A Graph 1

B Graph 2

C Graph 4

D Graph 5

(e) A step fixed cost – when the vertical axis represents cost incurred.

A Graph 3

B Graph 4

C Graph 5

D Graph 6

5 Analysing costs

It is important that you are able to identify whether a cost is fixed, variable or semi-variable from data given.

Illustration 2

Consider the following costs:

	100 units	*200 units*
Material	$500	$1,000
Labour	$1,000	$2,000
Rent	$2,000	$2,000
Electricity	$700	$900

Required:

Identify if the costs are fixed, variable or semi-variable.

Solution

To determine the type of cost, consider the cost behaviour over a range of activity levels.

Material: Material would normally be a variable cost – the total cost is increasing as the number of units increases. To check if it is a linear variable cost, divide the total cost by the number of units and the unit cost should be the same for each level:

Material is $500 for 100 units, therefore $5 per unit, and $1,000 for 200 units, therefore $5 per unit. This suggests that **material is a variable cost**.

Labour: If you look at labour, you can see that **labour is a variable cost** of $10 per unit.

Rent: Rent is normally a fixed cost and in the example the total rent cost is $2,000 for each level of activity. This suggests that **rent is a fixed cost**.

Electricity: For electricity the total cost is increasing as the number of units increase, but if we work out the unit cost we can see that it varies at each level. Electricity is $700 for 100 units, therefore $7 per unit and $900 for 200 units, therefore $4.50 per unit. This suggests that **electricity is a semi-variable cost.**

(3) The point where the extrapolation of this line cuts the vertical axis (the intercept) is then read off as the total fixed cost element. The variable cost per unit is given by the gradient of the line.

From the above diagram the fixed cost contained within this set of data is adjudged to be **$200**.

The variable cost is calculated as follows:

Cost for zero units	=	$200
Cost for 150 units	=	$500

$$\text{Gradient (i.e. variable cost)} = \frac{500 - 200}{150 - 0} = \textbf{\$2 per unit}$$

Test your understanding 7

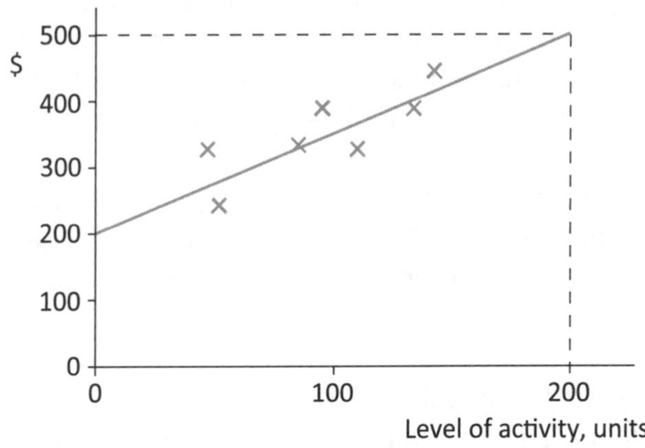

Required:

Based on the above scattergraph:

(a) the period fixed cost is $ ________.

(b) the variable cost per unit is $ ________.

Problems with using historical data to predict the future

The main problem which arises in the determination of cost behaviour is that the estimates are usually based on data collected in the past. **Events in the past may not be representative of the future** and managers should be aware of this if they are using the information for planning and decision making purposes.

It is important to think about the time period under consideration when we are analysing cost behaviour patterns. For example, over a long period of time all costs might be considered to be variable.

In an assessment you should assume that the time period under consideration is neither very long nor very short, unless you are given clear instructions to the contrary.

The time period under consideration

Over a number of years, if activity reduces an organisation can move to smaller premises to reduce rent costs and they can reduce the number of supervisors to reduce supervisor salary cost. Thus costs which we might normally classify as fixed costs are, in the longer term, becoming more variable in relation to the level of activity.

However, in the shorter term costs such as rent and supervisors' salaries are fixed. If demand for a product reduces, the expenditure on rent and on supervisors' salaries cannot be reduced immediately in response to the reduction in output. Such decisions require planning and consideration of factors such as whether the reduction in output is temporary or actions that might be taken to increase output again.

Similarly, over a number of years if activity increases then rent costs and supervisor salary costs will increase in response to the change in activity, again demonstrating more variable behaviour patterns in the longer term.

However, the rent and salary cost is not likely to increase in the longer term in a linear fashion in the way that we have depicted linear variable costs earlier in this chapter. In fact the behaviour of such costs over a longer period of time is likely to follow the pattern of the stepped fixed cost.

Think also about a cost that we would normally classify as variable, such as direct labour cost. In the very short term, for example one day, this cost could be regarded as a fixed cost. If for some reason, perhaps a machine breakdown, we do not produce any output on a particular day it is unlikely that at short notice we can send home all the work force and not pay them. Thus the direct labour cost is a fixed cost in the very short term.

6 Chapter summary

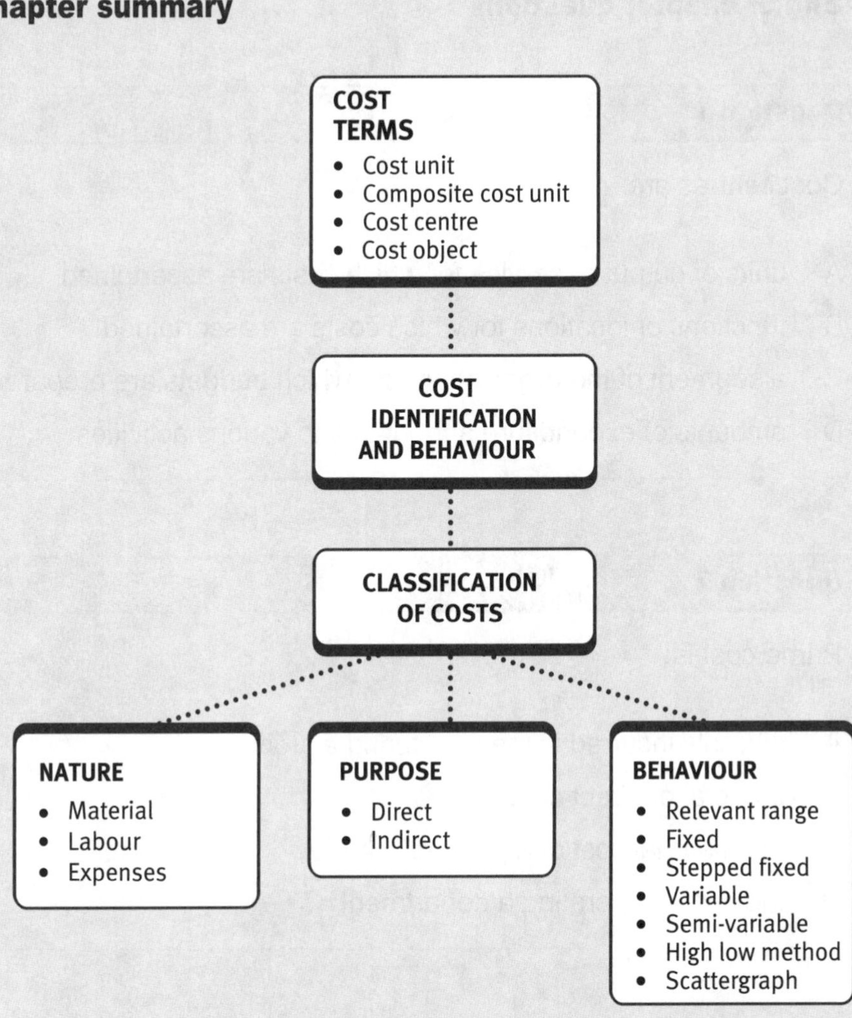
COST TERMS
• Cost unit
• Composite cost unit
• Cost centre
• Cost object
COST IDENTIFICATION AND BEHAVIOUR
CLASSIFICATION OF COSTS
NATURE
• Material
• Labour
• Expenses
PURPOSE
• Direct
• Indirect
BEHAVIOUR
• Relevant range
• Fixed
• Stepped fixed
• Variable
• Semi-variable
• High low method
• Scattergraph

7 End of chapter questions

Question 1

Cost centres are:

A units of output or service for which costs are ascertained

B functions or locations for which costs are ascertained

C a segment of the organisation for which budgets are prepared

D amounts of expenditure attributable to various activities

Question 2

Prime cost is:

A all costs incurred in manufacturing a product

B the total of direct costs

C the material cost of a product

D the cost of operating a department

Question 3

Fixed costs are conventionally deemed to be:

A constant per unit of output

B constant in total when production volume changes

C outside the control of management

D those unaffected by inflation

Question 4

Which of the following are stepped fixed costs? Select all that apply.

(a) Machine rental costs

(b) Direct material costs

(c) Royalties payable on units produced

(d) Depreciation on delivery vehicles

Question 5

Over long time periods of several years, factory rent costs will tend to behave as:

A linear variable costs

B fixed costs

C step fixed costs

D curvilinear variable costs

Question 6

P Ltd is preparing the production budget for the next period. Based on previous experience, it has found that there is a linear relationship between production volume and production costs. The following cost information has been collected in connection with production:

Volume (units)	*Cost ($)*
1,600	23,200
2,500	25,000

What would be the production cost for a production volume of 2,700 units?

A $5,400

B $25,400

C $27,000

D $39,150

Question 7

A company increases its activity within the relevant range. Tick the correct boxes below to indicate the effect on costs.

Total variable costs will:	increase	□
	decrease	□
	remain the same	□
Total fixed cost will:	increase	□
	decrease	□
	remain the same	□
The variable cost per unit will:	increase	□
	decrease	□
	remain the same	□
The fixed cost per unit will:	increase	□
	decrease	□
	remain the same	□

Question 8

The following data have been collected for four cost types, W, X, Y and Z, at two activity levels:

Cost type	*Cost 100 units* $	*Cost 140 units* $
W	8,000	10,560
X	5,000	5,000
Y	6,500	9,100
Z	6,700	8,580

The overhead costs of each production cost centre are then divided by the quantity of production achieved to calculate the amount of overhead cost to be attributed to each unit.

This is known as the overhead absorption rate (OAR):

$$\textbf{Overhead absorption rate (OAR)} = \frac{\textbf{Production cost centre overhead}}{\textbf{Quantity of absorption base (units/labour hours/machine hours)}}$$

Illustration 3

Continuing with our WHW Ltd example:

The output of the machining department is to be measured using the number of machine hours, while the output of the assembly and finishing departments is to be measured using the number of direct labour hours. The reasons for this can be seen from the number of machine and direct labour hours for each department shown in the original data for the example. The machining department is clearly machine-intensive, whereas the other departments are labour-intensive.

The absorption rates are calculated by dividing the costs attributed to the department by its appropriate measure of output.

	Machining	*Assembly*	*Finishing*
Production overhead costs (from illustration 2)	$40,864	$47,400	$10,100
Number of:			
machine hours	32,000		
direct labour hours		32,000	4,000
Absorption rates:			
per machine hour	$1.277		
per labour hour		$1.481	$2.525

The overhead absorption rates (OARs) have been calculated as follows:

Machining – using machine hours:

OAR = $40,864/32,000 = **$1.277 per machine hour**

Assembly – using labour hours:

OAR = $47,400/32,000 = **$1.481 per labour hour**

Finishing – using labour hours:

OAR = $10,100/4,000 = **$2.525 per labour hour**

Applying the overhead absorption rate

When using an absorption method based either on direct labour hours or on machine hours the cost attributed to each unit is obtained by multiplying the time taken per unit by the absorption rate per hour.

For example, if a particular cost unit took three machine hours in the machining department, and five direct labour hours in each of the assembly and finishing departments, the overhead cost absorbed by the cost unit would be as follows:

	$
Machining: 3 hours × $1.277	3.83
Assembly: 5 hours × $1.481	7.41
Finishing: 5 hours × $2.525	12.63
Overhead absorbed by cost unit	23.87

Overhead absorption methods

In addition to the three bases of absorption mentioned above (physical units produced, labour hours worked, machine hours operated), a percentage rate based on any of the following may be used:

- direct material cost;
- direct labour cost;
- prime cost.

In our WHW Ltd example, if a direct labour cost percentage is used the absorption rates would be as follows:

	Machining	*Assembly*	*Finishing*
	$	$	$
Production overhead costs	40,864	47,400	10,100
Direct wages cost	32,600	67,200	7,200
Direct labour cost percentage	125%	71%	140%

If our cost unit had a labour cost of $12 in the machining department, and $20 in each of the assembly and finishing departments, the overhead cost absorbed by the cost unit using this method would be as follows:

	$
Machining: 125% × $12	15.00
Assembly: 71% × $20	14.20
Finishing: 140% × $20	28.00
Overhead absorbed by cost unit	57.20

The direct material cost and the prime cost methods work in a similar way.

The WHW Ltd example demonstrates how the calculated total production cost of a particular cost unit can be dramatically different, depending on the overhead absorption method selected. It is important that the selected method results in the most **realistic** charge for overhead, reflecting the incidence of overheads in the cost centre as closely as possible within the limits of the available data.

You must not make the common mistake of thinking that the best absorption method in this example would be the one which results in the lowest overhead charge to our cost unit. Remember that the same total cost centre overhead is being shared out over the cost units produced, whichever absorption method is selected. If one cost unit is given a lower charge for overhead, then other cost units will be charged with a higher amount so that the total overhead is absorbed overall.

A major factor in selecting the absorption rate to be used is a consideration of the practical applicability of the rate. This will depend on the ease of collecting the data required to use the selected rate.

It is generally accepted that a time-based method should be used wherever possible, that is, the machine hour rate or the labour hour rate. This is because many overhead costs increase with time, for example indirect wages, rent and rates. Therefore, it makes sense to attempt to absorb overheads according to how long a cost unit takes to produce. The longer it takes, the more overhead will have been incurred in the cost centre during that time.

In addition to these general considerations, each absorption method has its own advantages and disadvantages:

Rate per unit. This is the easiest method to apply but it is only suitable when all cost units produced in the period are identical. Since this does not often happen in practice this method is rarely used.

Direct labour hour rate. This is a favoured method because it is time-based. It is most appropriate in labour-intensive cost centres, which are becoming rarer nowadays and so the method is less widely used than it has been in the past.

Machine hour rate. This is also a favoured method because it is time-based. It is most appropriate in cost centres where machine activity predominates and is therefore more widely used than the direct labour hour rate. As well as absorbing the time-based overheads mentioned earlier, it is more appropriate for absorbing the overheads relating to machine activity, such as power, maintenance, repairs and depreciation.

Direct wages cost percentage. This method may be acceptable because it is to some extent time-based. A higher direct wages cost may indicate a longer time taken and therefore a greater incidence of overheads during this time. However, the method will not produce equitable overhead charges if different wage rates are paid to individual employees in the cost centre. If this is the case, then there may not be a direct relationship between the wages paid and the time taken to complete a cost unit.

Direct materials cost percentage. This is not a very logical method because there is no reason why a higher material cost should lead to a cost unit apparently incurring more production overhead cost. The method can be used if it would be too costly and inconvenient to use a more suitable method.

Prime cost percentage. This method is not recommended because it combines the direct wages cost percentage and direct materials cost percentage methods and therefore suffers from the combined disadvantages of both.

5 Predetermined overhead absorption rates

Overhead absorption rates are usually predetermined, that is, they are calculated in advance of the period over which they will be used, **using budgeted or expected costs and activity levels**.

The main reason for this is that overhead costs are not incurred evenly throughout the period. In some months the actual expenditure may be very high and in others it may be relatively low. The actual overhead rate per hour or per unit will therefore be subject to wide fluctuations. If the actual rate was used in product costing, then product costs would also fluctuate wildly. Such product costs would be very difficult to use for planning and control purposes.

Fluctuations in the actual level of production would also cause the same problem of fluctuating product costs.

A further advantage of using predetermined rates is that managers have an overhead rate permanently available which they can use in product costing, price quotations and so on. The actual overhead costs and activity levels are not known until the end of the period. It would not be desirable for managers to have to wait until after the end of the period before they had a rate of overhead that they could use on a day-to-day basis.

Under- or over-absorption of overheads

The problem with using predetermined overhead absorption rates is that the actual figures for overhead and for the absorption base are likely to be different from the estimates used in calculating the absorption rate.

At the end of the period, the company must determine if it has absorbed too much or too little overhead into the products. Two things could have changed during the period:

- The amount of the overhead could be more or less than was budgeted.
- The quantity of the absorption base (units/labour hours/machine hours) could have been more or less than budgeted.

It is these differences which cause an under- or over-absorption of production overheads.

Illustration 4

We will now return to our WHW Ltd example to see how this is calculated, assuming that machine/labour hour rates have been used to absorb the overheads.

We will assume that all of the values used in the calculations in our example so far are estimates based on WHW Ltd's budgets.

The *actual* costs for the same four-week period have now been allocated and apportioned using the same techniques and bases as shown in our earlier example, with the following total actual costs being attributed to each cost centre:

	Machining	*Assembly*	*Finishing*
	$	*$*	*$*
Actual costs	43,528	49,575	9,240

Actual labour and machine hours recorded against each cost centre were:

	Machining	*Assembly*	*Finishing*
Machine hours	32,650		
Labour hours		31,040	3,925

The amount of **overhead cost absorbed** into each department's total number of saleable cost units will be calculated as follows:

Overhead absorbed = budgeted OAR × actual hours

The budgeted OARs were calculated in illustration 3.

Amount absorbed:	*Machining*	*Assembly*	*Finishing*
	$	*$*	*$*
32,650 hours × $1.277	41,694		
31,040 hours × $1.481		45,970	
3,925 hours × $2.525			9,911

This is compared to the **actual cost incurred** and the difference is the under-/over-absorption of production overhead:

	Machining	*Assembly*	*Finishing*
	$	$	$
Amount absorbed	41,694	45,970	9,911
Actual cost incurred	43,528	49,575	9,240
Over-/(Under-)absorption	(1,834)	(3,605)	671

If the amount absorbed exceeds the amount incurred, then an **over-absorption** arises; the opposite is referred to as an **under-absorption**. The terms *under-recovery* and *over-recovery* are sometimes used.

We will return to the under- and over-absorption of overheads in Chapter 9 when we learn how under- or over-absorptions are accounted for in the bookkeeping records.

Under- and over-absorption

The under- or over-absorption in illustration 4 has arisen because the actual overhead incurred per hour was different from the predetermined rate per hour. There are two possible causes of this:

(1) The actual number of hours (machine or direct labour) was different from the number contained in the budget data. If this happens, then we would expect the variable element of the overhead to vary in direct proportion to the change in hours, so this part of the absorption rate would still be accurate. However, the fixed overhead would not alter with the hours worked and this means that the actual overhead cost per hour would be different from the predetermined rate.

(2) The actual production overhead incurred may be different from the estimate contained in the predetermined rate.

The problems caused by under- or over-absorption of overheads

If overheads are under-absorbed then managers have been working with unit rates for overheads which are too low. Prices may have been set too low and other similar decisions may have been taken based on inaccurate information. If the amount of under-absorption is significant, then this can have a dramatic effect on reported profit.

Do not make the common mistake of thinking that over-absorption is not such a bad thing because it leads to a boost in profits at the period end. If overhead rates have been unnecessarily high, then managers may have set selling prices unnecessarily high, leading to lost sales. Other decisions would also have been based on inaccurate information.

Although it is almost impossible to avoid under- and over-absorption altogether, it is possible to minimise the amount of adjustment necessary at the year end. This is achieved by conducting regular reviews of the actual expenditure and activity levels which are arising. The overhead absorption rate can thus be reviewed to check that it is still appropriate to absorb the overheads sufficiently accurately by the year end. If necessary the overhead absorption rate can be adjusted to reflect more recent estimates of activity and expenditure levels.

Test your understanding 3

Budgeted labour hours	8,500
Budgeted overheads	$148,750
Actual labour hours	7,928
Actual overheads	$146,200

(a) What is the labour hour overhead absorption rate?

A $17.50 per hour

B $17.20 per hour

C $18.44 per hour

D $18.76 per hour

(b) What is the amount of overhead under-/over-absorbed?

A $2,550 under-absorbed

B $2,529 over-absorbed

C $2,550 over-absorbed

D $7,460 under-absorbed

Test your understanding 4

Production overhead in department A is absorbed using a predetermined rate per machine hour. Last period, the production overhead in department A was under-absorbed. Which of the following situations could have contributed to the under-absorption? (*Tick all that apply.*)

□ the actual production overhead incurred was lower than budgeted

□ the actual production overhead incurred was higher than budgeted

□ the actual machine hours were lower than budgeted

□ the actual machine hours were higher than budgeted

6 Reciprocal servicing

In our original example of apportionment and reapportionment, there was only one service cost centre. In many examples there will be more than one and this can create a complication when it comes to reapportionment of overheads from the service cost centres to the production cost centres. The complication arises when the service cost centres use each other's services.

For example, if two services cost centres were canteen and maintenance, it is possible that the maintenance staff could use the services of the canteen and should therefore pick up a share of the canteen's costs. It is also possible that the canteen uses the services of the maintenance department and should therefore also pick up a share of the maintenance department costs. This is known as **reciprocal servicing**.

This can lead to a complicated situation because we do not know the total of the maintenance costs until a proportion of the canteen costs has been charged to it. Similarly, we do not know the total of the canteen costs until the total of the maintenance costs has been apportioned.

There are two methods which can be used to solve this problem. Your *Fundamentals of Management Accounting* syllabus requires you to be able to use only the **repeated distribution method**. We will use the following example to illustrate this. The other method, using algebra, is outside the scope of your syllabus.

Illustration 5

A company reapportions the costs incurred by two service cost centres – Stores and Inspection – to three production cost centres – Machining, Finishing and Assembly.

The following are the overhead costs which have been allocated and apportioned to the five cost centres:

	$000
Machining	400
Finishing	200
Assembly	100
Stores	100
Inspection	50

Estimates of the benefits received by each cost centre are as follows:

	Machining	*Finishing*	*Assembly*	*Stores*	*Inspection*
	%	%	%	%	%
Stores	30	25	35	–	10
Inspection	20	30	45	5	–

These percentages indicate the use which each of the cost centres makes of Stores and Inspection facilities.

Required:

Calculate the charge for overhead to each of the three production cost centres, including the amounts reapportioned from the two service centres.

Solution

The task of allocating and apportioning the overheads to all cost centres has already been done (the primary apportionment). The problem now is to reapportion the costs of the service centres (the secondary apportionment).

Using the repeated distribution method the service cost centre costs are apportioned backwards and forwards between the cost centres until the figures become very small. At this stage it might be necessary to round the last apportionments.

In the workings that follow we have chosen to begin the secondary apportionment by apportioning the Inspection costs. The $50,000 inspection cost is reapportioned according to the percentages provided, then the total of Stores department is reapportioned and so on. The final result would have been the same if we had chosen instead to begin by apportioning Stores costs first.

	Machining	*Finishing*	*Assembly*	*Stores*	*Inspection*
	$	$	$	$	$
Initial allocation	400,000	200,000	100,000	100,000	50,000
Apportion Inspection	10,000	15,000	22,500	2,500	(50,000)
Apportion Stores	30,750	25,625	35,875	(102,500)	10,250
Apportion Inspection	2,050	3,075	4,612	513	(10,250)
Apportion Stores	154	128	180	(513)	51
Apportion Inspection*	11	16	24	–	(51)
Total charge for overhead	442,965	243,844	163,191	0	0

* When the service department cost reduces to a small amount, the final apportionment is adjusted for roundings.

The objective has been achieved and all of the overheads have been apportioned to the production cost centres, using the percentages given.

Reciprocal servicing

The task of accounting for reciprocal servicing can be fairly laborious, particularly if it must be performed manually. Managers must therefore ensure that the effort is worthwhile.

Generally, if the service centre costs are significant and they make considerable use of each other's services, then accounting for reciprocal servicing is probably worthwhile. In other cases the reciprocal servicing could be ignored, or alternatively the service centre which does the most work for the other service centres could be apportioned first. The other service centres could then be apportioned directly to the production cost centres.

The overriding consideration must be the usefulness to managers of the resulting information. If the improved accuracy of the overhead absorption rates is deemed to be worthwhile, then reciprocal servicing should be taken into account in service cost reapportionment.

A spreadsheet or similar software package would obviously be helpful here!

In the assessment, you must never ignore the existence of reciprocal servicing unless you are specifically instructed to do so.

Test your understanding 5

DC Ltd has commenced the preparation of its fixed production overhead cost budget for year 2 and has identified the following costs:

	$000
Machining	600
Assembly	250
Finishing	150
Stores	100
Maintenance	80
	1,180

The stores and maintenance departments are production service departments. An analysis of the services they provide indicates that their costs should be apportioned as follows:

	Machining	*Assembly*	*Finishing*	*Stores*	*Maintenance*
Stores	40%	30%	20%	–	10%
Maintenance	55%	20%	20%	5%	–

Required:

After the apportionment of the service department costs, the total overheads of the production departments will be (*to the nearest $500*):

Machining $ _______
Assembly $ _______
Finishing $ _______

Activity-based costing

Activity-based costing (ABC) is a more recent development in cost analysis. It is based on the idea that to use a single absorption base of either labour or machine hours does not accurately reflect the cause of the overhead costs being incurred.

Using an ABC approach, overhead costs are accumulated initially in activity ***cost pools***. These might include, for example, order placing or material handling. Costs would then be collected and analysed for each activity cost pool and a ***cost driver*** would be identified for each activity. Cost drivers are the factors which cause the cost of an activity to increase.

Using estimates of the costs attributed to each activity cost pool and the number of cost drivers associated with it, a **cost driver rate** is calculated. This is similar in principle to the calculation of absorption rates. For example, if the total cost of the activity of setting up a machine is $5,000 for a period and the number of machine set-ups for the period is 250, the cost per set-up is $20 ($5,000/250). Each product that requires the use of this machine is regarded as having incurred $20 of overhead cost each time the machine is set up for the product.

This analysis of overhead costs into activities, and their absorption using a variety of cost drivers, is believed to produce more accurate product costs. The ABC technique can also be applied to non-production costs as well as to the determination of the costs of services provided.

Note: Students are not expected to have a detailed knowledge of ABC.

7 The use of costing information in pricing decisions

There are several methods which companies use to determine the selling price for a product. The way overheads are treated will have a big impact on the selling price calculated.

Marginal cost pricing

With marginal costing, we look at the cost of making and selling one additional unit. This can be very useful when deciding the selling price for a special order. With marginal costing, the variable costs will be incurred if one additional unit is made, but the fixed cost may not change (if the unit to be made falls within the relevant range). Marginal cost is often thought of as variable cost.

It is easier than absorption costing in that we do not have to absorb the overhead into the product cost. The problem with marginal cost pricing is that it is difficult to decide on the mark-up that must be added to the marginal cost in order to ensure that the other costs such as administration overheads are covered and that the organisation makes a profit.

Marginal cost pricing is useful in a one-off special price decision, but it does not help us to decide on the price to be charged in routine product pricing decisions, in order to cover all costs and earn a profit.

You will study marginal costing in much more detail in the later management accounting papers.

Full cost (absorption) pricing

With absorption costing, as we have seen, the overhead absorption rate can be used to trace indirect costs to cost units in order to obtain the unit's full cost.

The full cost of production can be used to determine the selling price.

When deciding on the selling price for a job, organisations often use **mark-up** or **margin**. Firstly, the total costs of the job will be estimated then the profit can be calculated using either mark-up or margin. The selling price can be calculated by adding the costs to the profit.

Profit mark-up

Profit mark-up is calculated as a **percentage of costs**. This can be marginal cost or total cost. This is also referred to as **cost-plus**.

Example

ABG Co. uses profit mark-up to calculate selling prices. The mark-up is 20% of total cost. If the total cost of Job 35 is $8,400, what selling price would ABG quote for the job?

Solution

Selling price = Total cost + 20%.

Total cost	$8,400
Profit	$1,680 (20% of costs)
Selling price	$10,080

Profit margin

Profit margin can calculated as a **percentage return on sales**, or it can be calculated as a **percentage return on investment**.

When using return on sales, the profit can be calculated as:

Total cost × (required margin ÷ (1 – required margin))

or the selling price can be calculated as:

Total cost ÷ (1 – required margin)

Example: Full-cost pricing to achieve a specified return on sales

This pricing method involves determining the full cost of a cost unit and then adding a mark-up that represents a specified percentage of the final selling price.

WP Ltd manufactures product A. Data for product A are as follows:

Direct material cost per unit	$7
Direct labour cost per unit	$18
Direct labour hours per unit	2 hours
Production overhead absorption rate	$6 per direct labour hour
Mark-up for non-production overhead costs	5% of total production cost

WP Ltd requires a 15% return on sales revenue from all products.

Calculate the selling price for product A, to the nearest cent.

Solution

	$ per unit
Direct material cost	7.00
Direct labour cost	18.00
Total direct cost	25.00
Production overhead absorbed (2 hours × $6)	12.00
Total production cost	37.00
Mark-up for non-production costs (5% × $37.00)	1.85
Full cost	38.85
Profit mark-up (15/85* × $38.85)	6.86
Selling price	45.71

*Always read the question data carefully. The 15% required return is expressed as a percentage of the sales revenue, not as a percentage of the cost.

Example: Full-cost pricing to achieve a specified return on investment

This method involves determining the amount of capital invested to support a product. For example, some fixed or non-current assets and certain elements of working capital such as inventory and trade receivables can be attributed to individual products.

The selling price is then set to achieve a specified return on the capital invested on behalf of the product. The following example will demonstrate how the method works.

LG Ltd manufactures product B. Data for product B are as follows:

Direct material cost per unit	$62
Direct labour cost per unit	$14
Direct labour hours per unit	4 hours
Production overhead absorption rate	$16 per direct machine hour
Mark-up for non-production overhead costs	8% of total production cost

LG Ltd sells 1,000 units of product B each year. Product B requires an investment of $400,000 and the target rate of return on investment is 12% per annum.

Calculate the selling price for one unit of product B, to the nearest cent.

Solution

	$ *per unit*
Direct material cost	62.00
Direct labour cost	14.00
Total direct cost	76.00
Production overhead absorbed (4 hours × $16)	64.00
Total production cost	140.00
Mark-up for non-production costs (8% × $140)	11.20
Full cost	151.20
Profit mark-up (see working)	48.00
Selling price	199.20

Working:

Target return on investment in product B = $400,000 × 12% = $48,000

Target return per unit of product B = $48,000/1,000 units = $48

Test your understanding 6

GY Ltd budgets to produce and sell 3,800 units of product R in the forthcoming year. The amount of capital investment attributable to product R will be $600,000 and GY Ltd requires a rate of return of 15% on all capital invested.

Further details concerning product R are as follows:

Direct material cost per unit	$14
Direct labour cost per unit	$19
Variable overhead cost per unit	$3
Machine hours per unit	8

Fixed overhead is absorbed at a rate of $11 per machine hour.

Required:

Calculate all answers to the nearest cent.

(a) The variable cost of product R is $ ________ per unit.

(b) The total (full) cost of product R is $ ________ per unit.

(c) The selling price of product R which will achieve the specified return on investment is $ ________ per unit.

8 Chapter summary

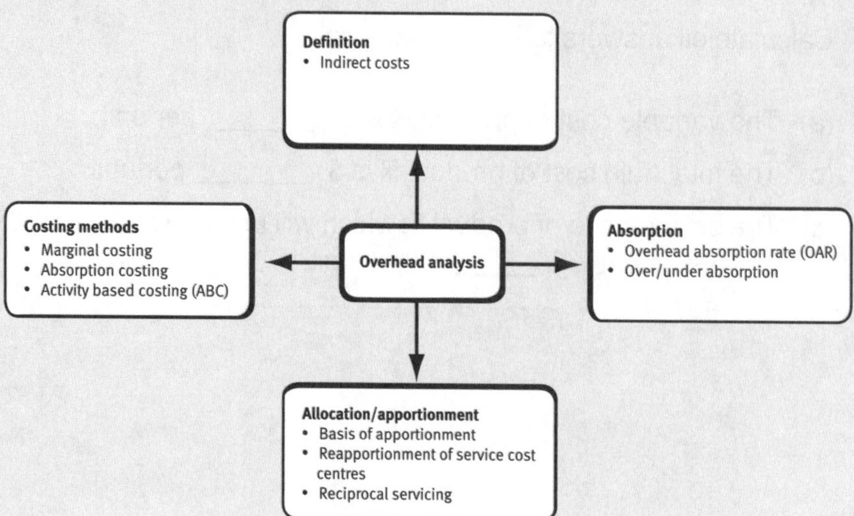

9 End of chapter questions

Question 1

A method of dealing with overheads involves spreading common costs over cost centres on the basis of benefit received. This is known as:

A overhead absorption

B overhead apportionment

C overhead allocation

D overhead analysis

Question 2

An overhead absorption rate is used to:

A share out common costs over benefiting cost centres

B find the total overheads for a cost centre

C charge overheads to products

D control overheads

Question 3

Over-absorbed overheads occur when:

A absorbed overheads exceed actual overheads

B absorbed overheads exceed budgeted overheads

C actual overheads exceed budgeted overheads

D budgeted overheads exceed absorbed overheads

Question 4

A management consultancy recovers overheads on chargeable consulting hours. Budgeted overheads were $615,000 and actual consulting hours were 32,150. Overheads were under-recovered by $35,000.

If actual overheads were $694,075, what was the budgeted overhead absorption rate per hour?

A $19.13

B $20.50

C $21.59

D $22.68

Question 5

P Ltd absorbs overheads on the basis of direct labour hours. The overhead absorption rate for the period has been based on budgeted overheads of $150,000 and 50,000 direct labour hours.

During the period, overheads of $180,000 were incurred and 60,000 direct labour hours were used.

Which of the following statements is correct?

A Overhead was $30,000 over-absorbed

B Overhead was $30,000 under-absorbed

C No under- or over-absorption occurred

D None of the above

Question 6

The budgeted fixed overhead absorption rate for last period was $5 per direct labour hour. Other data for the period are as follows:

Actual fixed overhead expenditure	$234,500
Actual direct labour hours	51,300
Budgeted fixed overhead expenditure	$212,900

The number of direct labour hours budgeted to be worked last period was __________.

Question 7

Activity in the packing department of a company manufacturing fine china involves operatives bubble-wrapping finished items and placing them in boxes which are then sealed and labelled. Most of the boxes are sealed and labelled by specialised machines, but about a quarter of them have to be sealed and labelled by hand. Budgeted activity levels for next period are 3,800 machine hours and 3,600 direct labour hours. The most appropriate production overhead absorption rate for the packing department would be:

Tick the correct box.

Machine hour rate ☐
Direct labour hour rate ☐

Question 8

Data for the machining cost centre are as follows:

Budgeted cost centre overhead	$210,000
Actual cost centre overhead	$230,000
Budgeted machine hours	42,000
Actual machine hours	43,000

Required:

Complete the following calculation

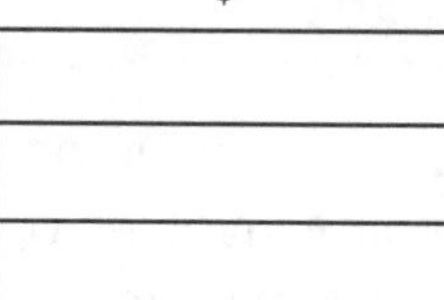

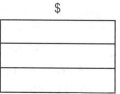

	$
Overhead absorbed	
Actual overhead incurred	
Overhead under-/over-absorbed	

The overhead is under-/over-absorbed. (*delete as appropriate*)

Question 9

The Utopian Hotel is developing a cost accounting system. Initially it has decided to create four cost centres: Residential and Catering deal directly with customers, while Housekeeping and Maintenance are internal service cost centres.

The management accountant is in the process of calculating overhead absorption rates for the next period. An extract from the overhead analysis sheet is as follows:

	Basis of apportionment	*Residential*	*Catering*	*House-keeping*	*Mainte-nance*	*Total*
		$	$	$	$	$
Consumables	Allocated	14,000	23,000	27,000	9,000	73,000
Staff costs	Allocated	16,500	13,000	11,500	5,500	46,500
Rent				A		37,500
Insurance	Value of equip.		B			14,000
Utilities		C				18,500

Other information

The following information is also available:

	Residential	*Catering*	*House-keeping*	*Mainte-nance*	*Total*
Floor area (sq. metres)	2,750	1,350	600	300	5,000
Value of equipment	$350,000	$250,000	$75,000	$75,000	$750,000

Required:

(a) The entries on the overhead analysis sheet shown as A to C are:

A $ ________ (to the nearest $)
B $ ________ (to the nearest $)
C $ ________ (to the nearest $)

(b) The initial overhead allocation and apportionment has now been completed. The cost centre overhead totals are as follows:

	Residential	*Catering*	*House-keeping*	*Mainte-nance*	*Total*
	$	$	$	$	$
Initial allocation and apportionment	85,333	68,287	50,370	23,010	227,000

Housekeeping works 70% for Residential and 30% for Catering, and Maintenance works 20% for Housekeeping, 30% for Catering and 50% for Residential.

After the reapportionment of the Housekeeping and Maintenance cost centres, the total cost centre overheads for Residential and Catering will be, (*to the nearest $*):

Residential $ __________
Catering $ __________

Question 10

QRS Ltd has three main departments – Casting, Dressing and Assembly – and has prepared the following production overhead budgets for period 3.

	Casting	*Dressing*	*Assembly*
Production overheads	$225,000	$175,000	$93,000
Expected production hours	7,500	7,000	6,200

During period 3, actual results were as follows:

	Casting	*Dressing*	*Assembly*
Production overheads	$229,317	$182,875	$92,500
Production hours	7,950	7,280	6,696

Required:

(a) The departmental overhead absorption rates per production hour for period 3 are:

Casting $ _______
Dressing $ _______
Assembly $ _______

(b) (i) The overheads in the Casting department were (tick the correct box and insert the value of the over-/under-absorption):

under-absorbed □ over-absorbed □

by $ _______

(ii) The overheads in the Dressing department were (tick the correct box and insert the value of the over-/under-absorption):

under-absorbed □ over-absorbed □

by $ _______

(c) The overheads in the Assembly department were over-absorbed. Which of the following factors contributed to the over-absorption?

□ the actual overheads incurred were lower than budgeted.
□ the actual production hours were higher than budgeted.

Question 11

DC Ltd's overhead absorption rates for year 1 are as follows:

Machining	$13.83 per machine hour
Assembly	$9.98 per labour hour
Finishing	$9.45 per labour hour

Job no. XX34 is to be started and completed in year 1. Details of the job are as follows:

Direct materials cost $2,400
Direct labour cost $1,500

Machine hours and labour hours required for the job are:

	Machine hours	*Labour hours*
Machining department	45	10
Assembly department	5	15
Finishing department	4	12

Required:

Complete the following statements (to the nearest cent):

(i) The total production overhead cost of job no. XX34 is $________.

(ii) The total production cost of job no. XX34 is $_______.

Question 12

A company manufactures a range of products one of which, product Y, incurs a total cost of $20 per unit. The company incurs a total cost of $600,000 each period and the directors wish to achieve a return of 18% on the total capital of $800,000 invested in the company.

Required:

Based on this information the cost-plus selling price of one unit of product Y should be $ ________.

Question 13

After the initial overhead allocation and apportionment has been completed, the overhead analysis sheet for a car repair workshop is as follows:

Total overhead cost	*Vehicle servicing*	*Crash repairs*	*Tyre fitting*	*Canteen and vending*
$	*$*	*$*	*$*	*$*
233,000	82,000	74,000	61,000	16,000

The costs of the canteen and vending activity are to be reapportioned to the other activities on the basis of the number of personnel employed on each activity.

	Vehicle servicing	*Crash repairs*	*Tyre fitting*	*Canteen and vending*
Number of personnel	20	15	5	2

The canteen and vending cost to be apportioned to the crash repair activity is $ ________.

Question 14

The number of machine and labour hours budgeted for three production cost centres for the forthcoming period is as follows:

	Machining	*Assembly*	*Finishing*
Machine hours	50,000	4,000	5,000
Labour hours	10,000	30,000	20,000

The most appropriate production overhead absorption basis for each cost centre would be (tick the correct box):

	Machining	*Assembly*	*Finishing*
Rate per machine hour	☐	☐	☐
Rate per labour hour	☐	☐	☐

Question 15

The Crayfield Hotel has completed its initial allocation and apportionment of overhead costs and has established that the total budgeted annual overhead cost of its linen services activity is $836,000.

The cost unit used to plan and control costs in the hotel is an occupied room night. The hotel expects the occupancy rate of its 400 rooms, which are available for 365 nights each year, to be 85% for the forthcoming year.

Required:

To the nearest cent, the overhead absorption rate for the linen services activity is $ __________ per occupied room night.

Test your understanding answers

Test your understanding 1

(a) Canteen costs – Number of employees

(b) Cleaning of factory premises – Floor area

(c) Power – Machine running hours

(d) Rent – Floor area

(e) Insurance of plant and machinery – Plant and equipment at cost

Test your understanding 2

Overhead cost item	*Total*	*Machining*	*Assembly*	*Finishing*
	$	*$*	*$*	*$*
Maintenance cost	38,000	19,000	13,300	5,700

Working:

$$\text{Overhead cost per maintenance hour} = \frac{\$38,000}{(1,000 + 700 + 300)} = \$19$$

Maintenance cost for Machining = ($19 × 1,000) = **$19,000**

The other apportionments are calculated in the same way.

Test your understanding 3

(a) **A**

Labour hour overhead absorption rate = $148,750/8,500 = **$17.50 per hour**.

(b) **D**

	$
Overhead incurred	146,200
Overhead absorbed ($17.50 × 7,928 hours)	138,740
Under-absorption	**7,460**

Test your understanding 4

Two of the stated factors could have contributed to the under-absorption:

- ***the actual production overhead incurred was higher than budgeted****;* if this did happen then the predetermined absorption rate would be too low and there would be a potential under-absorption;
- ***the actual machine hours were lower than budgeted****;* if this occurred then there would be fewer than expected hours to absorb the production overhead, potentially leading to under-absorption.

Test your understanding 5

Machining: **$691,500**
Assembly: **$299,500**
Finishing: **$189,000**

Workings:

	Machining	*Assembly*	*Finishing*	*Stores*	*Maintenance*
	$000	$000	$000	$000	$000
Allocated costs	600.00	250.00	150.00	100.00	80.00
Stores apportionment	40.00	30.00	20.00	(100.00)	10.00
Maintenance apportionment	49.50	18.00	18.00	4.50	(90.00)
Stores apportionment	2.00	1.50	1.00	(4.50)	–
Total	**691.50**	**299.50**	**189.00**	–	–

Test your understanding 6

(a) The variable cost per unit of product R is $36.00 per unit.

Direct material $14 + direct labour $19 + variable overhead $3 = **$36**.

(b) The total (full) cost of product R is $124.00 per unit.

Variable cost $36 + fixed overhead (8 hours × $11) = **$124**.

(c) The selling price of product R which will achieve the specified return on investment is $147.68 per unit.

Working:

Required return from investment in product R
= $600,000 × 15% = $90,000

Required return per unit sold = $90,000/3,800 units = $23.68

Required selling price = $124.00 full cost + $23.68 = **$147.68**

Question 1

B

Answer (A) describes the final stage of charging overheads to cost units. (C) describes the allotment of whole items of cost to a single cost unit or cost centre. (D) describes the whole process of overhead allocation, apportionment and absorption.

Question 2

C

An overhead absorption rate is a means of attributing overhead to a product or service based, for example, on direct labour hours.

Question 3

A

Over- or under-absorption of overhead is the difference between absorbed overheads and actual overheads. Under-absorption occurs when actual overheads exceed absorbed overheads.

Question 4

B

Let $x = budgeted overhead absorption rate per hour:

	$
Overhead incurred	694,075
Overhead absorbed ($694,075 – $35,000)	659,075
Under-absorption	35,000

$$\$x = \frac{659,075}{32,150} = \mathbf{\$20.50}$$

Question 5

C

	$
Absorbed: ($150,000/50,000) = $3/hour × 60,000	180,000
Actual incurred	180,000
Under-/over-absorption	–

Question 6

Direct labour hours budgeted to be worked last period = **42,580**.

$$\text{Budgeted overhead absorption rate} = \frac{\text{Budgeted fixed overhead expenditure}}{\text{Budgeted direct labour hours}}$$

$$\$5 = \frac{\$212{,}900}{\text{Budgeted direct labour hours}}$$

Budgeted direct labour hours = $212,900/$5 = **42,580**.

Question 7

The most appropriate production overhead absorption rate for the packing department would be a ***direct labour hour rate***.

Although the number of machine hours in the cost centre is significant, we are told that a quarter of the output is not placed on the machines. No machine hours would be recorded for this output and the use of a machine hour rate would mean that this part of the output received no charge for the overheads of the packing cost centre.

Question 8

	$
Overhead absorbed ($5* × 43,000)	215,000
Actual overhead incurred	230,000
Overhead under-/over-absorbed	**15,000**

The overhead is **under-absorbed**.

$$* \text{ Overhead absorption rate} = \frac{\$210{,}000}{42{,}000} = \$5 \text{ per machine hour}$$

Question 9

(a) A **$4,500**
B **$4,667**
C **$10,175**

Workings:

A Using floor area as the apportionment basis, the rent cost apportioned to Housekeeping = (600/5,000) × $37,500 = **$4,500**.

B (250,000/750,000) × $14,000 = **4,667**.

C Using floor area as the apportionment basis, the utilities cost apportioned to Residential = (2,750/5,000) × $18,500 = **$10,175**.

(b) Residential $135,318
Catering $91,682

Workings:

	Residential	*Catering*	*Housekeeping*	*Maintenance*
	$	$	$	$
Initial allocation and apportionment	85,333	68,287	50,370	23,010
Maintenance reapportioned				
50% to Residential	11,505			
30% to Catering		6,903		
20% to Housekeeping			4,602	(23,010)
	96,838	75,190	54,972	–
Housekeeping reapportioned				
70% to Residential	38,480			
30% to Catering		16,492	(54,972)	
	135,318	**91,682**	–	

Note: This is an example of an application of absorption costing in a non-manufacturing situation. Do not be put off by this. In an assessment you must be prepared to deal with all sorts of unfamiliar situations. The principles of overhead analysis that you have learned in this chapter can be applied in the same way in this non-manufacturing environment. Residential and Catering are the equivalent of the production cost centres that you have learned about, whereas Housekeeping and Maintenance are internal service departments whose costs will need to be reapportioned.

As well as an understanding of two charts:

- Breakeven chart
- PV chart

Students will require a good knowledge of all of these calculations and charts.

3 Contribution

In Chapter 2 you learned that variable costs are those that vary with the level of activity. If we can identify the variable costs associated with producing and selling a product or service we can highlight a very important measure: ***contribution.***

CONTRIBUTION = SALES VALUE – VARIABLE COSTS

Variable costs are sometimes referred to as marginal costs and the two terms are often used interchangeably.

Contribution is so called because it literally does contribute towards fixed costs and profit. Once the contribution from a product or service has been calculated, the fixed costs associated with the product or service can be deducted to determine the profit for the period.

Illustration 1

Consider a product with a variable cost per unit of $26 and selling price of $42. Fixed costs for the period are $12,000.

(a) What is the contribution per unit for the product?

(b) If 1,000 units are sold, what is the total contribution?

(c) What is the total profit and the profit per unit at this level of sales?

(d) Calculate the total profit for the following levels of sales:
   - 500
   - 900
   - 1,200

(e) Calculate the contribution per unit and profit per unit for each level of sales.

Solution

(a) Contribution per unit = sales value – variable costs
$42 – $26 = **$16**

(b) Total contribution = contribution per unit × number of units
$16 × 1,000 = **$16,000**

(c) Total profit = total contribution – fixed costs
$16,000 – $12,000 = **$4,000**

Profit per unit = total profit/number of units
$4,000/1,000 = **$4**

(d) It is easier to use a table for these calculations:

Units	*500*	*900*	*1,200*
	$	*$*	*$*
Sales	21,000	37,800	50,400
Variable cost	13,000	23,400	31,200
Total contribution	8,000	14,400	19,200
Fixed costs	12,000	12,000	12,000
Total Profit/(Loss)	**(4,000)**	**2,400**	**7,200**

(e) Contribution per unit	$16	$16	$16
Profit per unit	**($8)**	**$2.67**	**$6**

You can see from this that the contribution per unit does not change, but that the profit per unit can change significantly as the volume changes. This makes contribution much more useful than profit in many decisions. In the above example, it would have been quicker to start with contribution when working out the profit, as shown below. This saves some unnecessary calculations:

	$	*$*	*$*
Contribution per unit	16	16	16
× units	500	900	1,200
Total contribution	8,000	14,400	19,200
Fixed costs	12,000	12,000	12,000
Total Profit/(Loss)	**(4,000)**	**2,400**	**7,200**

4 Breakeven point

An important concept for decision-makers is breakeven. At a level of zero sales, the company's total contribution will be zero, therefore they will make a total loss equal to the level of their fixed costs. As sales revenues grow, the contribution will grow and will start to cover the fixed costs. Eventually a point will be reached where neither profit nor loss is made, this is the **breakeven point**. At this point the total contribution must exactly match the fixed costs. Any additional contribution made above this level will constitute profit.

If we know how much contribution is earned from each unit sold, then we can calculate the number of units required to break even as follows:

$$\textbf{Breakeven point in units} = \frac{\textbf{Fixed costs}}{\textbf{Contribution per unit}}$$

For example, suppose that an organisation manufactures a single product, incurring variable costs of $30 per unit and fixed costs of $20,000 per month. If the product sells for $50 per unit, then the breakeven point can be calculated as follows:

$$\textbf{Breakeven point in units} = \frac{\$20{,}000}{(\$50 - \$30)} = \textbf{1,000 units per month}$$

Test your understanding 1

AB Company manufactures a single product. The unit costs of the product are as follows:

	$
Direct Materials	36
Direct Labour	12
Direct Expenses	9
Variable Overheads	13

The product sells for $95. The fixed costs for the period were $55,000.

Calculate the breakeven number of units.

5 The margin of safety

The margin of safety is the difference between the expected level of sales and the breakeven point. The larger the margin of safety, the more likely it is that a profit will be made, that is, if sales start to fall there is more leeway before the organisation begins to incur losses (assuming projected sales are greater than breakeven sales).

Margin of safety can be expressed in units or as a % of projected sales:

Margin of safety = projected sales – breakeven sales

or

$$\textbf{Margin of safety \%} = \frac{\textbf{Projected sales – breakeven sales}}{\textbf{Projected sales}}$$

Example: if a company has a breakeven level of sales of 1,000 and is forecasting sales of 1,700, the margin of safety can be calculated as follows:

Margin of safety = 1,700 – 1,000 = 700 units

or

Margin of safety % = (1,700 – 1,000) / 1,700 = 0.41 = 41%

Using the margin of safety % puts it in perspective. To quote a margin of safety of 700 units without relating it to the projected sales figure is not giving the full picture.

Illustration 2

RT organisation manufactures one product. The product sells for $250, and has variable costs per unit of $120. Fixed costs for the month were $780,000. The monthly projected sales for the product were 8,000 units. The margin of safety can be calculated as:

First calculate the breakeven sales:

$$\textbf{Breakeven point in units} = \frac{\textbf{Fixed costs}}{\textbf{Contribution per unit}}$$

$$= \frac{\$780{,}000}{(\$250-\$120)} = \textbf{6,000 units}$$

Margin of safety in units = **projected sales – breakeven sales**
= 8,000 – 6,000 = **2,000 units**

Margin of safety % = **(projected sales – breakeven sales) / projected sales**
= (8,000 – 6,000) / 8,000 = **25%**

The margin of safety can also be used as one route to a profit calculation. We have seen that the contribution goes towards fixed costs and profit. Once breakeven point is reached the fixed costs have been covered. After the breakeven point there are no more fixed costs to be covered and all of the contribution goes towards making profits grow. From the above example, the monthly profit from sales of 8,000 units would be **$260,000.** This can be calculated in the normal way:

Contribution	$130
Total Contribution ($130 × 8,000)	$1,040,000
Fixed costs	$780,000
Profit	**$260,000**

Or using margin of safety:

Margin of safety	= 2,000 units per month
Monthly profit	= 2,000 × contribution per unit
	= 2,000 × $130
	= **$260,000**

Test your understanding 2

OT Ltd plans to produce and sell 4,000 units of product C each month, at a selling price of $18 per unit. The unit cost of product C is as follows:

	$ per unit
Variable cost	8
Fixed cost	4
	—
	12
	—

To the nearest whole number, the monthly margin of safety, as a percentage of planned sales is __________ %.

6 The contribution to sales (C/S) ratio

The contribution to sales ratio is a useful calculation in CVP analysis. It is usually expressed as a percentage. It can be calculated as follows.

$$\textbf{C/S ratio} = \frac{\textbf{Contribution}}{\textbf{Sales}}$$

The C/S ratio can be calculated using contribution and sales at either a unit level, or at a total level.

A higher contribution to sales ratio means that contribution grows more quickly as sales levels increase. Once the breakeven has been passed, profits will accumulate more quickly than for a product with a lower contribution to sales ratio.

You might sometimes see this ratio referred to as the **profit-volume (P/V) ratio**.

Using the RT example from Illustration 2, the C/S ratio can be calculated as:

$$\textbf{C/S ratio} = \frac{\textbf{Contribution}}{\textbf{Sales}}$$

C/S ratio = 130/250 = 0.52 = **52%**

If we can assume that a unit's variable cost and selling price remain constant then the C/S ratio will also remain constant.

The C/S ratio can be used in the calculation of the breakeven point. When we use the C/S ratio on the bottom of the breakeven formula, we get the answer in $ of sales revenue, rather than in units:

$$\textbf{Breakeven point in \$ of sales revenue} = \frac{\textbf{Fixed costs}}{\textbf{C/S ratio}}$$

Using the data from Illustration 2:

$$\textbf{Breakeven point in \$ of sales revenue} = \frac{\textbf{Fixed costs}}{\textbf{C/S ratio}} = \frac{\textbf{\$780,000}}{\textbf{0.52}} = \textbf{\$1,500,000}$$

Note: This could have been calculated as: breakeven point × selling price

= 6,000 × $250 =**$1,500,000**

Sales required for a target profit

A further calculation which is used as part of CVP analysis is the calculation of the level of sales required to achieve a certain level of profit. As with the breakeven point, this can be calculated in sales units or in $ of sales revenue.

The calculations are as follows:

$$\textbf{Sales units required to achieve a profit of X} = \frac{\textbf{(Fixed costs + X)}}{\textbf{Contribution per unit}}$$

or

$$\text{Sales revenue required to achieve a profit of X} = \frac{\text{(Fixed costs + X)}}{\text{C/S ratio}}$$

Test your understanding 3

A company manufactures and sells a single product which has the following cost and selling price structure

	$/unit	*$/unit*
Selling price		120
Direct material	22	
Direct labour	36	
Variable overhead	14	
Fixed overhead	12	
	—	
		84
		—
Profit per unit		36
		—

The fixed overhead absorption rate is based on the normal capacity of 2,000 units per month. Assume that the same amount is spent each month on fixed overheads.

Budgeted sales for next month are 2,200 units.

You are required to calculate:

(i) the breakeven point, in sales units per month;

(ii) the margin of safety for next month;

(iii) the budgeted profit for next month;

(iv) the sales required to achieve a profit of $96,000 in a month.

7 Breakeven charts

A basic breakeven chart records costs and revenues on the vertical axis (y) and the level of activity on the horizontal axis (x). Lines are drawn on the chart to represent costs and sales revenue. The breakeven point can be found where the sales revenue line cuts the total cost line.

We will use a basic example to demonstrate how to draw a breakeven chart. Data from JB Limited's budget is given below:

Selling price	$50 per unit
Variable cost	$30 per unit
Fixed costs	$20,000 per month
Forecast sales	1,700 units per month

The completed graph is shown below:

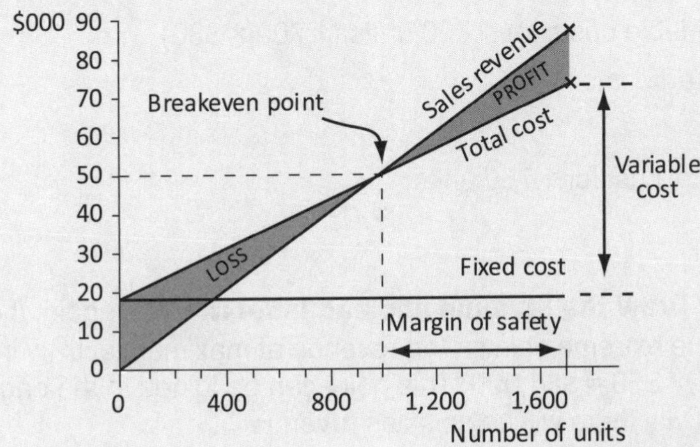

While you will not be required to draw a graph to scale in the assessment, you may need to do so in your working life or in future examinations for other subjects. Learning to draw a chart to scale will provide a firm foundation for your understanding of breakeven charts. To give yourself some practice, it would be a good idea to follow the step-by-step guide which follows to produce your own chart on a piece of graph paper.

Step 1: Select appropriate scales for the axes and draw and label them. Your graph should fill as much of the page as possible. This will make it clearer and easier to read. You can make sure that you do this by putting the extremes of the axes right at the end of the available space.

The highest point on the vertical axis will be the monthly sales revenue, that is,

1,700 units × $50 = $85,000

The highest point on the horizontal axis will be monthly sales volume of 1,700 units.

Make sure that you do not need to read data for volumes higher than 1,700 units before you set these extremes for your scales.

Step 2: Draw the fixed cost line and label it. This will be a straight line parallel to the horizontal axis at the $20,000 level.

The $20,000 fixed costs are incurred in the short term even with zero activity.

Step 3: Draw the total cost line and label it. The best way to do this is to calculate the total costs for the maximum sales level, which is 1,700 units in our example. Mark this point on the graph and join it to the cost incurred at zero activity, that is, $20,000.

	$
Variable costs for 1,700 units (1,700 × $30)	51,000
Fixed costs	20,000
Total cost for 1,700 units	71,000

Step 4: Draw the revenue line and label it. Once again, the best way is to plot the extreme points. The revenue at maximum activity in our example is 1,700 × $50 = $85,000. This point can be joined to the origin, since at zero activity there will be no sales revenue.

Step 5: Mark any required information on the chart and read off solutions as required. You can check that your chart is accurate by reading off the breakeven point and then checking this against the calculation for breakeven:

$$\textbf{Breakeven point in units} = \frac{\textbf{Fixed costs}}{\textbf{Contribution per unit}}$$

$$= \frac{\$20,000}{(\$50\text{-}\$30)} = \textbf{1,000 units}$$

The margin of safety can be seen as the area to the right of the breakeven point up to the forecast sales level of 1,700.

The contribution breakeven chart

One of the problems with the conventional or basic breakeven chart is that it is not possible to read contribution directly from the chart. A contribution breakeven chart is based on the same principles but it shows the variable cost line instead of the fixed cost line. The same lines for total cost and sales revenue are shown so the breakeven point and profit can be read off in the same way as with a basic breakeven chart. However, with this chart it is also possible to read the contribution for any level of activity.

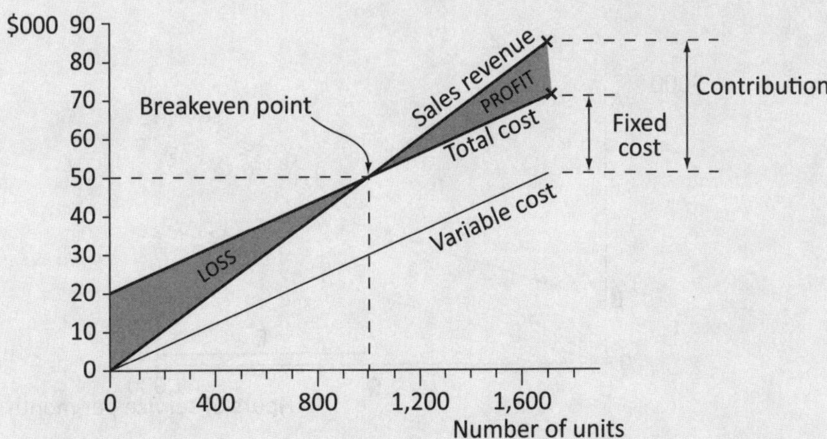

Using the same basic example as for the conventional chart, the total variable cost for an output of 1,700 units is 1,700 × $30 = $51,000. This point can be joined to the origin since the variable cost is nil at zero activity.

The contribution can be read as the difference between the sales revenue line and the variable cost line.

This form of presentation might be used when it is desirable to highlight the importance of contribution and to focus attention on the variable costs.

Ensure you are familiar with these charts and that you are able to identify all the component parts.

Test your understanding 4

Breakeven charts

The following data are available concerning HF Ltd's single service Q.

	$ per hour of service	*$ per hour of service*
Selling price		50
Variable cost		
Direct material	7	
Direct labour	8	
Variable overhead	5	
	–	20
		—
Contribution		30
Fixed overhead		15
		—
Profit		15
		—

1,000 hours of service Q are provided to customers each month.

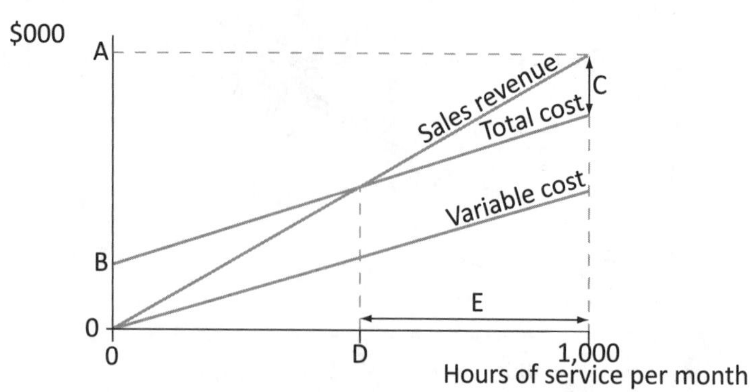

Required:

The management accountant of HF Ltd has prepared the above contribution breakeven chart for service Q.

The values or quantities indicated by A to E on the chart are:

A $ [ ]

B $ [ ]

C $ [ ]

D [ ] hours

E [ ] hours

8 The profit–volume chart

Another form of breakeven chart is the profit–volume chart. This chart plots a single line depicting the profit or loss at each level of activity. The breakeven point is where this line cuts the horizontal axis. A profit–volume chart for the JB Limited example is shown below:

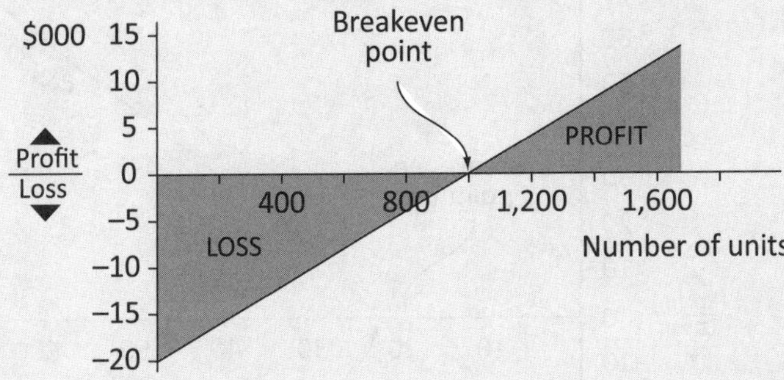

The vertical axis shows profits and losses and the horizontal axis, showing units, is drawn at zero profit or loss.

At zero activity the loss is equal to $20,000, that is, the amount of fixed costs. The second point used to draw the line could be the calculated breakeven point or the calculated profit for sales of 1,700 units.

The profit–volume graph is also called a profit graph or a contribution–volume graph.

The main advantage of the profit–volume chart is that it is capable of depicting clearly the effect on profit and breakeven point of any changes in the variables.

PV chart illustration

A company manufactures a single product which incurs fixed costs of $30,000 per annum. Annual sales are budgeted to be 70,000 units at a sales price of $30 per unit. Variable costs are $28.50 per unit.

(a) Draw a profit–volume graph, and use it to determine the breakeven point.

The company is now considering improving the quality of the product and increasing the selling price to $35 per unit. Sales volume will be unaffected, but fixed costs will increase to $45,000 per annum and variable costs to $33 per unit.

(b) On the same graph as for part (a), draw a second profit–volume graph and comment on the results.

Solution

The profit–volume charts are shown below:

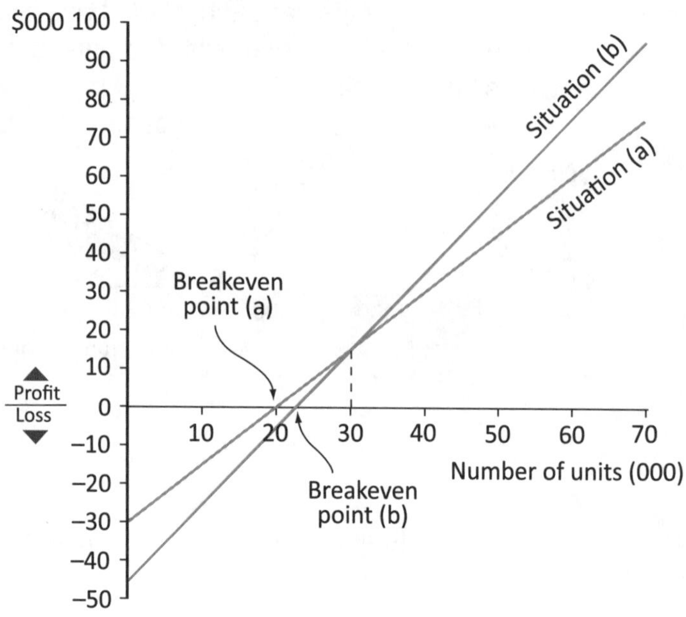

The two lines have been drawn as follows:

- *Situation (a).* The profit for sales of 70,000 units is $75,000.

	$000
Contribution 70,000 × $(30 – 28.50)	105
Fixed costs	30
Profit	75

This point is joined to the loss at zero activity, $30,000, that is, the fixed costs.

- *Situation (b).* The profit for sales of 70,000 units is $95,000.

	$000
Contribution 70,000 × $(35 – 33)	140
Fixed costs	45
Profit	95

This point is joined to the loss at zero activity, $45,000, that is, the fixed costs.

Comment on the results. The chart clearly shows the potentially larger profits available from option (b). It also shows that the breakeven point increases from 20,000 units to 22,500 units but that this is not a large increase when viewed in the context of the projected sales volume. It is also possible to see that for sales volumes above 30,000 units the profit achieved will be higher with option (b). For sales volumes below 30,000 units option (a) will yield higher profits (or lower losses).

The profit–volume graph is the clearest way of presenting information like this. If we attempted to draw two conventional breakeven charts on one set of axes the result would be difficult to interpret.

Test your understanding 5

Select *true* or *false* for each of the following statements about a profit–volume chart.

(a) The profit line passes through the origin.

True □
False □

(b) Other things being equal, the angle of the profit line becomes steeper when the selling price increases.

True □
False □

(c) Contribution cannot be read directly from the chart.

True □
False □

(d) The point where the profit line crosses the vertical axis is the breakeven point.

True □
False □

(e) Fixed costs are shown as a line parallel to the horizontal axis.

True □
False □

(f) The angle of the profit line is directly affected by the P/V ratio.

True □
False □

The economist's breakeven chart

An economist would probably depict a breakeven chart as shown below:

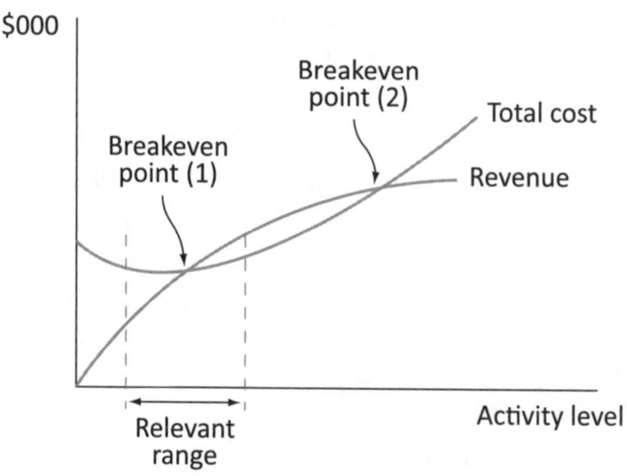

The total cost line is not a straight line which climbs steadily as in the accountant's chart. Instead it begins to reduce initially as output increases because of the effect of economies of scale. Later it begins to climb upwards according to the law of diminishing returns.

The revenue line is not a straight line as in the accountant's chart. The line becomes less steep to depict the need to give discounts to achieve higher sales volumes.

However, you will see that within the middle range the economist's chart does look very similar to the accountant's breakeven chart. This area is marked as the relevant range on the chart.

For this reason, it is unreliable to assume that the cost–volume–profit relationships depicted in breakeven analysis are relevant across a wide range of activity. In particular, the economist's chart shows that the constant cost and price assumptions are likely to be unreliable at very high or very low levels of activity. Managers should therefore ensure that they work within the relevant range, that is, within the range over which the depicted cost and revenue relationships are more reliable.

The relevant range in the context of cost behaviour patterns was discussed in chapter 2.

9 The limitations of breakeven (or CVP) analysis

The limitations of the practical applicability of breakeven analysis and breakeven charts stem mostly from the assumptions which underlie the analysis:

- Costs are assumed to behave in a linear fashion. Unit variable costs are assumed to remain constant and fixed costs are assumed to be unaffected by changes in activity levels. The charts can in fact be adjusted to cope with non-linear variable costs or steps in fixed costs but too many changes in behaviour patterns can make the charts very cluttered and difficult to use.
- Sales revenues are assumed to be constant for each unit sold. This may be unrealistic because of the necessity to reduce the selling price to achieve higher sales volumes. Once again the analysis can be adapted for some changes in selling price but too many changes can make the charts unwieldy.
- It is assumed that activity is the only factor affecting costs, and factors such as inflation are ignored. This is one of the reasons why the analysis is limited to being essentially a short-term decision aid.
- Apart from the unrealistic situation of a constant product mix, the charts can only be applied to a single product or service. Not many organisations have a single product or service and if there is more than one, then the apportionment of fixed costs between them becomes arbitrary.
- The analysis seems to suggest that as long as the activity level is above the breakeven point, then a profit will be achieved. In reality certain changes in the cost and revenue patterns may result in a second breakeven point after which losses are made.

10 Chapter summary

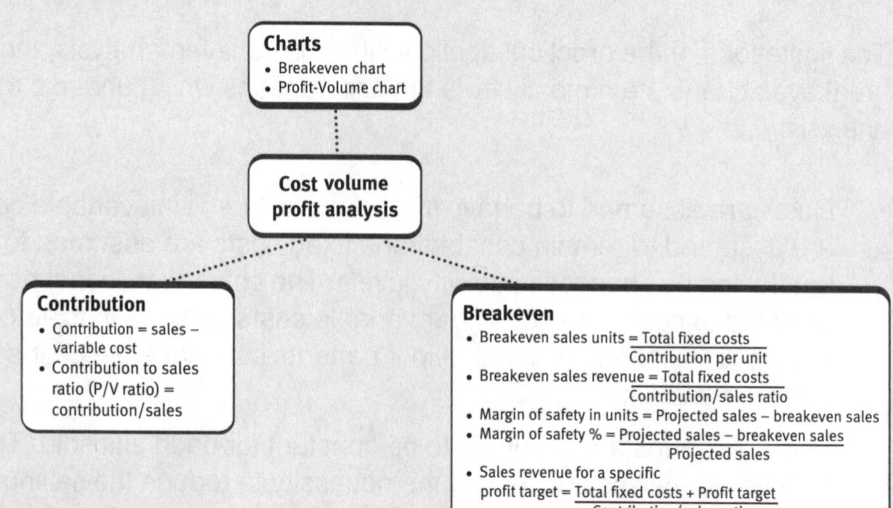

Charts
• Breakeven chart
• Profit-Volume chart
Cost volume profit analysis
Contribution
• Contribution = sales – variable cost
• Contribution to sales ratio (P/V ratio) = contribution/sales
Breakeven
• Breakeven sales units = Total fixed costs / Contribution per unit
• Breakeven sales revenue = Total fixed costs / Contribution/sales ratio
• Margin of safety in units = Projected sales – breakeven sales
• Margin of safety % = Projected sales – breakeven sales / Projected sales
• Sales revenue for a specific profit target = Total fixed costs + Profit target / Contribution/sales ratio

11 End of chapter questions

Question 1

A Ltd has fixed costs of $60,000 per annum. It manufactures a single product which it sells for $20 per unit. Its contribution to sales ratio is 40%.

A Ltd's breakeven point in units is:

A 1,200

B 3,000

C 5,000

D 7,500

Question 2

For the forthcoming year, E plc's variable costs are budgeted to be 60% of sales value and fixed costs are budgeted to be 10% of sales value.

If E plc increases its selling prices by 10%, but if fixed costs, variable costs per unit and sales volume remain unchanged, the effect on E plc's contribution would be:

A a decrease of 2%

B an increase of 5%

C an increase of 10%

D an increase of 25%

Question 3

An organisation currently provides a single service. The cost per unit of that service is as follows:

	$
Selling price	130
	—
Direct materials	22
Direct labour	15
Direct expenses	3
Variable overheads	10
	—
Total variable cost	50
	—

Total fixed costs for the period amount to $1,600,000. How many units of service (to the nearest whole unit) will the organisation need to provide to customers to generate a profit of $250,000?

A 20,000

B 20,555

C 23,125

D 26,428

Question 4

The P/V ratio is the ratio of profit generated to the volume of sales.

True ☐

False ☐

Question 5

Product J generates a contribution to sales ratio of 30%. Fixed costs directly attributable to product J amount to $75,000 per month. The sales revenue required to achieve a monthly profit of $15,000 is $ ______.

Question 6

A manufacturer of mobile phones is considering the following actions. Which of these is likely to increase their C/S ratio? (Tick all that apply.)

(i) □ taking advantage of quantity discounts for bulk purchases of material

(ii) □ introducing training programmes designed to improve labour efficiency

(iii) □ following the actions of a competitor who has cut prices substantially

(iv) □ reducing exports to countries where there is intense price competition

(v) □ offering retailers a lower price if they display the product more prominently.

Question 7

BSE Veterinary Services is a specialist laboratory carrying out tests on cattle to ascertain whether the cattle have any infection. At present, the laboratory carries out 12,000 tests each period but, because of current difficulties with the beef herd, demand is expected to increase to 18,000 tests a period, which would require an additional shift to be worked.

The current cost of carrying out a full test is:

	$ per test
Materials	115
Technicians' wages	30
Variable overhead	12
Fixed overhead	50

Working the additional shift would:

(i) require a shift premium of 50% to be paid to the technicians on the additional shift;

(ii) enable a quantity discount of 20% to be obtained for all materials if an order was placed to cover 18,000 tests;

(iii) increase fixed costs by $700,000 per period.

The current fee per test is $300.

Required:

(a) The profit for the period at the current capacity of 12,000 tests is $__________.

(b) A framework for a profit statement if the additional shift was worked and 18,000 tests were carried out is as follows (complete the boxes to derive the period profit):

$000

(i) Sales
(ii) Direct materials
(iii) Direct labour
(iv) Variable overhead
(v) Fixed costs
(vi) Profit

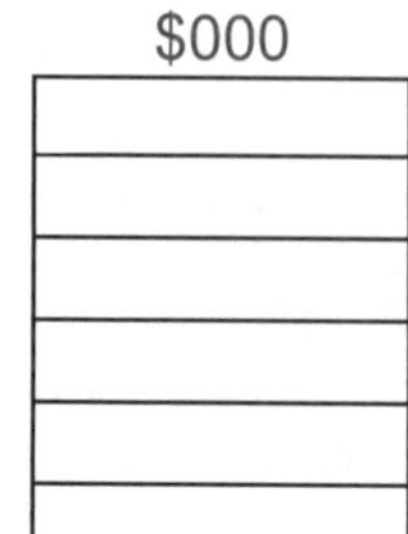

(c) It has been determined that for a capacity of 15,000 tests per period, the test fee would be $300. Variable costs per test would amount to $140, and period fixed costs would be $1,200,000. The breakeven number of tests at this capacity level is ________ tests.

Question 8

B Ltd manufactures a single product which it sells for $9 per unit. Fixed costs are $54,000 per month and the product has a variable cost of $6 per unit.

In a period when projected sales revenue was $180,000, B Ltd's margin of safety, in units, was:

A 2,000

B 14,000

C 18,000

D 20,000

Question 9

A summary of a manufacturing company's budgeted profit statement for its next financial year, when it expects to be operating at 75% capacity, is given below:

	$	$
Sales 9,000 units at $32		288,000
Less:		
direct materials	54,000	
direct wages	72,000	
production overhead – fixed	42,000	
– variable	18,000	
		186,000
Gross profit		102,000
Less: admin., selling and dist'n costs:		
– fixed	36,000	
– varying with sales volume	27,000	
		63,000
Net profit		39,000

It has been estimated that:

(i) if the selling price per unit were reduced to $28, the increased demand would utilise 90% of the company's capacity without any additional advertising expenditure;

(ii) to attract sufficient demand to utilise full capacity would require a 15% reduction in the current selling price and a $5,000 special advertising campaign.

Required:

(a) Calculate the breakeven point in units, based on the original budget.

(b) Calculate the profit and breakeven point which would result from each of the two alternatives and compare them with the original budget.

(c) If the manufacturing company decided to proceed with the original budget, how many units must be sold to achieve a profit of $45,500.

Question 10

Match the following terms with the labels **a** to **d** on the graph. Write a, b, c or d in the relevant boxes.

☐	Margin of safety
☐	Fixed cost
☐	Contribution
☐	Profit

Question 11

MC Ltd manufactures one product only, and for the last accounting period has produced the simplified statement of profit or loss below:

	$	$
Sales		300,000
Costs:		
Direct materials	60,000	
Direct wages	40,000	
Prime cost	100,000	
Variable production overhead	10,000	
Fixed production overhead	40,000	
Fixed administration overhead	60,000	
Variable selling overhead	40,000	
Fixed selling overhead	20,000	
		270,000
Net profit		30,000

Required:

(a) A profit–volume graph is to be drawn for MC Ltd's product.

(i) The profit line drawn on the graph would cut the vertical axis (y-axis) at the point where y is equal to $ _______.

(ii) The profit line drawn on the graph would cut the horizontal axis (x-axis) at the point where x is equal to $ _______.

(iii) The margin of safety indicated by the graph would be $ _______.

(b) The effect of various changes in variables is to be indicated separately on the profit–volume graph. For each change, indicate whether the angle of the profit line and the breakeven point will increase, decrease or remain unchanged.

Variable changed	*The angle of the profit line will:*		
	Increase	*Decrease*	*Remain unchanged*
(i) Increase in selling price	☐	☐	☐
(ii) Increase in fixed cost	☐	☐	☐
(iii) Decrease in variable cost per unit	☐	☐	☐

	The breakeven point will:		
	Increase	*Decrease*	*Remain unchanged*
(i) Increase in selling price	☐	☐	☐
(ii) Increase in fixed cost	☐	☐	☐
(iii) Decrease in variable cost per unit	☐	☐	☐

Test your understanding answers

Test your understanding 1

Contribution = Selling price – Variable costs
= $95 – ($36 + $12 + $9 + $13) = $25

Breakeven point in units = $\dfrac{\textbf{Fixed costs}}{\textbf{Contribution per unit}}$

= $\dfrac{\$55{,}000}{\$25}$ = **2,200 units**

Test your understanding 2

First calculate the monthly fixed costs: 4,000 units × $4 = $16,000.

Then calculate the contribution per unit: sales – variable costs = (18 – 8) = $10.

Then calculate the breakeven point in units:

Breakeven point in units = $\dfrac{\textbf{Fixed costs}}{\textbf{Contribution per unit}}$

= $\dfrac{\$16{,}000}{\$10}$ = **1,600 units**

Margin of safety %: (Projected sales – Breakeven sales) / Projected sales = (4,000 – 1,600) / 4,000 = 0.6 = **60%**.

Test your understanding 3

(i) To calculate the breakeven point, first determine the contribution per unit.

Contribution = $120 – ($22 + $36 + $14) = $48

Note: The fixed costs are based on the budgeted level of output.

$$\textbf{Breakeven point} = \frac{\textbf{Fixed costs}}{\textbf{Contribution per unit}}$$

$$= \frac{\$12 \times 2{,}000}{\$48} = \textbf{500 units}$$

(ii) Margin of safety = Projected sales – Breakeven sales

= 2,200 – 500

= **1,700 units**

(iii) Once the breakeven point has been reached, all of the contribution goes towards profits because all of the fixed costs have been covered.

Budgeted profit = 1,700 units margin of safety × $48 contribution per unit

= **$81,600**

(iv) To achieve the desired level of profit, sufficient units must be sold to earn a contribution which covers the fixed costs and leaves the desired profit for the month.

$$\textbf{Sales units required for a profit of X} = \frac{\textbf{(Fixed costs + X)}}{\textbf{Contribution per unit}}$$

$$= \frac{(\$12 \times 2{,}000) + \$96{,}000}{\$48}$$

= **2,500 units**

Test your understanding 4

A Total sales revenue for 1,000 hours of service = **$50,000** (1,000 hours × $50 selling price)

B Fixed cost at zero activity = **$15,000** (1,000 hours × $15 fixed overhead absorption rate)

C Profit for 1,000 hours = **$15,000** (see workings below)

D Breakeven point = **500 hours** (see workings below)

E Margin of safety = **500 hours** (1,000 hours – 500 hours)

Workings:

	$	$
Sales value for 1,000 hours = 1,000 × $50		50,000
Total cost for 1,000 hours:		
variable cost 1,000 × $20	20,000	
fixed cost 1,000 × $15	15,000	
		35,000
Profit for 1,000 hours		**15,000**

$$\textbf{Breakeven point} = \frac{\textbf{Fixed costs}}{\textbf{Contribution per hour}} = \frac{\$15{,}000}{\$30} = \textbf{500 hours}$$

Test your understanding 5

(a) **False.** The profit line passes through the breakeven point on the horizontal axis, and cuts the vertical axis at the point where the loss is equal to the fixed costs.

(b) **True.** Profits increase at a faster rate if the selling price is higher.

(c) **True.** A contribution breakeven chart is needed for this.

(d) **False.** The point where the profit line crosses the vertical axis is the total loss, which is equal to the level of fixed costs. The breakeven point is where the profit line cuts the horizontal axis.

(e) **False.** No fixed cost line is shown on a profit–volume chart.

(f) **True.** The higher the P/V ratio or contribution to sales ratio, the higher will be the contribution earned per $ of sales and the steeper will be the angle of the profit line.

Question 1

D

Contribution per unit = 40% of selling price = $8

$$\textbf{Breakeven point} = \frac{\$60{,}000}{\$8} = 7{,}500 \text{ units}$$

Question 2

D

Fixed costs are not relevant because they do not affect contribution. Taking a selling price of, say, $100 per unit, the cost structures will look like this:

	Before change *$ per unit*		*After change* *$ per unit*
Sales price	100	+10%	110
Variable cost	60		60
	—		—
Contribution	40		50
	—		—

Contribution per unit increases by 25%. If sales volume remains unchanged then total contribution will also increase by 25%.

Question 3

$$\textbf{Sales units required to achieve a profit of X} = \frac{\textbf{(Fixed costs + X)}}{\textbf{Contribution per unit}}$$

$$= \frac{(\$1{,}600{,}000 + \$250{,}000)}{(\$130 - \$50)}$$

$$= \textbf{23,125 units}$$

Question 4

False. The P/V ratio is another term for the C/S ratio. It measures the ratio of the contribution to sales.

Question 5

$$\textbf{Required sales revenue} = \frac{\textbf{Fixed costs + Required profit}}{\textbf{C/S ratio}} = \frac{\$75{,}000 + \$15{,}000}{0.30}$$

= **$300,000**

Question 6

(i), (ii) and (iv) will increase the C/S ratio.

(i) Higher C/S ratio (lower variable costs per unit, higher contribution per unit)

(ii) Higher C/S ratio (lower variable costs per unit, higher contribution per unit)

(iii) Lower C/S ratio (lower selling price per unit, lower contribution per unit)

(iv) Higher C/S ratio (higher average contribution per unit)

(v) Lower C/S ratio (lower selling price per unit, lower contribution per unit)

Question 7

- In part (b) do not be tempted to use unit rates to calculate the new level of fixed costs. The current level of fixed costs is $600,000 *per period*. This will increase by $700,000.
- Also in part (b), notice that the shift premium applies only to the technicians working on the additional shift. It does not apply to all technicians' wages.

(a) **$1,116,000**

Workings: Profit statement for current 12,000 capacity

		$000
Sales	12,000 tests @ $300/test	3,600
Direct materials	12,000 tests @ $115/test	(1,380)
Direct labour	12,000 tests @ $30/test	(360)
Variable overhead	12,000 tests @ $12/test	(144)
Contribution		1,716
Fixed costs	12,000 tests @ $50/test	(600)
Profit		1,116

(b) **Profit statement for 18,000 capacity, with additional shift**

		$000	$000
Sales	18,000 tests @ $300/test		5,400 (i)
Direct materials	18,000 tests @ $92/test		(1,656) (ii)
Direct labour	12,000 tests @ $30/test	(360)	
	6,000 tests @ $45/test	(270)	
			(630) (iii)
Variable overhead	18,000 tests @ $12/test		(216) (iv)
Contribution			2,898 (v)
Fixed Costs			(1,300) (v)
Profit			1,598 (vi)

(c) **Breakeven volume** $= \dfrac{\textbf{\$1,200,000}}{\textbf{(\$300 – \$140)}}$ = **7,500 tests**

Question 8

A

You have to do a few preliminary calculations before calculating the margin of safety. You will first need to calculate the contribution per unit, then the breakeven point, then the projected sales in units before you can calculate the margin of safety.

Contribution per unit = \$9 – \$6 = \$3

$$\textbf{Breakeven point in units} = \frac{\textbf{Fixed costs}}{\textbf{Contribution per unit}}$$

$$= \frac{\$54,000}{\$3} = \textbf{18,000 units}$$

Projected sales = projected sales revenue/sales price = \$180,000/\$9 = 20,000 units

Margin of safety = Projected sales – Breakeven sales

= 20,000 – 18,000 = **2,000 units**

Question 9

(a) First calculate the current contribution per unit.

Contribution = Sales – Variable costs

Total contribution = 288,000 – (54,000 + 72,000 + 18,000 + 27,000) = $117,000

Contribution per unit = $117,000/9,000 units = $13

Now you can use the formula to calculate the breakeven point:

$$\textbf{Breakeven point} = \frac{\textbf{Fixed costs}}{\textbf{Contribution per unit}}$$

$$= \frac{\$42,000 + \$36,000}{\$13} = \textbf{6,000 units}$$

(b) *Alternative (i)*

Budgeted contribution per unit	$13
Reduction in selling price ($32 – $28)	$4
Revised contribution per unit	$9
Revised breakeven point = $78,000/$9	**8,667 units**
Revised sales volume = 9,000 × (90%/75%)	10,800 units
Revised contribution = 10,800 × $9	$97,200
Less fixed costs	$78,000
Revised profit	**$19,200**

Alternative (ii)

Budgeted contribution per unit	$13.00
Reduction in selling price (15% × $32)	$4.80
Revised contribution per unit	$8.20

Revised breakeven point $= \dfrac{\$78{,}000 + \$5{,}000}{\$8.20}$ **10,122 units**

Revised sales volume = 9,000 units × (100%/75%)	12,000 units
Revised contribution = 12,000 × $8.20	$98,400
Less fixed costs	$83,000
Revised profit	**$15,400**

Neither of the two alternative proposals is worthwhile. They both result in lower forecast profits. In addition, they will both increase the breakeven point and will therefore increase the risk associated with the company's operations.

This exercise has shown you how an understanding of cost behaviour patterns and the manipulation of contribution can enable the rapid evaluation of the financial effects of a proposal.

(c) In this case the contribution must be sufficient to cover both the fixed costs and the required profit. If we divide this amount by the contribution earned from each unit, we can determine the required sales volume.

$$\textbf{Required sales} = \frac{\textbf{Fixed costs + Required profit}}{\textbf{Contribution per unit}}$$

$$= \frac{(\$42{,}000 + \$36{,}000 + \$45{,}500)}{\$13} = \underline{\textbf{9,500 units}}$$

Question 10

c Margin of safety

a Fixed cost

b Contribution

d Profit

Question 11

(a) (i) – $120,000 (The profit line cuts the vertical axis at the point equal to the fixed costs, that is, the loss when no sales are made)

(ii) $240,000 (The profit line cuts the horizontal axis at the breakeven point)

(iii) $ 60,000 (The margin of safety is the difference between the projected sales and the breakeven level of sales)

Workings:

Total fixed costs = $40,000 + $60,000 + $20,000 = **$120,000**

C/S ratio = (300,000 – 100,000 – 10,000 – 40,000)/300,000 = 50%

$$\textbf{Breakeven point} = \frac{\textbf{Fixed costs}}{\textbf{C/S ratio}} = \frac{\$40{,}000 + 60{,}000 + 20{,}000}{0.5} = \$240{,}000$$

Margin of safety = Projected sales – Breakeven sales
= $300,000 – $240,000 = **$60,000**

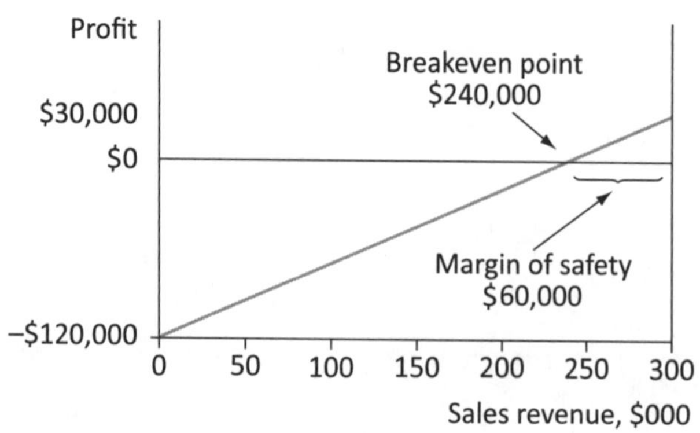

		The angle of the profit line will:	*The break-even point will:*
(b)	(i) Increase in selling price	Increase	Decrease
	(ii) Increase in fixed cost	Remain unchanged	Increase
	(iii) Decrease in variable cost per unit	Increase	Decrease

chapter

5

Decision making

Chapter learning objectives

After completing this chapter, you should be able to:

- explain relevant costs and cash flows:
- explain make or buy decisions:
- calculate the profit maximising product sales mix using limiting factor analysis.

1 Session content diagram

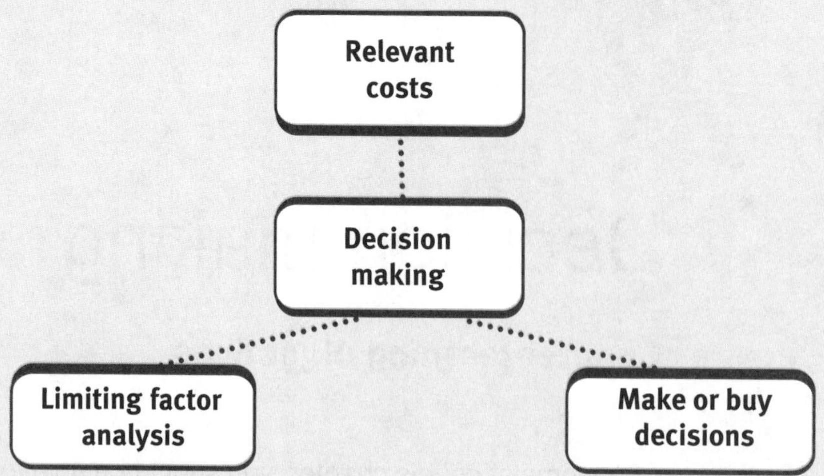

2 Decision making using relevant costs

Organisations face many decisions, and they often must choose between two or more alternatives. Decisions will generally be based on taking the decision that maximises shareholder value. In all decision making, only **relevant costs and revenues** should be used.

Relevant costs and revenues are those costs and revenues that *change* as a direct result of a decision taken.

Relevant costs and revenues have the following features:

- **They are future costs and revenues** – as it is not possible to change what has happened in the past, then relevant costs and revenues must be future costs and revenues.
- **They are incremental** – relevant costs are incremental costs and it is the increase in costs and revenues that occurs as a direct result of a decision taken that is relevant. Common costs can be ignored for the purposes of decision making. Look out for costs detailed as *differential, specific or avoidable.*
- **They are cash flows** – in addition, future costs and revenues must be cash flows arising as a direct consequence of the decision taken. Relevant costs do not include items which do not involve cash flows (depreciation for example).

In an examination, unless told otherwise, assume that variable costs are relevant costs.

Non-relevant costs

Costs which are not relevant to a decision are known as non-relevant costs and include:

- **Sunk costs** are past costs or historical costs which are not directly relevant in decision making, for example development costs or market research costs.
- **Committed costs** are future costs that cannot be avoided, whatever decision is taken.
- **Non-cash flow costs** are costs which do not involve the flow of cash, for example, depreciation.
- **Notional costs** are costs that will not result in an outflow of cash either now or in the future, for example sometimes the head office of an organisation may charge a 'notional' rent to its branches. This cost will only appear in the accounts of the organisation but will not result in a 'real' cash expenditure. Another example would be notional interest which could be charged to departments for the use of internally generated funds.
- **General fixed overheads** are usually not relevant to a decision. However, some fixed overheads may be relevant to a decision, for example stepped fixed costs may be relevant if fixed costs increase as a direct result of a decision being taken.
- **Net book values** are not relevant costs because like depreciation, they are determined by accounting conventions rather than by future cash flows.

Test your understanding 1

In a short-term decision making context, which ONE of the following would be a relevant cost?

A Specific development costs already incurred

B The cost of special material which will be purchased

C Depreciation on existing equipment

D The original cost of raw materials currently in inventory that will be used on the project.

Opportunity costs

The *CIMA terminology* defines **opportunity cost** as 'the value of the benefit sacrificed when one course of action is chosen in preference to an alternative. The opportunity cost is represented by the forgone potential benefit from the best rejected course of action'

Opportunity cost is an important concept in decision making. The opportunity cost emphasises that decision making is concerned with alternatives and that a cost of taking one decision is the profit or contribution forgone by not taking the next best alternative.

If resources to be used on projects are scarce (e.g. labour, materials, machines), then consideration must be given to profits or contribution which could have been earned from alternative uses of the resources.

For example, the skilled labour which may be needed on a new project might have to be withdrawn from normal production. This withdrawal would cause a loss in contribution which is obviously relevant to the project appraisal. rent, then it is not an opportunity cost.

When considering relevant costs, the cash flows of a single department or division cannot be looked at in isolation. The effects on cash flows of the whole organisation must be considered.

Test your understanding 2

GHT Ltd currently produces two products, K and R. Details of the two products for last year are given below:

	K	*R*
Selling price	$40	$25
Variable cost per unit	$31	$17
Sales units	4,000	2,000

Fixed costs for the year were $35,000.

GHT is now considering expanding production of K. If the expansion goes ahead, the fixed costs will increase by $22,000 per annum. The selling prices of the two products will remain the same, but it is anticipated that the variable cost of product K will fall to $28 per unit. The sales of K are budgeted to increase to 5,500, but the additional sales of K will result in a fall in sales of R by 300 units.

The factory space which will be used to house the expansion is currently rented out to a local business at a rent of $500 per month.

Required:

Advise GHT if the expansion is worthwhile. Calculate the resulting increase or decrease in profit.

3 Relevant cost of materials

Many relevant cost questions will involve the use of materials. There are a number of alternative costs which could be relevant for materials: purchase price, replacement cost, net realisable value or opportunity cost. The relevant cost will depend on the given situation.

The following decision tree can help to determine the relevant cost of materials.

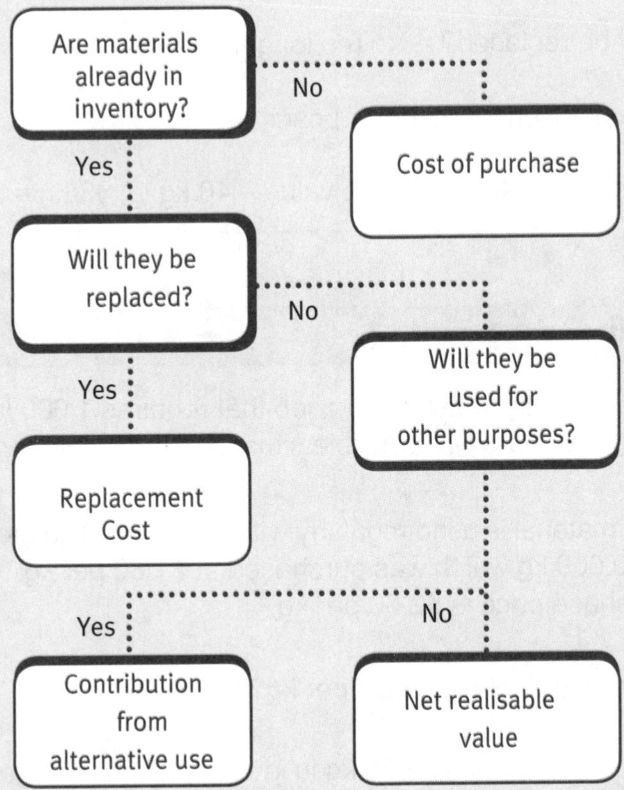

Note: The contribution from alternative use is the **opportunity cost.**

Illustration 1

Z Ltd has 50 kg of material P in inventory which was bought five years ago for $70. It is no longer used but could be sold for $3/kg.

Z Ltd is currently pricing a job that could use 40 kg of material P.

The relevant cost of material P that should be included in the contract is $ __________.

Solution

Using the decision tree:

Are materials already in inventory? – Yes

Will they be replaced? – No (no longer used)

Will they be used for other purposes? – No

Relevant cost = Net realisable value – 40 kg @ $3/kg = **$120**

Test your understanding 3

A firm is currently considering a job that requires 1,000 kg of raw material. There are two possible situations.

(a) The material is used regularly within the firm. The present inventory is 10,000 kg which was purchased at $1.80 per kg. The current purchase price is $2.00 per kg.

What is the relevant cost per kg?

(b) The company has 2,000 kg in inventory, bought 2 years ago for $1.50 per kg, but no longer used for any of the firm's products. The current market price for the material is $2.00, but the company could sell it for $0.80 per kg.

What is the relevant cost for material?

Test your understanding 4

A new contract requires the use of 50 tons of metal ZX. There are 25 tons of ZX in inventory at the moment, which were bought for $200 per ton. The company no longer has any use for metal ZX. The current purchase price is $210 per ton, and the metal could be disposed of for net scrap proceeds of $150 per ton. What cost should be charged to the new contract for metal ZX?

4 Relevant cost of labour

As with material, it can be difficult to determine the relevant cost of labour. With questions involving labour costs, the key question is whether spare capacity exists. The following decision tree can help to determine the relevant cost of labour.

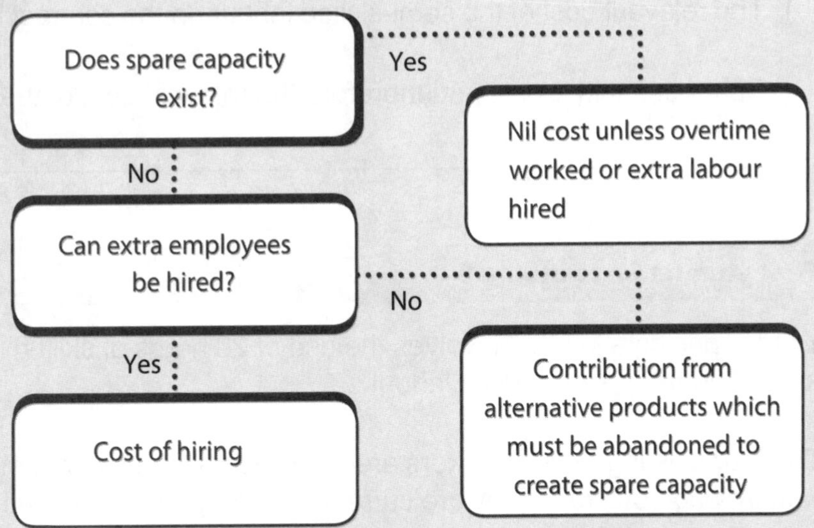

Note: When there is no spare capacity and no alternative labour can be hired, labour must be taken from existing projects. This is the **opportunity cost**. In this case, remember to add on the direct labour cost:

Relevant cost = Contribution forgone from alternative product **PLUS** direct labour cost.

Illustration 2

(a) 100 hours of unskilled labour are needed for a contract. The company has no surplus capacity at the moment, but additional temporary staff could be hired at $6.50 per hour.

What is the relevant cost of the unskilled labour on the contract?

(b) 100 hours of semi-skilled labour are needed for a contract. The company currently has 300 hours worth of spare capacity. There is a union agreement that there are no lay-offs. The workers are paid $8.50 per hour.

What is the relevant cost of the semi-skilled labour on the contract?

Solution

(a) The relevant cost of the unskilled labour on the contract is $650.

Using the decision tree, spare capacity does not exist, but extra employees can be hired, therefore the relevant cost is the cost of hiring temporary staff at $6.50 per hour.

The relevant cost for the contract is 100 hours × $6.50 = **$650**.

(b) The relevant cost of the semi-skilled labour on the contract is NIL.

Spare capacity exists and therefore the relevant cost of the semi-skilled labour is **$0**.

Test your understanding 5

Z Ltd is pricing a job that involves the use of 20 hours of skilled labour and 50 hours of semi-skilled labour.

The four existing skilled workers are paid $15 per hour with a minimum weekly wage of $450. They are currently working 24 hours a week.

The semi-skilled workforce is currently fully utilised. They are each paid $10 per hour, with overtime payable at time and a half. Additional workers may be hired for $12 per hour.

Calculate the relevant labour cost for Z Ltd's job.

Test your understanding 6

A mining operation uses skilled labour costing $14 per hour, which generates a contribution (after deducting the labour costs) of $3 per hour.

A new project is now being considered which requires 5,000 hours of skilled labour. There is a shortage of the required labour and no additional labour can be hired. What is the relevant cost of using the skilled labour on the project?

The relevant cost of overheads

In addition to calculating the relevant cost of materials and labour, you may also be required to calculate the relevant cost of overheads.

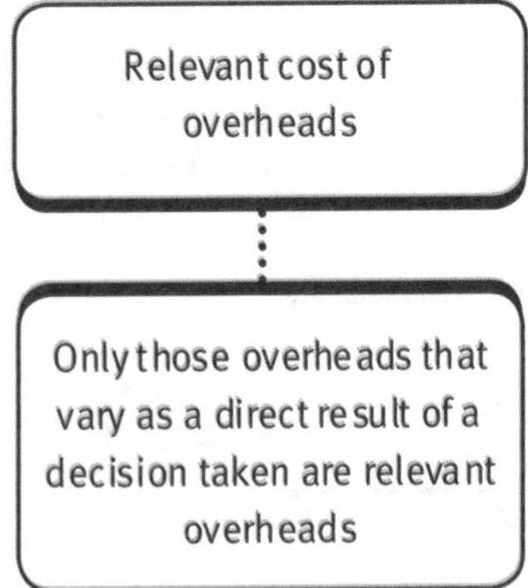

Example

JB Ltd absorbs overheads on a machine hour rate, currently $20/hour, of which $7 is for variable overheads and $13 for fixed overheads. The company is deciding whether to undertake a contract in the coming year. If the contract is undertaken, it is estimated that fixed costs will increase for the duration of the contract by $3,200.

Required:

Identify the relevant fixed and variable overhead costs for the contract.

Solution

- The variable cost per hour of overheads is relevant since this cost would be avoidable if the contract were not undertaken. The relevant cost of variable overheads is therefore **$7 per machine hour**.
- Actual fixed costs would not increase by $13 per hour, but by $3,200 in total, so the relevant cost of fixed overheads is therefore **$3,200**.

5 Relevant cost of non-current assets

The relevant costs associated with non-current assets, such as plant and machinery, are determined in a similar way to the relevant costs of materials.

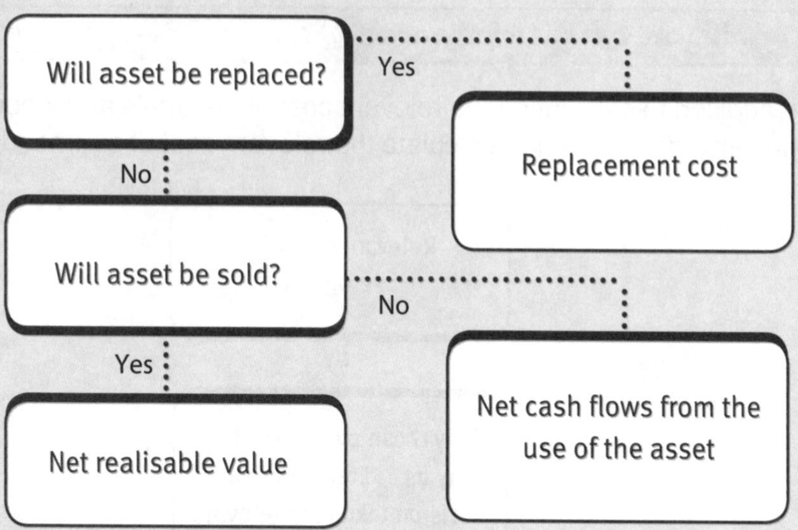

Where there is a choice between selling an asset, or using the asset, the higher of the net realisable value and the cash flows from the use of the asset (the economic value) should be selected as the relevant cost.

Illustration 3

A machine which cost $10,000 four years ago has a written-down value of $6,000 and the depreciation to be charged this year is $1,000. It has no alternative use, but it could be sold now for $3,000. In one year's time it will have no resale value.

Relevant cost of the machine = 

Solution

- The $10,000 (the cost of the machine four years ago) is a sunk cost and is not relevant to the decision.
- The $6,000 (written-down value of the machine) is not relevant because it is determined by accounting conventions and not by future cash flows.
- The $1,000 (depreciation charge this year) is not relevant because this is a non-cash flow cost.
- The $3,000 (sale proceeds if the machine were sold now) is a relevant cost (future cash flow).

The cost of keeping the machine and selling it in a year's time is $3,000 because this is the amount that you will miss out on if you don't sell it now.

Test your understanding 7

Equipment owned by a company has a net book value of $1,800 and has been idle for some months. It could now be used on a six month contract that is being considered. If not used on this contract, the equipment would be sold now for a net amount of $2,000. After use on the contract, the equipment would have no resale value and would be dismantled.

What is the total relevant cost of the equipment to the contract?

Relevant cost forms the foundation for much of the decision making organisations undertake. Remember to use COMMON SENSE in these questions.

Two common decisions are:

- Limiting factor decisions – where the company tries to operate at the maximum profitability despite being constrained in some way.
- Make or buy decisions – where a company decides whether to make components in house, or buy them from an external supplier.

6 Limiting factor analysis

In most business situations only a limited number of business opportunities may be undertaken. Some factor will limit the ability to undertake all the alternatives. This factor is referred to as the **limiting factor.**

A limiting factor is any factor which is in scarce supply and which stops the organisation from expanding its activities further, that is, it limits the organisation's activities.

The limiting factor for many trading organisations is sales volume because they cannot sell as much as they would like. However, other factors may also be limited, especially in the short term. For example, machine capacity or the supply of skilled labour may be limited for one or two periods until some action can be taken to alleviate the shortage.

Illustration 4

X makes a single product (Z) that requires $5 of materials and two hours of labour. There are only 80 hours of labour available each week and the maximum amount of material available each week is $500.

Assuming unlimited demand for product Z, which of these two factors is a limiting factor on production?

Solution

It can be said that the supply of both labour hours and materials is limited and that therefore they are both scarce resources. The maximum production within these constraints can be shown to be:

Materials: $500/$5 = 100 units
Labour hours: 80 hours/2 hours = 40 units

Thus the shortage of labour hours is the limiting factor.

Note: In *Fundamentals of Management Accounting*, questions will only examine single limiting factors. Therefore always establish which factor is the limiting factor and base all calculations on this. Later CIMA papers will examine situations with more than one limiting factor.

Decisions involving a single limiting factor

The concept of **contribution** can be used to make decisions about the best use of a limited resource.

If an organisation is faced with a single limiting factor, for example machine capacity, then it must ensure that a production plan is established which maximises the profit from the use of the available capacity. Assuming that fixed costs remain constant, this is the same as saying that the contribution must be maximised from the use of the available capacity. The machine capacity must be allocated to those products which earn the most contribution per machine hour.

This decision rule can be stated as:
'maximising the contribution per unit of limiting factor'.

To calculate the contribution per unit of limiting factor:

$$\frac{\textbf{Contribution per unit}}{\textbf{Units of limiting factor required per unit}}$$

When limiting factors are present, contribution (and therefore profits) are maximised when products earning the highest amount of contribution per unit of limiting factor are manufactured first. The profit-maximising production mix is known as the **optimal production plan**.

The optimal production plan is established as follows.

- **Step 1** If not clearly given in the question, establish the single limiting factor
- **Step 2** Calculate the contribution per unit for each product.
- **Step 3** Calculate the contribution per unit of limiting factor.
- **Step 4** Rank the products according to their contribution per unit of limiting factor.
- **Step 5** Allocate the limiting factor to the highest-ranking product.
- **Step 6** Once the demand for the highest-ranking product is satisfied, move on to the next highest-ranking product and so on until the (limiting factor) scarce resource is used up.

Illustration 5

LMN Ltd manufactures three products L, M and N. The company which supplies the two raw materials which are used in all three products has informed LMN that their employees are refusing to work overtime. This means that supply of the materials is limited to the following quantities for the next period:

Material A	1,030 kg
Material B	1,220 kg

No other source of supply for materials A and B can be found for the next period.
Information relating to the three products manufactured by LMN Ltd is as follows:

	L	*M*	*N*
Quantity of material used per unit manufactured:			
Material A (kg)	2	1	4
Material B (kg)	5	3	7
Maximum sales demand (units)	120	160	110
Contribution per unit sold	$15	$12	$17.50

Required:

Recommend a production mix which will maximise the profits of LMN Ltd for the forthcoming period.

Solution

- **Step 1:** Check whether the supply of each material is adequate or whether either or both of them represent a limiting factor.

Material A required to produce the total sales demand of products L,M and N:

(120 × 2) + (160 × 1) + (110 × 4) = **840kg** (available: 1,030kg)

Therefore material A is not a limiting factor.

Material B required to produce the total sales demand of products L,M and N:

(120 × 5) + (160 × 3) + (110 × 7) = **1,850kg** (available: 1,220 kg)

Therefore material B is the liming factor.

- **Step 2:** Calculate the contribution per unit of product. This is given in the question:

	L	*M*	*N*
Contribution per unit sold	$15	$12	$17.50

- **Step 3:** Calculate the **contribution per unit of limiting factor**.

	L	M	N
Contribution per unit sold	$15	$12	$17.50
Material B consumed (kg)	5	3	7
Contribution per kg of material B	$3	$4	$2.50

- **Step 4:** Rank the products

	L	M	N
Contribution per kg of material B	$3	$4	$2.50
Ranking	**2**	**1**	**3**

- **Step 5/6**: Allocate material B to the products according to this ranking. Once the demand for the highest ranking product is satisfied, move to the next highest ranking product, and so on, until all of material B is used up.

Product	*Production (units)*	*Material B utilised (kg)*	
M	160 (max)	480	(160 × 3)
L	120 (max)	600	(120 × 5)
N	20	140	(balance)
		1,220	

The available material B is able to satisfy the maximum market demand for products M and L. The balance of available material is allocated to the last product in the ranking, product N.

The optimum production mix is to produce:

160 units of M

120 units of L

20 units of N

If required by the question, calculate the maximum profit (or contribution if the question has no fixed costs). It is best to use total contribution for this calculation:

Product M	*Product L*	*Product N*	*Total*
(160 × 12) +	(120 × 15) +	(20 × 17.50) =	**$4,070**

Note: This is the maximum profit which can be made given the limiting factor. No other combination can achieve a higher profit.

Test your understanding 8

ABC Ltd makes three products, all of which use the same machine, which is available for 50,000 hours per period.

The unit costs of the product are:

	Product A	*Product B*	*Product C*
	$	*$*	*$*
Direct materials	70	40	80
Direct labour:			
Machinists ($8/hour)	48	32	56
Assemblers ($6/hour)	36	40	42
Total variable cost	154	112	178
Selling price per unit	200	158	224
Maximum demand (units)	3,000	2,500	5,000

Fixed costs are $300,000 per period.

Required:

(a) The deficiency in machine hours for the next period is ________ hours.

(b) The optimum production plan that will maximise ABC Ltd's profit for the next period is:

Product A [ ] units

Product B [ ] units

Product C [ ] units

7 Make or buy decisions

Businesses may be faced with the decision about whether to make components or products themselves (in house) or to obtain these from outside suppliers.

If the items are bought in from external suppliers, their purchase cost is wholly marginal (i.e. direct). However, if it is decided to manufacture the items internally, the comparative costs of doing so will be the **variable production cost** (direct materials and direct labour costs, plus the variable factory overhead). Allocated fixed costs will not be relevant to the decision as they will not change, but any **specific** or **avoidable** fixed costs incurred in the production of the item under consideration would be included as part of the internal manufacturing cost.

Note: Relevant costing principles are behind all decisions, remember to look out for opportunity costs.

If the total internally manufactured cost is greater than the cost of obtaining similar items elsewhere, it is obviously uneconomic to produce these items internally and they would be purchased externally. An item should be made in house only if the relevant cost of making the product in house is less than the cost of buying the product externally.

If spare capacity exists:

The relevant cost of making the product in house = the variable cost of internal manufacture plus any fixed costs directly related to that product.

If no spare capacity exists:

The relevant cost of making the product in house = the variable cost of internal manufacture plus any fixed costs directly related to that product **plus** the opportunity cost of internal manufacture (e.g. lost contribution from another product).

Illustration 6

Albax Ltd manufactures three components (A, B and C) All the components are manufactured using the same general purpose machinery. The following production cost data are available, together with the purchase prices from an outside supplier.

	A	*B*	*C*
Production cost:	$	$	$
Direct material	14	20	10
Direct labour	24	13	12
Variable overhead	8	7	8
Allocated fixed overhead	9	6	4
	—	—	—
Total	55	46	34
Purchase price from outside supplier	54	50	28

Required:

Which, if any, components should be purchased from the outside supplier?

Solution

When comparing internal production costs and external buy in costs, the relevant cost to use for the internal production cost is the **variable cost of production.**

	A	B	C
	$	$	$
Internal production cost (variable production costs only)	46	40	30
Purchase price from outside supplier	54	50	28
Incremental (cost)/saving	(8)	(10)	2

In this case, Albax should purchase component C externally. Components A and B should be manufactured internally.

Test your understanding 9

Following on from illustration 7, further details of A, B and C are now available:

	A	B	C
Machine hours per unit	2	5	4

The external price of C has risen to $42.

Manufacturing requirements show a need for 1,500 units of each component per week. The maximum number of general purpose machinery hours available per week is 15,000.

What should be purchased from the outside supplier?

8 Chapter summary

Relevant costs
- Cash flows
- Incremental costs
- Ignore sunk costs
- Opportunity costs
- Notional costs

Decision making

Limiting factor analysis
- Limiting factor
- Contribution per unit of limiting factor
- Optimum production plan

Make or buy decisions
- Internal production costs
- Limiting factors

9 End of chapter questions

Question 1

P Ltd provides plumbing services. Due to a shortage of skilled labour next period the company is unable to commence all the plumbing jobs for which customers have accepted estimates.

When deciding which plumbing jobs should be commenced, the jobs should be ranked according to the:

A Contribution to be earned from each job.

B Profit to be earned from each job.

C Contribution to be earned per hour of skilled labour on each job.

D Profit to be earned per hour of skilled labour on each job.

Question 2

Z Ltd manufactures three products, the selling price and cost details of which are given below:

	Product X	*Product Y*	*Product Z*
	$	$	$
Selling price per unit	75	95	95
Costs per unit:			
Direct materials ($5/kg)	10	5	15
Direct labour ($8/hour)	16	24	20
Variable overhead	8	12	10
Fixed overhead	24	36	30

In a period when direct materials are restricted in supply, the most and the least profitable uses of direct materials are:

	Most profitable	*Least profitable*
A	X	Z
B	Y	Z
C	Z	Y
D	Y	X

Question 3

PH Ltd has spare capacity in its factory. A supermarket chain has offered to buy a number of units of product XZ each month, and this would utilise the spare capacity. The supermarket is offering to purchase XZ at a price of $8 per unit. The cost structure of XZ is as follows:

	$ per unit
Direct material	3
Direct labour	2
Variable overhead	1
Fixed overhead	3
	9

Fixed costs would not be affected by the supermarket contract.

On a purely financial basis, should the supermarket's offer be accepted or rejected?

Question 4

The following tasks are undertaken when deciding on the optimum production plan when a limiting factor exists. Write 1, 2, 3 or 4 in the boxes to indicate the correct sequence of tasks.

- □ Rank the products according to the contribution per unit of limiting factor used.
- □ Calculate each product's contribution per unit of limiting factor used.
- □ Identify the limiting factor.
- □ Allocate the limited resource according to the ranking.

Question 5

The following statements relate to relevant cost concepts in decision making:

(i) Materials can never have an opportunity cost whereas labour can.

(ii) The annual depreciation charge is not a relevant cost.

(iii) Fixed costs would have a relevant cost element if a decision causes a change in their total expenditure.

Which statements are correct?

A (i) and (ii) only

B (ii) and (iii) only

C (i), (ii) and (iii)

Question 6

A contract is under consideration that requires 800 labour hours. There are 450 hours of spare labour capacity for which the workers are still being paid the normal rate of pay. The remaining hours required for the contract can be found either by overtime working paid at 50% above the normal rate of pay or by diverting labour from the manufacture of product OT.

If the contract is undertaken and labour is diverted, then sales of product OT will be lost. Product OT takes seven labour hours per unit to manufacture and makes a contribution of $14 per unit. The normal rate of pay for labour is $8 per hour.

What is the total relevant labour cost to the contract?

A $3,500

B $4,200

C $4,500

D $4,900

Question 7

A company has an asset that originally cost $58,000, but would now cost just $37,000 to replace. The asset could be sold for scrap to earn $11,000. Alternatively, it could be used in a small project that would earn net income of $17,500. The asset has no other use.

What is the relevant value of the asset?

A $6,500

B $11,000

C $17,500

D $37,000

Question 8

A company manufactures and sells two products (X and Y) both of which require the same raw material. For the coming period, the supply of material is limited to 5,000 kg. Data relating to each product are as follows:

	X	*Y*
Selling price per unit	$25	$46
Total variable cost per unit	$15	$10
Material per unit (kg)	2.5	6
Maximum demand (units) per period	1,500	600

In order to maximise profit in the coming period, how many units of each product should the company manufacture and sell?

A 1,500 units of X and 208 units of Y

B 1,000 units of X and 417 units of Y

C 1,500 units of X and 600 units of Y

D 560 units of X and 600 units of Y

Question 9

A mining operation uses skilled labour costing $4 per hour, which generates a contribution (after deducting the labour costs) of $3 per hour.

A new project is now being considered which requires 5,000 hours of skilled labour. There is a surplus of the required labour which is sufficient to cope with the new project. The workers who are currently idle are being paid full wages. What is the relevant cost of using the skilled labour on the project?

Question 10

PQ Ltd manufactures three products, production cost details per unit are given:

	R	*S*	*T*
Direct material (kg)	10	12	6
Direct labour ($)	20	16	12
Specific fixed costs ($)	4	2	–
Allocated fixed overhead ($)	13	16	21

The direct material cost per kg is $2.50 and variable production overheads are 150% of direct labour.

An external company have offered to provide the 3 products for:

R $75
S $75
T $50

Which products should be purchased externally?

Question 11

A sunk cost is:

A a cost committed to be spent in the current period

B a past cost which is irrelevant for decision making

C a cost connected with oil exploration in the North Sea

D a cost unaffected by fluctuations in the level of activity.

Question 12

A company is evaluating a project that requires two types of material (T and V).

Data relating to the material requirements are as follows:

Material	*Quantity needed for project*	*Quantity in inventory*	*Original cost*	*Current purchase price*	*Current resale price*
	kg	*kg*	*$/kg*	*$/kg*	*$/kg*
T	500	100	$40	$45	$44
V	400	200	$55	$52	$40

Material T is regularly used by the company in normal production. Material V is no longer in use by the company and has no alternative use within the business.

What is the total relevant cost of materials for the project?

Question 13

20 hours of skilled labour are needed for production of new product Q. The skilled labour force is working at full capacity at the moment and the workers would have to be taken off production of product G in order to work on the client's contract. The details of product G are shown below:

	$/unit
Selling price	600
Direct materials	100
Direct labour	1 hour @ $10/hour
Variable overheads	150
Fixed overheads	150

The skilled workers' pay rate would not change, regardless of which product they worked on.

The relevant cost of the skilled labour on the contract is $ ______

Question 14

A machine which originally cost $80,000 has an estimated useful life of 10 years and is depreciated at the rate of $8,000 per annum. The net book value of the machine is currently $40,000 and the net sale proceeds if it were to be sold today are $25,000.

Required:

Identify whether the costs associated with the machine are relevant or not. If you think they are not relevant, give reasons.

Question 15

Gill Ltd manufactures three products E, F and G. The products are all finished on the same machine. This is the only mechanised part of the process. During the next period the production manager is planning an essential major maintenance overhaul of the machine. This will restrict the available machine hours to 1,400 hours for the next period. Data for the three products are:

	Product E	*Product F*	*Product G*
	$ per unit	*$ per unit*	*$ per unit*
Selling price	30.00	17.00	21.00
Variable cost	13.00	6.00	9.00
Fixed production cost	10.00	8.00	6.00
Other fixed cost	2.00	1.00	3.50
Profit	5.00	2.00	2.50
Maximum demand (units/period)	250	140	130

No inventories are held.

Fixed production costs are absorbed using a machine hour rate of $2 per machine hour.

Required:

Determine the production plan that will maximise profit for the forthcoming period.

Question 16

Unit production details of the three products manufactured by ZX Company are as follows:

	X	Y	Z
Direct material ($)	14	18	10
Direct labour (hours)	5	4	6
Specific fixed costs ($)	6	10	3
Allocated fixed overhead ($)	9	6	4

The direct labour rate is $8 per hour, and variable production overheads are 150% of direct labour.

An external company has offered to provide the three products for:

X $115
Y $110
Z $130

Which products should be purchased externally?

Question 17

A factory produces two products GG and HH. The production costs for the GG are as follows:

Variable costs	$15,000
Fixed costs	$50,000

An external supplier has offered to supply the required units GG for $38,000.

If the GG is purchased externally, the spare capacity can be used to expand the production of the HH. This would earn a contribution of $25,000.

Should the GG be purchased externally? State the maximum the company would be willing to pay for the external units.

Question 18

Explain why fixed overhead absorption rates are assumed to be irrelevant to a decision and variable overhead absorption rates are assumed to be relevant to the same decision.

Test your understanding answers

Test your understanding 1

B

This material will be purchased solely for use in this project, making it relevant. If the decision is not taken then the material will not be purchased.

Specific development costs have already been incurred and are therefore sunk costs.

Depreciation on existing equipment depreciation is a non-cash item.

The original cost of raw materials currently in inventory is a sunk cost.

Test your understanding 2

GHT should not to go ahead with the expansion as it will result in a loss of $400

It is possible to calculate this type of question by looking at the profit before any expansion and then comparing it to the profit after the expansion, but this is time consuming. The quickest way to tackle this sort of question is to use an incremental approach:

	$
Product K:	
Additional contribution on existing units (4,000 × $3)[1]	12,000
Contribution on additional units (1,500 × $12)[2]	18,000
Product R:	
Lost contribution (300 × $8)	(2,400)
Increase in fixed costs	(22,000)
Opportunity cost - loss of rental income ($500 × 12)[3]	(6,000)
Incremental profit (loss)	**(400)**

Notes:

(1) Additional contribution on product K = new contribution – original contribution

Additional contribution = $12 – $9 = **$3**

(2) The contribution on the additional units should be calculated using the new contribution.

(3) The loss of rental income is an opportunity cost and must be included in the calculation. If GHT go ahead with the expansion, they can no longer obtain the rental income.

Test your understanding 3

(a) **The relevant cost per kg is $2.00**

The material is in inventory and is used regularly by the company. It will therefore be replaced at the current purchase price of $2.00. The relevant cost per kg is therefore the current purchase cost of $2.00.

(b) **The relevant cost is $800**

The materials are in inventory, but are no longer in use therefore will not be replaced. There is no alternative use for the material, therefore the relevant cost will be the net realisable value of $0.80 per kg. The relevant cost of material = 1,000 kg × $0.80 = $800.

Test your understanding 4

$9,000 should be charged to the contract

The only alternative use for the material held in inventory is to sell it for scrap. To use 25 tons on the contract is to give up the opportunity of selling it for:

25 × $150 = $3,750

The organisation must then purchase a further 25 tons, and assuming this is in the near future, it will cost $210 per ton.

The contract must be charged with:

	$
25 tons × $150	3,750
25 tons × $210	5,250
	9,000

Test your understanding 5

The relevant labour cost for Z Ltd's job = **$600**.

Skilled workers – 20 hours required.

Minimum weekly wage covers $450/$15 = 30 hours work.

Each worker is currently working 24 hours, therefore has 6 hours per week spare capacity which is already paid for.

In total, the four workers will have 6 × 4 = 24 hours available, which is sufficient for the job. Relevant cost is therefore = **$0**.

Semi-skilled workers – 50 hours required.

There is no spare capacity, therefore either additional staff must be hired, or overtime must be worked.

Hiring additional staff will cost $12 per hour.

Working overtime will cost: $10 × 1.5 = $15 per hour.

It is therefore cheaper to hire additional workers. Relevant cost is therefore = 50 hours × $12 = **$600**.

Test your understanding 6

The contract should be charged with $85,000

Using the decision tree, spare capacity does not exist, and no additional labour can be hired so the labour must be taken from the existing activity

How much contribution is lost if the labour is transferred from the existing activity?

	$
Contribution per hour lost	3
PLUS: labour cost per hour	14
Relevant cost per labour hour as a result of the labour transfer	17
The contract should be charged with 5,000 hours × $17	$85,000

Test your understanding 7

The relevant cost of the equipment is $2,000

The asset will not be replaced, but it could be sold now for $2,000. If not sold now, it would have no other value. Therefore the relevant cost is the opportunity cost now = **$2,000**.

Test your understanding 8

(a) Deficiency in machine hours for next period is **13,000 hours**

	Product A	*Product B*	*Product C*	*Total*
Machine hours per unit	48/8 = 6	32/8 = 4	56/8 = 7	
Maximum demand (units)	3,000	2,500	5,000	
Total machine hours to meet maximum demand	18,000	10,000	35,000	63,000
Machine hours available				50,000
Deficiency of machine hours				13,000

(b) To maximise profits, the company should make:

Product A – **3,000 units**

Product B – **2,500 units**

Product C – **3,142 units**

	Product A	Product B	Product C
	$	$	$
Selling price per unit	200	158	224
Variable cost per unit	(154)	(112)	(178)
Contribution per unit	46	46	46
Machine hours required per unit	6	4	7
Contribution per machine hour	$7.67	$11.50	$6.57
Ranking	**2**	**1**	**3**

Therefore, make

	Machine hours
2,500 units of product B (4 × 2,500)	10,000
3,000 units of product A (6 × 3,000)	18,000
	28,000
3,142 units of product C (balance = 22,000/7)	22,000
	50,000

Test your understanding 9

300 units of B should be purchased externally

	A	B	C
Variable production cost	$46	$40	$30
External cost	$54	$50	$42
Incremental cost	($8)	($10)	($12)
Hours per unit	2	5	4
Incremental cost per hour	($4)	($2)	($3)
Ranking – lowest cost	**3rd**	**1st**	**2nd**

It is now cheaper to make ALL the components within the factory, however there is a limit on the number of machinery hours available.

First check if all components can be made in house:

Hours required to make 1,500 units of each component:

(1,500 × 2) + (1,500 × 5) + (1,500 × 4) = 16,500 hours

The company only has 15,000 hours available. So, 1,500 hours of work must be sub-contracted. The CHEAPEST component per hour must be bought externally. This is component B.

1,500 hours of time on B equates to 1,500 ÷ 5 = 300 units of B to be purchased externally.

Question 1

C

The decision rule in a limiting factor situation is to maximise the contribution per unit of limiting factor.

Question 2

B

	X	Y	Z
Contribution/unit	$41.00	$54.00	$50.00
Materials (kg/unit)	2	1	3
Contribution/kg	$20.50	$54.00	$16.66
Ranking	**2**	**1**	**3**

Question 3

Accept the offer.

On a purely financial basis, the price of $8 per unit exceeds the variable cost of $6 per unit. Since the fixed cost would not be affected, the units sold to the supermarket will each earn a contribution of $2.

Question 4

3 Rank the products according to the contribution per unit of limiting factor used.

2 Calculate each product's contribution per unit of limiting factor used.

1 Identify the limiting factor.

4 Allocate the limited resource according to the ranking.

Question 5

B

Materials can have an alternative use that can exceed their value in the project being considered.

Question 6

A

800 labour hours required. The relevant cost must be considered in two parts:

Spare capacity: 450 hours of spare capacity exists. The relevant cost for these 450 hours would be **$0** as the workers are being paid whether they work these hours or not.

No spare capacity: a further 350 hours are required for the contract. Either workers need to be diverted from the production of product OT, or overtime must be worked.

The relevant cost of diverting workers from the manufacture of product OT will be the contribution lost per hour plus the direct labour rate:

Contribution lost per hour ($14 ÷ 7 hours) $2 + Direct labour rate $8 = $10 per hour

Working overtime will cost: $8 × 1.5 = $12 per hour

It is therefore cheaper to divert workers from the manufacture of product OT. The relevant cost is therefore 350 hours × $10 = **$3,500**.

Question 7

C

The relevant value of a non-current asset is the higher of its net realisable value from disposal ($11,000) and its economic value in use ($17,500).

The historical cost is irrelevant. The asset would not be replaced, because replacement cost is more than the asset is worth to the business. The opportunity cost of the asset is the value of its most profitable alternative use, which is on the project to earn $17,500.

Question 8

D

	X	Y
Contribution per unit	$10	$36
Contribution per kg	$4	$6
Ranking	2nd	1st

Product	*Units*	*Hours per unit*	*Hours*
Y	600	6	3,600
X	560	2.5	1,400 (balance)
			5,000

Question 9

The relevant cost is **NIL**.

The question states that there is surplus of skilled labour. This suggests that the existing labour force will be able to undertake this project at no extra cost to the company.

Question 10

R should be purchased externally, but S and T are cheaper to produce internally.

	R	*S*	*T*
Direct material	25	30	15
Direct labour	20	16	12
Variable overheads	30	24	18
Specific fixed costs	4	2	–
Total internal production cost	79	72	45
External purchase price	75	75	50

Question 11

B

A sunk cost is a past cost and is therefore not relevant for future decisions.

Question 12

Material	$
T *(500 × $45)*	22,500
V *(200 × $40) + (200 × $52)*	18,400
Total relevant cost	**40,900**

Material T is in constant use, therefore if it is used for this project it will be replaced. In this case the relevant cost is the current purchase price $45.

400 units of material V is required and there are 200 units in inventory. Deal with this in two parts:

Material in inventory: 200 units are in inventory but they are no longer in use so will not be replaced. The only alternative for these units is to sell them, therefore the relevant cost for the 200 units in inventory is the realisable value of $40.

Material not in inventory: The project requires 400 units, so the 200 units which are not in inventory will have to be purchased at the current purchase price $52.

Question 13

The relevant cost of the skilled labour on the contract is **$7,000**

Using the decision tree, spare capacity does not exist, and no additional labour can be hired so the labour must be taken from the production of product G.

How much contribution is lost if the labour is transferred from product G?

Contribution earned from product G per hour
= $(600 – 100 – 10 – 150) = $340.

	$
Contribution per hour lost from product G	340
PLUS: labour cost per hour	10
Relevant cost per labour hour as a result of the labour transfer	350
The contract should be charged with 20 hours × $350	$7,000

Question 14

- The $80,000 (the original cost of the machine four years ago) is a sunk cost and is **not relevant** to the decision.
- The $40,000 (written-down value of the machine) is **not relevant** because it is determined by accounting conventions and not by future cash flows.
- The $8,000 (annual depreciation charge) is **not relevant** because this is a non-cash flow cost.
- The $25,000 (sale proceeds if the machine were sold now) is a **relevant** cost (future cash flow).

Question 15

The optimum production plan is to produce: 130 units of G and 202 units of E.

The first step is to calculate how many machine hours are required for each product. We can then determine whether machine hours are really a limiting factor.

	Product E	*Product F*	*Product G*	*Total*
Fixed production cost per unit × $2 per hour	$10	$8	$6	
Machine hours per unit	5	4	3	
Maximum demand (units)	250	140	130	
Maximum hours required	1,250	560	390	2,200

Since 2,200 machine hours are required and only 1,400 hours are available, machine hours are a limiting factor.

The optimum production plan is the plan which maximises the contribution from the *limiting factor.*

The next step is to calculate the contribution per machine hour from each of the products. The products can then be ranked on that basis.

	Product E	*Product F*	*Product G*
	$	*$*	*$*
Selling price per unit	30	17	21
Variable cost per unit	13	6	9
	—	—	—
Contribution per unit	17	11	12
	—	—	—
Machine hours per unit	5	4	3
Contribution per hour	$3.40	$2.75	$4.00
Ranking	**2**	**3**	**1**

The available hours can be allocated according to this ranking.

	Units to be produced	*Machine hours required*
Product G (maximum demand)	130	390
Product E (balance of hours)	202	1,010
		1,400

Question 16

X and Z should be purchased externally, but Y is cheaper to produce internally.

	X	*Y*	*Z*
	$	*$*	*$*
Direct material	14	18	10
Direct labour ($8 per hour)	40	32	48
Variable overheads	60	48	72
Specific fixed costs	6	10	3
Internal production cost	120	108	133
External purchase price	$115	$110	$130

Question 17

GG should be bought externally. The company would pay up to $40,000.

If GG is bought externally:

Saving of variable cost:	$15,000
Additional contribution	$25,000
	$40,000
External purchase cost	$38,000

The company will make a saving of $2,000, therefore it is worth buying the GG units from the external company. The company would be willing to pay up to $40,000 for the external units.

Question 18

Fixed overhead absorption rates are not considered to be relevant costs in decision making because fixed overhead absorption is not a cash flow and does not represent 'real' spending.

Variable overheads, on the other hand, will increase as activity levels increase and will result in additional expenditure being incurred. Such expenditure will represent 'real' cash spending.

chapter

6

Investment appraisal

Chapter learning objectives

After completing this chapter you should be able to:

- explain the process of valuing long term investments;
- calculate the net present value, internal rate of return and payback for an investment.

1 Session content diagram

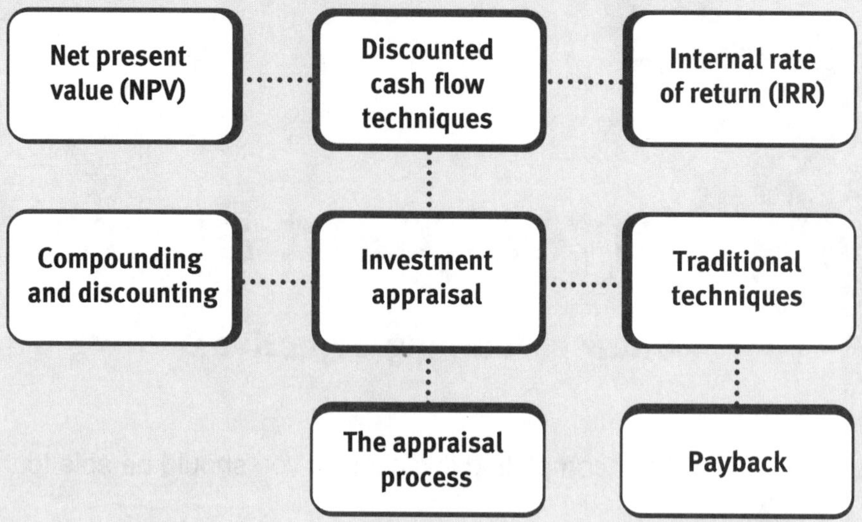

2 The Capital Investment Process

Capital investment decisions normally represent the most important decisions that an organisation makes, since they normally commit a substantial proportion of a firm's resources to actions that are likely to be irreversible. Many different capital investment projects exist including; replacement of assets, cost-reduction schemes, new product/service developments, product/service expansions, statutory, environmental and welfare proposals, etc.

3 Investment appraisal methods

To appraise a potential capital project:

- Estimate the costs and benefits from the investment
- Select an appraisal method and use it to ascertain if the investment is financially worthwhile
- Decide whether or not to go ahead with the project

It is important to note that the costs and benefits from the investment are estimates. Many take place in the future and many assumptions are made in calculating these figures. The costs and benefits for the investment are called **cash flows**. Remember that all the rules of relevant cost apply to investment decision, only **relevant cash flows** should be used.

To recap the main relevant cost rules:

- Sunk costs should be ignored.
- Only incremental costs should be included (i.e. those which will change as a result of the decision).
- Non-cash flows are excluded (including depreciation, provisions or allocated fixed costs).
- Opportunity costs should be included.

Appraisal methods

There are a number of appraisal methods which are used to assess how financially worthwhile investments are. The three techniques covered in this paper are:

- Payback.
- Net present value (NPV).
- Internal rate of return (IRR).

Each of the methods uses a different calculation, it is important to know how to do each of the calculations, and the decision rule used in each. The different methods can give different answers. In practice, most organisations use more than one appraisal method.

Based on the decision rule of the method used, a decision can be made as to whether the investment is financially worthwhile, although there will be other, non-financial considerations which must also be taken into account.

4 Payback

The payback technique considers the time a project will take to pay back the money invested in it. It is based on expected cash flows. To use the payback technique a company must set a **target payback period**.

Decision criteria

- Compare the payback period to the company's target return time and if the payback for the project is quicker the project should be accepted.
- Faced with mutually exclusive projects choose the project with the quickest payback.

Illustration 1

KLJ are considering purchasing a new machine. The machine will cost $550,000. The management accountant of KLJ has estimated the following additional cash flows will be received over the next 6 years if the new machine is purchased:

Year 1: $40,000
Year 2: $65,000
Year 3: $140,000
Year 4: $175,000
Year 5: $160,000
Year 6: $70,000

KLJ have a target payback period of 4 years. Calculate the payback period for the new machine and advise KLJ whether or not to proceed with the investment.

Solution

Note: The investment is shown as year 0. We treat year 0 as today and assume that the investment is made today. Show the initial investment as a negative cash flow for year 0. Work out the **cumulative cash flow** for each year until the cash flow becomes positive. This will highlight when payback has been achieved.

Year	*Cash flow*	*Cumulative cash flow*
	$000	$000
0	(550)	(550)
1	40	(510)
2	65	(445)
3	140	(305)
4	175	(130)
5	160	30
6	70	100

You can see that payback is achieved between years 4 and 5.

The payback period is usually given in years and months. To calculate the payback in years and months you should go to the year where the cumulative cash flow becomes positive. In this case year 5, so payback is 4 years plus a number of months. To calculate the months, take the cumulative cash flow from the previous year (year 4) divided by the cash flow in the year (year 5), then multiply the decimal fraction of a year by 12 to calculate the number of months. **Note:** The number of months calculated should be rounded up.

Here the cumulative cash flow becomes positive in year 5, so payback is 4 years plus (130/160 × 12) months = 4 years 10 months.

KLJ have a target payback period of 4 years. The payback is after this target, so the advice to KLJ would be to **not undertake the investment.**

Test your understanding 1

Snocold Limited (SL) are considering two projects. Both cost $450,000 and only one may be undertaken. SL use the payback method for appraising investments and require payback within three years.

The details of the cash flows for the two projects are given:

Year	*Project A*	*Project B*
	$000	$000
1	200	50
2	150	120
3	100	190
4	50	310
5	20	260

Advise SL which project they should undertake.

Calculation with constant annual cash flows

In some cases, the cash flows estimated for the project are the same each year. We call these **constant annual cash flows**. In these cases, the payback calculation can be simplified by using the following formula:

$$\textbf{Payback period} = \frac{\textbf{Initial investment}}{\textbf{Annual cash flow}}$$

Example

A project will cost \$300,000. The annual cash flows are estimated at \$90,000 per annum. Calculate the payback period.

$$\textbf{Payback period} = \frac{\textbf{Initial investment}}{\textbf{Annual cash flow}}$$

$$= \frac{\$300{,}000}{\$90{,}000} = \textbf{3.33 years}$$

3 years 4 months

Test your understanding 2

An investment of \$1 million is expected to generate net cash inflows of \$200,000 each year for the next 7 years.

Calculate the payback period for the project.

Advantages and disadvantages of payback

Advantages	Disadvantages
• Simple to understand.	• It is not a measure of absolute profitability.
• Payback is a simple measure of risk. A project with a long payback period tends to be riskier than one with a short payback period.	• Ignores the time value of money. It assumes that \$100 received in year 5 would be worth the same as \$100 received in year 1. We will look at this in more detail later in the chapter.
• Uses cash flows, not subjective accounting profits.	• Does not take account of cash flows beyond the payback period.
• If payback is used in selecting projects, companies may avoid liquidity problems.	
• Attaches greater importance to cash flows in earlier years.	

5 The time value of money

One characteristic of all capital expenditure projects is that the cash flows arise over the long term (a period usually greater than 12 months). Under this situation it becomes necessary to carefully consider the time value of money.

Money received today is worth more than the same sum received in the future, i.e. it has a time value.

If you were offered $1,000 today or $1,000 in 2 years, you would select to receive the money now as you believe it is worth more.

When we looked at the payback method, we recognised that one of its disadvantages was that it did not take account of the time value of money. The other two appraisal methods covered in this chapter (Net present value and Internal rate of return) do take account of the time value of money. These methods use **discounted cash flows** in their calculations.

Before looking at discounting, we have to firstly understand **compounding.**

Compounding

A sum invested today will earn interest. Compounding calculates the future value of a given sum invested today for a number of years.

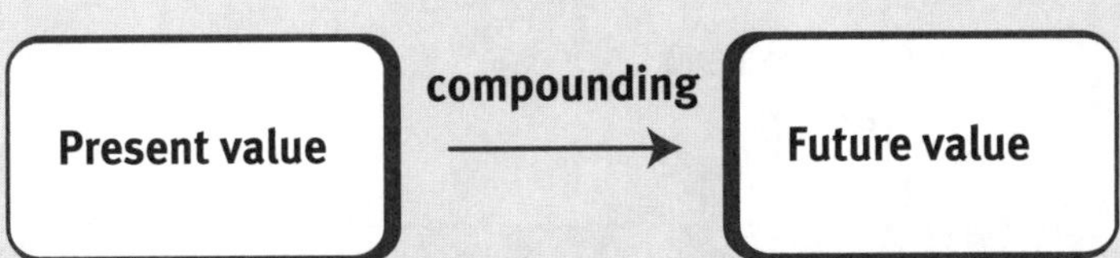

Illustration 2

$100 is invested in an account for five years. The interest rate is 10% per annum (p.a.). Find the value of the account after five years.

To compound a sum, the figure is increased by the amount of interest it would earn over the period.

If $100 is invested, by the end of the first year this will be worth:

Year 1: $100 + 10% = **$110**.

If the $110 is now invested for a further year, by the end of the 2nd year it will be worth:

Year 2: $110 + 10% = **$121**

If this is continued for 5 years, at the end of 5 years it will be worth:

Year 3: \$121 + 10% = **\$133.10**

Year 4: \$133.10 + 10% = **\$146.41**

Year 5: \$146.41 + 10% = **\$161.05**

There is a formula to speed up this calculation:

Formula for compounding

$$V = X(1+r)^n$$

Where:
- V = Future value
- X = Initial investment (present value)
- r = Interest rate (expressed as a decimal)
- n = Number of time periods

Using the example in Illustration 2:

$$V = X(1 + r)^n$$
$$= 100(1 + 0.1)^5$$
$$= \$161.05$$

Test your understanding 3

\$5,000 is invested in an account earning 2.75% interest p.a. Calculate the fund value after 12 years.

Test your understanding 4

\$5,000 is invested for 10 years in an account earning 5% interest p.a. Calculate how much this will be worth at the end of the 10 years.

Discounting

Discounting performs the opposite function to compounding. Compounding finds the future value of a sum invested now, whereas discounting considers a sum receivable in the future and establishes its equivalent value today. This value in today's terms is known as the **Present Value.**

In investment projects, cash flows will arise at many different points in time. Calculating the present value of future cash flows will be a key technique in investment appraisal decisions.

Formula for discounting

The formula is simply a rearrangement of the compounding formula:

$$\text{Present value (X)} = \frac{\text{Future value (V)}}{(1 + r)^n}$$

This can be presented as:

$$\text{Present value} = \text{Future value x } \frac{1}{(1 + r)^n}$$

$$\text{or Present value} = \text{Future value x } (1 + r)^{-n}$$

$$\text{where } \frac{1}{(1 + r)^n} \text{ or } (1 + r)^{-n}$$

Is known as the **discount factor**

We can therefore simplify the formula as:

Present value = Future value × Discount factor

Illustration 3

How much should be invested now in order to have $250 in 8 years' time? The account pays 12% interest per annum.

Solution

Present value = Future value × Discount factor

= $\$250 \times (1 + 0.12)^{-8}$
= $250 × 0.404
= **$101**

The discount factor, $(1 + r)^{-n}$ can be looked up in tables which are given in the assessment. Copies of the tables are at the front of this text book.

On the **present value table**, look along the top row for the interest rate (12%) and down the columns for the number of years (8), where the two intersect you can read off the discount factor (0.404).

Test your understanding 5

Find the present value of $2,000 receivable in 6 years' time, if the interest rate is 10% p.a.

Test your understanding 6

HJK Ltd can either receive $12,000 in 2 years time or $14,000 in 4 years time. The interest rate is 6% p.a. Advise HJK which they should select.

Present value table

The present value table covers whole interest rates from 1% to 20% for years 1 to 20. If a question requires an interest rate which is not a whole number or is higher than 20%, then the formula must be used to calculate the discount factor.

Note: At the top of the present value table, you are given the formula for calculating the discount factor.

Test your understanding 7

A project costing $350,000 has the following expected cash flows:

Year:	1	2	3	4
Annual cash flows ($000)	100	150	120	100

Required:

Calculate the Net Present Value for the project if the relevant rate of interest is 8.5%.

Interest rate

In the above calculations we have referred to the rate of interest. There are a number of alternative terms used to refer to the rate a firm should use to take account of the time value of money:

- Cost of capital
- Discount rate
- Required return

Whatever term is used, the rate of interest used for discounting reflects the cost of the finance that will be tied up in the investment.

We can now move on to the investment appraisal methods which use discounting. The two methods which use discounted cash flow (DCF) techniques are:

- **Net Present Value (NPV)**
- **Internal Rate of Return (IRR)**

6 Net Present Value (NPV)

Discounting future cash flows into present value terms is extremely valuable when appraising financial investment opportunities.

Typically an investment opportunity will involve a significant capital outlay initially with cash benefits being received in the future for several years. To compare all these cash flows on an equitable basis (like with like) it is usual practice to convert all future cash flows into present values. Hence a net present value can be established.

The NPV represents the surplus funds (after funding the investment) earned on the project. This tells us the impact the project has on shareholder wealth.

Decision criteria

- Any project with a positive NPV is viable – it will increase shareholder wealth
- Faced with mutually-exclusive projects, choose the project with the highest NPV.

Initial assumptions in NPV calculations

(1) All cash inflows and outflows are known with certainty.

(2) All cash flows are assumed to occur at the end of the year.

(3) Sufficient funds are available to undertake all profitable investments.

(4) There is zero inflation.

(5) There is zero taxation.

Illustration 4

Consider the following cash flows for a project with an initial investment of $30,000.

Year	*Cash flow*
1	$ 5,000
2	$ 8,000
3	$10,000
4	$ 7,000
5	$ 5,000

If we added up all of the cash flows, the total is $35,000. Given the initial investment of $30,000, it looks like the project has generated an additional $5,000. (total cash inflows less initial investment), but this assumes that the $5,000 received in year 5 is worth exactly the same as the $5,000 received in year 1. We know that this is not the case due to the time value of money. The technique used here – total cash inflows less initial investment is a sound one, but first we must discount all the cash flows back to the present value.

Assume an interest rate of 10%.

When you have a number of cash flows to discount, it is easier to use a table to lay out your workings:

Year	*Cash flow ($)*	*Discount factor (10%)*	*Present value (future value × discount factor)*
0	(30,000)	1	(30,000)
1	5,000	0.909	4,545
2	8,000	0.826	6,608
3	10,000	0.751	7,510
4	7,000	0.683	4,781
5	5,000	0.621	3,105
		NPV =	**(3,451)**

Note: The initial investment is shown as a negative in year zero. Year zero is today, so this figure is already in present day terms, therefore **the discount factor in year zero is always 1**.

We can now add the cash flows together as they are all in present value terms.

The present value of the total cash inflows less initial investment is called the **Net Present Value (NPV)**.

In this example the NPV is negative $3,451. The decision rule is that projects with a positive NPV should be accepted and those with a negative NPV should be rejected, therefore in this case **the project should be rejected**.

Test your understanding 8

MKP Ltd is considering two mutually exclusive projects with the following details:

	Project A ($000)	*Project B ($000)*
Initial investment	45	10
Scrap value in year 5	2	1
Cash flow year 1	20	5
Cash flow year 2	15	4
Cash flow year 3	10	3
Cash flow year 4	10	2
Cash flow year 5	10	2

Assume that the initial investment is made at the start of the project and the annual cash flows are at the END of each year. The scrap values should be treated as cash inflows in year 5.

Required:

Calculate the Net Present Value for Projects A and B if the relevant cost of capital is 10%.

		Project A		*Project B*	
Year	*Discount factor 10%*	*Cash flow $000*	*PV $000*	*Cash flow $000*	*PV $000*
0					
1					
2					
3					
4					
5					

Which project would you recommend using the NPV technique?

Test your understanding 9

A project requires an initial investment of $500,000. The following cash flows have been estimated for the life of the project:

Year	*Cash flow*
1	$ 120,000
2	$ 150,000
3	$ 180,000
4	$ 160,000

The company uses NPV to appraise projects. Using a discount rate of 7%, calculate the NPV of the project and recommend whether the project should be undertaken.

Advantages and disadvantages of NPV

Advantages	Disadvantages
• Considers the time value of money.	• Fairly complex.
• It is a measure of absolute profitability.	• Not well understood by non-financial managers.
• Uses cash flows and not subjective accounting profits.	• It may be difficult to determine the cost of capital.
• Considers the whole life of the project.	
• Should maximise shareholder wealth.	

Advantages and disadvantages of NPV

When appraising projects or investments, NPV is considered to be superior (in theory) to most other methods. This is because it:

- Considers the time value of money – discounting cash flows back to present value takes account of the impact of interest. This is ignored by the payback method.
- Is an absolute measure of return – the NPV of an investment represents the actual surplus raised by the project. This allows a business to plan more effectively.
- Is based on cash flows not profits – the subjectivity of profits makes them less reliable than cash flows and therefore less appropriate for decision making.
- Considers the whole life of the project – methods such as payback only considers the earlier cash flows associated with the project. NPV takes account of all relevant flows. Discounting the flows takes account of the fact that later flows are less reliable.
- Should lead to the maximisation of shareholder wealth. If the cost of capital reflects the shareholders' required return then the NPV reflects the theoretical increase in their wealth. For a commercial company, this is considered to be the primary objective of business.

However there are several potential drawbacks:

- It is difficult to explain to managers. To understand the meaning of the NPV calculation requires an understanding of discounting. The method is not as intuitive as methods such as payback.
- It requires knowledge of the cost of capital. The calculation of the cost of capital is, in practice, a complex calculation.
- It is relatively complex – for the reasons explained above NPV may be rejected in favour of simpler techniques.

7 Internal Rate of Return (IRR)

The next investment appraisal technique, which is linked to NPV, is Internal Rate of Return (IRR).

IRR calculates the rate of return at which the project has an NPV of zero. The IRR is compared to the company's cost of capital (this is the target rate).

Decision criteria

- If the IRR is greater than the cost of capital the project should be accepted.
- Faced with mutually exclusive projects choose the project with the higher IRR.

Calculating IRR

The steps are:

(1) Calculate two NPVs for the project at two different costs of capital.

(2) Use the following formula to find the IRR:

$$IRR \approx L + \frac{N_L}{N_L - N_H}(H - L)$$

where: L = lower discount rate

H = higher discount rate

N_l = NPV at the lower discount rate

N_H = NPV at the higher discount rate.

Illustration 5

You are given the following data on Project Z:

At 10% the NPV is \$33,310
At 20% the NPV is \$8,510
At 30% the NPV is – \$9,150

Calculate the IRR for project Z.

Note: It does not matter what two discounts rates you use, but different rates will give slightly different answers. (This method for calculating IRR is an approximation). Normally we try to use one NPV which is positive and one which is negative. **The higher the discount rate – the lower the NPV will be.**

In this case we will use 10% and 30%.

H = 30%

L = 10%

N_H = (\$9,150)

N_L = \$33,310

$$IRR \approx L + \frac{N_L}{N_L - N_H}(H - L)$$

$$IRR = 10 + \frac{33{,}310}{33{,}310 - (-9{,}150)} \times (30 - 10)$$

IRR = 25.7%

Test your understanding 10

The NPV of a project has been calculated at two different discount rates:

At 10% the NPV is \$13,725
At 15% the NPV is – \$40,520

Calculate the IRR.

Advantages and disadvantages of IRR:

Advantages	Disadvantages
• Considers the time value of money.	• It is not a measure of absolute profitability.
• % measure – easy to understand.	• Fairly complicated to calculate.
• Uses cash flows, not subjective accounting profits.	• Calculation only provides an estimate.
• Considers the whole life of the project.	
• Should maximise shareholder wealth.	

Advantages and disadvantages of IRR

IRR is closely linked to the NPV method and shares most of the advantages of NPV:

- Considers the time value of money – discounting cash flows to present value takes account of the impact of interest. This is ignored by the payback method.
- Is based on cash flows not profits – the subjectivity of profits makes them less reliable than cash flows and therefore less appropriate for decision making.
- Considers the whole life of the project – methods such as payback only considers the earlier cash flows associated with the project. As IRR is based on NPV, it takes account of all relevant flows. Discounting the flows takes account of the fact that later flows are less reliable.
- Should lead to the maximisation of shareholder wealth. If all projects which generate a rate of return higher than the cost of capital are accepted, this should increase shareholder's wealth. For a commercial company, this is considered to be the primary objective of business.

Where IRR differs from NPV is that it is a relative (%) measure rather than an absolute measure. This makes IRR easy to understand and aids comparisons between projects of different sizes.

However there are several potential drawbacks:

- It is difficult to explain to managers. To understand the meaning of IRR, users must first understand the NPV calculation and this requires an understanding of discounting. The method is not as intuitive as methods such as payback.
- The IRR calculation does not yield an exact answer, but is an approximation.
- Unlike NPV it is not an absolute measure. It does not give an indication of absolute profitability as NPV does.

Given the choice of methods, NPV is seen as the superior method.

Projects with equal annual cash flows

In the special case where a project has equal annual cash flows, the discounted cash flow can be calculated in a quicker way. There are two types of equal annual cash flows:

Annuity – a constant annual cash flow for a number of years

Perpetuity – a constant annual cash flow that continues indefinitely

Note: Students should be aware of annuities and perpetuities, but will not be required to calculate them.

Illustration using annuities

Annuity

Pluto Ltd has been offered a project costing $30,000. The returns are expected to be $10,000 each year for 5 years. Cost of capital is 7%. Calculate the NPV of the project and recommend if it should be accepted.

Solution, using the normal discounting method.

Year	*Cash flow* ($)	*Discount factor* (7%)	*Present value* ($)
0	(30,000)	1	(30,000)
1	10,000	0.935	9,350
2	10,000	0.873	8,730
3	10,000	0.816	8,160
4	10,000	0.763	7,630
5	10,000	0.713	7,130
		NPV =	**11,000**

You can see from this that there is a lot of repetition as we multiply each of the discount factors by the same amount. If we add up all of the discount factors from years 1 to 5 we get 4.100. This is known as the 5 year **annuity factor.**

Like the discount factor, the annuity factor can be looked up on a table – the cumulative present value table. This table is given in the exam. Copies of the tables are at the front of this text book. Look along the top row for the interest rate (7%) and down the columns for the number of years (5), where the two intersect you can read off the annuity factor (0.4100). (there can be small differences due to roundings)

It would have been quicker to calculate the NPV as follows, using the annuity method:

Year	*Cash flow* ($)	*Annuity factor* *(7%)*	*Present value* ($)
0	(30,000)	1	(30,000)
1 – 5	10,000	4.100	41,000
		NPV =	**11,000**

In this case, the NPV is positive, therefore **the project should be accepted.**

Illustration using perpetuities

Perpetuity

The present value of a perpetuity can be found using the formula:

$$PV = \text{cash flow} \times \frac{1}{r}$$

Where r = interest rate.

Example

In order to earn a perpetuity of $2,000 per annum how much would need to be invested today? The account will pay 10% interest.

Solution

Initial investment required = $2,000 ÷ 0.10 = **$20,000**

8 Chapter summary

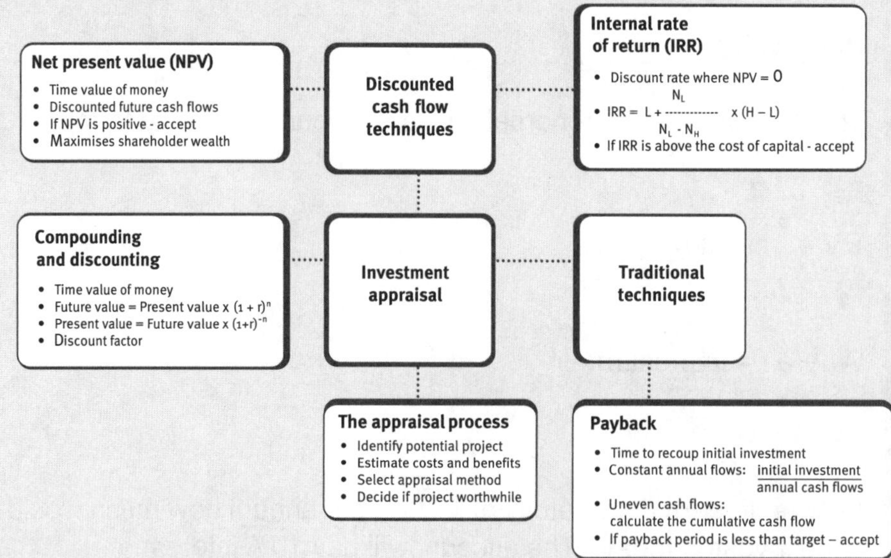

Net present value (NPV)
• Time value of money
• Discounted future cash flows
• If NPV is positive - accept
• Maximises shareholder wealth
Discounted cash flow techniques
Internal rate of return (IRR)
• Discount rate where NPV = 0
• IRR = L + $\frac{N_L}{N_L - N_H}$ x (H – L)
• If IRR is above the cost of capital - accept
Compounding and discounting
• Time value of money
• Future value = Present value x $(1 + r)^n$
• Present value = Future value x $(1+r)^{-n}$
• Discount factor
Investment appraisal
Traditional techniques
The appraisal process
• Identify potential project
• Estimate costs and benefits
• Select appraisal method
• Decide if project worthwhile
Payback
• Time to recoup initial investment
• Constant annual flows: $\frac{\text{initial investment}}{\text{annual cash flows}}$
• Uneven cash flows: calculate the cumulative cash flow
• If payback period is less than target – accept

9 End of chapter questions

Question 1

A company is considering a project with a 3 year life producing the following costs and revenues:

	$
Cost of machine	100,000
Annual depreciation of machine (for 3 years)	20,000
Residual value of machine	40,000
Annual cost of direct labour	25,000
Annual charge for foreman (10% apportionment)	7,000
Annual cost of components required	13,000
Annual net revenues from machine	80,000
Cost of capital	20%

The net present value of the cash flows relating to the machine is closest to:

A ($13,000)

B ($11,380)

C $11,620

D $22,370

Question 2

The internal rate of return is the interest rate that equates the present value of expected future net cash flows to:

A the initial cost of the investment outlay

B the depreciation value of the investment

C the terminal (compounded) value of future cash receipts

D the firm's cost of capital

Question 3

An investment of $15 million is expected to generate net cash inflows of $3.5 million each year for the next 6 years.

Calculate the payback period for the project.

Question 4

A company is considering two projects. Both cost $900,000 and only one may be undertaken. The payback method for appraising investments is used and the company requires payback within 4 years.

The details of the cash flows for the two projects are given:

Year	*Project A*	*Project B*
	$000	$000
1	200	100
2	200	200
3	200	300
4	200	400
5	200	100

Which project should be undertaken?

Question 5

$90,000 is invested for 8 years in an account earning 4.5% interest p.a. Calculate how much this will be worth at the end of the 8 years.

Question 6

Find the present value of $15,500 receivable in 5 years' time, if the interest rate is 7% p.a.

Question 7

Details of two projects are given.

Project A

Initial investment	$450,000				
Year:	1	2	3	4	5
Annual cash flows ($000)	250	150	100	100	100

Project B

Initial investment	$100,000				
Year:	1	2	3	4	5
Annual cash flows ($000)	50	40	30	20	20

Required:

Calculate the net present value for Projects A and B if the relevant cost of capital is 10% and recommend which project should be undertaken.

Question 8

The NPV of a project has been calculated at two different discount rates:

At 10% the NPV is $7,100

At 15% the NPV is – $5,140

Calculate the IRR.

Question 9

A project requires an initial investment of $19,000. The company has a cost of capital of 10%. The following cash flows have been estimated for the life of the project:

Year	*Cash flow*
1	$ 4,000
2	$ 8,000
3	$ 7,000
4	$ 5,000

Calculate the IRR of the project and recommend whether the project should be undertaken.

Question 10

Abbly Machines (AM) are considering making an investment of $1.2m on launching a new product. They have undertaken some market research and have estimated that the new product could generate the following cash flows:

Year 1: $140,000
Year 2: $265,000
Year 3: $340,000
Year 4: $560,000
Year 5: $290,000

AM require payback within 4 years. Advise if they should go ahead with the investment.

Question 11

How much would $40,000 receivable in 4 years time be worth in today's value, if the interest rate is 7%?

Question 12

SH Company have decided to expand their manufacturing facility. The cost of this expansion will be $2.3m. Expected cash flows from the expansion are estimated as $600,000 for the first 2 years and $800,000 for the following 2 years. The company uses a discount rate of 5% when appraising investment projects.

Calculate the NPV of the project and advise SH if they should go ahead with the expansion.

Question 13

A project requires an initial investment of $23,000. The company has a cost of capital of 10%. The following cash flows have been estimated for the life of the project:

Year	*Cash flow*
1	$ 6,000
2	$ 10,000
3	$ 8,000
4	$ 4,000

Calculate the IRR of the project and recommend whether the project should be undertaken.

Test your understanding answers

Test your understanding 1

SL should undertake project A.

Project A:

Year	0	1	2	3	4	5
Annual cash flow ($000)	(450)	200	150	100	50	20
Cumulative cash flow	(450)	(250)	(100)	0	50	70

Project B:

Year	0	1	2	3	4	5
Annual cash flow ($000)	(450)	50	120	190	310	260
Cumulative cash flow	(450)	(400)	(280)	(90)	220	480

SL require a payback of 3 years.

Project A pays back in exactly 3 years

Project B pays back in 3 years plus (90/310 × 12) months = 3 years 4 months

Note: This question demonstrates a problem with using payback as an investment appraisal method. You can see from the above tables that project B is in fact more financially worthwhile than project A. Over the 5 years project A has net cash flows of $70,000, while project B has $480,000. Using payback method, SL would select project A as it pays back the initial investment sooner. This highlights one of the problems with payback, which is that it does not take account of the cash flows over the whole project, but only looks at the cash flows up to the target payback period.

Test your understanding 2

The payback period is 5 years.

$$\text{Payback period} = \frac{\text{Initial investment}}{\text{Annual cash flow}}$$

= 1,000,000/200,000 = 5 years

Test your understanding 3

Future Value (V) = $5,000 $(1.0275)^{12}$ = **$6,923.92**

Test your understanding 4

Future value (V) = $5,000 $(1.05)^{10}$ = **$8,144.47**

Test your understanding 5

Present value = Future value × Discount factor

= $2,000 × 0.564 = **$1,128**

Test your understanding 6

It would be better to receive $14,000 in 4 years time.

Receive $12,000 in 2 years time:

Present value = Future value × Discount factor

= $12,000 × 0.89 = **$10,680**

Receive $14,000 in 4 years time:

Present value = Future value × Discount factor

= $14,000 × 0.792 = **$11,088**

Test your understanding 7

The NPV is $35,710.

Year	*Discount factor*	*Cash flow $000*	*Present value $000*
0	1	(350)	(350.00)
1	0.9217	100	92.17
2	0.8495	150	127.43
3	0.7829	120	93.95
4	0.7216	100	72.16
		NPV =	**35.71**

The discount factor for 8.5% is not given in the present value tables, so the formula must be used to calculate the discount factor:

Year 1: discount factor = $(1+0.085)^{-1}$ = 0.9217
Year 2: discount factor = $(1+0.085)^{-2}$ = 0.8495
Year 3: discount factor = $(1+0.085)^{-3}$ = 0.7829
Year 4: discount factor = $(1+0.085)^{-4}$ = 0.7216

Test your understanding 8

Both projects have positive NPVs, so both are worth doing. Project A has an NPV of $7,360 and Project B has an NPV of $3,330 so **Project A should be selected.**

		Project A		*Project B*	
Year	*Discount factor*	*Cash flow $000*	*Present value $000*	*Cash flow $000*	*Present value $000*
0		(45)	(45)	(10)	(10)
1	0.909	20	18.18	5	4.55
2	0.826	15	12.39	4	3.30
3	0.751	10	7.51	3	2.25
4	0.683	10	6.83	2	1.37
5	0.621	10 +2 = 12	7.45	2+1 = 3	1.86
		NPV =	**7.36**	**NPV =**	**3.33**

Test your understanding 9

The project has a positive NPV of $12,110, therefore **the project should be undertaken.**

Year	*Cash flow ($)*	*Discount factor (7%)*	*Present value ($) (future value × discount factor)*
0	(500,000)	1	(500,000)
1	120,000	0.935	112,200
2	150,000	0.873	130,950
3	180,000	0.816	146,880
4	160,000	0.763	122,080
		NPV =	**12,110**

Test your understanding 10

IRR = 11.3%.

H = 15%

L = 10%

N_H = ($40,520)

N_L = $13,725

$$IRR \approx L + \frac{N_L}{N_L - N_H}(H - L)$$

$$IRR = 10 + \frac{13,725}{13,725 - (40,520)} \times (15 - 10)$$

IRR = 11.3%

Question 1

C

Remember only to use the relevant cash flows:

Revenue – Components – Labour = $80,000 – $13,000 – $25,000 = $42,000

Depreciation is excluded as it a non-cash item.

The apportionment of the foreman's wages is also excluded as it is not an incremental cost.

The residual value is included as a cash flow in year 3.

Year	*Cash flow $000*	*Discount factor (20%)*	*Present value ($000)*
0	(100)	1	(100)
1	42	0.833	34.99
2	42	0.694	29.15
3	42 + 40 = 82	0.579	47.48
		NPV =	**11.62**

Net present value = **$11,620**

Question 2

A

At the IRR, PV of future net cash flows = initial capital outlay, i.e. where the NPV = zero.

Question 3

The payback period is **4 years 4 months.**

$$\text{Payback period} = \frac{\text{Initial investment}}{\text{Annual cash flow}}$$

= 15,000,000/3,500,000 = 4.28

The payback period is 4 years + (0.28 × 12) months = 4 years 4 months.

Question 4

Project B should undertaken.

Project A:

Year	0	1	2	3	4	5
Annual cash flow ($000)	(900)	200	200	200	200	200
Cumulative cash flow	(900)	(700)	(500)	(300)	(100)	100

Project B:

Year	0	1	2	3	4	5
Annual cash flow ($000)	(900)	100	200	300	400	100
Cumulative cash flow	(900)	(800)	(600)	(300)	100	200

The target payback period is 4 years.

Project A pays back in 4 years plus (100/200 × 12) months = 4 years 6 months

Project B pays back in 3 years plus (300/400 × 12) months = 3 years 9 months

Question 5

Future value (V) = $90,000 $(1.045)^8$ = **$127,989**

Question 6

Present value - Future value × Discount factor

PV = $15,500 × 0.713 = **$11,052**

Question 7

Project A should be selected.

		Project A		*Project B*	
Year	*Discount factor*	*Cash flow $000*	*Present value $000*	*Cash flow $000*	*Present value $000*
0		(450)	(450)	(100)	(100)
1	0.909	250	227.25	50	45.45
2	0.826	150	123.9	40	33.04
3	0.751	100	75.1	30	22.53
4	0.683	100	68.3	20	13.66
5	0.621	100	62.1	20	12.42
		NPV =	**106.65**	**NPV =**	**27.10**

Both projects have positive NPVs, so both are worth doing.

Project A has an NPV of **$106,650**

Project B has an NPV **of $27,100**

Question 8

IRR = 12.9%

H = 15%

L = 10%

N_H = ($5,140)

N_L = $7,100

$$IRR \approx L + \frac{N_L}{N_L - N_H}(H - L)$$

$$IRR = 10 + \frac{7{,}100}{7{,}100 - (-5{,}140)} \times (15 - 10)$$

IRR = 12.9%

Question 9

The IRR is less than the cost of capital, therefore **the project should be rejected.**

		Discount factor 10%		*Discount factor 5%*	
Year	*Cash flow* $	*DF (10%)*	*Present value* $	*DF (5%)*	*Present value* $000
0	(19,000)	1	(19,000)	1	(19,000)
1	4,000	0.909	3,636	0.952	3,808
2	8,000	0.826	6,608	0.907	7,256
3	7,000	0.751	5,257	0.864	6,048
4	5,000	0.683	3,415	0.823	4,115
		NPV =	**(84)**	**NPV =**	**2,227**

L = 5%

H = 10%

N_L = \$2,227

N_H = (\$84)

$$IRR \approx L + \frac{N_L}{N_L - N_H}(H - L)$$

$$IRR = 5 + \frac{2,227}{2,227 - (-84)} \times (10 - 5)$$

IRR = 9.8%

Question 10

The investment should be undertaken.

Year	Cash flow	Cumulative cash flow
	$000	$000
0	(1,200)	(1,200)
1	140	(1,060)
2	265	(795)
3	340	(455)
4	560	105
5	290	395

Payback is achieved between years 3 and 4.

Payback is 3 years plus (455/560 × 12) months = 3 years 10 months.

This is less than the target payback period of 4 years, therefore the investment should be undertaken.

Question 11

Present value = Future value × Discount factor

= $40,000 × 0.763 = **$30,520**

Question 12

On the basis of the positive NPV of $165,000, **the project should be undertaken.**

Year	Cash flow ($000)	Discount factor (5%)	Present value ($000) (future value × discount factor)
0	(2,300)	1	(2,300)
1	600	0.952	571.2
2	600	0.907	544.2
3	800	0.864	691.2
4	800	0.823	658.4
		NPV =	**165**

Question 13

The IRR is less than the cost of capital**, therefore the project should be rejected.**

		Discount factor 10%		*Discount factor 5%*	
Year	*Cash flow* $	*DF (10%)*	*Present value* $	*DF (5%)*	*Present value* $000
0	(23,000)	1	(23,000)	1	(23,000)
1	6,000	0.909	5,454	0.952	5,712
2	10,000	0.826	8,260	0.907	9,070
3	8,000	0.751	6,008	0.864	6,912
4	4,000	0.683	2,732	0.823	3,292
		NPV =	**(546)**	**NPV =**	**1,986**

so:

L = 5%

H = 10%

N_L = \$1,986

N_H = (\$546)

$$IRR \approx L + \frac{N_L}{N_L - N_H}(H - L)$$

$$IRR = 5 + \frac{1,986}{1,986 - (546)} \times (10 - 5)$$

IRR = 8.9%

chapter

7

Standard costing

Chapter learning objectives

After completing this chapter, you should be able to:

- explain the difference between ascertaining costs after the event and establishing standard costs in advance;
- explain why planned standard costs, prices and volumes are useful in setting a benchmark;
- calculate standard costs for the material, labour and variable overhead elements of the cost of a product or service;
- calculate variances for materials, labour, variable overhead, sales prices and sales volumes;
- prepare a statement that reconciles budgeted contribution with actual contribution;
- prepare variance statements.

1 Session content diagram

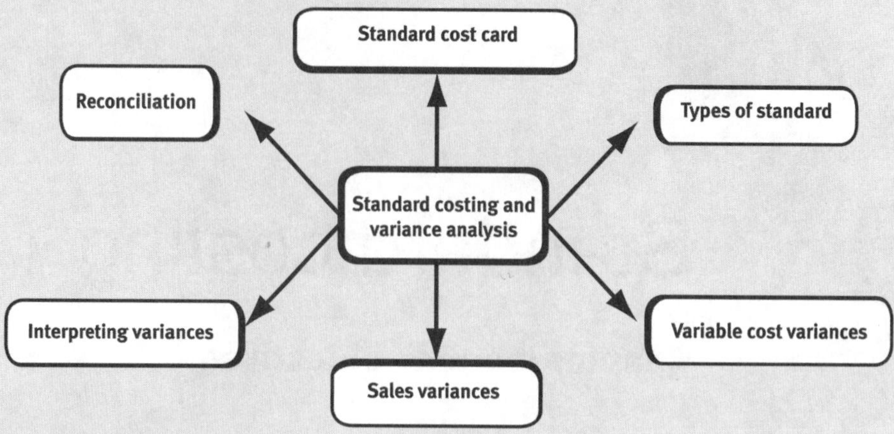

2 Standard costing

A standard cost is a carefully **pre-determined** unit cost which is prepared for each cost unit. It contains details of the standard amount and price of each resource that will be utilised in providing the service or manufacturing the product.

The standard becomes a **target** against which performance can be measured.

The actual costs incurred are measured after the event and compared to the pre-determined standards.

The difference between the standard and the actual is known as a **variance**. Analysing variances can help managers focus on the areas of the business requiring the most attention. This is known as **management by exception**.

The *CIMA Terminology* defines **standard costing** as a 'control technique that reports variances by comparing actual costs to pre-set standards facilitating action through management by exception'.

3 Standard cost card

A standard cost card showing the variable elements of production cost might look like this.

Standard cost card: product 176

	$ *per unit*
Direct materials: 30 kg @ $4.30	129.00
Direct labour: 12 hours @ $11.80	141.60
Prime cost	270.60
Variable production overhead:	
12 hours @ $0.75	9.00
Variable production cost	279.60

Look at each item in detail, it is essential that you recognise the detail given on the standard cost card. Ensure you learn the terminology.

For each of the variable costs, the standard amount and the standard price are given.

Direct material – $129.00 per unit, made up of **standard quantity** (30kg) × **standard price** ($4.30)

Direct labour – $141.60 per unit, made up of **standard hours** (12 hours) × **standard rate** ($11.80)

Variable production overheads – $9.00 per unit, made up of **standard hours** (12 hours) × **standard rate** ($0.75)

Note: The standard hours for labour and overheads are usually the same since we normally assume that variable overheads vary in direct proportion to the number of direct labour hours worked.

Some standard cost cards will also include the fixed overhead and the standard selling price.

These standard data provide the information for a detailed variance analysis, as long as the actual data are collected at the same level of detail.

Measurable cost units

In order to be able to apply standard costing it must be possible to identify a measurable cost unit. This can be a unit of product or service but it must be capable of being standardised, for example standardised tasks must be involved in its creation. The cost units themselves do not necessarily have to be identical. For example, standard costing can be applied in situations such as costing plumbing jobs for customers where every cost unit is unique. However, the plumbing jobs must include standardised tasks for which a standard time and cost can be determined for monitoring purposes.

It can be difficult to apply standard costing in some types of service organisation, where cost units may not be standardised and they are more difficult to measure.

The standard cost may be stored on a physical card, but nowadays it is more likely to be stored on a computer, perhaps in a database. Alternatively it may be stored as part of a spreadsheet so that it can be used in the calculation of variances.

Illustration 1

The following data are given for one unit:

Direct materials: 40 square metres @ $6.48/sq m
Direct labour: Bonding department – 48 hours @ $12.50/hour
Direct labour: Finishing department – 30 hours @ $11.90/hour

The following are the budgeted costs and labour hours per annum for variable production overhead:

	$	*hours*
Bonding department	375,000	500,000
Finishing department	150,000	300,000

Required:

From the information given, prepare a standard cost card extract for one unit and enter on the standard cost card the costs to show subtotals for prime cost and variable production cost.

Solution

Standard cost card extract

	$ *per unit*
Direct materials: 40 sq m @ $6.48	259.20
Direct labour:	
Bonding – 48 hours @ $12.50	600.00
Finishing – 30 hours @ $11.90	357.00
Prime cost	1,216.20
Variable production overhead:	
Bonding – 48 hours @ $0.75 (1)	36.00
Finishing – 30 hours @ $0.50 (2)	15.00
Variable production cost	1,267.20

(1) Bonding department overhead absorption rate = $375,000/500,000 hours = $0.75

(2) Finishing department overhead absorption rate = $150,000/300,000 hours = $0.50

Test your understanding 1

A standard cost is:

A the planned unit cost of a product, component or service in a period

B the budgeted cost ascribed to the level of activity achieved in a budget centre in a control period

C the budgeted production cost ascribed to the level of activity in a budget period

D the budgeted non-production cost for a product, component or service in a period.

4 Types of standards

The *CIMA Terminology* defines a **standard** as a 'benchmark measurement of resource usage or revenue or profit generation, set in defined conditions'.

There are four main types of standards:

Ideal standard

Standards may be set at ideal levels, which make no allowance for inefficiencies such as losses, waste and machine downtime. This type of ideal standard is achievable only under the most favourable conditions and can be used if managers wish to highlight and monitor the full cost of factors such as waste, etc. However, this type of standard will almost always result in adverse variances since a certain amount of waste, etc., is usually unavoidable. This can be very demotivating for individuals who feel that an adverse variance suggests that they have performed badly.

Attainable standard

Standards may also be set at attainable levels which assume efficient levels of operation, but which include allowances for factors such as losses, waste and machine downtime. This type of standard does not have the negative motivational impact that can arise with an ideal standard because it makes some allowance for unavoidable inefficiencies. Adverse variances will reveal whether inefficiencies have exceeded this unavoidable amount.

Current standard

Standards based on current performance levels (current wastage, current inefficiencies) are known as current standards. Their disadvantage is that they do not encourage any attempt to improve on current levels of efficiency.

Basic standard

Standards set for the long term and remain unchanged over a period of years. This standard is often retained as a minimum standard and can be used for long term comparisons of performance.

Bases for setting standards

CIMA's definition of standards goes on to describe a number of bases which can be used to set the standard. These bases include:

- a prior period level of performance by the same organisation;
- the level of performance achieved by comparable organisations;
- the level of performance required to meet organisational objectives.

Use of the first basis indicates that management feels that performance levels in a prior period have been acceptable. They will then use this performance level as a target and control level for the forthcoming period.

When using the second basis management is being more outward looking, perhaps attempting to monitor their organisation's performance against 'the best of the rest'.

The third basis sets a performance level which will be sufficient to achieve the objectives which the organisation has set for itself.

Test your understanding 2

Tick the correct box.

A standard which assumes efficient levels of operation, but which includes allowances for factors such as waste and machine downtime, is known as an:

attainable standard □
ideal standard □

Information for setting standard costs

Setting standard costs

You have already seen that each element of a unit's standard cost has details of the price and quantity of the resources to be used. In this section, we will list some of the sources of information which may be used in setting the standard costs.

Standard material price

Sources of information include:

(a) quotations and estimates received from potential suppliers;

(b) trend information obtained from past data on material prices;

(c) details of any bulk discounts which may be available;

(d) information on any charges which will be made for packaging and carriage inwards;

(e) the quality of material to be used: this may affect the price to be paid;

(f) for internally manufactured components, the pre-determined standard cost for the component will be used as the standard price.

Standard material usage

Sources of information include:

(a) the basis to be used for the level of performance;

(b) if an attainable standard is to be used, the allowance to be made for losses, wastage, etc. (work study techniques may be used to determine this);

(c) technical specifications of the material to be used.

Standard labour rate

Sources of information include:

(a) the HR department, for the wage rates for employees of the required grades with the required skills;

(b) forecasts of the likely outcome of any trades union negotiations currently in progress;

(c) details of any bonus schemes in operation. For example, employees may be paid a bonus if higher levels of output are achieved.

Standard labour times

Sources of information include:

(a) the basis to be used for the level of performance;

(b) if an attainable standard is to be used, the allowance to be made for downtime, etc.;

(c) technical specifications of the tasks required to manufacture the product or provide the service;

(d) the results of work study exercises which are set up to determine the standard time to perform the required tasks and the grades of labour to be employed.

Variable production overhead costs

In Chapter 3 you learned how pre-determined hourly rates were derived for production overhead. These overhead absorption rates represent the standard hourly rates for overhead in each cost centre. They can be applied to the standard labour hours or machine hours for each cost unit.

The overheads will be analysed into their fixed and variable components so that a separate rate is available for fixed production overhead and for variable production overhead. This is necessary to achieve adequate control over the variable and fixed elements. Your *Fundamentals of Management Accounting* syllabus requires you to deal only with standard variable overhead costs.

5 Standard costing in the modern business environment

There has recently been some criticism of the appropriateness of standard costing in the modern business environment. The main criticisms include the following:

- Standard costing was developed when the business environment was more stable and operating conditions were less prone to change. In the present dynamic environment, such stable conditions cannot be assumed. If conditions are not stable, then it is difficult to set a standard cost which can be used to control costs over a period of time.
- Attainment of standard used to be judged as satisfactory, but in today's climate constant improvement must be aimed for in order to remain competitive.
- The emphasis on labour variances is no longer appropriate with the increasing use of automated production methods.

Using standards

The main purpose of standard costing is to provide a yardstick or benchmark against which actual performance can be monitored. If the comparison between actual and standard cost is to be meaningful, then the standard must be valid and relevant.

It follows that the standard cost should be kept as up to date as possible. This may necessitate frequent updating of standards to ensure that they fairly represent the latest methods and operations, and the latest prices which must be paid for the resources being used.

The standards may not be updated for every small change: however, any significant changes should be adjusted for as soon as possible.

An organisation's decision to use standard costing depends on its effectiveness in helping managers to make the correct decisions. It can be used in areas of most organisations, whether they are involved with manufacturing, or with services such as hospitals or insurance. For example, a pre-determined standard could be set for the labour time to process an insurance claim. This would help in planning and controlling the cost of processing insurance claims.

Standard costing may still be useful even where the final product or service is not standardised. It may be possible to identify a number of standard components and activities for which standards may be set and used effectively for planning and control purposes. In addition, the use of demanding performance levels in standard costs may help to encourage continuous improvement.

6 Variance analysis

Variance analysis involves breaking down the total variance to explain how much of it is caused by the usage of resources being different from the standard, and how much of it is caused by the price of resources being different from the standard. These variances can be combined to reconcile the total cost difference revealed by the comparison of the actual and standard cost.

If resource price or usage is above standard, or if sales volume or selling price is below standard, an **adverse** variance will result. If resource price or usage is below standard, or if sales volume or selling price is above standard, a **favourable** variance will result.

Variable cost variances

There are six main variable cost variances as shown below:

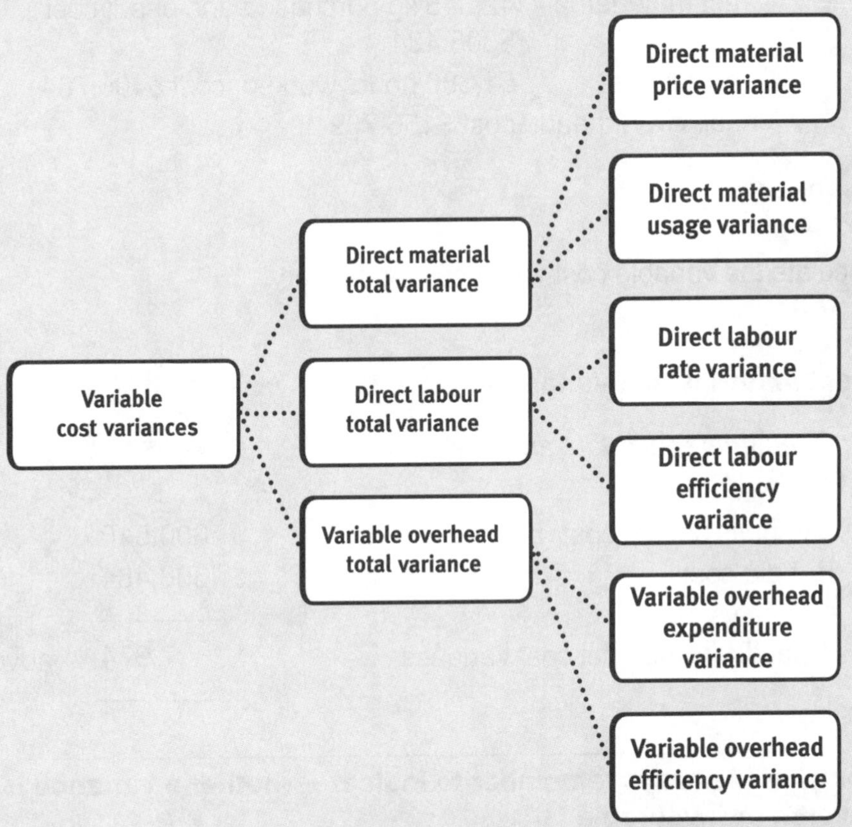

Ensure you learn the names of the six variable cost variances as questions may ask you to calculate just one or two variances.

We will use a simple example to demonstrate how the variances are calculated for direct material, direct labour and variable overhead:

Example

A company manufactures a single product for which the standard variable cost is:

	$ *per unit*
Direct material: 81 kg × $7 per kg	567
Direct labour: 97 hours × $8 per hour	776
Variable overhead: 97 hours × $3 per hour	291
	1,634

During January, 530 units were produced and the costs incurred were as follows:

Direct material:	42,845 kg purchased and used; cost $308,484
Direct labour:	51,380 hours worked; cost $400,764
Variable overhead:	cost $156,709

Required:

Calculate the variable cost variances for January.

Direct material cost variances

(a) *Direct material total variance*

	$	
530 units should cost (530 × 567)	300,510	
But did cost	308,484	
Total direct material cost variance	7,974	adverse

You should always remember to indicate whether a variance is adverse or favourable.

This direct material total variance can now be analysed into its 'price' and 'quantity' elements.

(b) *Direct material price variance*

The direct material price variance reveals how much of the direct material total variance was caused by paying a different price for the materials used.

	$	
42,845 kg purchased should have cost (× $7)	299,915	
But did cost	308,484	
Direct material price variance	8,569	adverse

The adverse price variance indicates that expenditure was $8,569 more than standard because a higher than standard price was paid for each kilogram of material.

(c) *Direct material usage variance*

The direct material usage variance reveals how much of the direct material total variance was caused by using a different quantity of material, compared with the standard allowance for the production achieved.

	kg	
530 units produced should have used (× 81 kg)	42,930	
But did use	42,845	
Variance in kg	85	favourable
× standard price per kg ($7): Direct material usage variance	$595	favourable

The favourable usage variance of $595 is the saving in material cost (at standard prices) resulting from using a lower amount of material than the standard expected for this level of output.

Check: $8,569 adverse + $595 favourable = $7,974 adverse (the correct total variance).

All of the 'quantity' variances are always valued at the standard price. Later in this example you will see that the 'quantity' variances for labour and for variable overhead – the efficiency variances – are valued at the standard rate per hour.

Complication in material variances

One slight complication sometimes arises with the calculation of the direct material price variance. In this example, the problem did not arise because the amount of material purchased was equal to the amount used.

However, when the two amounts are not equal then the direct material price variance could be based either on the material purchased or on the material used. In the example we used the following method – we will call it method A:

Method A Direct material price variance

	$
Material **purchased** should have cost	X
But did cost	X
Direct material price variance	X

Alternatively, we could have calculated the variance as follows – we will call it method B.

Method B Direct material price variance

	$
Material **used** should have cost	X
But did cost	X
Direct material price variance	X

Obviously, if the purchase quantity is different from the usage quantity, then the two methods will give different results.

So how do you know which method to use? The answer lies in the inventory valuation method.

If inventory is valued at standard cost, then method A is used. This will ensure that all of the variance is eliminated as soon as purchases are made and the inventory will be held at standard cost.

If inventory is valued at actual cost, then method B is used. This means that the variance is calculated and eliminated on each bit of inventory as it is used up. The remainder of the inventory will then be held at actual price, with its price variance still 'attached', until it is used and the price variance is calculated.

If this seems confusing you might find it easier to return and consider the reasoning after you have studied integrated accounting systems in Chapter 9, where you will learn which method is generally preferred.

Test your understanding 3

The standard cost card for product F shows that each unit requires 3 kg of material at a standard price of $9 per kilogram. Last period, 200 units of F were produced and $5,518 was paid for 620 kg of material that was bought and used.

Required:

Calculate the following variances and tick the correct box to indicate whether each variance is adverse or favourable.

	Adverse	*Favourable*
(a) the direct material price variance is $	☐	☐
(b) the direct material usage variance is $	☐	☐

Direct labour cost variances

(a) *Direct labour total variance*

	$	
530 units should cost (× $776)	411,280	
But did cost	400,764	
Total direct labour cost variance	10,516	favourable

This variance can now be analysed into its 'price' and 'quantity' elements. The 'price' part is called the labour rate variance and the 'quantity' part is called the labour efficiency variance.

(b) *Direct labour rate variance*

The direct labour rate variance reveals how much of the direct labour total variance was caused by paying a different rate per hour for the labour hours worked.

	$	
51,380 hours should have cost (× $8)	411,040	
But did cost	400,764	
Direct labour rate variance	10,276	favourable

The favourable rate variance indicates that expenditure was $10,276 less than standard because a lower than standard rate was paid for each hour of labour.

Notice the similarity between the method used to calculate the labour rate variance and the method used to calculate the material price variance.

(c) *Direct labour efficiency variance*

The direct labour efficiency variance reveals how much of the direct labour total variance was caused by using a different number of hours of labour, compared with the standard allowance for the production achieved.

	Hours
530 units produced should take (× 97 hours)	51,410
But did take	51,380
Variance in hours	30 favourable
× standard labour rate per hour ($8)	
Direct labour efficiency variance	$240 favourable

The favourable efficiency variance of $240 is the saving in labour cost (at standard rates) resulting from using fewer labour hours than the standard expected for this level of output.

Check: $10,276 favourable + $240 favourable = $10,516 favourable (the correct total variance).

Variable overhead cost variances

(a) *Variable overhead total variance*

	$	
530 units should cost (× $291)	154,230	
But did cost	156,709	
Total variable overhead cost variance	2,479	adverse

This variance can now be analysed into its 'price' and 'quantity' elements. The 'price' part is called the variable overhead expenditure variance and the 'quantity' part is called the variable overhead efficiency variance.

(b) *Variable overhead expenditure variance*

The variable overhead expenditure variance reveals how much of the variable overhead total variance was caused by paying a different hourly rate of overhead for the hours worked.

	$	
51,380 hrs of variable overhead should cost (× $3)	154,140	
But did cost	156,709	
Variable overhead expenditure variance	2,569	adverse

The adverse expenditure variance indicates that expenditure was $2,569 more than standard because a higher than standard hourly rate was paid for variable overhead.

(c) *Variable overhead efficiency variance*

The variable overhead efficiency variance reveals how much of the variable overhead total variance was caused by using a different number of hours of labour, compared with the standard allowance for the production achieved. Its calculation is very similar to the calculation of the labour efficiency variance.

Variance in hours (from labour efficiency variance)	30 hours	favourable
× standard variable overhead rate per hour ($3)		
Variable overhead efficiency variance	$90	favourable

The favourable efficiency variance of $90 is the saving in variable overhead cost (at standard rates) resulting from using fewer labour hours than the standard expected for this level of output.

Check: $2,569 adverse + $90 favourable = $2,479 adverse (the correct total variance)

Test your understanding 4

Budgeted production of product V is 650 units each period. The standard cost card for product V contains the following information.

		$ per unit
Ingredients	12 litres @ $4 per litre	48
Direct labour	3 hours @ $9 per hour	27
Variable production overhead	3 hours @ $2 per hour	6

During the latest period 670 units of product V were produced. The actual results recorded were as follows:

Ingredients purchased and used	8,015 litres	$33,663
Direct labour	2,090 hours	$17,765
Variable production overhead		$5,434

(a) The ingredients price variance is:

A $1,503 favourable

B $1,503 adverse

C $1,603 favourable

D $1,603 adverse

(b) The ingredients usage variance is:

A $100 favourable

B $100 adverse

C $105 favourable

D $860 adverse

(c) The labour rate variance is

A $325 favourable

B $325 adverse

C $1,045 favourable

D $1,045 adverse

(d) The labour efficiency variance is

A $680 adverse

B $720 adverse

C $720 favourable

D $1,260 adverse

(e) The variable overhead expenditure variance is:

A $1,254 favourable

B $1,254 adverse

C $1,534 favourable

D $1,534 adverse

(f) The variable overhead efficiency variance is:

A $151 adverse

B $160 adverse

C $160 favourable

D $280 adverse

Sales variances

Now that we have seen how to analyse the variable cost variances we will turn our attention to sales variances. The *Fundamentals of Management Accounting* syllabus requires you to be able to calculate two variances for sales: the sales price variance and the sales volume contribution variance:

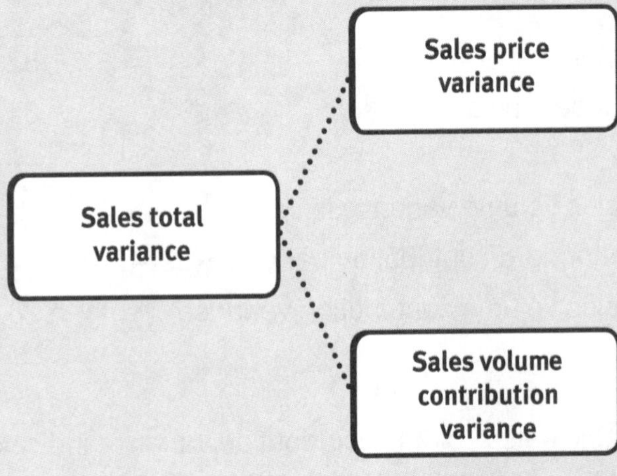

We will demonstrate the calculation of these variances using the following data.

Budget	Sales and production volume	81,600 units
	Standard selling price	$59 per unit
	Standard variable cost	$24 per unit
Actual results	Sales and production volume	82,400 units
	Actual selling price	$57 per unit
	Actual variable cost	$23 per unit

Sales price variance

The sales price variance reveals the difference in total revenue caused by charging a different selling price from standard.

	$	
82,400 units should sell for (× $59)	4,861,600	
But did sell for (82,400 units × $57)	4,696,800	
Sales price variance	164,800	adverse

The adverse sales price variance indicates that the 82,400 units were sold for a lower price than standard, which we can see from the basic data.

Sales volume contribution variance

The sales volume contribution variance reveals the contribution difference which is caused by selling a different quantity from that budgeted.

Actual sales volume	82,400	units
Budget sales volume	81,600	units
Sales volume variance in units	800	favourable
× standard contribution per unit $(59 – 24)	× $35	
Sales volume contribution variance	$28,000	favourable

The favourable sales volume contribution variance indicates that 800 additional units were sold than was budgeted, earning an additional standard contribution of $28,000.

Sales volume contribution variance

Since the analysis of variable cost variances explains all of the variations caused by differences between actual costs and standard costs, the calculation of the sales volume variance is based on the standard contribution not on the actual contribution.

Test your understanding 5

The following data relate to product R for the latest period.

Budgeted sales revenue	$250,000
Standard selling price per unit	$12.50
Standard contribution per unit	$5.00
Actual sales volume (units)	19,500
Actual sales revenue	$257,400

The sales variances for the period are:

	Adverse	*Favourable*
(a) Sales price variance $	☐	☐
(b) Sales volume contribution variance $	☐	☐

7 Variances working backwards

It is essential that you are comfortable with the calculation of variances. In some questions the variance will already have been calculated and you will be asked to work back to one of the components of the calculation such as the actual material used, or the actual hours worked.

Illustration 2

XYZ Ltd uses standard costing. It makes an assembly for which the following standard data are available:

Standard labour hours per assembly	24
Standard labour cost per hour	$8

During a period 850 assemblies were made, there was a nil direct labour rate variance and an adverse direct labour efficiency variance of $4,400.

Required:

How many actual labour hours were worked?

Solution

You are given the direct labour efficiency variance and the item you are looking for, the actual hours worked, is part of that calculation. Put all the information you have into your calculation and "work back" to the part that is missing.

850 units should take (850 × 24)	20,400 hours
Did take	?
Variance in hours	?
× standard labour rate per hour (× $8)	
Direct labour efficiency variance	$4,400 adverse

Work back – the variance in hours must have been 4,400/8 = 550 hours adverse

Therefore the actual hours must have been 20,400 + 550 = **20,950 hours**.

Test your understanding 6

ABC Ltd uses standard costing. It purchases a small component for which the following information is available:

Actual purchase quantity	6,800 units
Standard allowance for actual production	5,440 units
Standard price	$0.85 per unit
Material price variance (adverse)	($544)

What was the actual purchase price per unit?

A $0.75

B $0.77

C $0.93

D $0.95

Test your understanding 7

During a period 17,500 labour hours were worked at a standard cost of $6.50 per hour. The labour efficiency variance was $7,800 favourable. The number of standard labour hours expected for the output achieved was:

A 1,200

B 16,300

C 17,500

D 18,700

8 Idle time variances

You may come across a situation which involves idle time. Idle time occurs when labour is available for production but is not engaged in active production due to, for example:

- shortage of work
- shortage of material
- machine breakdown

During idle time, direct labour wages are being paid but no output is being produced. The cost of this can be highlighted separately in an idle time variance, so that it is not 'hidden' in an adverse labour efficiency variance. In this way, management attention can be directed towards the cost of idle time.

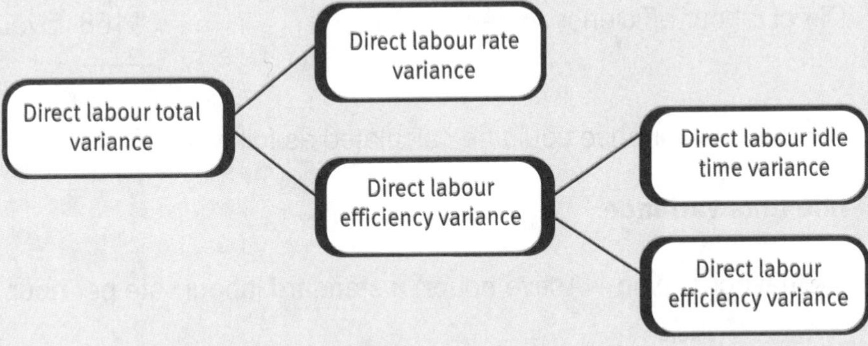

Note: The idle time variance will always be adverse.

Illustration 3

You are given the following extract from WQ Ltd's operation for April.

Standard cost:	*$ per unit*
Direct labour (5 hours at $6 per hour)	30
Variable production overhead	10

The variable production overhead is incurred in direct proportion to the direct labour hours worked. The number of units produced and sold in the month was 1,750.

Actual results for April:	$
Direct labour: 8,722 hours	47,971
Variable production overhead	26,166

Of the 8,722 hours of direct labour paid for, only 8,222 were active because of a shortage of material supplies.

First calculate the direct labour efficiency variance as normal:

Direct labour efficiency variance

	Hours	
1,750 units produced should take (× 5 hours)	8,750	
But did take	8,722	
Variance in hours	28	favourable
× standard labour rate per hour ($6)		
Direct labour efficiency variance	$168	favourable

An idle time variance could be calculated as follows:

Idle time variance

(Actual hours paid – Active hours) × standard labour rate per hour

= (8,722 – 8,222) × $6

= $3,000 adverse

This is the standard cost of wages incurred during the idle time.

These idle hours must be eliminated from the calculation of the labour efficiency variance, so that the efficiency of labour is being measured only during the hours when they were actually working. This gives a much more meaningful measure of labour efficiency.

Direct labour efficiency variance

	Hours	
1,750 units produced should have taken (× 5 hours)	8,750	
But did take (active hours)	8,222	
Variance in hours	528	favourable
× standard labour rate per hour ($6)		
Direct labour efficiency variance	$3,168	favourable

The total of these two variances is the same as the original labour efficiency variance ($168 favourable).

Variable overhead variances with idle time

Variable production overhead variances can also be affected by idle time. It is usually assumed that variable production overhead expenditure is incurred in active hours only – for example, only when the machines are actually running, incurring power costs, etc. –therefore variable production overhead expenditure is not being incurred during idle hours. The variable production overhead efficiency variance is affected in the same way as the labour efficiency variance.

Following on from the WQ Ltd example in Illustration 3, we can now calculate the variable overhead variances.

Idle time will impact on both parts of the variable production overhead variances. First calculate the variances as normal:

Variable production overhead expenditure variance

	$
8,722 hours of variable production overhead should cost (× $2)	17,444
But did cost	26,166
Variable production overhead expenditure variance	8,722 adverse

Variable production overhead efficiency variance

Variance in hours (from labour efficiency variance)	28 favourable
× standard variable overhead rate per hour ($2)	
Variable production overhead efficiency variance	$56 favourable

The effect on the variable production overhead variances would be as follows:

Variable production overhead expenditure variance

	$
8,222 active hours of variable production overhead should cost (× $2)	16,444
But did cost	26,166
Variable production overhead expenditure variance	9,722 adverse

Variable production overhead efficiency variance

	Hours
1,750 units produced should have taken (35 hours)	8,750
But did take (active hours)	8,222
Variance in hours	528 favourable
× standard variable overhead rate per hour ($2)	
Variable production overhead efficiency variance	$1,056 favourable

The total of $8,666 adverse for the two variable production overhead variances is not affected by the idle time (you should check this for yourself). However, we have now measured efficiency during active hours only, and we have allowed variable production overhead expenditure only for active hours.

Test your understanding 8

The standard direct labour cost of one unit of product Q is $3.00 (0.25 hours × $12.00).

The eight employees who make the product work a 7 hour day. In a recent 3 day period, results were as follows:

Actual units produced: 650 units

Actual labour cost: $2,275

During this period, there was a power failure. This means that all work had to stop for 2 hours.

(a) If the company reports idle time separately, the labour efficiency variance for the period is:

A 126 favourable

B $142 favourable

C $66 adverse

D $126 adverse

(b) The labour rate variance for the period is:

A $259 favourable

B $259 adverse

C $325 favourable

D $325 adverse

(c) The idle time variance for the period is:

A $24 adverse

B $24 favourable

C $192 adverse

D $192 favourable

9 Reconciling actual contribution with budgeted contribution

Now that you have seen how to calculate the variable cost and sales variances, you should be in a position to produce a statement which reconciles the actual and budget contribution for the period.

Illustration 4

The following variances have been calculated for period 4:

Direct material price	$1,954	Adverse
Direct material usage	$580	Adverse
Direct labour rate	$4,361	Favourable
Direct labour efficiency	$168	Favourable
Variable production overhead expenditure	$8,772	Adverse
Variable production overhead efficiency	$56	Favourable
Sales price	$8,750	Favourable
Sales volume contribution	$14,500	Adverse

The budgeted contribution for period 4 was $116,000 and the actual contribution for the period was $103,579.

Required:

Present the variances in a statement which reconciles the budget and actual contribution for period 4.

Solution

A reconciliation statement, known as an **operating statement**, begins with the original budgeted contribution. It then adds or subtracts the variances (depending on whether they are favourable or adverse) to arrive at the actual contribution for the month.

Contribution reconciliation statement for Period 4

	$	$
Original budgeted contribution:		116,000
Sales volume contribution variance		(14,500)
		———
Standard contribution from actual sales volume		101,500
Sales price variance		8,750
		———
		110,250

Cost variances:			
Direct material:	price	(1,954)	
	usage	(580)	
			(2,534)
Direct labour:	rate	4,361	
	efficiency	168	
			4,529
Variable production overhead:	expenditure	(8,722)	
	efficiency	56	
			(8,666)
Actual contribution			103,579

Note: Variances in brackets are adverse.

Test your understanding 9

The budgeted contribution for last month was $43,900 but the following variances arose:

	$	
Sales price variance	3,100	adverse
Sales volume contribution variance	1,100	adverse
Direct material price variance	1,986	favourable
Direct material usage variance	2,200	adverse
Direct labour rate variance	1,090	adverse
Direct labour efficiency variance	512	adverse
Variable overhead expenditure variance	1,216	favourable
Variable overhead efficiency variance	465	adverse

The actual contribution for last month was $ ________.

10 Interpreting variances

There are many possible causes of variances, ranging from errors in setting the standard cost to efficiencies and inefficiencies of operations. The following shows some of the possible causes of variances.

Variance	Favourable	Adverse
Material price	• Standard price set too high	• Standard price set too low
	• Lower quality material used	• Higher quality material used
	• Unexpected discounts available	• Unexpected price increase
Material usage	• Standard usage set too high	• Standard usage set too low
	• Higher quality material used	• Lower quality material used
	• More skilled workers	• Less skilled workers
	• Stricter quality control	• Theft
Labour rate	• Standard rate set too high	• Standard rate set too low
	• Lower pay rises	• Higher pay rises
Labour efficiency	• Standard hours set too high	• Standard hours set too low
	• More skilled workers	• Less skilled workers
	• Higher grade of material	• Lower grade of material
	• More efficient working	• Less efficient working
Sales price	• Higher quality product	• Increased competition
	• Higher selling price	• Lower selling price
Sales volume contribution	• Increased marketing activity	• Quality control problems
	• Higher sales volume	• Lower sales volume

In an assessment question, you should review the information given and select any feasible cause that is consistent with the variance in question: that is, if the variance is favourable you must select a cause that would result in a favourable variance.

Interpreting the variable overhead variances

The variable overhead expenditure variance is caused by the standard absorption rate being set at too high, or too low a level.

The variable overhead efficiency variance will be affected by all of the same factors as the labour efficiency variance.

When interpreting the variable overhead expenditure variance, remember that overheads consist of a number of items: indirect materials, indirect labour, maintenance costs, power, etc., which may change because of rate changes or variations in consumption. Consequently, any meaningful interpretation of the variable overhead expenditure variance must focus on individual cost items.

The inter-relations between variances

Adverse variances in one area of the organisation may be interrelated with favourable variances elsewhere, or vice versa. For example, if cheaper material is purchased this may produce a favourable material price variance. However, if the cheaper material is of lower quality and difficult to process, this could result in adverse variances for material usage and labour efficiency. There could also be an impact on the sales variances if the cheaper material affects the overall quality of the final product. Sales volume could reduce resulting in an adverse sales volume contribution variance, or the sales price may have to be reduced which would result in an adverse sales price variance.

It is important that students can identify any inter-relations between variances.

Test your understanding 10

The direct material usage variance for last period was $3,400 adverse. Which of the following reasons could have contributed to this variance? *(Tick all that apply.)*

(a) Output was higher than budgeted □

(b) The purchasing department bought poor quality material □

(c) The original standard usage was set too high □

(d) Market prices for the material were higher than expected □

(e) An old, inefficient machine was causing excess wastage □

Standard hour

Sometimes it can be difficult to measure the output of an organisation which manufactures a variety of dissimilar items. For example, if a company manufactures metal saucepans, utensils and candlesticks, it would not be meaningful to add together these dissimilar items to determine the total number of units produced. It is likely that each of the items takes a different amount of time to produce and utilises a different amount of resource.

A standard hour is a useful way of measuring output when a number of dissimilar items are manufactured. A standard hour or minute is the amount of work achievable, at standard efficiency levels, in an hour or minute.

The best way to see how this works is to look at an example.

Example

A company manufactures tables, chairs and shelf units. The standard labour times allowed to manufacture one unit of each of these are as follows:

	Standard labour hours per unit
Table	3 hours
Chair	1 hour
Shelf unit	5 hours

Production output during the first two periods of this year was as follows:

	Units produced	
	Period 1	*Period 2*
Table	7	4
Chair	5	2
Shelf unit	3	5

It would be difficult to monitor the trend in total production output based on the number of units produced. We can see that 15 units were produced in total in period 1 and 11 units in period 2. However, it is not particularly meaningful to add together tables, chairs and shelf units because they are such dissimilar items. You can see that the mix of the three products changed over the two periods and the effect of this is not revealed by simply monitoring the total number of units produced.

Standard hours present a useful output measure which is not affected by the mix of products. The standard hours of output for the two periods can be calculated as follows:

		Period 1		*Period 2*	
	Standard hours per unit	*Units produced*	*Standard hours*	*Units produced*	*Standard hours*
Table	3	7	21	4	12
Chair	1	5	5	2	2
Shelf unit	5	3	15	5	25
			—		—
Total standard labour hours produced			41		39
			—		—

Expressing the output in terms of standard labour hours shows that in fact the output level for period 2 was very similar to that for period 1.

It is important for you to realise that the actual labour hours worked during each of these periods was probably different from the standard labour hours produced. The standard hours figure is simply an expression of how long the output should have taken to produce, to provide a common basis for measuring output.

The difference between the actual labour hours worked and the standard labour hours produced will be evaluated as the labour efficiency variance.

11 Chapter summary

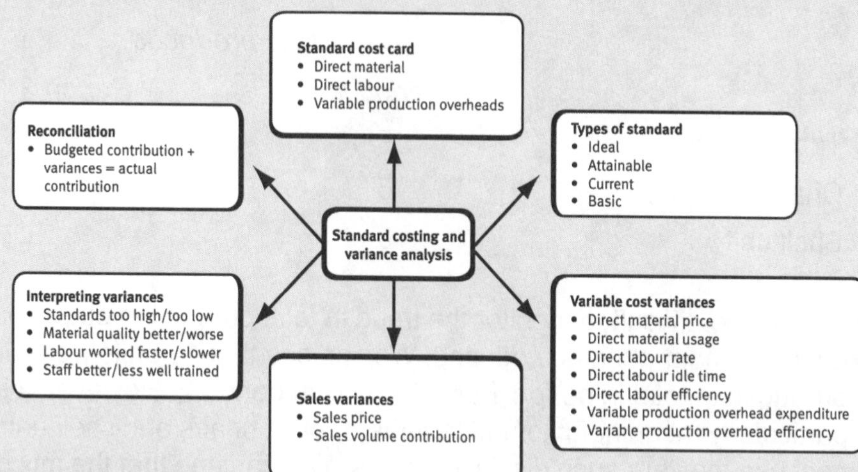

12 End of chapter questions

Question 1

The standard cost card for product K shows that each unit requires four hours of direct labour at a standard rate of $8 per hour. Last period, 420 units were produced and the direct labour cost amounted to $15,300. The direct labour efficiency variance was $160 adverse.

The actual rate paid per direct labour hour is $ _______.

Question 2

Is the following statement *true* or *false*?

Standard costing cannot be applied in an organisation that manufactures specialist furniture to customers' specifications because every cost unit is unique.

Question 3

The budgeted sales of product Y are 230 units per period at a standard sales price of $43 per unit. Last period the sales volume contribution variance was $1,100 favourable and all units were actually sold for $46 per unit. The sales price variance was $840 favourable.

The standard variable cost per unit of product Y is $ _______.

Question 4

Carshine services employs a number of people providing a car cleaning and valeting service which operates in the car parks of local supermarkets and railway stations. In an attempt to control costs and revenues the company has established the following standard cost and fee per car cleaned and valeted:

	$ per car
Materials: shampoo/polish: 0.5 litres @ $2.00 per litre	1.00
Labour: 0.75 hour @ $6 per hour	4.50
Total variable cost	5.50
Standard contribution	4.50
Standard fee per car	10.00

Carshine services expects to clean and valet 3,000 cars each month. In March, a total of 2,800 cars were cleaned and the following costs and revenues were recorded:

	$	$
Sales revenue		28,050
Shampoo/polish: 1,460 litres	2,800	
Labour: 2,020 hours	12,726	
		15,526
Contribution		12,524

Required:

Calculate the cost and sales variances to be recorded for March. Tick the box to indicate whether each variance is adverse or favourable:

			Adverse	*Favourable*
(a) material price:	$		☐	☐
(b) material usage:	$		☐	☐
(c) labour rate:	$		☐	☐
(d) labour efficiency:	$		☐	☐
(e) sales price:	$		☐	☐
(f) sales volume contribution:	$		☐	☐

Question 5

Using the data from Question 4, and your calculated variances, prepare a statement reconciling the budgeted contribution to the actual contribution for March.

Question 6

If employees are more skilled than had been allowed for in the original standard cost, which *four* of the following variances are most likely to result?

(a) favourable material usage ☐

(b) adverse material usage ☐

(c) favourable labour efficiency ☐

(d) adverse labour efficiency ☐

(e) favourable labour rate ☐

(f) adverse labour rate ☐

(g) favourable variable overhead efficiency ☐

(h) adverse variable overhead efficiency ☐

Question 7

PP Ltd has prepared the following standard cost information for one unit of product X:

Direct materials	2 kg @ $13/kg	$26.00
Direct labour	3.3 hours @ $12/hour	$39.60
Variable overheads	3.3 hours @ $2.50	$8.25

Actual results for the period were recorded as follows:

Production	12,000 units
Materials – 26,400 kg	$336,600
Labour – 40,200 hours	$506,520
Variable overheads	$107,250

All of the materials were purchased and used during the period.

(a) The direct material price and usage variances are:

	Material price	*Material usage*
A	$6,600F	$31,200A
B	$6,600F	$31,200F
C	$31,200F	$6,600A
D	$31,200A	$6,600A

(b) The direct labour rate and efficiency variances are:

	Labour rate	*Labour efficiency*
A	$24,120F	$7,200F
B	$24,120A	$7,200A
C	$24,120A	$7,560A
D	$31,320A	$7,200A

(c) The variable overhead expenditure and efficiency variances are:

	Expenditure	*Efficiency*
A	$6,750A	$1,500A
B	$6,750A	$1,500F
C	$8,250A	$1,500A
D	$8,250F	$1,500F

Question 8

Budgeted sales of product V are 4,800 units per month. The standard selling price and variable cost of product V are $45 per unit and $22 per unit respectively.

During June the sales revenue achieved from actual sales of 4,390 units of product V amounted to $231,900.

(a) The sales price variance for product V for June was $ _______ adverse/favourable (delete as appropriate).

(b) The sales volume contribution variance for product V for June was $ _______ adverse/favourable (delete as appropriate).

Question 9

The following variances have been calculated for the latest period:

	$
Sales volume contribution variance	11,245 (F)
Material usage variance	6,025 (F)
Labour rate variance	3,100 (A)
Variable overhead expenditure variance	2,415 (A)

All other variances were zero. The budgeted contribution for the period was $48,000.

The actual contribution reported for the period was $ _______.

Question 10

The following extract is taken from the standard cost card of product H.

		$ per unit
Direct labour	4 hours @ $12 per hour	48
Variable production overhead		8

During the latest period the number of direct labour hours worked to produce 490 units of product H was 1,930. The variable production overhead cost incurred was $3,281.

The variable production overhead variances for the period are:

	Adverse	Favourable
(a) Variable production overhead expenditure variance $__________	☐	☐
(b) Variable production overhead efficiency variance $ __________	☐	☐

Question 11

The standard cost of providing a meal in a fast food restaurant is as follows:

	$
Ingredient cost	1.80
Direct labour cost	0.30
Variable overhead cost	0.20

The standard price of the meal is $4.50 and the budgeted sales volume is 4,650 meals each period.

During period 9 a total of 4,720 meals were sold for $20,768. The actual total variable cost per meal was $2.30.

(a) The sales price variance for period 9 was:

A $465 favourable

B $465 adverse

C $472 favourable

D $472 adverse

(b) The sales volume contribution variance for period 9 was:

A $147 favourable

B $147 adverse

C $154 favourable

D $154 adverse

Question 12

Extracts from the standard cost card for product N are as follows:

	$
Direct labour: 14 hours @ $11 per hour	154
Variable production overhead: 14 hours @ $3 per hour	42

During the latest period, 390 units of product N were produced. Details concerning direct labour and variable production overhead are as follows:

Direct labour: amount paid for 5,720 hours = $68,640
Variable production overhead cost incurred = $16,280

Of the 5,720 labour hours paid for, 170 hours were recorded as idle time due to a machine breakdown.

Calculate the following variances and indicate whether each variance is adverse or favourable:

(a) the direct labour rate variance is $ _______

(b) the direct labour efficiency variance is $ _______

(c) the idle time variance is $ _______

(d) the variable production overhead expenditure variance is $ _______

(e) the variable production overhead efficiency variance is $ _______

Question 13

Inter-relationship may exist between variances. Explain a possible inter-relationship that might exist:

(i) between cost variances;

(ii) between the sales price and sales volume contribution variance;

(iii) between cost and sales variances.

Test your understanding answers

Test your understanding 1

A

A standard cost is a carefully pre-determined unit cost which is prepared for each cost unit.

Test your understanding 2

A standard which assumes efficient levels of operation, but which includes allowances for factors such as waste and machine downtime is known as an **attainable** standard.

Test your understanding 3

(a) the direct material price variance is **$62 favourable**.

(b) the direct material usage variance is **$180 adverse**.

	$
620 kg should have cost (× $9)	5,580
But did cost	5,518
Direct material price variance	**62 favourable**

	kg
200 units produced should have used (× 3 kg)	600
But did use	620
Variance in kg	20 adverse
× standard price per kg ($9):	
Direct material usage variance	**$180 adverse**

Test your understanding 4

(a) **D**

	$	
8,015 litres should cost (× $4)	32,060	
But did cost	33,663	
Ingredients price variance	1,603	adverse

(b) **A**

	Litres	
670 units produced should use (× 12)	8,040	
But did use	8,015	
Variance in litres	25	favourable
× standard price per litre ($4)		
Ingredients usage variance	$100	favourable

(c) **C**

	$	
2,090 hours should cost (× $9)	18,810	
But did cost	17,765	
Labour rate variance	1,045	favourable

(d) **B**

	Hours	
670 units produced should take (× 3)	2,010	
But did take	2,090	
Variance in hours	80	adverse
× standard labour rate per hour ($9)		
Labour efficiency variance	$720	adverse

(e) **B**

	$	
2,090 hours should cost (× $2)	4,180	
But did cost	5,434	
Variable overhead expenditure variance	1,254	adverse

(f) **B**

Variance in hours (from labour efficiency variance)	80 hours	adverse
× standard variable overhead rate per hour ($2)		
Variable overhead efficiency variance	$160	adverse

Test your understanding 5

	$	
19,500 units should sell for ($12.50)	243,750	
But did sell for	257,400	
Sales price variance	13,650	favourable

Actual sales volume	19,500	
Budget sales volume ($250,000/$12.50)	20,000	
Sales volume variance in units	500	adverse
× standard contribution per unit	× $5	
Sales volume contribution variance	$2,500	adverse

Test your understanding 6

C

	$	
6,800 litres should cost (× $0.85)	5,780	
But did cost	?	
Material price variance	544	adverse

Working back, materials must have cost ($5,780 + $544) = $6,324

Therefore the actual purchase price per unit = material cost ÷ actual quantity purchased

Actual purchase price per unit = $6,324 ÷ 6,800 = **$0.93 per unit**.

Test your understanding 7

D

X units should take	?
Did take	17,500 hours
Variance in hours	?
× standard labour rate per hour (× $6.50)	
Direct labour efficiency variance	$7,800 fav

Work back – the variance in hours must have been $7,800/$6.50 = 1,200 hours fav

The actual hours were 17,500, therefore the standard hours expected must have been 17,500 + 1,200 = **18,700 hours**.

Test your understanding 8

(a) **A**

650 units should take (× 0.25 hours)	162.5	active hours
But did take[1]	152.0	active hours
Variance in hours	10.5	favourable
× standard labour rate ($12)		
Labour efficiency variance	**$126**	**favourable**

Note[1]: Actual hours = (7 hours × 3 days × 8 employees) – (8 × 2 hours) = 152 hours

(b) **B**

	$	
168 hours should cost (× $12.00)	2,016	
But did cost	2,275	
Labour rate variance	**259**	**adverse**

(c) **C**

Idle time variance = (Actual hours paid – Active hours) × standard labour rate per hour

= (168 – 152) × $12 = **$192 adverse**.

Test your understanding 9

The actual contribution for last month was $38,635.

Workings:

When working from the budgeted contribution to the actual contribution, adverse variances are deducted from the budgeted contribution and favourable variances are added.

The actual contribution for last month was $(43,900 – 3,100 – 1,100 + 1,986 – 2,200 – 1,090 – 512 + 1,216 – 465) = **$38,635**.

Test your understanding 10

The reasons which could have contributed to the adverse direct material usage variance are:

(b) Poor quality material could have led to higher wastage.
(e) Excess wastage causes an adverse material usage variance.

(a) A higher output would not in itself cause an adverse usage variance, because the expected usage of material would be based on the actual output achieved.

(c) Setting the original standard usage too high is likely to lead to favourable usage variances.

(d) Higher market prices would cause adverse material price variances.

Question 1

The actual rate paid per direct labour hour is **$9 per hour**.

420 units should take (420 × 4)	1,680 hours
Did take	?
Variance in hours	?
× standard labour rate per hour (× $8)	
Direct labour efficiency variance	$160 adverse

Work back – the variance in hours must have been 160/8 = 20 hours adverse

Therefore the actual hours must have been 1,680 + 20 = 1,700 hours.

If the actual direct labour cost was $15,300 for 1,700 hours. The actual rate must have been ($15,300/1,700) = $9 per hour.

Question 2

False.

Even though each cost unit is unique, each could involve standardised tasks for which a standard time and/or cost can be determined for control purposes.

Question 3

The standard variable cost per unit of product Y is **$21**.

This calculation involves a number of steps.

First, using the sales price variance, calculate the actual volume of sales:

	$	
Standard selling price per unit	43	
Actual selling price per unit	46	
	—	
Sales price variance per unit	3	favourable
× actual number of units sold	?	
	—	
Total sales price variance	840	favourable

Therefore the actual number of units sold = $840 ÷ $3 = **280 units**

Now use the sales volume contribution variance to calculate the standard contribution:

	units	
Actual sales volume	280	
Budget sales volume	230	
	—	
Sales volume variance in units	50	
× standard contribution per unit	?	
	——	
Sales volume contribution variance	$1,100	favourable

Therefore the standard contribution per unit = $1,100 ÷ 50 = **$22**

Finally calculate the standard variable cost per unit:

Standard variable cost per unit = standard selling price – standard contribution

= $43 – $22 = **$21**

Question 4

(a) **$120 favourable**

(b) **$120 adverse**

(c) **$606 adverse**

(d) **$480 favourable**

(e) **$50 favourable**

(f) **$900 adverse**

Workings:

Material price variance

	$
1,460 litres should have cost (× $2)	2,920
But did cost	2,800
Material price variance	**120 favourable**

Material usage variance

	Litres
2,800 cars should have used (× 0.5 litres)	1,400
But did use	1,460
Variance in litres	60 adverse
× standard price per litre ($2)	
Material usage variance	**$120 adverse**

Labour rate variance

	$
2,020 hours should have cost (× $6)	12,120
But did cost	12,726
Labour rate variance	**$606 adverse**

Labour efficiency variance

	Hours
2,800 cars should have taken (× 0.75 hour)	2,100
But did take	2,020
Variance in hours	80 favourable
× standard rate per hour ($6)	
Labour efficiency variance	**$480 favourable**

Sales price variance

	$
Revenue for 2,800 cars should be (× $10)	28,000
But actual revenue was	28,050
Sales price variance	**$50 favourable**

Sales volume contribution variance

Actual cars cleaned	2,800 cars
Budgeted cars cleaned	3,000 cars
Sales volume variance in cars	200 adverse
× standard contribution per car	× $4.50
Sales volume contribution variance	**$900 adverse**

Question 5

Statement reconciling the budgeted contribution for March with the actual contribution achieved

		$
Budgeted contribution (3,000 cars × $4.50)		13,500
Sales volume contribution variance		(900)
Standard contribution from actual volume achieved		12,600
Sales price variance		50
		12,650
Cost variances		
Material price	120	
Material usage	(120)	
		–
Labour rate	(606)	
Labour efficiency	480	
		(126)
Actual contribution		12,524

Note: Variances in brackets are adverse

Question 6

(a), (c), (f) and (g) are most likely.

(a) Highly skilled employees may use material more efficiently.
(c) Highly skilled employees may work more quickly.
(f) Highly skilled employees are likely to be paid a higher hourly rate.
(g) Highly skilled employees may work more quickly.

Question 7

(a) **A**

Material price variance	$
Standard cost of materials used 26,400 kg × $13	343,200
Actual cost	336,600
Material price variance	**6,600 favourable**

Material usage variance	*Kg*
Standard usage 12,000 units × 2 kg	24,000
Actual usage	26,000
Material usage variance in kg	2,400 adverse
× standard price per kg	× $13
Material usage variance	**$31,200 adverse**

(b) **B**

Labour rate variance	$
Standard cost of hours used 40,200 × $12	482,400
Actual labour cost	506,520
Labour rate variance	**24,120 adverse**

Labour efficiency variance	*Hours*
Standard time 12,000 units × 3.3 hours	39,600
Actual time	40,200
labour efficiency variance in hours	600 actual
× standard rate per hour	× $12
Labour efficiency variance	**$7,200 actual**

(c) **A**

Variable overhead expenditure variance	$	
40,200 hours of variable overhead should cost (× $2.50)	100,500	
But did cost	107,250	
Variable overhead expenditure variance	**6,750**	**adverse**

Variable overhead efficiency variance		
Efficiency variance in hours, from labour efficiency variance	600	adverse
× standard variable overhead rate per hour	× $2.50	
Variable overhead efficiency variance	**$1,500**	**adverse**

Question 8

(a) The sales price variance for product V for June was **$34,350 favourable**.

(b) The sales volume contribution variance for product V for June was **$9,430 adverse**.

	$	
4,390 units should sell for (× $45)	197,550	
But did sell for	231,900	
Sales price variance	**34,350**	**favourable**
Actual sales volume	4,390	units
Budget sales volume	4,800	units
Sales volume variance in units	410	adverse
× standard contribution per unit $(45 – 22)	× $23	
Sales volume contribution variance	**$9,430**	**adverse**

Question 9

The actual contribution reported for the period was **$59,755**.

Adverse variances are deducted from the budgeted contribution to derive the actual contribution. Favourable variances are added because they would increase the contribution above the budgeted level.

$48,000 + $(11,245 + 6,025 – 3,100 – 2,415) = $59,755.

Question 10

(a) Variable production overhead expenditure variance **$579 favourable**.

(b) Variable production overhead efficiency variance **$60 favourable**.

	$
1,930 hours should cost (× $2)[1]	3,860
But did cost	3,281
Variable production overhead expenditure variance	579 favourable
	Hours
490 units should take (× 4)	1,960
But did take	1,930
Efficiency variance in hours	30 favourable
× standard variable overhead rate per hour (× $2)	
Variable production overhead efficiency variance	$60 favourable

Note [1]: The variable overhead rate per hour = $8 ÷ 4 hours = $2

Question 11

(a) **D**

	$	
4,720 meals should sell for (× $4.50)	21,240	
But did sell for	20,768	
Sales price variance	472	adverse

(b) **C**

Actual sales volume	4,720	meals
Budget sales volume	4,650	meals
Sales volume variance in meals	70	favourable
× standard contribution per meal [1]	× $2.20	
Sales volume contribution variance	$154	favourable

Note [1]: Standard contribution = $(4.50 – 1.80 – 0.30 – 0.20) = $2.20

Question 12

(a) Direct labour rate variance = **$5,720 adverse**

(b) Direct labour efficiency variance = **$990 adverse**

(c) Idle time variance = **$1,870 adverse**

(d) Variable production overhead expenditure variance = **$370 favourable**

(e) Variable production overhead efficiency variance = **$270 adverse**

Workings:

(a)

	$	
5,720 hours paid for should cost (× $11)	62,920	
But did cost	68,640	
Direct labour rate variance	**5,720**	**adverse**

(b)

	Hours	
390 units should take (× 14 hours)	5,460	
But did take (active hours = 5,720 – 170)	5,550	
Variance in hours	90	adverse
× standard labour rate per hour ($11)		
Direct labour efficiency variance	**$990**	**adverse**

(c) Idle time variance = 170 hours × $11 standard rate = **$1,870 adverse**

(d)

	$
Variable overhead cost of 5,550 active hours should be (× $3)	16,650
Actual variable overhead cost	16,280
Variable production overhead expenditure variance	**370 favourable**

(e)

Efficiency variance in hours	
(from labour efficiency variance)	90 adverse
× standard variable production overhead rate per hour (× $3)	
Variable production overhead efficiency variance	**$270 adverse**

Question 13

(1) **Possible inter-relationship between cost variances**
Employing a higher grade of labour than standard might produce an adverse labour rate variance. However, if these employees are more skilled than standard they may work more quickly and efficiently, resulting in a favourable labour efficiency variance and a favourable variable overhead efficiency variance.

(2) **Possible inter-relationship between the sales price and sales volume contribution variance**
Charging a higher selling price than standard will produce a favourable sales price variance. However, the higher price might deter customers and thus sales volumes might fall below budget, resulting in an adverse sales volume contribution variance.

(3) **Possible inter-relationship between cost and sales variances**
Purchasing a higher quality material than standard might produce an adverse material price variance. However, the quality of the finished product might be higher than standard and it might be possible to command higher selling prices, thus producing a favourable sales price variance. Furthermore, the higher quality product might attract more customers to buy which could result in a favourable sales volume contribution variance.

chapter

8

Budgeting

Chapter learning objectives

After completing this chapter, you should be able to:

- explain why organisations set out financial plans in the form of budgets, typically for a financial year;
- prepare functional budgets and budgets for capital expenditure and depreciation;
- prepare a master budget: based on functional budgets;
- explain budget statements;
- identify the impact of budgeted cash surpluses and shortfalls on business operations;
- prepare a flexible budget;
- calculate budget variances;
- distinguish between fixed and flexible budgets;
- prepare a statement that reconciles budgeted contribution with actual contribution.

1 Session content diagram

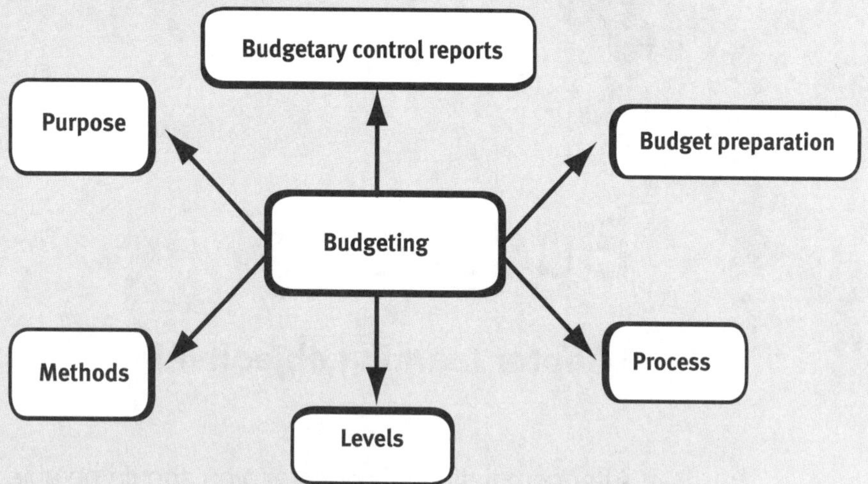

2 The purposes of budgeting

Budgets have several different purposes:

Planning – the budgeting process forces management to look ahead, set targets, anticipate problems and give the organisation purpose and direction.

Control – the budget provides the plan against which actual results can be compared.

Co-ordination – a sound budgeting system helps to co-ordinate the different activities of the business and to ensure that they are in harmony with each other.

Communication – budgets communicate targets to managers.

Motivation – the budget can influence behaviour and motivate managers.

Performance evaluation – the budget can be used to evaluate the performance of a manager.

Authorisation – budgets act as authority to spend.

What is a budget?

The *CIMA Terminology* defines a **budget** as ' a quantitative expression of a plan for a defined period of time'

The definition goes on to explain that budgets can be set for sales volumes and revenues, resource quantities, costs and expenses, assets, liabilities and cash flows.

For a budget to be useful it must be quantified. For example:

'*We plan to spend as little as possible in running the printing department this year*'

would not be particularly useful. This is simply a vague indicator of intended direction; it is not a quantified plan and would not provide much assistance in management's task of planning and controlling the organisation.

'*Budgeted revenue expenditure for the printing department for the year to 31st December 2013 is $60,000*'

is much better. The quantification of the budgets has provided:

- a definite target for planning purposes; and
- a yardstick for control purposes.

The budget period

The time period for which a budget is prepared and used is called the **budget period**. It can be any length to suit management purposes but it is usually one year.

The length of time chosen for the budget period will depend on many factors, including:

- the nature of the organisation
- the type of item being considered.

Each budget period can be subdivided into control periods, of varying lengths, depending on the level of control which management wishes to exercise. The usual length of a control period is one month.

More on the purposes of budgeting

Planning

Budgets compel planning. Without the annual budgeting process the pressures of day-to-day operational problems may tempt managers not to plan for future operations. The budgeting process encourages managers to anticipate problems before they arise, and hasty decisions that are made on the spur of the moment, based on expediency rather than reasoned judgements, will be minimised. Corporate planners would regard budgeting as an important technique whereby long-term strategies are converted into shorter-term action plans.

Control

The budget acts as a comparator for current performance, by providing a yardstick against which current activities can be monitored. Those results which are out-of-line with the budget can be further investigated and corrected. The comparison of actual results with a budgetary plan, and the taking of action to correct deviations, is known as **feedback control**.

Appropriate control action can be taken if necessary to correct any deviations from the plan.

Co-ordination

The budget serves as a vehicle through which the actions of the different parts of an organisation can be brought together and reconciled into a common plan. Without any guidance managers may each make their own decisions believing that they are working in the best interests of the organisation. Budgeting forces managers to appreciate how their activities relate to those of other managers within the organisation.

Communication

Through the budget, top management communicates its expectations to lower-level management so that all members of the organisation may understand these expectations and can co-ordinate their activities to attain them.

Motivation

The budget can be a useful device for influencing managerial behaviour and motivating managers to perform in line with the organisational objectives.

Performance evaluation

The performance of managers is often evaluated by measuring their success in achieving their budgets. The budget might quite possibly be the only quantitative reference point available.

Consider two divisions within a company, A and B. You are told that both achieved profits of $1 million during the year. If you are now told that division A had a budgeted profit of $2 million and division B had budgeted for a profit of $500,000, you now have much more information about the two divisions and their performances.

Authorisation

A budget may act as formal authorisation to a manager for expenditure, the hiring of staff and the pursuit of the plans contained in the budget.

Levels of budgeting

It is useful at this stage to distinguish in broad terms between three different types of planning:

(1) strategic planning;

(2) budgetary planning;

(3) operational planning.

These three forms of planning are interrelated. The main distinction between them relates to their time span which may be short term, medium term or long term.

The short term for one organisation may be the medium or long term for another, depending on the type of activity in which it is involved.

Strategic planning

Strategic planning is concerned with preparing long-term action plans to attain the organisation's objectives.

Strategic planning is also known as corporate planning or long-range planning.

Budgetary planning

Budgetary planning is concerned with preparing the short- to medium-term plans of the organisation. It will be carried out within the framework of the strategic plan. An organisation's annual budget could be seen as an interim step towards achieving the long-term or strategic plan.

Operational planning

Operational planning refers to the short-term or day-to-day planning process. It is concerned with planning the utilisation of resources and will be carried out within the framework set by the budgetary plan.

3 The budget process

The process of preparing and using budgets will differ from organisation to organisation. However there are a number of key requirements in the budgetary planning and control process.

The budget committee

The need for coordination in the planning process is paramount. For example, the purchasing budget cannot be prepared without reference to the production budget. The best way to achieve this coordination is to set up a budget committee. The budget committee should comprise representatives from all functions in the organisation.

The budget committee should meet regularly to review the progress of the budgetary planning process and to resolve problems that have arisen. These meetings will effectively bring together the whole organisation in one room, to ensure a coordinated approach to budget preparation.

The budget manual

Effective budgetary planning relies on the provision of adequate information to the individuals involved in the planning process.

A budget manual is a collection of documents which contains key information for those involved in the planning process.

The contents of the budget manual

Typical contents could include the following:

- An introductory explanation of the budgetary planning and control process including a statement of the budgetary objective and desired results.

  Participants should be made aware of the advantages to them and to the organisation of an efficient planning and control process. This introduction should give participants an understanding of the workings of the planning process, and of the sort of information that they can expect to receive as part of the control process.
- A form of organisation chart to show who is responsible for the preparation of each functional budget and the way in which the budgets are interrelated.
- A timetable for the preparation of each budget. This will prevent the formation of a 'bottleneck', with the late preparation of one budget holding up the preparation of all others.

- Copies of all forms to be completed by those responsible for preparing budgets, with explanations concerning their completion.
- A list of the organisation's account codes, with full explanations of how to use them.
- Information concerning key assumptions to be made by managers in their budgets, for example, the rate of inflation, key exchange rates, etc.
- The name and location of the person to be contacted concerning any problems encountered in preparing budgetary plans. This will usually be the coordinator of the budget committee (the **budget officer**) and will probably be a senior accountant.

The principal budget factor

The principal budget factor (key factor) is the factor which limits the activities of the organisation. The principal budget factor is also known as the **limiting factor**.

The early identification of this factor is important in the budgetary planning process because it indicates which budget should be prepared first.

For example, if sales volume is the principal budget factor, then the sales budget must be prepared first. All other budgets should then be linked to this.

Failure to identify the principal budget factor at an early stage could lead to delays at a later stage when managers realise that the targets they have been working with are not feasible.

The interrelationship of budgets

The critical importance of the principal budget factor stems from the fact that all budgets are interrelated. For example, if sales is the principal budget factor this is the first budget to be prepared. This will then provide the basis for the preparation of several other budgets including the selling expenses budget and the production budget.

However, the production budget cannot be prepared directly from the sales budget without a consideration of inventory policy. For example, management may plan to increase finished goods inventory in anticipation of a sales drive. Production quantities would then have to be higher than the budgeted sales level. Similarly, if a decision is taken to reduce the level of material inventories held, it would not be necessary to purchase all of the materials required for production.

The budget committee, with representatives from all areas of the organisation should help to ensure the coordination of all budgets within the organisation.

Using computers in budget preparation

A vast amount of data can be involved in the budgetary planning process and managing this volume of data in a manual system is an onerous and cumbersome task.

A computerised budgetary planning system will have the following advantages over a manual system:

- computers can easily handle the volume of data involved;
- a computerised system can process the data more rapidly than a manual system;
- a computerised system can process the data more accurately than a manual system;
- computers can quickly and accurately access and manipulate the data in the system.

Organisations may use specially designed budgeting software. Alternatively, a well-designed spreadsheet model can take account of all of the budget interrelationships described above.

The model will contain variables for all of the factors about which decisions must be made in the planning process, for example, sales volume, unit costs, credit periods and inventory volumes.

If managers wish to assess the effect on the budget results of a change in one of the decision variables, this can be accommodated easily by amending the relevant variable in the spreadsheet model. The effect of the change on all of the budgets will be calculated instantly so that managers can make better informed planning decisions.

This process of reviewing the effect of changes in the decision variables is called '**what-if?**' analysis. For example, managers can rapidly obtain the answer to the question, 'What if sales volumes are 10% lower than expected?'.

Budgetary planning is an iterative process. Once the first set of budgets has been prepared, those budgets will be considered by senior management. The criteria used to assess the suitability of budgets may include adherence to the organisation's long-term objectives, profitability and liquidity. Computerised spreadsheet models provide managers with the ability to amend the budgets rapidly, and adjust decision variables until they feel that they have achieved the optimum plan for the organisation for the forthcoming period.

4 Functional budgets and the master budget

A master budget for the entire organisation brings together the departmental or activity budgets for all the departments or responsibility centres within the organisation.

The master budget is a summary of all the functional budgets. It usually comprises the budgeted statement of profit or loss, budgeted statement of financial position and budgeted cash flow statement (cash budget).

It is this master budget which is submitted to senior management for approval because they should not be burdened with an excessive amount of detail. The master budget is designed to give the summarised information that they need to determine whether the budget is an acceptable plan for the forthcoming period.

The structure of a budget depends on the nature of the organisation and its operations. In a manufacturing organisation, the budgeting process will probably consist of preparing several functional budgets, beginning with a sales budget. (Sales is usually the principal budget factor).

Budget preparation

The stages in budget preparation for a manufacturing company are illustrated in the following diagram.

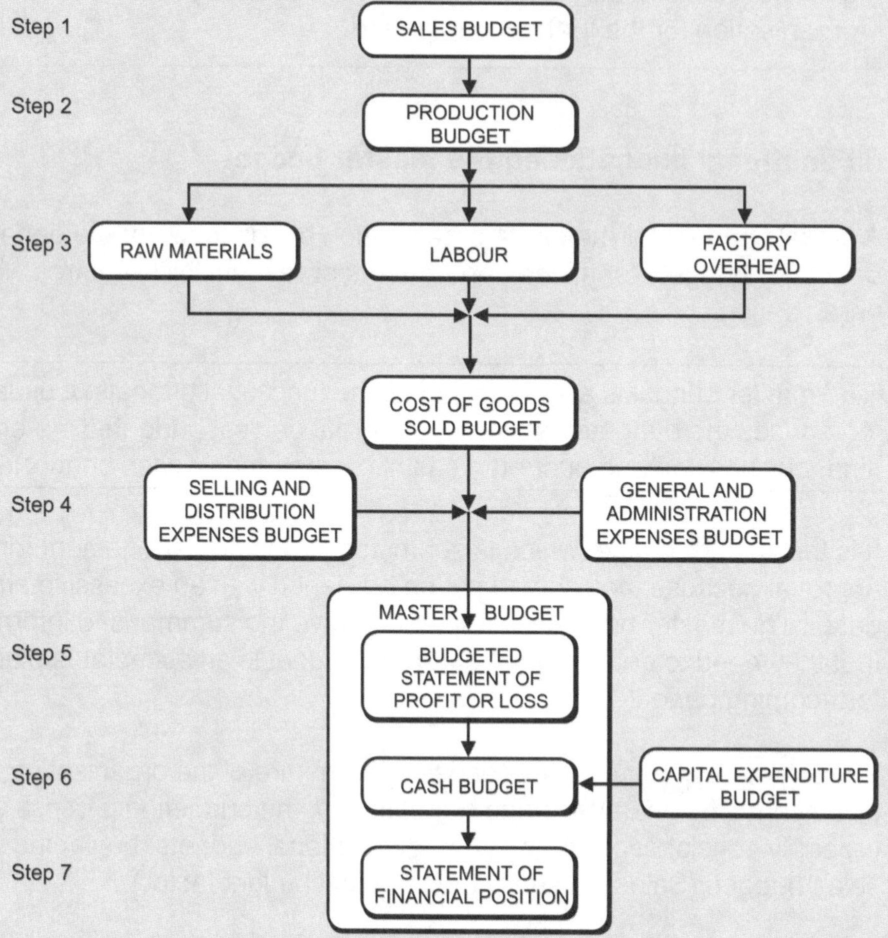

You can see from this that the principal budget factor is the starting point in the process. It is generally sales, as shown in the diagram.

Step 1: The sales budget considers how many units can be sold.

Step 2: The production budget considers how many units must be produced to meet the budgeted sales level.

Note: The difference between the sales and the production budgets is the inventory of finished goods.

Step 3: The material, labour and overhead budgets can be established, based on the production budget.

Note: The material budget is generally calculated in two parts, firstly the quantity of material required in production, then the quantity of material required to be purchased. The difference between these will be the inventory of raw materials.

Material losses in production and idle time must be taken account of in the material and labour budgets.

Step 4: Non-production budgets. Budgets for non-production costs, such as selling and distribution costs, must also be considered.

Steps 5, 6 and 7: The master budget, comprising the statement of profit or loss, cash budget and statement of financial position can be pulled together from the individual budgets.

More detail on functional budgets and the master budget

Sales budget. Budget for future sales, expressed in revenue terms and possibly also in terms of units of sale. The budget for the organisation as a whole might combine the sales budgets of several sales regions or products.

Production budget. A production budget follows on from the sales budget, since production quantities are determined by sales volume. The production volume will differ from sales volume by the amount of any planned increase or decrease in inventories of finished goods (and work in progress).

In order to express the production budget in financial terms (production cost), subsidiary budgets must be prepared for materials, labour and production overheads. Several departmental managers could be involved in preparing these subsidiary budgets.

Direct materials usage budget. This is a budget for the quantities and cost of the materials required to produce the planned production quantities.

Materials purchasing budget. This is a budget for the cost of the materials to be purchased in the period. The materials purchased budget will differ from the material usage budget if there is a planned increase or decrease in direct materials inventory. The material purchases budget should also include the purchase costs of indirect materials.

Direct labour budget. This is a budget of the direct labour costs of production. If direct labour is a variable cost, it is calculated by multiplying the production quantities (in units) by the budgeted direct labour cost per unit. If direct labour is a fixed cost, it can be calculated by estimating the payroll cost for the period.

Production overhead budget. Budgets can be produced for production overhead costs. Where a system of absorption costing is used, overheads are allocated and apportioned, and budgeted absorption rates are determined.

Administration and sales and distribution overhead budget. Other overhead costs should also be budgeted.

The master budget:

Budgeted statement of profit or loss, cash budget and statement of financial position. Having prepared the functional budgets for sales and costs, the master budget can be summarised as a statement of profit or loss for the period, a cash budget (or cash flow forecast) and a statement of financial position as at the end of the budget period.

If the budgeted profit, cash budget or statement of financial position are unsatisfactory, the budgets should be revised until a satisfactory planned outcome is achieved.

The best way to see how budgets are prepared is to work through an example.

Illustration 1

A company manufactures two products, Aye and Bee. Standard cost data for the products for next year are as follows:

	Product Aye per unit	*Product Bee* per unit
Direct materials:		
X at $2 per kg	24 kg	30 kg
Y at $5 per kg	10 kg	8 kg
Z at $6 per kg	5 kg	10 kg
Direct labour:		
Unskilled at $6 per hour	10 hours	5 hours
Skilled at $10 per hour	6 hours	5 hours

Budgeted inventories for next year are as follows:

	Product Aye units	*Product Bee units*
Opening	400	800
Closing	500	1,100

	Material X	Material Y	Material Z
	kg	kg	kg
Opening	30,000	25,000	12,000
Closing	35,000	27,000	12,500

Budgeted sales for next year: product Aye 2,400 units; product Bee 3,200 units.

Required:

Prepare the following budgets for next year:

(a) production budget, in units;

(b) material usage budget, in kilos;

(c) material purchases budget, in kilos and $;

(d) direct labour budget, in hours and $.

Solution

(a) **Production budget**

	Product Aye	Product Bee
	units	units
Sales units required	2,400	3,200
Closing inventory	500	1,100
	2,900	4,300
Less opening inventory	400	800
Production units required	2,500	3,500

(b) **Material usage budget**

	Material X	Material Y	Material Z
	kg	kg	kg
Requirements for production:			
Product Aye[1]	60,000	25,000	12,500
Product Bee	105,000	28,000	35,000
Total material usage	165,000	53,000	47,500

Note [1]: Material X for product Aye:

2,500 units produced × 24 kg = 60,000 kg

The other material requirements are calculated in the same way.

(c) **Material purchases budget**

	Material X	*Material Y*	*Material Z*
	kg	*kg*	*kg*
Material required for production	165,000	53,000	47,500
Closing inventory	35,000	27,000	12,500
	200,000	80,000	60,000
Less opening inventory	30,000	25,000	12,000
Material purchases (kg)	170,000	55,000	48,000
Standard price per kg	$2	$5	$6
Material purchases ($)	$340,000	$275,000	$288,000

Total material purchases = ($340,000 + $275,000 + $288,000) = **$903,000**

(d) **Direct labour budget**

	Unskilled labour hours	*Skilled labour hours*	*Total*
Requirements for production:			
Product Aye[1]	25,000	15,000	
Product Bee	17,500	17,500	
Total hours required	42,500	32,500	
Standard rate per hour	$6	$10	
Direct labour cost	$255,000	$325,000	$580,000

Note [1]: Unskilled labour for product Aye:

2,500 units produced × 10 hours = 25,000 hours

The other labour requirements are calculated in the same way.

Test your understanding 1

An ice cream manufacturer is in the process of preparing budgets for the next few months, and the following draft figures are available:

Sales forecast	
June	6,000 cases
July	7,500 cases
August	8,500 cases
September	7,000 cases
October	6,500 cases

Each case uses 2.5 kg of ingredients and it is policy to have inventories of ingredients at the end of each month to cover 50% of next month's production.

There are 750 cases of finished ice cream in inventory on 1 June and it is policy to have inventories at the end of each month to cover 10% of the next month's sales.

Required:

(a) The production budget (in cases) for June and July will be:

June: _______ cases

July: _______ cases

(b) The ingredient purchases budget (in kg) for August will be _______ kg

5 The cash budget

The cash budget is one of the most vital planning documents in an organisation. It will show the cash effect of all of the decisions taken in the planning process.

Management decisions will have been taken concerning such factors as inventory policy, credit policy, selling price policy and so on. All of these plans will be designed to meet the objectives of the organisation. However, if there are insufficient cash resources to finance the plans, they may need to be modified or perhaps action might require to be taken to alleviate the cash constraint.

A cash budget can give forewarning of potential problems that could arise so that managers can be prepared for the situation or take action to avoid it.

The use of forecasts to modify actions so that potential threats are avoided or opportunities exploited is known as **feedforward control**.

There are four possible cash positions that could arise:

	Possible management action
Short-term deficit	Arrange a bank overdraft, reduce receivables and inventories, increase payables
Long-term deficit	Raise long-term finance, such as long-term loan capital or share capital
Short-term surplus	Invest short term, increase receivables and inventories to boost sales, pay suppliers early to obtain cash discount
Long-term surplus	Expand or diversify operations, replace or update non-current assets

Notice that the type of action taken by management will depend not only on whether a deficit or a surplus is expected, but also on how long the situation is expected to last.

For example, management would not wish to use surplus cash to purchase non-current assets, if the surplus was only short term and the cash would soon be required again for day-to-day operations.

Preparing cash budgets

A few basic principles when preparing cash budgets:

- **The format for cash budgets**

  There is no definitive format which should be used for a cash budget. However, whichever format you decide to use it should include the following:

  (i) **A clear distinction between the cash receipts and cash payments for each control period** and a subtotal clearly shown for each.

  (ii) **A figure for the net cash flow for each period**. This makes the cash budget easier to prepare and use. In practice, managers find the figure for the net cash flow helps to draw attention to the cash flow implications of their actions during the period.

  (iii) **The closing cash balance for each control period**. The closing balance for each period will be the opening balance for the following period.

- **Depreciation is not included in cash budgets**

  Remember that depreciation is not a cash flow. It may be included in your data for overheads and must therefore be excluded before the overheads are inserted into the cash budget.

- **Allowance must be made for bad and doubtful debts**

  Bad debts will never be received, and doubtful debts may not be received. When you are forecasting the cash receipts from customers you must remember to adjust for these items.

Illustration 2

Watson Ltd is preparing budgets for the next quarter. The following information has been prepared so far:

Sales value	June (estimate)	$12,500
	July	$13,600
	August	$17,000
	September	$16,800
Direct wages	$1,300 per month	
Direct material purchases	June (estimate)	$3,450
	July	$3,780
	August	$2,890
	September	$3,150

Other information

- Watson sells 10% of its goods for cash. The remainder of customers receive one month's credit.
- Payments to material suppliers are made in the month following purchase.
- Wages are paid as they are incurred.
- Watson takes one month's credit on all overheads.
- Production overheads are $3,200 per month.
- Selling, distribution and administration overheads amount to $1,890 per month.
- Included in the amounts for overhead given above are depreciation charges of $300 and $190, respectively.
- Watson expects to purchase a delivery vehicle in August for a cash payment of $9,870.
- The cash balance at the end of June is forecast to be $1,235.

Required:

Prepare a cash budget for each of the months July to September.

Solution

Watson Ltd cash budget for July to September

	July	*August*	*September*
	$	$	$
Sales receipts:			
10% in cash	1,360	1,700	1,680
90% in one month	11,250	12,240	15,300
Total receipts	12,610	13,940	16,980

	July	*August*	*September*
	$	$	$
Material purchases (one month credit)	3,450	3,780	2,890
Direct wages	1,300	1,300	1,300
Production overheads[1]	2,900	2,900	2,900
Selling, distribution and administration overhead[1]	1,700	1,700	1,700
Delivery vehicle	–	9,870	–
Total payments	9,350	19,550	8,790
Net cash inflow/(outflow)	3,260	(5,610)	8,190
Opening cash balance	1,235	4,495	(1,115)
Closing cash balance	4,495	(1,115)	7,075

Note [1]: Depreciation has been excluded from the overhead figures because it is not a cash item.

Interpretation of the cash budget

The cash budget produced for Watson Ltd, in illustration 2, forewarns the management that their plans will lead to a cash deficit of $1,115 at the end of August. They can also see that it will be a short-term deficit and can take appropriate action.

They may decide to delay the purchase of the delivery vehicle or perhaps negotiate a period of credit before the payment will be due. Alternatively overdraft facilities may be arranged for the appropriate period.

The important point to appreciate is that management should take appropriate action for a forecast short-term deficit. For example, it would not be appropriate to arrange a five year loan to manage a cash deficit that is expected to last for only one month.

If it is decided that overdraft facilities are to be arranged, it is important that due account is taken of the timing of the receipts and payments within each month.

For example, all of the payments in August may be made at the beginning of the month but receipts may not be expected until nearer the end of the month. The cash deficit could then be considerably greater than it appears from looking only at the month-end balance.

If the worst possible situation arose, the overdrawn balance during August could become as large as $4,495 – $19,550 = $15,055. If management had used the month-end balances as a guide to the overdraft requirement during the period then they would not have arranged a large enough overdraft facility with the bank. It is important therefore, that they look in detail at the information revealed by the cash budget, and not simply at the closing cash balances.

Test your understanding 2

The following details have been extracted from the receivables collection records of C Ltd:

Invoice paid in the month after sale	60%
Invoice paid in the second month after sale	25%
Invoice paid in the third month after sale	12%
Bad debts	3%

Invoices are issued on the last day of each month.

Customers paying in the month after sale are entitled to deduct a 2% settlement discount.

Credit sales values for June to September are budgeted as follows:

June	*July*	*August*	*September*
$35,000	$40,000	$60,000	$45,000

The amount budgeted to be received from credit sales in September is

A $47,280

B $47,680

C $48,850

D $49,480

6 Approaches to budgeting

There are many approaches used in budgeting. It is useful to think of these pairs:

- Rolling and periodic budgets
- Incremental and zero-based budgeting (ZBB)
- Participative and imposed budgeting

Rolling budgets

The *CIMA Terminology* defines a **rolling budget** as a 'budget continuously updated by adding a further accounting period (month or quarter) when the earliest accounting period has expired. Its use is particularly beneficial where future costs and/or activities cannot be forecast accurately.'

For example, a budget may initially be prepared for January to December. At the end of the first quarter, that is, at the end of March, year 1, the first quarter's budget is deleted. A further quarter is then added to the end of the remaining budget, for January to March, year 2. The remaining portion of the original budget is updated in the light of current conditions. This means that managers have a full year's budget always available and the rolling process forces them continually to plan ahead.

A system of rolling budgets is also known as *continuous budgeting.*

Advantages

(1) Budgeting should be more accurate, uncertainties should be reduced.

(2) Managers are forced to reconsider their budgets on a much more regular basis, taking into account current conditions.

(3) Planning and control are based on a more recent, more realistic budget.

(4) There is always a budget extending 9 –12 months into the future.

Disadvantages

(1) Budgets are prepared several times a year meaning more time, money and effort in budget preparation.

(2) Managers doubt the usefulness of preparing one budget after another.

In practice, most organisations carry out some form of updating process on their budgets, so that the budgets represent a realistic target for planning and control purposes. The formalised budgetary planning process will still be performed on a regular basis to ensure a coordinated approach to budgetary planning.

Periodic budget

A periodic budget shows the costs and revenue for one period of time, e.g. one year and is updated on a periodic basis, e.g. every 12 months.

Incremental budgeting

The traditional approach to budgeting is to take the previous year's budget and to add on a percentage to allow for inflation and other cost increases. In addition there may be other adjustments for specific items such as an extra worker or extra machine.

In times of recession, the opposite process will take place, i.e. last year's budget minus a certain percentage.

Advantages

(1) Relatively easy to do, even for non-accountants.

(2) Can be performed relatively quickly.

(3) Less likely to miss required items.

Disadvantages

(1) Consideration will not be given to the justification for each activity. They will be undertaken merely because they were undertaken the previous year. Different ways of achieving the objective will not be examined.

(2) Past inefficiencies will be continued and it may result in **budget slack,** which is unnecessary expenditure being built into the budget.

(3) Managers know that if they fail to spend their budget, it is likely to be reduced next period. They therefore try to spend the whole budget, regardless of whether or not the expenditure is justified.

Zero-based budgeting

Zero-based budgeting (ZBB) was developed as an alternative to the incremental approach.

The *CIMA Terminology* defines **zero-based budgeting** as a 'method of budgeting that requires all costs to be specifically justified by the benefits expected.'

Zero-based budgeting is so called because it requires each budget to be prepared and justified from zero, instead of simply using last year's budget or actual results as a base. Incremental levels of expenditure on each activity are evaluated according to the resulting incremental benefits. Available resources are then allocated where they can be used most effectively.

The major advantage of ZBB is that managers are forced to consider alternative ways of achieving the objectives for their activity and they are required to justify the activities which they currently undertake. This helps to eliminate or reduce the incidence of budget slack.

Advantages and disadvantages of ZBB

Advantages

(1) Inefficient or obsolete operations can be identified and discontinued.

(2) It creates an inquisitorial attitude, rather than one which assumes current practices represent value for money.

(3) Wasteful expenditure is avoided.

(4) Managers are forced to consider alternative methods of achieving their objectives.

(5) Knowledge and understanding of the cost behaviour patterns of the organisation will be enhanced.

(6) Resources should be allocated efficiently and economically.

Disadvantages

(1) The time involved and the cost of preparing the budget is much greater than for less elaborate budgeting methods.

(2) It may emphasise short-term benefits to the detriment of long-term benefits.

(3) There is a need for management to possess skills that may not be present in the organisation.

(4) It is difficult to compare and rank completely different types of activity.

(5) The budgeting process may become too rigid and the company may not be able to react to unforeseen opportunities or threats.

(6) Incremental costs and benefits of alternative courses of action are difficult to quantify accurately.

Note: A detailed discussion of ZBB is outside the scope of your *Fundamentals of Management Accounting* syllabus, but you should be aware that there are a number of different approaches to budgetary planning.

Participative budgeting

The *CIMA Terminology* defines **participative budgeting** as a 'budgeting process where all budget holders have the opportunity to participate in setting their own budgets'.

This may also be referred to as '*bottom-up budgeting*'.

Advantages

(1) Improved quality of forecasts to use as the basis for the budget. Managers who are doing a job on a day-to-day basis are likely to have a better idea of what is achievable, what is likely to happen in the forthcoming period, local trading conditions, etc.

(2) Improved motivation. Budget holders are more likely to want to work to achieve a budget that they have been involved in setting themselves, rather than one that has been imposed on them by more senior managers. They will own the budget and accept responsibility for the achievement of the targets contained.

Disadvantages

(1) Extended and complex budgetary process. It is a lengthy process to get every manager's input to the process.

(2) Slack may be built in to the budget. Where managers are involved in setting their own budgets, they may deliberately make the budgets easier to achieve.

Imposed budgeting

The *CIMA Terminology* defines **imposed budgeting** as 'A budget allowance which is set without permitting the ultimate budget holder to have the opportunity to participate in the budgeting process'.

This may also be referred to as 'top down budgeting'.

Advantages

(1) Involving managers in the setting of budgets is more time consuming than if senior managers simply imposed the budgets.

(2) Managers may not have the skills or motivation to participate usefully in the budgeting process.

(3) Senior managers have a better overall view of the company and its resources and may be better placed to create a budget which utilises those scarce resources to best effect. They may offer a more objective, fresher perspective.

Disadvantages

(1) Lack of ownership of the budget. Managers may resent the budget being imposed and therefore may not try hard to meet it.

(2) Lack of detailed knowledge of each business area may result in an unrealistic budget.

Note: The behavioural aspects of budgeting is outside the scope of the *Fundamentals of Management Accounting* syllabus.

Test your understanding 3

The term 'budget slack' refers to:

A the extended lead time between the preparation of the functional budgets and the master budget

B the difference between the budgeted output and the breakeven output

C the additional capacity available which can be budgeted for

D the deliberate overestimation of costs and underestimation of revenues in a budget

Test your understanding 4

A system of budgeting whereby the budget is continuously updated by adding a further accounting period when the earliest accounting period has expired, is known as a system of (*tick the correct box*):

rolling budgets □

incremental budgets □

7 Budgetary control

Budgetary control is achieved by comparing the actual results with the budget. The differences are calculated as variances and management action may be taken to investigate and correct the variances if necessary or appropriate. As you learned earlier with standard cost variances:

- If costs are higher or revenues are lower than the budget, then the difference is an **adverse variance**.
- If costs are lower or revenues are higher than the budget, then the difference is a **favourable variance**.

Budget centres

The *CIMA Terminology* defines a **budget centre** as a 'section of an entity for which control may be exercised through prepared budgets'

Each budget centre is often a **responsibility centre**. Each centre will have its own budget and a manager will be responsible for managing the centre and controlling the budget. This manager is often referred to as the budget holder. Regular budgetary control reports will be sent to each budget holder so that they may monitor their centre's activities and take control action if necessary.

There are four classifications for responsibility centres, depending on what the manager of the centre has responsibility for:

- **Cost centre** – manager is responsible for operating costs.
- **Revenue centre** – manager is responsible for revenue.
- **Profit centre** – manager is responsible for operating costs and revenue and the resulting profit.
- **Investment centre** – manager is responsible for profit and the return on any investment made.

Budgetary control reports

If managers are to use budgets to control their areas effectively, they must receive regular control information.

The budgetary reporting system should ideally be based on the ***exception principle*** which means that management attention is focused on those areas where performance is significantly different from budget. Subsidiary information could be provided on those items which are in line with the budget.

Attributes of budgetary control reports

Budgetary control reports should be:

- **Timely**. The information should be made available as soon as possible after the end of the control period. Corrective action will be much more effective if it is taken soon after the event, and adverse trends could continue unchecked if budgetary reporting systems are slow.
- **Accurate**. Inaccurate control information could lead to inappropriate management action. There is often a conflict between the need for timeliness and the need for accuracy. More accurate information might take longer to produce. The design of budgetary reporting systems should allow for sufficient accuracy for the purpose to be fulfilled.
- **Relevant to the recipient**. Busy managers should not be swamped with information that is not relevant to them. They should not need to search through a lot of irrelevant information to reach the part which relates to their area of responsibility. The natural reaction of managers in this situation could be to ignore the information altogether.
- **Communicated to the correct manager**. Control information should be directed to the manager who has the responsibility and authority to act on it. If the information is communicated to the wrong manager its value will be immediately lost and any adverse trends may continue uncorrected. Individual budget holders' responsibilities must be clearly defined and kept up to date in respect of any changes.

Many control reports also segregate controllable and non-controllable costs and revenues, that is, the costs and revenues over which managers can exercise control are highlighted separately in the reports from those over which they have no control.

A number of accounting packages have the facility to record actual and budget details against each account code for each budget centre. These may then be printed in the form of a report.

8 Fixed and flexible budgets

When managers are comparing the actual results with the budget for a period, it is important to ensure that they are making a valid comparison. The use of flexible budgets can help to ensure that actual results are monitored against realistic targets.

Illustration 3

A company manufactures a single product and the following data show the actual results for costs for the month of April compared with the budgeted figures.

Operating statement for April

	Budget	*Actual*	*Variance*
Units produced	1,200	1,000	(200)
	$	$	$
Direct material	19,200	16,490	2,710
Direct labour	13,200	12,380	820
Production overhead	24,000	24,120	(120)
Administration overhead	21,000	21,600	(600)
Selling overhead	16,400	16,200	200
Total cost	93,800	90,790	3,010

Note: Variances in brackets are *adverse*.

Looking at the costs incurred in April, a cost saving of $3,010 has been made compared with the budget. However, the number of units produced was 200 less than budget so some savings in expenditure might be expected. It is not possible to tell from this comparison how much of the saving is due to efficient cost control, and how much is the result of the reduction in activity.

The type of budget being used here is a **fixed budget**. A fixed budget is one which remains **unchanged regardless of the actual level of activity.** In situations where activity levels are likely to change, and there is a significant proportion of variable costs, it is difficult to control expenditure satisfactorily with a fixed budget.

If costs are mostly fixed, then changes in activity levels will not cause problems for cost comparisons with fixed budgets.

A **flexible budget** can help managers to make more valid comparisons. It is designed to show the allowed expenditure for the actual number of units produced and sold. Comparing this flexible budget with the actual expenditure, it is possible to distinguish genuine efficiencies and inefficiencies.

Preparing a flexible budget

Before a flexible budget can be prepared, managers must identify the cost behaviour, i.e. which costs are fixed, which are variable and which are semi-variable. The allowed expenditure on variable costs can then be increased or decreased as the level of activity changes. You will recall that fixed costs are those costs which will not increase or decrease over the relevant range of activity. The allowance for these items will therefore remain constant. Semi-variable costs have both a fixed and a variable element.

We can now continue with the example.

Management has identified that the following budgeted costs are fixed:

	$
Direct labour	8,400
Production overhead	18,000
Administration overhead	21,000
Selling overhead	14,000

It is now possible to identify the expected variable cost per unit produced.

	Original budget	*Fixed cost*	*Variable cost*	*Variable cost per unit*
	(a)	*(b)*	*(c) = (a) –(b)*	*(c) ÷ 1,200*
Units produced	1,200			
	$	$	$	$
Direct material	19,200	–	19,200	16
Direct labour	13,200	8,400	4,800	4
Production overhead	24,000	18,000	6,000	5
Administration overhead	21,000	21,000	–	–
Selling overhead	16,400	14,000	2,400	2
	93,800	61,400	32,400	27

From this you can see that:

- administration overhead is fixed
- direct material is variable
- direct labour, production overhead and selling and distribution overheads are semi-variable

Now that managers are aware of the fixed costs and the variable costs per unit it is possible to 'flex' the original budget to produce a budget cost allowance for the actual 1,000 units produced.

The budget cost allowance (or flexed budget) for each item is calculated as follows:

Budget cost allowance = Budgeted fixed cost + (number of units produced × variable cost per unit)

The budget cost allowances can be calculated as follows:

Direct material = 0 + (1,000 × 16) = $16,000

Direct labour = 8,400 + (1,000 × 4) = $12,400

Production overhead = 18,000 + (1,000 × 5) = $23,000

Administration overhead = 21,000 + 0 = $21,000

Selling overhead = 14,000 + (1,000 × 2) = $16,000

A flexible budget statement can now be produced:

Flexible budget comparison for April

	Cost allowance	*Actual cost*	*Variance*
	$	$	$
Direct material	16,000	16,490	(490)
Direct labour	12,400	12,380	20
Production overhead	23,000	24,120	(1,120)
Administration overhead	21,000	21,600	(600)
Selling overhead	16,000	16,200	(200)
Total cost	88,400	90,790	(2,390)

Note: Variances in brackets are adverse.

This revised analysis shows that in fact the cost was $2,390 higher than would have been expected from a production volume of 1,000 units.

The cost variances in the flexible budget comparison are almost all adverse. These overspendings were not revealed when the fixed budget was used and managers may have been under the false impression that costs were being adequately controlled.

The total budget variance

If we now produce a statement showing the fixed budget, the flexible budget and the actual results together, it is possible to analyse the total variance between the original budget and the actual results.

	Fixed budget	*Flexible budget*	*Actual results*	*Expenditure variances*
	$	$	$	$
Direct material	19,200	16,000	16,490	(490)
Direct labour	13,200	12,400	12,380	20
Production overhead	24,000	23,000	24,120	(1,120)
Administrative overhead	21,000	21,000	21,600	(600)
Selling and distribution overhead	16,400	16,000	16,200	(200)
	93,800	88,400	90,790	(2,390)

5,400 Volume variance | (2,390) Expenditure variance

3,010 Total variance

The total variance is therefore made up of two parts:

(1) the volume variance of $5,400 favourable, which is the expected cost saving resulting from producing 200 units less than budgeted;

(2) the expenditure variance of $2,390 adverse, which is the net total of the over- and under-expenditure on each of the costs for the actual output of 1,000 units.

Notice that the volume variance is the saving in standard variable cost: 200 units × $27 per unit = $5,400.

When you looked at standard costing, you learned how some of the expenditure variances can be analysed between their price and usage elements – for example, how much of the variance is caused by paying a different price per hour of labour (the labour rate variance), or per kilogram of material (the material price variance), and how much is caused by using a different quantity of material or labour (the usage and efficiency variances).

Using flexible budgets for planning

You should appreciate that while flexible budgets can be useful for control purposes they are not particularly useful for planning. The original budget must contain a single target level of activity so that managers can plan such factors as the resource requirements and the product pricing policy. This would not be possible if they were faced with a range of possible activity levels, although managers will of course consider a range of possible activity levels before they select the target budgeted activity level.

The budget can be designed so that the fixed costs are distinguished from the variable costs. This will facilitate the preparation of a budget cost allowance (flexed budget) for control purposes at the end of each period, when the actual activity is known.

Test your understanding 5

G Ltd produces and sells a single product. The budget for the latest period is as follows.

	£
Sales revenue (12,600 units)	277,200
Variable costs:	
Direct material	75,600
Direct labour	50,400
Production overhead	12,600
Fixed costs:	
Production overhead	13,450
Other overhead	10,220
	162,270
Budgeted profit	114,930

The actual results for the period were as follows.

	£
Sales revenue (13,200 units)	303,600
Variable costs:	
Direct material	78,350
Direct labour	51,700
Production overhead	14,160
Fixed costs:	
Production overhead	13,710
Other overhead	10,160
	168,080
Actual profit	135,520

Required:

Prepare a flexible budget control statement and comment on the results.

Test your understanding 6

A flexible budget is:

A a budget which, by recognising different cost behaviour patterns, is designed to change as the volume of activity changes

B a budget for a defined period of time which includes planned revenues, expenses, assets, liabilities and cash flow

C a budget which is prepared for a period of one year which is reviewed monthly, whereby each time actual results are reported, a further forecast period is added and the intermediate period forecasts are updated

D a budget of semi-variable production costs only.

9 Reconciling actual contribution with budgeted contribution

In the same way as we did with standard costing in the last chapter, we can use the variances calculated in the budgetary control statements to reconcile the actual contribution with the budgeted contribution for the period.

Example

ABG Ltd has a budgeted contribution for May of $368,000. The following variances were calculated for the period:

Direct material total variance	$12,500 adverse
Direct labour total variance	$17,900 favourable
Variable production overhead total variance	$11,850 favourable

Required:

Calculate the actual contribution for May.

Solution

	$
Budgeted contribution	368,000
Direct material total variance	(12,500)
Direct labour total variance	17,900
Variable production overhead total variance	11,850
Actual contribution	385,250

Test your understanding 7

The budgeted contribution for last month was $45,500. The following variances arose:

	$	
Sales total variance	3,100	adverse
Direct material total variance	1,986	favourable
Direct labour total variance	1,090	adverse
Variable overhead total variance	465	adverse

The actual contribution for last month was $ ________.

10 Chapter summary

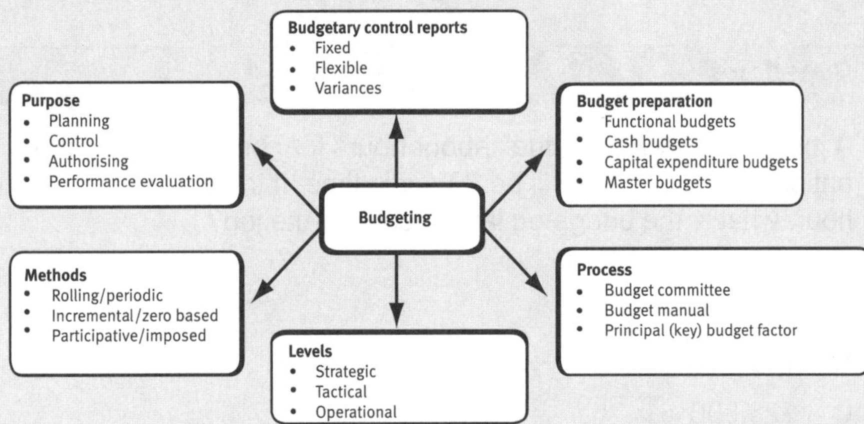

11 End of chapter questions

Question 1

A job requires 2,400 actual labour hours for completion and it is anticipated that there will be 20% idle time. If the wage rate is $10 per hour, what is the budgeted labour cost for the job?

A $19,200

B $24,000

C $28,800

D $30,000

Question 2

The following extract is taken from the production cost budget of S Ltd:

Production (units)	2,000	3,000
Production cost ($)	11,100	12,900

The budget cost allowance for an activity level of 4,000 units is

A $7,200

B $14,700

C $17,200

D $22,200

Question 3

Which of the following items of information would be contained in the budget manual? (Tick all that are correct.)

(a) An organisation chart. ☐

(b) The timetable for budget preparation. ☐

(c) The master budget. ☐

(d) A list of account codes. ☐

(e) Sample forms to be completed during the budgetary process. ☐

Question 4

Is the following statement *true* or *false*?

The principal budget factor is always the forecast sales volume.

Question 5

Assuming that sales volume is the principal budget factor, place the following budgets in the order that they would be prepared in the budgetary planning process. Indicate the correct order by writing 1, 2, 3, etc. in the boxes provided.

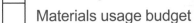

	Sales budget
	Materials purchases budget
	Materials inventory budget
	Production budget
	Finished goods inventory budget
	Materials usage budget

Question 6

Each finished unit of product H contains 3 litres of liquid L. 10% of the input of liquid L is lost through evaporation in the production process. Budgeted output of product H for June is 3,000 units. Budgeted inventories of liquid L are:

- Opening inventory 1,200 litres
- Closing inventory 900 litres

The required purchases of liquid L for June are_______ litres.

Question 7

The totals from KM Ltd's budgetary control report for February are as follows:

	Fixed budget	*Flexible budget*	*Actual results*
	$	$	$
Total sales revenue	124,310	135,490	134,580
Total variable costs	93,480	98,450	97,920
Total contribution	30,830	37,040	36,660

Complete the following table, ticking the box to indicate whether the variance is adverse or favourable.

	$	*Adverse*	*Favourable*
Sales price variance		☐	☐
Sales volume contribution variance		☐	☐
Total expenditure variance		☐	☐
Total budget variance		☐	☐

Question 8

Which of the following best describes the principle of reporting by exception?

A Sending budget reports only to those exceptional managers who are able to understand their content.

B Providing detailed reports only on those areas of the business that are performing exceptionally well and providing only subsidiary information about other areas of the business.

C Providing detailed reports only on those areas of the business that are not performing according to budget and providing only subsidiary information about aspects that are in line with budget.

Question 9

The following extract is taken from the catering costs budget of a company that provides training courses.

Number of delegates	120	170
Catering cost	$1,470	$2,020

In a flexible budget for 185 delegates, the budget cost allowance for catering costs will be $ _______.

Question 10

A small manufacturing firm is to commence operations on 1 July. The following estimates have been prepared:

	July	*August*	*September*
Sales (units)	10	36	60
Production (units)	40	50	50

It is planned to have raw material inventories of $10,000 at the end of July, and to maintain inventories at that level thereafter. There is no opening inventory.

Selling prices, costs and other information:

	Per unit
	$
Selling price	900
Material cost	280
Labour cost	160
Variable overheads	40

Fixed overheads are expected to be $5,000 per month, including $1,000 depreciation.

10% of sales are in cash, the balance payable the month following sale.

Labour is paid in the month incurred, and all other expenditures the following month.

Required:

(a) The budgeted cash receipts from sales are:

July	$	
August	$	
September	$	

(b) The budgeted cash payments for raw materials are:

July	$	
August	$	
September	$	

(c) The total of the budgeted cash payments for labour and overhead in August is $ ________.

(d) A cash budget can be used to give forewarning of potential cash problems that could arise so that managers can take action to avoid them. This is known as:

feedforward control ☐

feedback control ☐

(e) A cash budget is continuously updated to reflect recent events and changes to forecast events. This type of budget is known as a:

flexible budget ☐

rolling budget ☐

Question 11

The Arcadian Hotel operates a budgeting system and budgets expenditure over eight budget centres as shown below. Analysis of past expenditure patterns indicates that variable costs in some budget centres vary according to occupied room nights (ORN), while in others the variable proportion of costs varies according to the number of visitors (V).

The budgeted expenditures for a period with 2,000 ORN and 4,300 V were as follows:

Budget centre	*Variable costs vary with:*	*Budgeted expenditure* $	*Partial cost analysis* *Budget expenditure includes:*
Cleaning	ORN	13,250	$2.50 per ORN
Laundry	V	15,025	$1.75 per V
Reception	ORN	13,100	$12,100 fixed
Maintenance	ORN	11,100	$0.80 per ORN
Housekeeping	V	19,600	$11,000 fixed
Administration	ORN	7,700	$0.20 per ORN
Catering	V	21,460	$2.20 per V
General overheads	–	11,250	all fixed
		112,485	

In period 9, with 1,850 ORN and 4,575 V, actual expenditures were as follows:

Budget centre	*Actual expenditure* $
Cleaning	13,292
Laundry	14,574
Reception	13,855
Maintenance	10,462
Housekeeping	19,580
Administration	7,930
Catering	23,053
General overheads	11,325
	114,071

Required:

(a) The total budget cost allowances for the following costs for period 9 are:

	$
Cleaning	
Laundry	
Reception	
Maintenance	
Housekeeping	
General overheads	

(b) The total budget cost allowance in the flexible budget for period 9 is $113,521.

The total expenditure variance for period 9 is $ _______. The variance is:

adverse ☐

favourable ☐

Question 12

C Ltd makes two products, Alpha and Beta. The following data are relevant for year 3:

Material prices:	Material M	$2 per unit
	Material N	$3 per unit

Direct labour is paid $10 per hour.

Production overhead cost is estimated to be $200,000. Production overhead cost is absorbed into product costs using a direct labour hour absorption rate. Selling and administration overhead is budgeted to be $75,000.

Each unit of finished product requires:

	Alpha	*Beta*
Material M	12 units	12 units
Material N	6 units	8 units
Direct labour	7 hours	10 hours

The sales director has forecast that sales of Alpha and Beta will be 5,000 and 1,000 units, respectively, during year 3. The selling prices will be:

Alpha	$182 per unit
Beta	$161 per unit

She estimates that there will be opening inventory of 100 units of Alpha and 200 units of Beta. At the end of year 3 she does not intend holding any inventory of Alpha or Beta.

The production director estimates that the opening inventories of raw materials will be 3,000 units of material M and 4,000 units of material N. At the end of year 3 the inventories of these raw materials are to be:

M:	4,000 units
N:	2,000 units

Statement of financial position extracts for year 2:

Inventory of finished goods	$15,000
Inventory of raw materials	$20,000
Retained earnings	$81,000

The finance director advises that the rate of tax to be paid on profits during year 3 is likely to be 30%.

Required:

Prepare the company's budgets for year 3 including a budgeted statement of profit or loss for the year ended 31st December.

Question 13

B Ltd is preparing its budgets for year 2. The company's year end is 31st December.

The following information is available:

Budgeted statement of profit or loss for the year ended 31 December, year 2

	$	$
Revenue		1,203,500
Opening inventory of raw materials	32,000	
Purchases of raw materials	253,700	
	285,700	
Closing inventory of raw materials	17,000	
	268,700	
Direct wages	448,500	
Production overhead *	200,000	
Production cost of goods completed	917,200	
Opening inventory of finished goods	25,000	
	942,200	
Closing inventory of finished goods	37,800	
Production cost of goods sold		904,400
Gross profit		299,100
Selling and administration overhead *		75,000
Net profit before taxation		224,100
Taxation		67,230
		156,870
Retained earnings b/f		103,000
Retained earnings c/f		259,870

* Included in the production overhead cost is $25,000 for depreciation of property and equipment. Selling and administration overhead includes $5,000 for depreciation of equipment.

A quarterly cash-flow forecast has already been partly completed for year 2 and is set out below:

	1	2	3	4
Quarter, year 2	$	$	$	$
Receipts	196,000	224,000	238,000	336,000
Payments:				
Materials	22,000	37,000	40,000	60,000
Direct wages	100,000	110,500	121,000	117,000
Overhead	45,000	50,000	70,000	65,000
Taxation	5,000			

In addition to the above, the company plans to purchase a new machine during the year which will cost $120,000. This will be paid for in quarter 3.

The company's statement of financial position as at 31st December, year 1, is expected to be as follows:

	$	$	$
Assets	*Cost*	*Depreciation*	*Net*
Non-current assets			
Land	50,000	–	50,000
Buildings and equipment	400,000	75,000	325,000
	450,000	75,000	375,000
Current assets			
Inventories			
– raw materials	32,000		
– finished goods	25,000		
		57,000	
Receivables		25,000	
Cash at bank		10,000	
			92,000
			467,000

Capital and liabilities

Capital		
Share capital		350,000
Retained earnings		103,000
		453,000
Current liabilities		
Payables	9,000	
Taxation	5,000	
		14,000
		467,000

No changes to share capital will be made during the year.

Required:

Prepare the company's quarterly cash budget for the year ended 31st December, year 2 and a budgeted statement of financial position as at 31 December, year 2.

Question 14

When preparing a production budget, the quantity to be produced equals

A sales quantity + opening inventory + closing inventory

B sales quantity – opening inventory + closing inventory

C sales quantity – opening inventory – closing inventory

D sales quantity + opening inventory – closing inventory

Question 15

A master budget comprises

A the budgeted statement of profit or loss

B the budgeted cash flow, budgeted statement of profit or loss and budgeted statement of financial position

C the budgeted cash flow

D the entire set of budgets prepared

Question 16

Budgeted sales of product Y next period are 8,690 units. Each unit of product Y requires 8 kg of material Z. Budgeted inventories are as follows:

	Product Y	*Material Z*
	units	*kg*
Opening inventory	875	6,300
Closing inventory	920	6,180

The budgeted purchases of material Z (in kg) next period are:

A 8,615 kg

B 69,280 kg

C 69,760 kg

D 69,880 kg

Question 17

The following information relates to XY Ltd:

	Wages incurred	*Materials purchases*	*Overhead*	*Sales*
Month	$000	$000	$000	$000
February	6	20	10	30
March	8	30	12	40
April	10	25	16	60
May	9	35	14	50
June	12	30	18	70
July	10	25	16	60
August	9	25	14	50

(a) It is expected that the cash balance on 31 May will be $22,000.

(b) The wages may be assumed to be paid within the month they are incurred.

(c) It is company policy to pay suppliers for materials three months after receipt.

(d) Credit customers are expected to pay two months after delivery.

(e) Included in the overhead figure is $2,000 per month which represents depreciation on two cars and one delivery van.

(f) There is a one-month delay in paying the overhead expenses.

(g) 10% of the monthly sales are for cash and 90% are sold on credit.

(h) A commission of 5% is paid to agents on all the credit sales but this is not paid until the month following the sales to which it relates; this expense is not included in the overhead figures shown.

(i) It is intended to repay a loan of $25,000 on 30 June.

(j) Delivery is expected in July of a new machine costing $45,000 of which $15,000 will be paid on delivery and $15,000 in each of the following two months.

(k) Assume that overdraft facilities are available if required.

Required:

Prepare a cash budget for June, July and August.

Question 18

Of the four costs shown below, which would not be included in the cash budget of an insurance firm?

A Depreciation of non-current assets.

B Commission paid to agents.

C Office salaries.

D Capital cost of a new computer.

Question 19

PR Ltd's cash budget forewarns of a short-term surplus. Which of the following would be appropriate actions to take in this situation? (Select all that are correct.)

(a) Increase receivables and inventory to boost sales ☐

(b) Purchase new non-current assets ☐

(c) Repay long-term loans ☐

(d) Pay suppliers early to obtain a cash discount ☐

Question 20

Tick the correct box.

A participative budgeting system may also be described as a:

bottom-up budget ☐
top-down budget ☐

Question 21

Lawrence Ltd operates a system of flexible budgets and the flexed budgets for expenditure for the first two quarters of year 3 were as follows:

Flexed budgets – quarters 1 and 2

	Quarter 1	*Quarter 2*
Activity		
Sales units	9,000	14,000
Production units	10,000	13,000
Budget cost allowances	$	$
Direct materials	130,000	169,000
Production labour	74,000	81,500
Production overhead	88,000	109,000
Administration overhead	26,000	26,000
Selling and distribution overhead	29,700	36,200
Total budget cost allowance	347,700	421,700

Despite a projected increase in activity, the cost structures in quarters 1 and 2 are expected to continue during quarter 3 as follows:

(a) The variable cost elements behave in a linear fashion in direct proportion to volume. However, for production output in excess of 14,000 units the unit variable cost for production labour increases by 50%. This is due to a requirement for overtime working and the extra amount is payable only on the production above 14,000 units.

(b) The fixed cost elements are not affected by changes in activity levels.

(c) The variable elements of production costs are directly related to production volume.

(d) The variable element of selling and distribution overhead is directly related to sales volume.

Required:

Prepare a statement of the budget cost allowances for quarter 3, when sales were 14,500 units and production was 15,000 units.

Question 22

A recent budgetary control report shows the following information:

	Fixed budget	*Flexible budget*	*Actual results*
	$	$	$
Total sales revenue	585,847	543,776	563,945
Total variable costs	440,106	418,482	425,072
Total contribution	145,741	125,294	138,873

The sales volume contribution variance for the period was:

A $6,868 adverse

B $13,579 favourable

C $20,447 adverse

D $42,071 adverse

Question 23

F Ltd uses a flexible budgeting system to control the costs incurred in its staff canteen. The budget cost allowance for consumable materials is flexed according to the average number of employees during the period.

Required:

Complete the following equation by inserting '+', '–' or '×' as appropriate in the gaps:

Flexible budget cost allowance for consumable materials = budgeted fixed cost _____ (budgeted variable cost per employee ______ average number of employees)

Test your understanding answers

Test your understanding 1

(a) June: **6,000 cases**
    July: **7,600 cases**

(b) August: **19,125 kg**

Use a clear columnar layout for your budget workings. Although your workings will not earn marks, clear workings help you to avoid arithmetical errors because 100% accuracy is vital.

Do not forget to adjust for the budgeted movement in inventory in parts (a) and (b). A common error is to get the opening and closing inventory calculations the wrong way round.

Workings:

Production budget (in cases)

	June	*July*	*August*	*September*
Sales	6,000	7,500	8,500	7,000
Closing inventory[1]	750	850	700	650
Opening inventory	(750)	(750)	(850)	(700)
Production budget	6,000	7,600	8,350	6,950

Note [1]: Closing inventory for June is calculated as 10% of July sales (7,500 × 10%) = 750. All other months are calculated in the same way.

Ingredients purchases budget (in kg)

		August
Quantity to be used in production	(8,350 × 2.5kg)	20,875
Closing inventory	(6,950 × 2.5kg × 50%)	8,687.5
Opening inventory	(8,350 × 2.5kg × 50%)	(10,437.5)
Ingredients purchases budget		19,125.0kg

Test your understanding 2

D

Amount to be received in September is:

	$
60% of August sales less 2% discount: ($60,000 × 60% × 98%)	35,280
25% of July sales: ($40,000 × 25%)	10,000
12% of June sales: ($35,000 × 12%)	4,200
	49,480

Test your understanding 3

D

A manager might build some slack into a budget to provide some 'leeway' to disguise unnecessary spending.

Test your understanding 4

A system of budgeting whereby the budget is continuously updated by adding a further accounting period when the earliest accounting period has expired is known as a system of **rolling budgets**. It is also known as a continuous budgeting system.

Test your understanding 5

Flexible budget control statement for the latest period

	Original budget	*Flexed budget*	*Actual results*	*Variance*
Activity (units)	12,600	13,200	13,200	
	$	$	$	$
Sales revenue	277,200	290,400	303,600	13,200
Variable costs:				
Direct material	75,600	79,200	78,350	850
Direct labour	50,400	52,800	51,700	1,100
Production overhead	12,600	13,200	14,160	(960)
Fixed costs:				
Production overhead	13,450	13,450	13,710	(260)
Other overhead	10,220	10,220	10,160	60
	162,270	168,870	168,080	790
Profit	114,930	121,530	135,520	13,990

Note: Variances in brackets are adverse.

Comments

(1) The total budget variance can be analysed as follows.

	$	$
Sales volume variance ($121,530 – $114,930)		6,600
Sales price variance	13,200	
Expenditure variance	790	
		13,990
Total budget variance ($135,520 – $114,930)		20,590

(2) The favourable sales price variance indicates that a higher selling price than standard was charged for the units sold. Despite the higher price, the sales volume achieved was higher than budgeted.

(3) Expenditure on direct material, direct labour and other overhead costs was lower than the budget cost allowance for the activity level achieved. It is not possible to tell from the data provided whether the savings were achieved as a result of a lower price or a lower usage of resources.

(4) Expenditure on production overhead costs, both fixed and variable, was higher than the budget cost allowance for the activity level achieved.

Test your understanding 6

A

A flexible budget is designed to show the budgeted costs and revenues at different levels of activity.

Test your understanding 7

The actual contribution for last month was **$42,831**.

	$
Budgeted contribution	45,500
Sales variance	(3,100)
Direct material variance	1,986
Direct labour variance	(1,090)
Variable production overhead variance	(465)
Actual contribution	42,831

Question 1

D

Idle time is 20% of the total hours to be paid for.

Therefore, hours to be paid for = 2,400/0.8 = 3,000. Budgeted labour cost = 3,000 × $10 = **$30,000**.

Question 2

B

Production cost is a semi-variable cost. Use the high-low method to work out the variable and fixed elements.

$$\text{Variable cost per unit} = \frac{\text{increase in cost}}{\text{increase in production}}$$

$$\text{Variable cost per unit} = \frac{(\$12{,}900 - \$11{,}100)}{(3{,}000 - 2{,}000)} = \$1.80 \text{ per unit}$$

Fixed cost = total cost – (variable cost per unit × number of units)

Fixed cost = $12,900 – ($1.80 × 3,000) = $7,500

Budget cost allowance for 4,000 = $7,500 + ($1.80 × 4,000) = **$14,700**

Question 3

(a), (b), (d) and (e) would be contained in a budget manual.

The master budget (c) is the end result of the budgetary planning process.

Question 4

False.

The forecast sales volume will often be the principal budget factor or limiting factor, but this is not always the case.

Question 5

1	Sales budget
6	Materials purchases budget
5	Materials inventory budget
3	Production budget
2	Finished goods inventory budget
4	Materials usage budget

Question 6

The required purchases of liquid L for June are **9,700 litres**.

	Litres
Liquid L required (3,000 × 3 litres)	9,000
Evaporation loss (9,000 × 10/90)*	1,000
Total required input of liquid L	10,000
Closing inventory	900
Less: opening inventory	(1,200)
Required purchases of liquid L	9,700

* evaporation loss is 10 % of input

Question 7

Sales price variance	**$910**	**adverse**
Sales volume contribution variance	**$6,210**	**favourable**
Total expenditure variance	**$530**	**favourable**
Total budget variance	**$5,830**	**favourable**

Notes:

(1) The sales price variance is the difference between the sales revenue that was achieved and the sales revenue that would be expected for the actual activity level that occurred (that is, the sales revenue in the flexible budget).

$(134,580 - 135,490) = **$910 adverse**

(2) The sales volume contribution variance is the additional standard contribution that arose as a result of the change in the sales volume from the original budget.

$(37,040 - 30,830) = **$6,210 favourable**

(3) The expenditure variance is the difference between the actual expenditure and the expenditure that would be expected for the actual activity achieved.

$(98,450 - 97,920) = **$530 favourable**

(4) The total budget variance is the difference between the original budget contribution and the actual contribution achieved.

$(36,660 - 30,830) = **$5,830 favourable**

Question 8

C

Exception reporting involves providing detailed reports only on those areas of the business that are not performing according to budget and providing only subsidiary information about aspects that are in line with budget. This ensures that management do not receive too much information and that their attention is focused where control action is most needed.

Question 9

In a flexible budget for 185 delegates the budget cost allowance for catering costs will be **$2,185**

Delegates	$
170	2,020
120	1,470
50	550

Variable catering cost per delegate = $550/50 = $11 per delegate

Fixed catering cost = $2,020 – $(170 × 11) = $150

Budget cost allowance for 185 delegates = $150 + $(185 × 11) = **$2,185**.

Question 10

(a)	July	**$900**
	August	**$11,340**
	September	**$34,560**

Workings:

	$	$
July: 10% × (10 × $900)		900
August: 90% × July sales (10 × $900)	8,100	
10% × August sales (36 × $900)	3,240	
		11,340
September: 90% × August sales (36 × $900)	29,160	
10% × September sales (60 × $900)	5,400	
		34,560

(b)	July	**$0**
	August	**$21,200**
	September	**$14,000**

Workings:

Cash payments each month are for the previous month's purchases. Therefore, no payments are made in July.

	$	$
August: payment for July closing inventory	10,000	
payment for July usage (40 × $280)	11,200	
		21,200
September: payment for August usage (50 × $280)		14,000

(c) **$13,600**

Workings:

	$
August labour cost paid in month incurred (50 × $160)	8,000
July variable overhead cost paid in August (40 × $40)	1,600
Fixed overhead cash cost ($5,000 – $1,000 depreciation)	4,000
	13,600

(d) This is known as **feedforward** control.

(e) This type of budget is known as a **rolling** budget.

Question 11

(a)

	$
Cleaning	**12,875**
Laundry	**15,506**
Reception	**13,025**
Maintenance	**10,980**
Housekeeping	**20,150**
General overheads	**11,250**

Workings:

	Activity (ORN/V)	*Variable cost per unit*	*Variable cost allowance*	*Fixed cost allowance*	*Total budget cost allowance*
		$	$	$	$
Cleaning	1,850	2.50	4,625	8.250[1]	12,875
Laundry	4,575	1.75	8,006	7.500[2]	15,506
Reception	1,850	0.50[3]	925	12,100	13,025
Maintenance	1,850	0.80	1,480	9.500[4]	10,980
Housekeeping	4,575	2.00[5]	9,150	11,000	20,150
General o/heads	–	–	–	11,250	11,250

Notes:

	$
(1) Total budget cost allowance for 2,000 ORN	13,250
Less variable allowance (2,000 × $2.50)	5,000
Fixed cost allowance	8,250

(2) $15,025 – (4,300 × $1.75) = $7,500

(3)

	$
Total budget cost allowance for 2,000 ORN	13,100
Less fixed allowance	12,100
Variable cost allowance for 2,000 ORN	1,000

Variable cost allowance per ORN: $\frac{\$1,000}{2,000}$ = $0.50 per ORN

(4) $11,100 – (2,000 × $0.80) = $9,500

(5)

	$
Total budget cost allowance for 4,300 V	19,600
Less fixed allowance	11,000
Variable cost allowance for 4,300 V	8,600

Variable cost allowance per V: $\frac{\$8,600}{4,300}$ = $2 per visitor

(b) **$550 adverse**

Workings:

	$	
Flexible budget expenditure	113,251	
Actual expenditure	114,071	
Expenditure variance	550	adverse

Question 12

Sales budget for the year ended 31 December, year 3

	Alpha	*Beta*	*Total*
Sales volume	5,000	1,000	
Selling price	$182	$161	
Sales revenue	$910,000	$161,000	$1,071,000

Production budget for the year ended 31 December, year 3

	Alpha units	*Beta units*
Required by sales	5,000	1,000
Required closing inventory	–	–
Less expected opening inventory	100	200
Production required	4,900	800

Raw materials usage budget for the year ended 31 December, year 3

	Material M units	*Material N units*
Required by production of Alpha[1]	58,800	29,400
Required by production of Beta	9,600	6,400
Total raw material usage	68,400	35,800

Note [1]: The material usage for Alpha is determined as follows:

	Units
Material M: 4,900 × 12	58,800
Material N: 4,900 × 6	29,400

The material requirements for Beta are calculated in the same way.

Raw materials purchases budget for the year ended 31 December, year 3

	Material M units	Material N units	Total
Raw materials required by production	68,400	35,800	
Required closing inventory	4,000	2,000	
Less expected opening inventory	3,000	4,000	
Quantity to be purchased	69,400	33,800	
Price per unit	$2	$3	
Value of purchases	$138,800	$101,400	$240,200

Direct labour budget for the year ended 31 December, year 3

	Labour hours	Rate per hour $	Labour cost $
Product Alpha – 4,900 units	34,300	10	343,000
Product Beta – 800 units	8,000	10	80,000
	42,300		423,000

Production cost budget:

$$\text{Production overhead absorption rate} = \frac{\$200{,}000}{42{,}300} = \$4.72813 \text{ per labour hour}$$

Overhead absorbed by Alpha = 34,300 hours × $4.728 = $162,175

Overhead absorbed by Beta = 8,000 hours × $4.728 = $37,825

Budgeted statement of profit or loss for the year ended 31 December, year 3

	$	$
Revenue		1,071,000
Opening inventory of raw materials	20,000	
Purchases of raw materials	240,200	
	260,200	
Closing inventory of raw materials[2]	14,000	
	246,200	
Direct wages	423,000	
Production overhead	200,000	
Production cost of goods completed	869,200	
Opening inventory of finished goods	15,000	
	884,200	
Closing inventory of finished goods	–	
Production cost of goods sold		884,200
Gross profit		186,800
Selling and administration overhead		75,000
Net profit before taxation		111,800
Taxation (30%)		33,540
		78,260
Retained earnings b/f		81,000
Retained earnings c/f		159,260

Note [2]: The closing inventories are calculated as follows:

	$
Raw materials:	
M: 4,000 × $2	8,000
N: 2,000 × $3	6,000
	14,000

Question 13

Cash budget for the year ended 31st December, year 2

Quarter	*1*	*2*	*3*	*4*
	$	$	$	$
Receipts	196,000	224,000	238,000	336,000
Payments:				
Materials	22,000	37,000	40,000	60,000
Direct wages	100,000	110,500	121,000	117,000
Overhead	45,000	50,000	70,000	65,000
Taxation	5,000			
Machinery purchase			120,000	
Total payments	172,000	197,500	351,000	242,000
Net cash inflow/(outflow)	24,000	26,500	(113,000)	94,000
Balance b/fwd[1]	10,000	34,000	60,500	(52,500)
Balance c/fwd	34,000	60,500	(52,500)	41,500

Note [1]: The balance b/fwd in quarter 1 is the cash at bank on the estimated statement of financial position for 31st December, year 1.

Budgeted statement of financial position at 31st December, year 2

Assets	*Cost* $	*Depreciation* $	*Net* $
Non-current assets			
Land	50,000	–	50,000
Buildings and equipment[2]	520,000	105,000	415,000
	570,000	105,000	465,000
Current assets			
Inventories			
– raw materials	17,000		
– finished goods	37,800		
		54,800	
Receivables[3]		234,500	
Cash at bank		41,500	
			330,800
			795,800
Capital and liabilities			
Capital			
Share capital			350,000
Retained earnings			259,870
			609,870
Current liabilities			
Payables[4]		118,700	
Taxation		67,230	
			185,930
			795,800

Note [2]: *Buildings and equipment*	$
Opening cost balance	400,000
Purchases during year	120,000
	520,000
Depreciation	$
Opening depreciation balance	75,000
Production depreciation	25,000
Selling depreciation	5,000
	105,000

Note [3]: *Receivables*	$
Opening balance	25,000
Sales	1,203,500
Receipts (from cash budget)	(994,000)
Closing balance of receivables	**234,500**

Note [4]: *Payables*	$
Opening balance of payables	9,000
Material purchases	253,700
Overhead, excluding depreciation:*	
Production	175,000
Selling and administration	70,000
	507,700
Less payments (from cash budget):	
Materials	159,000
Overhead	230,000
Closing balance of payables	**118,700**

* The depreciation must be excluded from the overhead because it is not a cash item, i.e. it is not a payment which is made to suppliers.

Question 14

B

Requirements for closing inventory increase the amount to be produced, so these must be added. The available opening inventory reduces production requirements, so this must be deducted.

Question 15

B

The master budget comprises the budgeted cash flow, budgeted statement of profit or loss and budgeted statement of financial position.

Question 16

C

Product Y production budget	*Units*
Sales volume	8,690
Closing inventory	920
Less opening inventory	(875)
Production required	8,735

Materials usage budget	kg
Production units 8,735 × 8 kg	69,880

Material Z purchases budget	kg
Required for production	69,880
Closing inventory	6,180
Less opening inventory	(6,300)
Budgeted purchases	69,760

Question 17

Cash budget for June, July and August

	June	July	August
	$	$	$
Receipts			
Receipts from credit sales[1]	54,000	45,000	63,000
Cash sales[2]	7,000	6,000	5,000
Total receipts	61,000	51,000	68,000
Payments			
Wages	12,000	10,000	9,000
Materials[3]	30,000	25,000	35,000
Overhead[4]	12,000	16,000	14,000
Commission[5]	2,250	3,150	2,700
Loan repayment	25,000		
Payments for new machine		15,000	15,000
	81,250	69,150	75,700
Net cash inflow/(outflow)	(20,250)	(18,150)	(7,700)
Opening balance	22,000	1,750	(16,400)
Closing balance	1,750	(16,400)	(24,100)

Explanatory notes

(1) The cash received from credit sales is 90% of the sales made two months before. Therefore for June, cash receipts = 90% of April sales (90% × $60,000) = $54,000.

(2) Cash sales are 10% of the sales made in the month.

(3) March purchases are paid for three months later in June, and so on.

(4) May overheads, less depreciation = $14,000 – $2,000 = $12,000. These are paid in cash in June, and so on.

(5)

	May	June	July
Credit sales (90%)	$45,000	$63,000	$54,000
5% commission	$2,250	$3,150	$2,700

These amounts for commission are paid one month later, that is, in June, July and August.

Question 18

A

Depreciation is not a cash flow.

Question 19

(a) and (d) would be appropriate actions in this situation. Actions (b) and (c) would not be appropriate because they would involve investing the surplus funds for too long.

Question 20

A participative budgeting system may also be described as a **bottom-up** budget.

Question 21

In this example you will need to investigate the cost behaviour patterns to determine which costs are fixed, which are variable and which are semi-variable.

The first step in investigating cost behaviour patterns is to look at the cost data. You should be able to easily spot any fixed costs because they remain constant when activity levels change.

The easiest way to identify the behaviour patterns of non-fixed costs is to divide each cost figure by the related activity level. If the cost is a linear variable cost, then the cost per unit will remain constant. For a semi-variable cost the unit rate will reduce as the activity level increases, because the same basic amount of fixed costs is being spread over a greater number of units.

You will then need to recall how to use the high–low method to determine the fixed and variable elements of any semi-variable costs. This was covered in Chapter 2.

If you divide each cost figure by the relevant activity figure, you will find that the only wholly variable cost is direct material, at $13 per unit.

You can also see that the only wholly fixed cost is administration overhead since this is a constant amount for both activity levels, $26,000.

For the remaining costs you will need to use the high–low method to determine the fixed and variable elements.

Production labour

	Production, units	$
Quarter 2	13,000	81,500
Quarter 1	10,000	74,000
Change	3,000	7,500

$$\text{Variable cost per unit} = \frac{\$7{,}500}{3{,}000} = \$2.50 \text{ per unit}$$

$$\text{Fixed cost} = \$81{,}500 - (\$2.50 \times 13{,}000) = \$49{,}000$$

Production overhead

	Production, units	$
Quarter 2	13,000	109,000
Quarter 1	10,000	88,000
Change	3,000	21,000

$$\text{Variable cost per unit} = \frac{\$21{,}000}{3{,}000} = \$7 \text{ per unit}$$

$$\text{Fixed cost} = \$109{,}000 - (\$7 \times 13{,}000) = \$18{,}000$$

Selling and distribution overhead

Note: The example says that selling and distribution overhead is related to sales volume.

	Sales, units	$
Quarter 2	14,000	36,200
Quarter 1	9,000	29,700
	5,000	6,500

$$\text{Variable cost per unit sold} = \frac{\$6,500}{5,000} = \$1.30 \text{ per unit}$$

Fixed cost = $36,200 – ($1.30 × 14,000) = $18,000

We can now prepare a statement of the budget cost allowances for quarter 3.

	Quarter 3	
	Budget cost allowance	
	$	$
Direct material (15,000 units × $13)		195,000
Production labour:[1]		
Fixed	49,000	
Variable up to 14,000 units (14,000 × $2.50)	35,000	
Variable above 14,000 units (1,000 × $3.75)	3,750	
		87,750
Production overhead:		
Fixed	18,000	
Variable (15,000 × $7)	105,000	
		123,000
Administration overhead: fixed		26,000
Selling and distribution overhead:		
Fixed	18,000	
Variable (14,500 × $1.30)[2]	18,850	
		36,850
Total budget cost allowance		468,600

Note [1]: The unit variable cost for production labour increases by 50% for production over 14,000 units.

Note [2]: The flexible budget allowance for selling and distribution overhead must be based on the sales volume of 14,500 units.

Question 22

C

The sales volume contribution variance is the reduction in the budgeted contribution for the period.

Sales volume contribution variance = \$(125,294 – 145,741) = \$20,447 adverse

Question 23

Flexible budget cost allowance for consumable materials = budgeted fixed cost __+__ (budgeted variable cost per employee __×__ average number of employees).

chapter

9

Integrated accounting systems

Chapter learning objectives

After completing this chapter, you should be able to:

- explain the principles of manufacturing accounts and the integration of the cost accounts with the financial accounting system;
- prepare a set of integrated accounts, showing standard cost variances.

1 Session content diagram

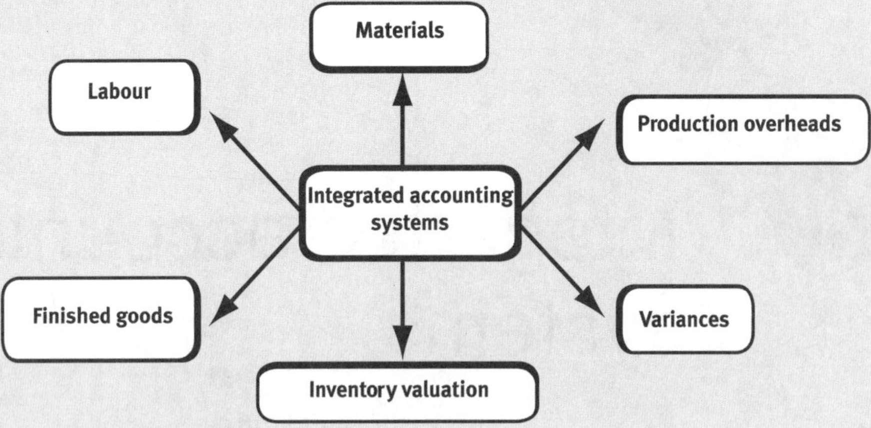

2 Integrated accounting systems

Each organisation will design its accounting system to suit its own needs, taking into account factors such as statutory accounting requirements and management information needs. The accounting systems that are in use range from very simple manual systems to sophisticated computerised systems capable of producing detailed reports as required by management.

In an integrated system the cost accounting function and the financial accounting function are combined in one system, rather than separating the two sets of accounts in two separate ledgers.

The *CIMA Terminology* defines **integrated accounts** as a 'set of accounting records that integrates both financial and cost accounts using a common input of data for all accounting purposes'.

Accounts required for an integrated accounting system:

- Raw materials control account
- Wages control account
- Production overhead control account
- Administration overhead control account
- Selling and distribution overhead control account
- Work in progress control account
- Finished goods control account
- Cost of sales control account

- Other accounts:
  - Sales account
  - Under-/over-absorption account
  - Statement of profit or loss

Control accounts are total or summary accounts. For example, the raw materials control account records the total materials received and the total materials issued.

Advantages of an integrated system

The main advantages of integrated systems are as follows:

- Duplication of effort is avoided and there is less work involved in maintaining the system than if two sets of accounts are kept.
- There is no need for the periodic reconciliation of the two sets of accounts which is necessary with non-integrated systems.
- Maintaining a single set of accounts avoids the confusion that can arise when two sets of accounts are in existence which each contain different profit figures.

The main disadvantage of integrated accounts is that a single system is used to provide information both for external and internal reporting requirements. The need to provide information for statutory purposes may influence the quality of information which can be made available for management purposes.

Financial accounting is required to record all transactions for the accounting period and to allow the organisation to produce the statutory accounts at the end of the period. Financial accounting is viewed as external in nature.

Cost accounting is the production of information for management of a company to aid planning, control and decision making. It is internal in nature and needs to be more detailed than the financial accounting.

3 Accounting for the cost of labour

Before we can begin to look at integrated accounts in operation, we need to spend some time discussing the detail of accounting for the cost of labour.

The cost of labour is made up of a number of components. It is important to recognise how these components are accounted for. Some will be treated as direct labour costs and some will be treated as indirect labour costs.

Gross wages

The total amount of pay for each employee is known as a gross wage. This is the total amount of pay, but this is not the amount received by the employee as a number of deductions are made first. Employees receive a net wage.

Net wage = Gross wage – Deductions

Deductions from employees' wages

In the United Kingdom, the following deductions will be made:

- *Income tax.* Employers deduct income tax from gross wages before they are paid to the employee. This is known as pay-as-you-earn (PAYE).
- *National Insurance*. Employers also deduct a social security tax called national insurance (NI).

The employer will pay the deducted tax and NI to the relevant authorities on behalf of the employee.

In addition, the employer pays *employer's* NI contributions based on the level of the employee's wages. This is an added cost of employment: it is often referred to as an *employment-related cost.*

Some organisations treat the cost of employer's NI as an indirect cost. However, others regard this related employment cost as part of the wage cost of each direct employee and would share it among the tasks completed by adding it to the gross wages value, thus treating it as part of direct wages cost.

Overtime premium

It is common for hours worked in excess of the basic working week to be paid at a higher rate per hour. The extra amount is usually referred to as *overtime premium.* The treatment of overtime premium depends on the reason for the overtime.

- **Specific customer request**. Where a customer requires a job to be completed early or at a specific time, they should be advised that overtime would be required and that this cost would be charged to them. In this situation the overtime premium is treated as a direct cost.
- **General circumstances**. Overtime may be required as a result of the organisation's need to complete work which would not be finished without the working of overtime. In his case the cost of the overtime premium is regarded as an indirect cost, even the premium that is paid to direct workers, because it cannot be identified with a specific cost unit.

Bonus earnings

The earning of bonuses, if paid on an individual task basis, can be clearly attributed to a particular task and so would be a direct labour cost of this task. However, if the bonus system accumulates the total standard time and hours worked for a particular pay period and then calculates the bonus based on these totals, any bonus will usually be treated as an indirect cost.

Idle time

Idle time payments are made when an employee is available for work and is being paid, but is not carrying out any productive work. Idle time can arise for various reasons including machine breakdown, lack of orders or unavailability of materials. Idle time must be recorded carefully and management must ensure that it is kept to a minimum. Idle time payments are treated as indirect costs in the analysis of wages.

Illustration 1

The wages analysis for cost centre 456 shows the following summary of gross pay:

		Direct employees	*Indirect employees*
		$	$
Basic pay	ordinary hours	48,500	31,800
Overtime pay	basic rate	1,600	2,800
	premium	800	1,400
Bonuses paid		5,400	8,700
Total gross pay		56,300	44,700

Direct employees are those directly involved in production, while indirect employees may be involved indirectly with production, or in support functions. Remember, direct labour costs can be associated directly with an individual cost unit but indirect labour costs cannot.

Required:

Which of these are direct labour costs and which are indirect labour costs?

Solution

There is no indication that the overtime and bonuses can be specifically identified with any particular cost unit. Therefore, the overtime premium and the bonuses are indirect costs, even the amounts which were paid to direct employees. The wages can be analysed as follows:

		Direct labour cost	*Indirect labour cost*
		$	$
Basic pay		48,500	31,800
Overtime pay	basic rate	1,600	2,800
	premium		2,200
Bonuses paid			14,100
		50,100	50,900

It would not be 'fair' to charge the overtime premium of direct workers to the cost unit which happened to be worked on during overtime hours if this unit did not specifically cause the overtime to be incurred. Therefore, the premium is treated as an indirect cost of all units produced in the period.

The direct labour cost of $50,100 can be directly identified with cost units and will be charged to these units based on the analysis of labour time. The indirect costs cannot be identified with any particular cost unit and will be shared out over all units, using the overhead absorption methods described in Chapter 3.

Test your understanding 1

Gross wages incurred in department 1 in June were $54,000. The wages analysis shows the following summary breakdown of the gross pay:

	Paid to direct labour	*Paid to indirect labour*
	$	$
Ordinary time	25,185	11,900
Overtime		
basic pay	5,440	3,500
premium	1,360	875
Shift allowance	2,700	1,360
Sick pay	1,380	300
	36,065	17,935

What is the direct wages cost for department 1 in June?

A $25,185

B $30,625

C $34,685

D $36,065

Double entry

For this chapter you will need an understanding of double entry, which you will cover in more detail in your financial accounting studies.

Transactions are entered into **ledgers**. A ledger exists for each type of cost or income which the organisation wishes to gather information about. Each ledger has two sides, **debit** and **credit**. All entries must have two equal parts, a debit and a credit.

A debit is an asset or an expense and a credit is a liability or an income.

We normally draw our ledgers as '**T accounts**' and show the debits on the left and the credits on the right.

Debit	Credit

Example

Purchase material by cash. The two ledger accounts are material and cash. In this case, we would debit the materials accounts and credit the cash account.

If we purchased materials on credit (pay later), we would debit the materials account and credit the payables account.

Balancing a ledger

Assume we have the following entries in the production overhead ledger at the end of the period:

	$		$
Bank	5,000	Work in progress	27,000
Wages control	10,000		
Raw materials control	9,000		

To balance the account, add up both sides, in this case the debit total is $24,000 and the credit total is $27,000. Put the largest total at the bottom of BOTH columns.

	$		$
Bank	5,000	Work in progress	27,000
Wages control	10,000		
Raw materials control	9,000		
Balance c/d	*3,000*		
	27,000		27,000

To make the account balance, $3,000 must be added to the debit side of the account. This is the closing balance of the account and we show it as Balance c/d (carried down) or c/f (carried forward).

Illustration 2

The following example will demonstrate the double-entry principles involved in an integrated system. Make sure that you understand which accounts are used to record each type of transaction, before you move on to the next example.

Example

The main accounting entries in an integrated system

The following shows the flow of accounting entries within an integrated system. The numbers in brackets refer to the numbers of the transactions described in the following pages:

raw materials control	
xxxxx(1)	xxxxx (2)
	xxxxx (3)

payables control	
	xxxxx (1)
	xxxxx (8)

work in progress control	
xxxxx(2)	xxxxx (13)
xxxxx(6)	
xxxxx(11)	

production overhead control	
xxxxx(3)	xxxxx (11)
xxxxx(7)	
xxxxx(8)	
xxxxx(9)	

wages control	
xxxxx(4)	xxxxx (6)
xxxxx(5)	xxxxx (7)

cash/bank	
	xxxxx (4)
	xxxxx (10)

PAYE/NI payable	
	xxxxx (5)

provision for depreciation	
	xxxxx (9)

administration overhead control	
xxxxx(10)	xxxxx (16)

receivables control	
xxxxx(12)	

sales account	
xxxxx(17)	xxxxx (12)

finished goods control	
xxxxx(13)	xxxxx (14)

cost of sales account	
xxxxx(14)	xxxxx (15)

statement of profit or loss	
xxxxx(15)	xxxxx (17)
xxxxx(16)	

(1) **The purchase of raw materials on credit terms.**

Debit	Raw materials control
Credit	Payables control

The cost of raw materials purchased is debited to the raw material control account.

(2) **The issue of direct materials to production.**

Debit	Work in progress control
Credit	Raw materials control

Direct materials costs are charged to the work in progress account.

(3) **The issue of indirect materials to production overheads.**

Debit	Production overhead control
Credit	Raw materials control

Indirect production costs (in this case indirect materials costs) are collected in the production overhead control account for later absorption into production costs.

From (2) and (3) you can see that the materials purchased in (1) have been split between direct (posted to work in progress control) and indirect (posted to production overhead control).

(4) **A cash payment of net wages.**

Debit	Wages control
Credit	Cash/Bank

Wages control is debited with the net amount of wages actually paid, after deductions.

(5) **The deductions for income tax (PAYE) and National Insurance (NI).**

Debit	Wages control
Credit	PAYE/NI payable

The total deductions for PAYE (pay as you earn) and NI are credited to the PAYE/NI payable account. This amount will be paid to the authorities at a later date.

The wages control account has now been debited with the gross amount of total wages. This gross amount must then be charged out according to whether it is direct or indirect wages:

(6) **The direct wages are charged to work in progress.**

Debit Work in progress control

Credit Wages control

Work in progress control is debited with the amount of direct wages.

(7) **The indirect wage costs are collected in the production overhead control account.**

Debit Production overhead control

Credit Wages control

We have now dealt with labour and materials, we will now deal with other expenses:

(8) **Electricity for production purposes, obtained on credit.**

Debit Production overhead control

Credit Payables control

(9) **Depreciation of machinery used for production.**

Debit Production overhead control

Credit Provision for depreciation

These last two items are both production overhead costs which are being accumulated for later absorption into production costs.

(10) **Cash paid for office expenses.**

Debit Administration overhead control

Credit Cash account

Once all of the production overhead has been accumulated in the overhead control account, a predetermined rate is used to absorb it into the cost of work in progress.

(11) **Absorption of production overhead, using a predetermined rate.**

Debit Work in progress control

Credit Production overhead control

The work in progress account now contains charges for direct costs and for absorbed production overheads.

(12) **The sale, on credit, of all goods produced in the month.**

Debit Receivables control

Credit Sales account

(13) **The transfer of completed goods to the finished goods account.**

Debit Finished goods control

Credit Work in progress control

This is usually done in stages as production is completed during the month. For demonstration purposes this has been simplified to show one transfer at the end of the month.

(14) **The transfer of finished goods from the inventory account to cost of sales.**

Debit Cost of sales account

Credit Finished goods control

This is also usually done in stages as inventory is sold during the month.

The summary statement of profit or loss is prepared for the month.

(15) **Transfer the costs of goods sold for the month from the cost of sales to the statement of profit or loss.**

Debit Statement of profit or loss

Credit Cost of sales account

(16) **Transfer the administration costs for the month from the administration overhead control account to the statement of profit or loss.**

Debit Statement of profit or loss

Credit Administration overhead control

(Alternatively, the administration overhead control account balance may first be transferred to the cost of sales account and from there to the statement of profit or loss).

(17) **The transfer of sales revenue to the statement of profit or loss.**

Debit Sales account

Credit Statement of profit or loss

The costs in the statement of profit or loss can now be offset against the sales revenue, and the profit for the period can be calculated.

This illustration has been simplified to demonstrate the main accounting flows. For example, in practice there would be more items of production overhead and administration overhead. There would also be expenditure on other types of overhead such as selling and distribution costs. Control accounts would be opened for these costs and they would be dealt with in the same way as the administration overhead in this example.

Test your understanding 2

A firm operates an integrated cost and financial accounting system. The accounting entries for an issue of direct materials to production would be:

	Debit	*Credit*
A	Work in progress control account	Material control account
B	Finished goods account	Material control account
C	Material control account	Work in progress control account
D	Cost of sales account	Work in progress control account

Test your understanding 3

During a period $35,750 was incurred for indirect labour. The correct entries to record this would be:

	Debit	*Credit*
A	Wages control account	Overhead control account
B	WIP control account	Wages control account
C	Overhead control account	Wages control account
D	Wages control account	WIP control account

Test your understanding 4

In an integrated cost and financial accounting system, the accounting entries for factory overhead absorbed would be:

	Debit	*Credit*
A	Work in progress control account	Overhead control account
B	Overhead control account	Work in progress control account
C	Overhead control account	Cost of sales account
D	Cost of sales account	Overhead control account

4 Accounting for under or over absorbed overheads

Take a moment to look back at the production overhead control account in Illustration 2.

You will see that the production overhead control account has acted as a collecting place for the production overheads incurred during the period. In this simplified example the account has been debited with the following overhead costs:

- indirect materials issued from stores
- the wages cost of indirect workers associated with production
- the cost of electricity for production purposes
- the depreciation of machinery used for production.

At the end of the period the production overhead cost is absorbed into work in progress costs using the predetermined overhead absorption rate. The amount absorbed is credited in the production overhead control account and debited in the work in progress account.

The remaining balance on the production overhead control account represents the amount of production overhead which is under-absorbed (debit balance) or over-absorbed (credit balance).

If overheads are over- or under-absorbed it effectively means that product costs have been overstated or understated.

Over-/under-absorption

When there has been an over- or under-absorption of overheads, it is not usually considered necessary to adjust individual unit costs and therefore inventory values are not altered. However, the cost of units sold will have been overstated or understated.

Any under absorption is charged to the statement of profit or loss for the period. The reverse is true for any over absorption, which is credited in the statement of profit or loss for the period.

Some organisations do not charge or credit the under- or over-absorption to the statement of profit or loss every period. Instead, the balance is carried forward in the control account and at the end of the year the net balance is transferred to the statement of profit or loss. This procedure is particularly appropriate when activity fluctuations cause under- and over-absorptions which tend to cancel each other out over the course of the year.

Illustration 3

ABC Company incurred the following production overheads in period 2:

	$
Indirect materials	40,300
Indirect labour	25,600
Utilities	14,200
Depreciation of machinery	10,700
Other production overheads	12,400

ABC absorbs overheads on the basis of machine hours. The following data are available for period 2:

Budgeted production overhead	$120,000
Budgeted machine hours	60,000

During period 2, actual machine hours were 55,000.

Required:

Prepare the production overhead control account and the over-/under-absorption account for period 2.

Solution

Production overhead control account

	$		$
Indirect materials	40,300	Work in progress	110,000
Indirect labour	25,600	($2* × 55,000)	
Utilities	14,200		
Depreciation of machinery	10,700		
Other production overheads	12,400		
Over-absorption	6,800		
	110,000		110,000

Production overhead over-absorption account

	$		$
		Production overhead control	6,800

* Overhead absorption rate = $120,000/60,000 = $2 per machine hour

Test your understanding 5

At the end of a period, in an integrated cost and financial accounting system the accounting entries for $18,000 overheads under-absorbed would be:

	Debit	*Credit*
A	Work in progress control account	Overhead control account
B	Statement of profit or loss	Work in progress control account
C	Statement of profit or loss	Overhead control account
D	Overhead control account	Statement of profit or loss

5 Recording variances in the ledger accounts

To be able to study this section effectively you must have a sound understanding of:

- the workings of an integrated accounting system;
- the calculation of cost variances in a standard costing system.

If you are not confident that you have a sound understanding of both of these subjects, then you should return and study them carefully before you begin on this section of the chapter.

General rules for recording variances

Although variations do exist, you will find the following general rules useful when you are recording variances in the ledger accounts:

- Variances are entered in the accounts at the point at which they arise
- The materials price variance is recorded in the materials control account. This is the procedure if the materials inventory is held at standard cost. We will learn more about this later in the chapter.
- The labour rate variance is recorded in the wages control account.
- The 'quantity' variances, that is, material usage, labour efficiency and variable production overhead efficiency, are recorded in the work in progress account.
- The variance for variable production overhead expenditure is usually recorded in the production overhead control account.
- Sales values are usually recorded at actual amounts and the sales variances are not shown in the ledger accounts.

The amount of the variance is recorded in the relevant variance account:
a debit for an adverse variance and
a credit for a favourable variance

Recording variances in ledgers

A ledger account is usually kept for each cost variance. As a general rule, all **variances are entered in the accounts at the point at which they arise**. For example:

- **labour rate variances** arise when the wages are paid. Therefore, they are entered in the **wages control account**. An adverse variance is debited in the account for wage rate variance and credited in the wages control account. For a favourable variance the entries would be the opposite way round;
- **labour efficiency variances** arise as the employees are working. Therefore, the efficiency variance is entered in the **work in progress account**. An adverse variance is debited in the account for labour efficiency variance and credited in the work in progress account. For a favourable variance the entries would be the opposite way round.

Illustration 4

Material variances

1000 kg of material is purchased at $5 per kg on 1st March and issued to production at the standard cost of $6 per kg on 10th March.

If the standard usage for producing the actual quantity of finished goods was 900 kg (but 1000kgs were actually consumed) then the entries in the raw material control account and the work in progress control account would be:

Raw material control

(1) payables (1000 × $5)	5,000	(2) work in progress (1000 × $6)	6,000
(4) material price variance	1,000		

Work in progress

(2) raw material control	6,000	(3) finished goods (900 × $6)	5,400
		(5) material usage variance	600

Material price variance

		(4) raw material control	1,000

Material usage variance

(5) work in progress	600		

(1) The actual purchases are debited to raw materials and credited to payables (1000 × $5).

(2) The issues to production are credited to the raw material account and debited to the work in progress account. Actual quantity at standard price (1000 × $6).

(3) Work in progress is transferred to finished goods. Standard quantity at standard price (900 × $6).

(4) The material price variance can be calculated as the balance on the raw material control account. This is transferred to the material price variance account. It is a **credit balance** on the variance account, therefore it is **favourable**.

(5) The material usage can be calculated as the balance on the work in progress account. This is transferred to the material usage variance account. It is a **debit balance** on the variance account, therefore it is **adverse**.

The statement of profit or loss

You will see that all of the variances are eliminated before any entries are made in the finished goods inventory account. The finished goods inventory is therefore held at standard cost and the transfer to the cost of sales account and to the statement of profit or loss will be made at standard cost.

At the end of the period the variance accounts are totalled and transferred to the statement of profit or loss. Adverse variances are debited to the statement of profit or loss and favourable variances are credited. In this way the actual cost (standard cost, plus or minus the variances) is charged against the sales value in the statement of profit or loss for the period.

Full worked example with variances

Work carefully through the following example of integrated standard cost bookkeeping. It will also give you some useful practice at calculating cost variances.

JC Ltd produces and sells one product only, product J, the standard variable cost of which is as follows for one unit:

	$
Direct material X: 10 kg at $20	200
Direct material Y: 5 litres at $6	30
Direct wages: 5 hours at $6	30
Variable production overhead	10
Total standard variable cost	270
Standard contribution	130
Standard selling price	400

During April, the first month of the financial year, the following were the actual results for production and sales of 800 units:

	$	$
Sales on credit: 800 units at $400		320,000
Direct materials:		
X 7,800 kg	159,900	
Y 4,300 litres	23,650	
Direct wages: 4,200 hours	24,150	
Variable production overhead	10,500	
		218,200
Contribution		101,800

The material price variance is extracted at the time of receipt and the raw materials stores control account is maintained at standard prices. The purchases, bought on credit, during the month of April were:

X 9,000 kg at $20.50 per kg from K Ltd
Y 5,000 litres at $5.50 per litre from C plc

Assume no opening inventories, and no opening bank balance.

All wages and production overhead costs were paid from the bank during April.

Required:

(a) Calculate the variable cost variances for the month of April.

(b) Show all the accounting ledger entries for the month of April. The work in progress account should be maintained at standard variable cost and each balance on the separate variance accounts is to be transferred to a statement of profit or loss (SOPL) which you are also required to show.

(c) Explain the reason for the difference between the actual contribution given in the question and the contribution shown in your statement of profit or loss (SOFL) extract.

Solution

(a) **Direct material price variance**

Material X	$	
9,000 kg purchased should have cost (× $20)	180,000	
But did cost (9,000 × $20.50)	184,500	
Direct material price variance	4,500	adverse

Material Y	$	
5,000 litres purchased should have cost (× $6)	30,000	
But did cost (5,000 × $5.50)	27,500	
Direct material price variance	2,500	favourable

Direct material usage variance

Material X	kg	
800 units produced should have used (× 10 kg)	8,000	
But did use	7,800	
Variance in kg	200	favourable
× standard price per kg ($20)		
Direct material usage variance	$4,000	favourable

Material Y	*Litres*	
800 units produced should have used (× 5 litres)	4,000	
But did use	4,300	
Variance in litres	300	adverse
× standard price per litre ($6)		
Direct material usage variance	$1,800	adverse

Direct labour rate variance

	$	
4,200 hours should have cost (× $6)	25,200	
But did cost	24,150	
Direct labour rate variance	1,050	favourable

Direct labour efficiency variance

	Hours	
800 units produced should have taken (× 5 hours)	4,000	
But did take	4,200	
Variance in hours	200	adverse
× standard labour rate per hour ($6)		
Direct labour efficiency variance	$1,200	adverse

Variable overhead expenditure variance

	$	
4,200 hours of variable overhead should cost (× $2)	8,400	
But did cost	10,500	
Variable overhead expenditure variance	2,100	adverse

Variable overhead efficiency variance

	$	
Variance in hours (from labour efficiency variance)	200	adverse
× standard variable overhead rate per hour	× $2	
Variable overhead efficiency variance	$400	adverse

(b) The easiest way to approach this question is probably to follow the production through: deal first with the purchase and then the issue of the material; then move on to deal with the information about the wages. Lastly, prepare the control account for overheads, before dealing with the transfer from the work in progress account.

Numbers in brackets refer to the notes following the accounts.

Raw materials stores control

	$		$
K Ltd: material X (1)	184,500	Direct material price variance:	
C plc: material Y (2)	27,500	material X (1)	4,500
Direct material price		Work in progress (3)	
variance: material Y (2)	2,500	material X (7,800 × $20)	156,000
		material Y (4,300 × $6)	25,800
		Closing inventory c/f	28,200
	214,500		214,500

K Ltd

	$		$
Balance c/f	184,500	Raw materials stores control (1)	184,500

C plc

	$		$
Balance c/f	27,500	Raw materials stores control (2)	27,500

Work in progress control

	$		$
Raw material stores: (3)		Direct material usage	
material X	156,000	variance: (3)	
material Y	25,800	material Y	1,800
		Direct labour efficiency variance (6)	1,200
Direct material usage variance: (3)		Variable overhead efficiency variance (7)	400
material X	4,000	Finished goods: (8)	
Wages control (5)	25,200	800 units × $270	216,000
Production overhead control (7)	8,400		
	219,400		219,400

Wages control

	$		$
Bank (4)	24,150	Work in progress	25,200
Labour rate variance (5)	1,050	(4,200 × $6) (5)	
	25,200		25,200

Bank

	$		$
		Wages control (4)	24,150
		Production overhead control (7)	10,500

Production overhead control

	$		$
Bank (7)	10,500	Work in progress (7) (4,200 × $2)	8,400
		Variable overhead expenditure variance (7)	2,100
	———		———
	10,500		10,500
	———		———

Finished goods control

	$		$
Work in progress (8)	216,000	Cost of sales (8)	216,000

Cost of sales

	$		$
Finished goods (8)	216,000	SOPL (8)	216,000

Sales

	$		$
SOPL	320,000	Receivables	320,000

Receivables

	$		$
Sales	320,000		

Direct material price variance

	$		$
Raw material stores control (1)	4,500	Raw material stores control (2)	2,500
		SOPL (9)	2,000
	———		———
	4,500		4,500
	———		———

Direct material usage variance

	$		$
Work in progress: material Y (3)	1,800	Work in progress: material X (3)	4,000
SOPL (9)	2,200		
	4,000		4,000

Direct labour rate variance

	$		$
SOPL (9)	1,050	Wages control (5)	1,050

Direct labour efficiency variance

	$		$
Work in progress control (6)	1,200	SOPL (9)	1,200

Variable overhead expenditure variance

	$		$
Production overhead control (7)	2,100	SOPL (9)	2,100

Variable overhead efficiency variance

	$		$
Production overhead control (7)	400	SOPL (9)	400

The statement of profit or loss could also be shown as a T-account. However, a vertical presentation is probably preferable.

Statement of profit or loss for April (extract)

	$	$	$
Sales			320,000
Cost of sales (8)			216,000
			104,000
Cost variances			
Direct material price	(2,000)		
Direct material usage	2,200		
		200	
Direct labour rate	1,050		
Direct labour efficiency	(1,200)		
		(150)	
Variable production overhead expenditure	(2,100)		
Variable production overhead efficiency	(400)		
		(2,500)	
			(2,450)
Contribution			101,550

Note: Variances in brackets are adverse.

Explanatory notes

(1) The actual cost of material X purchases is debited to the raw materials stores control and credited to K Ltd. The adverse price variance is credited to the raw materials stores control and debited to the variance account. The net effect of these two entries is that the material is held in the stores account at standard cost.

(2) The actual cost of material Y purchases is debited to the raw materials stores control and credited to C plc. To bring the inventory value of material Y up to standard cost, the favourable price variance is debited to the stores control account and credited to the variance account.

(3) The standard cost of the actual material usage is transferred from the raw materials inventory to work in progress. The usage variances are transferred from work in progress to the material usage variance account. An adverse variance is debited to the variance account and credited to work in progress. A favourable variance is credited to the variance account and debited to work in progress. The net balance for materials cost in the work in progress account is now equal to the standard material cost for 800 units. Check this for yourself.

(4) The wages paid are collected in the control account.

(5) The standard wages cost of the hours worked is debited to work in progress. The favourable labour rate variance is credited to the variance account.

(6) The adverse labour efficiency variance is transferred from work in progress to the relevant variance account.
The net balance for wages cost in the work in progress account is now equal to the standard wages cost for 800 units. Check this for yourself.

(7) The variable production overhead paid is collected in the production overhead control account. The standard variable overhead cost of the hours worked is then debited to work in progress. The adverse variable overhead expenditure variance is debited to the variance account. The adverse variable overhead efficiency variance is transferred from work in progress to the relevant variance account. Notice the similarity between the accounting entries for labour and for variable overhead.

(8) The standard variable production cost of 800 units (800 × $270 = $216,000) is transferred from work in progress to finished goods. Since no finished goods inventories are held (production is equal to sales), this amount is transferred at the end of the month to cost of sales, and from there to the statement of profit or loss.

(9) At the end of April, the balances on the variance accounts are transferred to the statement of profit or loss.

(c) The difference between the actual contribution given in the question and the contribution shown in the statement of profit or loss extract in the solution to part (b) is $250.

	$
Actual contribution given in question	101,800
Contribution shown in solution to part (b)	101,550
Difference	250

This difference is caused by the treatment of the direct material price variance.

In the actual results given in the question, the material price variance on only the material actually used has been charged against the sales value. In the bookkeeping entries in part (b), the material price variances on all of the purchases for the month have been recorded and transferred to the statement of profit or loss.

The difference is therefore represented by the price variance on the materials in inventory at the end of April.

Direct material	*Purchases*	*Usage*	*Inventory balance*	*Price variance per unit*	*Price variance in inventory*
X	9,000 kg	7,800 kg	1,200 kg	\$20 – \$20.50 = (\$0.50)	\$(600)
Y	5,000 litres	4,300 litres	700 litres	\$6 – \$5.50 = \$0.50	\$350
					\$(250)

Note: Variances in brackets are adverse.

Test your understanding 6

A firm uses standard costing and an integrated accounting system. The double entry for an adverse material usage variance is:

	Debit	*Credit*
A	Material control account	Work in progress control account
B	Material usage variance account	Material control account
C	Work in progress control account	Material usage variance account
D	Material usage variance account	Work in progress control account

Valuing inventory at actual cost

In Chapter 7 you saw that the material price variance is calculated using a different method if inventory is valued at actual cost. If material inventory had been valued at actual cost in the previous example the material price variance would have been calculated as:

Direct material price variance

	$	
Material X		
7,800 kg used should have cost (× $20)	156,000	
But did cost	159,900	
Direct material price variance	3,900	adverse

	$	
Material Y		
4,300 litres used should have cost (× $6)	25,800	
But did cost	23,650	
Direct material price variance	2,150	favourable

The raw materials stores control account would look like this:

Raw materials stores control

	$		$
K Ltd: material X		Work in progress:	
(9,000 × $20.50)	184,500	material X (7,800 × $20)	156,000
C plc: material Y		material Y (4,300 × $6)	25,800
(5,000 × $5.50)	27,500	Direct material price variance:	
Direct material price variance:		material X	3,900
material Y	2,150	Closing inventory c/f	28,450
	214,150		214,150

Notice that the transfer to the work in progress account is the same as before, therefore that account will not be altered by the raw material inventory valuation method.

Check that the raw material inventory balance carried forward into May is correctly valued at actual cost.

	$
Material X: 1,200 kg × $20.50	24,600
Material Y: 700 litres × $5.50	3,850
Actual cost of material inventory	28,450

Which inventory valuation method is generally preferred?

It is generally accepted that it is better to value the raw material inventory at standard cost, for the following reasons:

(a) The whole of the price variance is eliminated as soon as the raw materials are purchased. This means that inventories are valued at a uniform rate and that the price variances are highlighted earlier for management attention.

(b) Raw materials are often purchased in single batches, then broken into several smaller batches for issue to production. If raw materials inventories are valued at actual cost, then a separate variance calculation is required for each issue. With valuation at standard cost, one single calculation is required on purchase.

6 Chapter summary

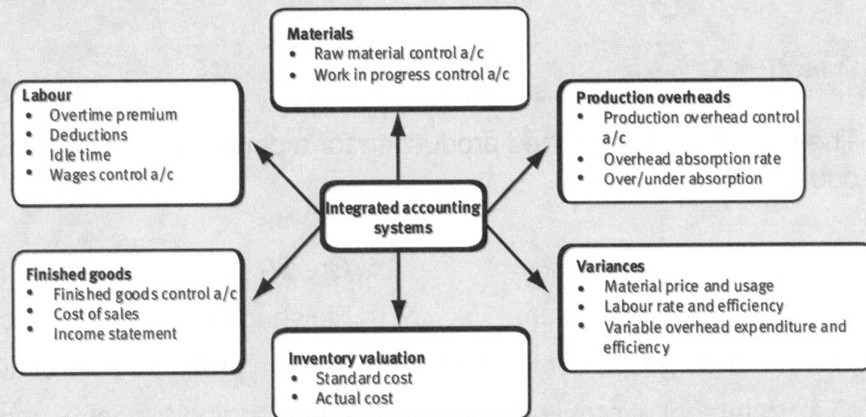

7 End of chapter questions

Question 1

The factory cost of finished production for a period was $873,190. The double entry for this is:

	Debit	*Credit*
A	Cost of sales account	Finished goods control account
B	Finished goods control account	Work in progress control account
C	Statement of profit or loss	Finished goods control account
D	Work in progress control account	Finished goods control account

Question 2

XYZ Ltd operates an integrated accounting system. The material control account at 31st March shows the following information:

Material control account

	$		$
Balance b/d	50,000	Production overhead control account	10,000
Payables	100,000	?	125,000
Bank	25,000	Balance c/d	40,000
	175,000		175,000

The $125,000 credit entry represents the value of the transfer to the

A Cost of sales account

B Finished goods account

C Statement of profit or loss

D Work in progress account

Question 3

In an integrated cost and financial accounting system the correct entries for the provision for depreciation of production machinery are:

	Debit	*Credit*
A	Provision for depreciation account	Work in progress account
B	Work in progress account	Provision for depreciation account
C	Overhead control account	Provision for depreciation account
D	Provision for depreciation account	Overhead control account

Question 4

The bookkeeping entries in a standard cost system when the actual price for raw materials is less than the standard price are:

	Debit	*Credit*
A	Raw materials control account	Raw materials price variance account
B	WIP control account	Raw materials control account
C	Raw materials price variance account	Raw materials control account
D	WIP control account	Raw materials price variance account

Question 5

In a standard cost bookkeeping system, when the actual hourly rate paid for labour is less than the standard hourly rate, the double entry to record this is:

	Debit	*Credit*
A	wages control account	labour rate variance account
B	work in progress control account	labour rate variance account
C	labour rate variance account	wages control account
D	labour rate variance account	work in progress control account

Question 6

A company purchased materials costing $30,000. Of these, materials worth $1,000 were issued to the maintenance department and materials worth $22,000 were issued to the production department. Which of the following accounting entries would arise as a result of these transactions? *(Tick all that are correct.)*

			$	
(a)	Debit	Raw materials control	29,000	□
(b)	Debit	Raw materials control	30,000	□
(c)	Debit	Work in progress control	22,000	□
(d)	Debit	Work in progress control	23,000	□
(e)	Debit	Work in progress control	30,000	□
(f)	Debit	Production overhead control	1,000	□
(g)	Credit	Raw materials control	23,000	□
(h)	Credit	Raw materials control	30,000	□

Question 7

Look at the following account and then identify whether statements (a) to (c) are true or false.

Wages control account

	$		$
Bank	82,500	Work in progress control	52,500
PAYE/NI payable	9,500	Production overhead control	39,500
	92,000		92,000

	True	False
(a) Gross wages for the period amounted to $82,500.	□	□
(b) Indirect wages incurred amounted to $39,500.	□	□
(c) Direct wages incurred amounted to $92,000.	□	□

Question 8

Details of the production wages for a company last period are as follows:

	Gross wages	PAYE/NI	Net wages
	$000	$000	$000
Direct wages paid	40	10	30
Indirect wages paid	20	6	14

Which of the following accounting entries would be used to record this data? (*Tick all that are correct.*)

		$000	☐
(a)	Debit wages control	44	☐
(b)	Debit work in progress	30	☐
(c)	Debit work in progress	40	☐
(d)	Debit production overhead control	14	☐
(e)	Debit production overhead control	20	☐
(f)	Debit wages control	16	☐
(g)	Debit wages control	60	☐
(h)	Credit bank	44	☐
(i)	Credit wages control	60	☐
(j)	Credit PAYE/NI payable	16	☐
(k)	Credit bank	60	☐

Question 9

Is the following statement *true* or *false*?

If material inventory is valued at standard cost then the material price variance calculation should be based on the materials actually used during the period.

Question 10

Inventories of material W are valued at their standard price of $7 per kg. Last period, 900 kg of W were purchased for $5,400, of which 800 kg were issued to production. Which of the following accounting entries would arise as a result of these transactions? *(Tick all that apply.)*

		$	
(a)	Raw material inventory	5,400 debit	□
(b)	Raw material inventory	6,300 debit	□
(c)	Work in progress	4,800 debit	□
(d)	Work in progress	5,600 debit	□
(e)	Material price variance	800 credit	□
(f)	Material price variance	800 debit	□
(g)	Material price variance	900 credit	□
(h)	Material price variance	900 debit	□

Question 11

D Ltd operates an integrated accounting system, preparing its annual accounts to 31 March each year. The following balances have been extracted from its trial balance at 31 October, year 3:

	$
Raw material control account	34,789 Dr
Wages control account	5,862 Cr
Production overhead control account	3,674 Cr
Work in progress control account	13,479 Dr

During the first week of November, year 3, the following transactions occurred:

	$
Purchased materials on credit	4,320
Incurred wages	6,450
Issued direct materials to production	2,890
Issued indirect materials to production	560
Incurred production overheads on credit	1,870
Absorbed production overhead cost	3,800
Cost of units completed	12,480
Paid wages	5,900

An analysis of the wages incurred shows that $5,200 is direct wages.

Required:

(a) The balance shown on the production overhead control account means that the production overhead at 31 October was:

under-absorbed □
over-absorbed □

(b) The raw material control account has been prepared for the first week of November:

Raw material control account

	$		$
Balance b/d	34,789	Work in progress	B
Payables	A	Production overhead	C
		Balance c/d	35,659
	–––––		–––––
	–––––		–––––

The values that would be entered as A, B and C would be:

A $ ☐
B $ ☐
C $ ☐

(c) The wages control account has been prepared for the first week of November:

Wages control account

	$		$
Bank	A	Balance b/d	5,862
		Work in progress	B
		Production overhead	C

The values that would be entered as A, B and C would be:

A $ ☐
B $ ☐
C $ ☐

(d) At the end of the week, the balance brought down on the production overhead control account will be a:

debit balance ☐

credit balance ☐

The value of the balance will be $ _______

(e) The work in progress control account has been prepared for the first week of November:

Work in progress control account

	$		$
Balance b/d	13,479	Finished goods	D
Raw materials	A	Balance c/d	12,889
Wages	B		
Production overhead	C		
	______		______
	______		______

The values shown in the account as A, B, C and D are:

A	$	
B	$	
C	$	
D	$	

Question 12

A manufacturing firm is very busy and overtime is being worked.

The amount of overtime premium contained in direct wages would normally be classified as:

A part of prime cost

B production overheads

C direct labour costs

D administrative overheads

Question 13

The following data relate to RTY company in June.

	$
Material purchased	15,500
of which:	
Direct	12,700
Indirect	2,800
Wages paid	23,900
of which:	
Direct	19,200
Indirect	4,700
Other production overheads incurred	6,400

Required:

Prepare the following ledger accounts for June:

(a) Material control

(b) Work in progress

(c) Production overhead control (assume that overhead absorbed = overhead incurred)

(d) Wages control

(e) Finished goods control

(f) Cost of sales

(g) Statement of profit or loss

Question 14

Data for the finishing department for the last quarter are as follows:

Budgeted cost centre overhead	$320,000
Actual cost centre overhead	$311,250
Budgeted direct labour hours	40,000
Actual direct labour hours	41,500

The accounting entries to record the under- or over-absorbed overhead for the quarter would be:

	Debit		*Credit*	
A	Overhead control account	$20,750	Statement of profit or loss	$20,750
B	Overhead control account	$8,750	Statement of profit or loss	$8,750
C	Statement of profit or loss	$20,750	Overhead control account	$20,750
D	Statement of profit or loss	$8,750	Overhead control account	$8,750

Question 15

The production overhead absorption rate is $3 per direct labour hour. During the period 23,000 direct labour hours were worked.

Production overhead control account

	$		$
Wages control	44,000	Work in progress control	A
Bank	22,000		
Depreciation	8,000		
Raw materials control	2,000		
	76,000		

(a) In the production overhead control account for the period shown above, the value to be inserted at A is $ ______

(b) Production overhead for the period was:

under-absorbed ☐

over-absorbed ☐

(c) The value of the under-/over-absorption was $ ______

Question 16

Q Ltd uses an integrated standard costing system. In October, when 2,400 units of the finished product were made, the actual material cost details were:

Material purchased	5,000 units @ $4.50 each
Material used	4,850 units

The standard cost details are that two units of the material should be used for each unit of the completed product, and the standard price of each material unit is $4.70.

The entries made in the variance accounts would be:

	Material price variance account	*Material usage* variance account
A	Debit $970	Debit $225
B	Debit $1,000	Debit $225
C	Credit $970	Debit $235
D	Credit $1,000	Debit $235

Test your understanding answers

Test your understanding 1

B

$25,185 + $5,440 = **$30,625**. The only direct costs are the wages paid to direct workers for ordinary time, plus the basic pay for overtime. Overtime premium and shift allowances are usually treated as overheads. However, if and when the overtime and shiftwork are incurred specifically for a particular cost unit, they are classified as direct costs of that cost unit. Sick pay is treated as an overhead and is therefore classified as an indirect cost.

Test your understanding 2

A

Direct costs of production are debited to the work in progress control account.

Test your understanding 3

C

Indirect costs, including indirect labour, are collected in the debit side of the overhead control account pending their later absorption into work in progress.

Test your understanding 4

A

The factory overhead is first collected in the overhead control account. It is then absorbed into production costs by debiting the work in progress account using the predetermined overhead absorption rate.

Test your understanding 5

C

Under-absorbed overhead is transferred from the overhead control account as a debit to the statement of profit or loss.

Test your understanding 6

D

An adverse variance is debited to the relevant variance account. This leaves us with options (B) or (D). The usage variance is eliminated where it arises, that is, in the work in progress account. Therefore, (D) is the correct answer.

Question 1

B

Answer (A) is the double entry for the production cost of goods sold. Answer (C) is also the entry for the production cost of goods sold, if a cost of sales account is not used. Answer (D) has entries in the correct accounts but they are reversed.

Question 2

D

Materials are issued from stores as either direct materials (to work in progress) or indirect materials (charged to the production overhead control account). The entry for the issue of indirect materials is already shown ($10,000 to production overhead). Therefore, the $125,000 must be the value of the issue of direct materials to work in progress.

Question 3

C

The provision for depreciation of production machinery is a production overhead cost. Therefore, it is debited to the production overhead control account to be accumulated with all other production overheads for the period. At the end of the period the production overhead will be absorbed into work in progress using the predetermined overhead absorption rate.

Question 4

A

If the actual price for raw materials is less than the standard price then the raw material price variance is favourable. The variance account would therefore be credited. The corresponding debit entry is made in the raw materials control account.

Question 5

A

The actual hourly rate is less than standard. Therefore, the rate variance is favourable and is credited to the variance account.

Question 6

The correct entries are (b), (c), (f) and (g):

(b) The purchased materials are debited in the raw materials control account.

(c) The direct materials are issued to the production department (work in progress).

(f) Materials issued to maintenance are indirect materials, debited to the production overhead control account.

(g) The total amount of materials issued is credited in the materials control account.

Question 7

(a) **False.** Gross wages are $92,000.

(b) **True.** Indirect wages are transferred to the production overhead control account.

(c) **False.** Direct wages are $52,500: the amount transferred to work in progress.

Question 8

(a) and (h)	The net wages paid are 'collected' in the wages control account and credited to the bank.
(f) and (j)	The deductions are 'collected' in the wages control account and credited to the PAYE/NI payable.

The total gross wages have now been debited to the wages control account.

(c), (e) and (i)	The gross wages are transferred to work in progress or to production overhead control according to whether they are direct or indirect wages.

Remember that the wages control account acts as a collecting place for the gross wages before they are transferred to work in progress or to production overhead control, according to whether they are direct wages or indirect wages. The gross wages are made up of two parts: the net wages that are paid from the bank, plus the PAYE/NI deductions.

Question 9

False.

When material inventory is valued at standard cost, the material price variance is based on the materials purchased.

Question 10

(a) Actual price of purchases is debited to the inventory account (900 × $6 = $5,400).

(d) Standard price of material issues is debited to work in progress (800 × $7 = $5,600).

(g) Favourable material price variance is credited to variance account:

	$	
900 kg purchased should cost (× $7)	6,300	
But did cost	5,400	
Material price variance	900	favourable

The complete raw material inventory account would look like this:

Raw material inventory account

Bank	5,400	Work in progress	5,600
Material price variance	900	Balance c/d (100 × $7)	700
	6,300		6,300

Question 11

(a) The credit balance shown on the production overhead control account means that there was **over absorption** of production overhead at 31 October. A debit balance would have indicated an under absorption of production overheads at that date.

(b) A **$4,320**
B **$2,890**
C **$560**

(c) A **$5,900**
B **$5,200**
C **$1,250**

Workings:

	$
Wages incurred	6,450
Direct wages to WIP	5,200
Indirect wages to production overhead	1,250

(d) At the end of the week, the balance on the production overhead control account will be a *credit* balance of **$3,794**.

Workings:

Production overhead control account

Raw materials	560	Balance b/d	3,674
Wages	1,250	Work in progress*	3,800
Payables	1,870		
Balance c/d	3,794		
	7,474		7,474

*Production overhead absorbed is transferred to work in progress. The over-absorbed balance is now $3,794, which is carried down to the next week.

(e) A $2,890
B $5,200
C $3,800
D $12,480

Question 12

B

Overtime premium is usually treated as an overhead cost if the overtime cannot be specifically identified with a particular cost unit.

Question 13

Raw materials control

(1) payables	15,500	(2) work in progress	12,700
		(3) production overhead	2,800
	———		———
	15,500		15,500
	———		———

Work in progress control

(2) payables	12,700	(9) finished goods	45,800
(5) wages control	19,200		
(8) production overhead	13,900		
	———		———
	45,800		45,800
	———		———

Wages control

(4) cash	23,900	(5) work in progress	19,200
		(6) production overhead	4,700
	———		———
	23,900		23,900
	———		———

Question 16

D

Price variance:	$
5,000 units should cost each	4.70
But actually cost	4.50
Saving	0.20

5,000 × $0.20 = $1,000 (F) – credited to variance account

Usage variance	*Material units*
2,400 finished units should use	4,800
Actual material usage	4,850
Variance in units	50 Adv

50 units × $4.70 (standard price) = $235 (Adv) – debited to variance account.

chapter

10

Costing systems

Chapter learning objectives

After completing this chapter, you should be able to:

- explain job, batch and process costing;
- prepare ledger accounts for job, batch and process costing systems.

1 Session content diagram

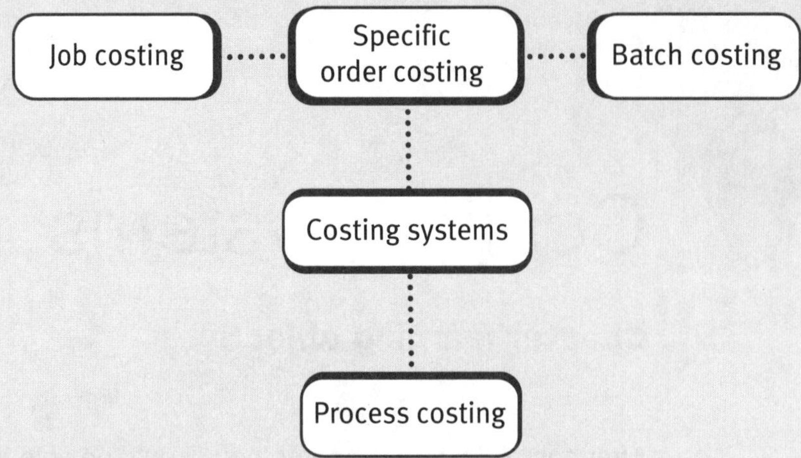

2 Costing systems

Every organisation will have its own costing system with characteristics which are unique to that particular system. However, although each system might be different, the basic costing method used by the organisation is likely to depend on the type of activity that the organisation is engaged in. The costing system would have the same basic characteristics as the systems of other organisations which are engaged in similar activities.

Specific order costing methods are appropriate for organisations which produce cost units which are separately identifiable from one another. **Job costing** and **batch costing** are types of specific order costing.

Process costing is used by organisations where a number of production processes are involved and the output of one process is the input to a later process, this continuing until the final product is completed. Examples of industries where process costing might be applied are food processing, chemicals and brewing. The final product is said to be homogeneous (i.e. each unit is identical and cannot be distinguished from another unit) and is usually manufactured for inventory from which sales are made to customers.

3 Job costing

Job costing applies where work is undertaken according to specific orders from customers. For example, a customer may request the manufacture of a single machine to the customer's own specification. Job costing can also be applied in service organisations, for example the repair of a vehicle or the preparation of a set of accounts for a client.

Job cost sheets

The main feature of a job costing system is the use of a **job cost sheet** or **job card** which is a detailed record used to collect the costs of each job. In practice this would probably be a file in a computerised system but the essential feature is that each job would be given a **specific job number** which identifies it from all other jobs. Costs would be allocated to this number as they are incurred on behalf of the job. Since the sales value of each job can also be separately identified, it is then possible to determine the profit or loss on each job.

Illustration 1: Job sheet

JOB COST SHEET

Job no.: 472

Estimate no.: 897

Job description: Instal shower Model no. 5856

Details: Mrs. P. Johnson
01734 692174
30 Hillside, Whyteham
Price estimate: £330

Date started: 15 June 20 ×6

MATERIALS					LABOUR						PRODUCTION OVERHEAD		
Date	Req. no.	Qty	Price $	Value $	Date	Emp. no.	Cost ctr	Hrs	Rate	$	Hours	Overhead absorption rate	$
14/6	641	1	128.00	128.00	15/6	17	4	8	10	80.00	9	4.50	40.50
15/6	644	2	3.10	6.20	15/6	12	3	1	10	10.00			
			Total c/f	134.20					Total c/f	90.00		Total c/f	40.50

EXPENSES	
Description	Cost $
Total c/f	

JOB COST SUMMARY		
Cost element	Actual $	Estimate $
Direct materials b/f	134.20	150.00
Direct labour b/f	90.00	80.00
Direct expenses b/f	–	–
Total direct cost	224.20	230.00
Production o/h b/f	40.50	36.00
Total production cost	264.70	266.00
Admin. o/h (5%)	13.24	13.30
Total cost	277.94	279.30
Price estimate	330.00	330.00
Job profit/loss)	52.06	50.70

Job card completed by: Guy

The job cost sheet would record details of the job as it proceeds. The items recorded would include:

- job number;
- description of the job; specifications, etc.;
- customer details;
- estimated cost, analysed by cost element;
- selling price, and hence estimated profit;
- delivery date promised;
- actual costs to date, analysed by cost element;
- actual delivery date, once the job is completed;
- sales details, for example delivery note no., invoice no.

The sheet has a separate section to record the details of each cost element. There is also a summary section where the actual costs incurred are compared with the original estimate. This helps managers to control costs and to refine their estimating process.

Completing the job cost sheet

Direct labour

The correct analysis of labour costs and their attribution to specific jobs depends on the existence of an efficient time recording and analysis system. For example, daily or weekly timesheets may be used to record how each employee's time is spent, using job numbers where appropriate to indicate the time spent on each job. The wages cost can then be charged to specific job numbers (or to overhead costs, if the employee was engaged on indirect tasks). In the job cost sheet shown in illustration 1, a total of nine direct labour hours were worked by two different employees.

Direct material

All documentation used to record movements of material within the organisation should indicate the job number to which it relates.

For example a **material requisition note**, which is a formal request for items to be issued from stores, should have a space to record the number of the job for which the material is being requisitioned. If any of this material is returned to stores, then the material returned note should indicate the original job number which is to be credited with the cost of the returned material. In the job cost sheet shown in illustration 1, two separate material requisitions were raised for material used on job number 472.

Sometimes items of material might be purchased specifically for an individual job. In this situation the job number must be recorded on the supplier's invoice or on the relevant cash records. This will ensure that the correct job is charged with the cost of the material purchased.

Direct expenses

Although direct expenses are not as common as direct material and direct labour costs, it is still essential to analyse them and ensure that they are charged against the correct job number.

For example, if a machine is hired to complete a particular job, then this is a direct expense of the job. The supplier's invoice should be coded to ensure that the expense is charged to the job. Alternatively, if cash is paid, then the cash book analysis will show the job number which is to be charged with the cost. We can see from the job cost sheet shown in illustration 1 that no direct expenses were incurred on behalf of job number 472.

Production overheads

The successful attribution of production overhead costs to cost units depends on the existence of well-defined cost centres and appropriate absorption bases for the overhead costs of each cost centre.

It must be possible to record accurately the units of the absorption base which are applicable to each job. For example, if machine hours are to be used as the absorption base, then the number of machine hours spent on each job must be recorded on the job cost sheet. The relevant cost centre absorption rate can then be applied to produce a fair overhead charge for the job.

The production overhead section of the job cost sheet for job 472 shows that the absorption rate is $4.50 per labour hour. The labour analysis shows that 9 hours were worked on this job, therefore the amount of production overhead absorbed by the job is $40.50.

Non-production overheads

The level of accuracy achieved in attributing costs such as selling, distribution and administration overheads to jobs will depend on the level of cost analysis which an organisation uses.

Many organisations simply use a predetermined percentage to absorb such costs, based on estimated levels of activity for the forthcoming period. The use of predetermined rates will lead to the problems of under- or over- absorbed overhead which we discussed in Chapter 3. The rates should therefore be carefully monitored throughout the period to check that they do not require adjusting to more accurately reflect recent trends in costs and activity.

Administrative overheads

For Job 472, administrative overheads have been included. These have been calculated as 5% of total production cost.

Illustration 2

Jobbing Ltd manufactures precision tools to its customers' own specifications. The manufacturing operations are divided into three cost centres: A, B and C.

Job number 427 was manufactured during the period and its job cost sheet reveals the following information relating to the job:

Direct material requisitioned	$6,780.10
Direct material returned to stores	$39.60

Direct labour recorded against job number 427:

Cost centre A:	146 hours at $4.80 per hour
Cost centre B:	39 hours at $5.70 per hour
Cost centre C:	279 hours at $6.10 per hour

Special machine hired for this job: hire cost $59.00

Machine hours recorded against job number 427:

Cost centre A:	411 hours
Cost centre B:	657 hours
Price quoted and charged to customer, including delivery	$17,200

Production overheads from the three cost centres are absorbed using the following overhead absorption rates:

Cost centre A:	$1.75 per machine hour
Cost centre B:	$3.80 per machine hour
Cost centre C:	$0.98 per labour hour

Jobbing Ltd absorbs non-production overhead using the following predetermined overhead absorption rates:

Administration and general overhead	10% of total production cost
Selling and distribution overhead	12% of selling price

You are required to present an analysis of the total cost and profit or loss attributable to job number 427.

Solution

Cost and profit analysis: job number 427	$	$
Direct material (note 1)		6,740.50
Direct labour:		
Cost centre A (146 hours × $4.80)	700.80	
Cost centre B (39 hours × $5.70)	222.30	
Cost centre C (279 hours × $6.10)	1,701.90	
		2,625.00
Direct expenses: hire of machine		59.00
Prime cost		9,424.50
Production overhead absorbed:		
Cost centre A (411 hours × $1.75)	719.25	
Cost centre B (657 hours × $3.80)	2,496.60	
Cost centre C (279 hours × $0.98)	273.42	
		3,489.27
Total production cost		12,913.77

Administration and general overhead (10% × $12,913.77)	1,291.38
Selling and distribution overhead (12% × $17,200)	2,064.00
Total cost	16,269.15
Profit	930.85
Selling price	17,200.00

Note 1: The figure for material requisitioned has been reduced by the amount of returns to give the correct value of the materials actually used for the job. ($6,780.10 – $39.60) = $6,740.50.

Test your understanding 1

A firm uses job costing and recovers overheads on direct labour cost.

Three jobs were worked on during a period, the details of which were:

	Job 1	*Job 2*	*Job 3*
	$	$	$
Opening work in progress	8,500	0	46,000
Material in period	17,150	29,025	0
Labour for period	12,500	23,000	4,500

The overheads for the period were exactly as budgeted: $140,000 and are absorbed on the basis of direct labour cost.

Jobs 1 and 2 were incomplete at the end of the period. What was the value of closing work in progress?

A $81,900

B $90,175

C $140,675

D $214,425

Test your understanding 2

Calculate the selling price for jobs A, B and C.

Job A: Total cost of job = $45. Profit mark-up is 25% of total cost.

Job B: Production cost of job = $38. 10% to be added to production cost to absorb general overheads. Profit mark-up is 20% of total job cost.

Job C: Total cost of job = $75. Profit margin is 15% of selling price.

4 Batch costing

The *CIMA Terminology* defines a **batch** as a 'group of similar units which maintains its identity throughout one or more stages of production and is treated as a cost unit'. An example would be a batch of printed leaflets.

Batch costing is very similar in nature to job costing which we have been studying so far in this chapter. It is a separately identifiable cost unit for which it is possible to collect and monitor the costs. The only difference is that a number of items are being costed together as a single unit, instead of a single item or service.

Once the cost of the batch has been determined, the cost per item within the batch can be calculated by dividing the total cost by the number of items produced.

Batch costing can be applied in many situations, including the manufacture of furniture, clothing and components. It can also be applied when manufacturing is carried out for the organisation's own internal purposes, for example, in the production of a batch of components to be used in production.

Batch costing example

Needlecraft Ltd makes hand embroidered sweatshirts to customer specifications.

The following detail is available from the company's budget.

Cost centre	*Budgeted overheads*	*Budgeted activity*
Cutting and sewing	$93,000	37,200 machine hours
Embroidering and packing	$64,000	16,000 direct labour hours

Administration, selling and distribution overhead is absorbed into batch costs at a rate of 8% of total production cost. Selling prices are set to achieve a rate of return of 15% of the selling price.

An order for 45 shirts, batch number 92, has been produced for Shaldene Community Choir. Details of activity on this batch are as follows:

Direct materials	$113.90
Direct labour	
Cutting and sewing (0.5 labour hours at $9 per hour)	$4.50
Embroidering and packing (29 labour hours at $11 per hour)	$319.00
Machine hours worked in cutting and sewing	2
Fee paid to designer of logo for sweat shirts	$140.00

Required:

Calculate the selling price per shirt in batch number 92.

Solution

Batch No. 92

	$	$
Direct material		113.90
Direct labour:		
Cutting and sewing	4.50	
Embroidering and packing	319.00	
	———	
		323.50
Direct expense: design costs		140.00
		———
Total direct cost		577.40

Production overhead absorbed:		
Cutting and sewing (W1) 2 machine hours × $2.50	5.00	
Embroidering and packing (W1) 29 labour hours × $4	116.00	
		121.00
Total production cost		698.40
Administration, etc. overhead $698.40 × 8%		55.87
Total cost		754.27
Profit margin 15/85 × $754.27		133.11
Total selling price of batch		887.38
Selling price per shirt $887.38/45		$19.72

Workings (W1):

Calculation of production overhead absorption rates:

Cutting and sewing = $93,000/37,200 = $2.50 per machine hour
Embroidering and packing = $64,000/16,000 = $4 per direct labour hour

Test your understanding 3

A firm uses job costing and recovers overheads on direct labour cost.

Three jobs were worked on during a period, the details of which were:

	Job 1	*Job 2*	*Job 3*
	$	$	$
Opening work in progress	8,500	0	46,000
Material in period	17,150	29,025	0
Labour for period	12,500	23,000	4,500

The overheads for the period were exactly as budgeted: $140,000.

Job 3 was completed during the period and consisted of a batch of 2,400 identical circuit boards. The firm adds 50% to total production costs to arrive at a selling price. What is the selling price of a circuit board?

A	It cannot be calculated without more information
B	$31.56
C	$41.41
D	$58.33

5 Process costing

Process costing is used in those industries where the end products are more or less identical and where goods and services result from a sequence of continuous or repetitive operations or processes to which costs are charged before being averaged over the output produced during the period.

In process costing, production moves from one process to the next until final completion occurs. Each production department performs some part of the total operation and transfers its completed production to the next department where it becomes the input for further processing. The completed production of the last department is transferred to the finished goods inventory.

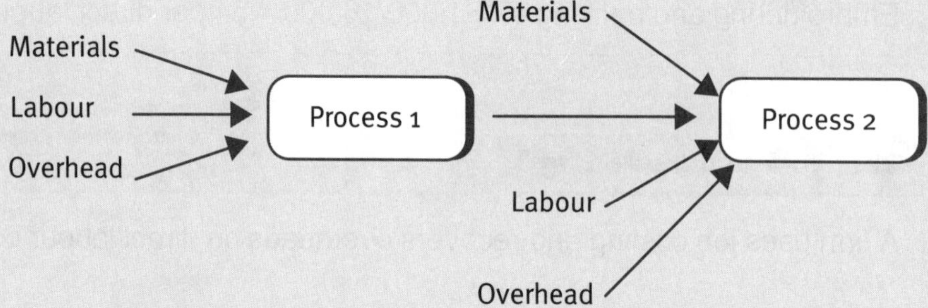

Process costing differs from job and batch costing in that the product is not customer specific and the range of products available is likely to be limited, but it is likely that the customer base will be large.

6 The process account

The costs for each process are gathered in a process account. This is shown as a T account:

Process account

Inputs to the process are shown on this side (debit)	Outputs from the process are shown on this side (credit)

In a process account there are two columns on each side, one for volume (kg, litres, units etc.) and one for cost:

	kg	$		kg	$

The purpose of the process account is to gather together all of the information for the process together and calculate the cost per unit.

Unit Cost = $\frac{\textbf{Total input costs}}{\textbf{Output units}}$

Note: This basic calculation will change as we add some complications to the process account.

Illustration 3

A company operates two processes, the output of process 1 is transferred to process 2 and the output of process 2 is the final product. Details for June are given:

	Process 1	*Process 2*
Direct materials	$10,000	$9,500
Direct Labour	$15,000	$7,500
Production Overheads	$12,000	$6,000
Input quantity	1,000 kg	500 kg
Output quantity	1,000 kg	1,500 kg

Required:

Complete the process accounts for process 1 and 2 for June.

Solution

Step 1: Set up the process account, and input all the information available from the question:

Process 1

	kg	$		kg	$
Material	1,000	10,000	Output *	1,000	
Labour		15,000			
Overhead		12,000			
	———	———		———	———
	———	———		———	———

* the output of process 1 will be the amount transferred to process 2

Step 2: Balance the quantity column, ensure that both sides agree:

Process 1

	kg	$		kg	$
Material	1,000	10,000	Output	1,000	
Labour		15,000			
Overhead		12,000			
	———	———		———	———
	1,000			1,000	
	———	———		———	———

Step 3: Calculate the cost per unit and value the output:

$$\textbf{Unit Cost} = \frac{\textbf{Total input costs}}{\textbf{Output units}}$$

= (10,000 + 15,000 + 12,000) / 1,000 = $37

So the value of the output is $37 × 1,000 = **$37,000**

Step 4: Finally balance the $ column.

Process 1

	Kg	$		Kg	$
Material	1,000	10,000	Output	1,000	37,000
Labour		15,000			
Overhead		12,000			
	1,000	37,000		1,000	37,000

Repeat the steps for process 2, remembering to include the transfer from process 1:

Process 2

	Kg	$		Kg	$
From Process 1	1,000	37,000	Output	1,500	60,000
Material	500	9,500			
Labour		7,500			
Overhead		6,000			
	1,500	60,000		1,500	60,000

The unit cost in process 2 is: 60,000/1,500 = **$40**.

So the value of the output = $40 × 1,500 = **$60,000**.

Test your understanding 4

During August a processing company incurred the following costs in its three processes:

	Process 1	*Process 2*	*Process 3*
	$	$	$
Direct materials	6,000	4,000	9,000
Direct labour	1,000	2,000	3,000
Direct expenses	2,000	3,000	4,000
Production overhead	1,000	2,000	3,000

The quantities of input and output were as follows:

	Process 1	*Process 2*	*Process 3*
	kg	kg	kg
Input	500	200	300
Output	500	700	1,000

The input quantities shown above do not include the output from the previous process. The output from process 1 is transferred to process 2, which in turn transfers its output to process 3 which after further processing results in the final product.

Required:

Show the process accounts.

7 Normal loss

Certain losses are inherent in the production process and cannot be eliminated, e.g. liquids may evaporate, part of the cloth cut to make a suit may be lost. These losses occur under efficient working conditions and are expected. They are known as **normal losses** and are often expressed as a percentage of the input.

Normal loss may have a small value, known as **scrap value**, if it can be sold. From the above examples, the offcuts of cloth from the suit manufacturer may be sold, but clearly the loss from evaporation could have no value.

Normal loss is shown on the credit side of the process account, it will have a quantity entry and may have a $ entry if it has a scrap value:

Process 1

	kg	$		kg	$
Materials			Output		
Labour			NORMAL LOSS		
Expenses					
Overheads					
	——	——		——	——
	——	——		——	——

We have to change the unit cost formula to take account of the normal loss:

$$\text{Unit Cost} = \frac{\textbf{Total input costs – scrap value of normal loss}}{\textbf{Expected output}}$$

The expected output can be calculated as the input units less normal loss units.

Illustration 4

A company operates a single process. The costs of the process are as follows:

	$
Direct materials	6,000
Direct labour	1,000
Production overhead	3,000

The input quantity was 500 kg and the expected or normal loss was 10% of input. The normal loss has no scrap value. Actual output was 450 kg.

Required:

Show the process account.

Solution

Step 1: Set up the process account, and input all the information available from the question:

Process 1

	Kg	$		Kg	$
Material	500	6,000	Output	450	
Labour		1,000	Normal loss	50	0
Overhead		3,000			
	_____	_____		_____	_____
	_____	_____		_____	_____

Step 2: Balance the quantity column, ensure that both sides agree:

Process 1

	Kg	$		Kg	$
Material	500	6,000	Output	450	
Labour		1,000	Normal loss	50	0
Overhead		3,000			
	500			500	

Step 3: Calculate the cost per unit and value the output:

$$\textbf{Unit Cost} = \frac{\textbf{Total input costs – scrap value of normal loss}}{\textbf{Expected output}}$$

= (6,000 + 1,000 + 3,000 – 0) / 450 = $22.22

So the value of the output = $22.22 × 450 = **$10,000**

Step 4: Finally balance the $ column.

Process 1

	Kg	$		Kg	$
Material	500	6,000	Output	450	10,000
Labour		1,000	Normal loss	50	0
Overhead		3,000			
	500	10,000		500	10,000

Normal loss with scrap value

Look at the previous example again, but this time assume the scrap can be sold for $5 per kg.

The normal loss will be shown with a value of $5 × 50 = $250.

Process 1

	Kg	$		Kg	$
Material	500	6,000	Output	450	
Labour		1,000	Normal loss	50	250
Overhead		3,000			
	500			500	

When we calculate the cost per unit this time, we must remember to deduct the scrap value from the input costs.

$$\textbf{Unit Cost} = \frac{\textbf{Total input costs – scrap value of normal loss}}{\textbf{Expected output}}$$

= (10,000 – 250) / 450 = $21.67

So the value of the output = $21.67 × 450 = $9,750

The complete process account will look like this:

Process 1

	Kg	$		Kg	$
Material	500	6,000	Output	450	9,750
Labour		1,000	Normal loss	50	250
Overhead		3,000			
	500	10,000		500	10,000

Accounting for scrap

The double entry for the normal loss is usually made in a scrap account. Note the scrap account is balanced off to receivables/cash.

Scrap account

	Kg	$		$
Process 1 normal loss	50	250	Receivable/cash	250

Test your understanding 5

NB Ltd manufactures paint in a 2-stage process. The normal loss in process 1 is 10% of input and can be sold for $2/kg. The following costs were incurred in May:

Materials 1,000 kg at $4.30/kg
Labour 500 hours at $6/hour
Overheads are absorbed at $2/labour hour

Losses were at the normal level.

Required:

Prepare the process account, clearly showing the cost per kg.

8 Abnormal losses and gains

We have seen that the normal loss is an estimate of the loss expected to occur in a particular process. This estimate may be incorrect and a different amount of loss may occur.

If the actual loss is greater than the normal loss then the excess loss is referred to as an **abnormal loss**.

If the actual loss is less than the normal loss then the difference is referred to as an **abnormal gain**.

Example

Input 10,000kg, normal loss 10%

If the actual loss is 1,200 kg – normal loss 1,000 kg and abnormal loss 200 kg.

Abnormal losses are shown on the credit side of the process account:

Process 1

	Kg	$		Kg	$
Materials			Output		
Labour			Normal loss	1,000	
Overheads			ABNORMAL LOSS	200	
	______	______		______	______
	______	______		______	______

If the actual loss is 900 kg – normal loss 1,000 kg and abnormal gain 100 kg.

Abnormal gains are shown on the debit side of the process account:

Process 1

	Kg	$		Kg	$
Materials			Output		
Labour			Normal loss	1,000	
Overheads					
ABNORMAL GAIN	100				
	______	______		______	______
	______	______		______	______

Abnormal losses and gains are treated differently from normal losses. In the process account, the normal loss is valued at scrap value, but the abnormal losses and gains are valued at the same rate as good output.

Illustration 5

The following example illustrates the calculations and entries in the process account when an **abnormal loss** occurs.

X Ltd has the following costs for process 1:

Materials (500 kg)	$6,000
Labour	$1,000
Expenses	$2,000
Overhead	$1,000

Normal loss is estimated to be 10% of input and losses may be sold as scrap for $5 per kg.

Actual output was 430 kg.

The process account is shown below.

Earlier in the chapter, we recommended that you should insert the units into the process account first, and then balance them off. In this example, this results in a balancing value on the credit side of 20 kg, which is the abnormal loss.

Process account

	kg	$		kg	$
Materials	500	6,000	Output	430	9,317
Labour		1,000	Normal loss	50	250
Expenses		2,000	Abnormal loss	20	433
Overheads		1,000			
	500	10,000		500	10,000

The cost per kg is calculated as follows:

$$\text{Unit Cost} = \frac{\text{Total input costs} - \text{scrap value of normal loss}}{\text{Expected output}}$$

Unit cost = (10,000 – 250)/450 = **$21.67**

The abnormal loss units are valued at the same rate per unit as the good output units, so the valuations are:

Output: (430 × $21.67) = $9,317
Abnormal loss: (20 × $21.67) = $433
The normal loss is valued at its scrap value only.

Accounting for scrap: The next step is to prepare the scrap and abnormal loss accounts. The normal loss is debited to the scrap account and the abnormal loss is debited to the abnormal loss account:

Scrap account

	$		$
Process – normal loss	250		
	–––		–––
	–––		–––

Abnormal loss account

	$		$
Process	433		
	–––		–––
	–––		–––

In reality the value of the abnormal loss is also scrap value, in this case (20 kg × $5) = $100, so we have to account for this. We show this by doing a double entry debiting the scrap account and crediting the abnormal loss account:

Scrap account

	$		$
Process – normal loss	250		
Abnormal loss transfer	100		
	–––		–––
	–––		–––

The scrap balance now represents the total of 70 kg scrapped, with a total scrap value of $350.

Abnormal loss account

	$		$
Process	433	Scrap account	100
	–––		–––
	–––		–––

The next step is to balance the scrap and the abnormal loss account. **Note**: The quantities are not required.

The scrap account is balanced to receivables/cash – this reflects the amount received from selling the scrap.

Scrap account

	$		$
Process – normal loss	250	Receivables/cash	350
Abnormal loss transfer	100		
	–––		–––
	350		350
	–––		–––

The abnormal loss account is balanced to the statement of profit or loss – this reflects the net cost of the excess loss (i.e. after deducting the scrap sales proceeds). It has now been highlighted separately for management attention, and the balance is transferred to the statement of profit or loss as an expense.

Abnormal loss account

	$		$
Process	433	Scrap account	100
		Statement of profit or loss	333
	–––		–––
	433		433
	–––		–––

Illustration 6

If the actual loss is smaller than the amount expected, then an **abnormal gain** is said to have occurred. If we consider the X Ltd example from illustration 5 again, except that the actual output achieved was 470 kg, we can see that the following process account results.

Process account

	kg	$		kg	$
Materials	500	6,000	Output	470	10,183
Labour		1,000			
Expenses		2,000	Normal loss	50	250
Overheads		1,000			
Abnormal gain	20	433			
	520	10,433		520	10,433

Note: The balancing value in the quantity column is now on the debit side. It represents the abnormal gain. The calculation of the cost per unit remains the same, but now there is an additional entry on the debit side.

Accounting for scrap: When we account for the scrap in this case, we need an abnormal gain account:

The normal loss is debited to the scrap account as before, but the abnormal gain has been debited to the process account, so the double entry is to credit the abnormal gain to the abnormal gain account.

As before, we do a double entry between the two accounts, this time we debit the abnormal gain account and credit the scrap account:

Abnormal gain account

	$		$
Scrap account	100	Process	433

Balance the scrap and the abnormal gain account.

The scrap account is balanced to receivables/cash as before.

The abnormal gain account is balanced to the statement of profit or loss – this reflects the net gain from the lower than expected process loss. It will be shown as an income in the statement of profit or loss.

Scrap account

	$		$
Process – normal loss	250	Abnormal gain transfer	100
		Receivables/cash	150
	250		250

Abnormal gain account

	$		$
Scrap account	100	Process	433
Statement of profit or loss	333		
	433		433

Test your understanding 6

A company operates a single process, Details for November are given:

Direct materials	$8,500
Direct labour	$2,500
Direct expenses	$7,000
Production overheads	$7,800

Input quantity 1,200 kg
Output quantity 1,100 kg

Normal loss is 10% of input and has a scrap value of $3.50 per kg.

Required:

Complete the process account for November and the scrap and abnormal gain or loss accounts.

Test your understanding 7

A company operates a single process, Details for November are given:

Direct materials	$8,500
Direct labour	$2,500
Direct expenses	$7,000
Production overheads	$7,800

Input quantity 1,200 kg
Output quantity 1,000 kg

Normal loss is 10% of input and has a scrap value of $3.50 per kg.

Required:

Complete the process account for November and the scrap and abnormal gain or loss accounts.

9 Work in progress: the concept of equivalent units

To calculate a unit cost of production, it is necessary to know how many units were produced in the period. In any given accounting period there are likely to be partially completed units, we call this **work in progress (WIP)**.

We have closing WIP at the end of the accounting period. This closing WIP is carried forward to the next accounting period as opening WIP.

Opening WIP and closing WIP are the final two entries in our process account. Opening WIP is shown as a debit and closing WIP is shown as a credit. The following shows all the potential entries in a process account:

Process 1

	kg	$		kg	$
OPENING WIP					
Materials			Output		
Labour			Normal loss		
Overheads			Abnormal loss *		
Abnormal gain *			CLOSING WIP		
	—	—		—	—
	—	—		—	—

* Remember a process account can only have either an abnormal loss OR an abnormal gain, it can never have both.

If some units were only partly processed at the end of the period, then these must be taken into account in the calculation of production output. The concept of equivalent units provides a basis for doing this. The work in progress (the partly finished units) is expressed in terms of how many equivalent complete units it represents.

If there are 500 units in progress which are 25% complete, these units would be treated as the equivalent of:
500 × 25% = 125 complete units.

A further complication arises if the work in progress has reached **different degrees of completion** in respect of each cost element. For example, you might stop the process of cooking a casserole just as you were about to put the dish in the oven. The casserole would probably be complete in respect of ingredients, almost complete in respect of labour, but most of the overhead cost would be still to come in terms of the cost of the power to cook the casserole.

It is common in many processes for the materials to be added in full at the start of processing and for them to be converted into the final product by the actions of labour and related overhead costs. For this reason, labour and overhead costs are often referred to as **conversion costs**.

The *CIMA Terminology* defines **conversion cost** as the 'cost of converting material into finished product, typically including direct labour, direct expense and production overhead'.

To overcome the problem of costs being incurred at different stages in the process, a separate equivalent units calculation is performed for each cost element.

Illustration 7

Details for PLC's single process for October are given:

Input materials	1,000 kg @ $9 per kg
Labour cost	$4,800
Overhead cost	$5,580
Outputs	Finished goods: 900 kg
	Closing work in progress: 100 kg

The work in progress is completed:

100% as to material
60% as to labour
30% as to overhead

For simplicity, losses have been ignored.

Now that you are beginning to learn about more complications in process costing, this is a good point to get into the habit of producing an **input/output reconciliation** as the first stage in your workings. This could be done within the process account, by balancing off the quantity columns in the way that we have done so far in this chapter. However, with more complex examples it is better to have total quantity columns in your working paper and do the 'balancing off' there.

In the workings table which follows, the first stage is to balance the input and output quantities, that is, check that the total kg input is equal to the total kg output. Then, each part of the output can be analysed to show how many equivalent kg of each cost element it represents.

				Equivalent kg to absorb cost		
Input	*kg*	*Output*	*kg*	*Materials*	*Labour*	*Overhead*
Materials	1,000	Finished goods	900	(100%) 900	(100%) 900	(100%) 900
		Closing WIP	100	(100%) 100	(60%) 60	(30%) 30
	1,000		1,000	1,000	960	930
		Costs		$9,000	$4,800	$5,580
		Cost/eq. unit		$9	$5	$6

For the equivalent unit calculations there is a separate column for each cost element. The number of equivalent units is found by multiplying the percentage completion by the number of kg in progress. For example, equivalent kg of labour in progress is 100 kg × 60% = 60 equivalent kg.

The number of equivalent units is then totalled for each cost element and a cost per equivalent unit is calculated.

These costs per equivalent unit are then used to value the finished output and the closing work in progress.

The process account is shown below, together with the calculation of the value of the closing work in progress. Note that this method may be used to value the finished output, but it is easier to total the equivalent unit costs ($9 + $5 + $6) and use the total cost of $20 multiplied by the finished output of 900 kg.

Closing WIP valuation		$
Materials	100 equivalent units × $9	900
Labour	60 equivalent units × $5	300
Overheads	30 equivalent units × $6	180
		1,380

Process account

	kg	$		kg	$
Materials	1,000	9,000	Finished goods	900	18,000
Labour		4,800	WIP	100	1,380
Overheads		5,580			
	1,000	19,380		1,000	19,380

Test your understanding 8

JM Limited operates a process system. Data for process 2 for period 5 was as follows:

Material	500 kg at $3/kg
Labour	650 at $10/hour
Production overheads	$8,070

Output for the period was 400 kg

There was no opening work in progress, but 100 kg were in progress at the end of the period, at the following stages of completion:

100% complete in terms of materials

70% complete in terms of conversion costs

Required:

Complete the process account for period 5.

Example with WIP and losses

Data concerning process 2 last month was as follows:

From process 1	$2,150 (400kg)
Materials added	$6,120 (3,000kg)
Conversion costs	$2,344
Output to finished goods	2,800 kg
Output scrapped	400 kg
Normal loss	10% of materials added in the period

The scrapped units were complete in materials added but only 50% complete in respect of conversion costs. All scrapped units have a value of $2 each.

There was no opening work in progress, but 200 kg were in progress at the end of the month, at the following stages of completion:

80% complete in terms of materials added
40% complete in terms of conversion costs

Required:

Write up the process 2 account for the period.

Solution

The first step is to produce an input/output reconciliation as in the last example. Notice that the losses are not complete. You will need to take account of this in the equivalent units columns. And remember that the normal loss units do not absorb any of the process costs. They are valued at their scrap value only, so they must not be included as part of the output to absorb costs.

Input	kg	Output	kg	Process 1	Materials	Conversion
				Equivalent kg to absorb cost		
from Process 1	400	Finished goods	2,800	(100%) 2,800	(100%) 2,800	(100%) 2,800
Materials	3,000	Closing WIP	200	(100%) 200	(80%) 160	(40%) 80
		Normal loss	300	–	–	–
		Abnormal loss (1)	100	(100%) 100	(100%) 100	(50%) 50
	3,400		3,400	3,100	3,060	2,930
		Costs		$2,150	$6,120	$2,344
		Scrap value (2)		$(600)		
				$1,550	$6,120	$2,344
		Cost/eq. unit	$3.30	$0.50	$2.00	$0.80

Notes:

(1) The abnormal loss is inserted in the output column as a balancing figure. Losses are 50% complete in conversion costs. Therefore, the 100kg of abnormal loss represents 50 equivalent complete kg in respect of conversion costs.

(2) By convention, the scrap value of normal loss is usually deducted from the first cost element.

For each cost element the costs incurred are divided by the figure for equivalent kg produced. For example, the cost per kg for materials added = $6,120/3,060 = $2 per kg.

The unit rates can now be used to value each part of the output. For example, the 160 equivalent kg of materials added in the work in progress are valued at 160 × $2 = $320. The 80 equivalent kg of conversion costs in work in progress are valued at 80 × $0.80 = $64.

Valuation	*Total*	*Process 1 transfer*	*Materials added*	*Conversion costs*
	$	$	$	$
Finished goods	9,240	1,400	5,600	2,240
Abnormal loss	290	50	200	40
Closing WIP	484	100	320	64

It is now possible to draw up the relevant accounts using these valuations of each part of the process output.

Process 2 account

	kg	$		kg	$
Process 1	400	2,150	Finished goods	2,800	9,240
Materials added	3,000	6,120	Normal loss	300	600
Conversion costs		2,344	Abnormal loss	100	290
			Work in progress	200	484
	3,400	10,614		3,400	10,614

Previous process costs

A common problem that students experience when studying process costing is understanding how to deal with previous process costs. An important point that you should have grasped by now is that production passes through a number of sequential processes. Unless the process is the last in the series, the output of one process becomes the input of the next. A common mistake is to forget to include the previous process cost as an input cost in the subsequent process.

You should also realise that all of the costs of the previous process (materials, labour and overhead) are combined together as a single cost of 'input material' or 'previous process costs' in the subsequent process.

We assumed that the work in progress must be 100% complete in respect of Process 1 costs. This is also an important point to grasp. Even if the Process 2 work had only just begun on these units, there cannot now be any more cost to add in respect of Process 1. Otherwise the units would not yet have been transferred out of Process 1 into Process 2.

10 Opening work in progress

Opening work in progress consists of incomplete units in process at the beginning of the period. Your syllabus requires you to know how to value work in progress using the **average cost method**. With this method, opening work in progress is treated as follows:

(1) The opening work in progress is listed as an additional part of the input to the process for the period.

(2) The cost of the opening WIP is added to the costs incurred in the period.

(3) The cost per equivalent unit of each cost element is calculated as before, and this is used to value each part of the output. The output value is based on the average cost per equivalent unit, hence the name of this method.

Test your understanding 9

The following information is available for process 2 in October:

			Degree of completion and cost					
			Process 1 input		*Materials added* in process 2		*Conversion* costs	
	Units	*Cost*						
		$	%	$	%	$	%	$
Opening WIP	600	1,480	100	810	80	450	40	220
Closing WIP	350		100		90		30	
Input costs:								
Input from process 1	4,000	6,280						
Materials added in process 2		3,109						
Conversion costs		4,698						

Normal loss is 5% of input from process 1.

300 units were scrapped in the month. The scrapped units had reached the following degrees of completion.

Materials added	90%
Conversion cost	60%

All scrapped units realised $1 each.

Output to the next process was 3,950 units.

Required:

Complete the account for process 2 and for the abnormal loss or gain in October.

Comparing process and specific order costing

Now that you have a clear picture of how process costing works you are in a position to think about the differences between process costing and specific order costing methods.

Remember that specific order costing is the collective term for the costing methods that you learned about earlier in the chapter: job and batch costing.

Process costing can be contrasted with specific order costing methods such as job and batch costing in a number of ways:

- since there is a continuous flow of identical units, individual cost units cannot be separately identified in a process costing environment. In a specific order costing environment, each cost unit is different from all others;
- costs incurred are averaged over the units produced in a process costing system. In contrast to a specific order costing system, it is not possible to allocate costs to specific cost units;
- each cost unit usually undergoes the same process or sequence of processes. In specific order costing environments, each cost unit often involves different operations or processes, depending on the customer's requirements;
- in process costing environments, items are usually produced to replenish inventory, rather than for a specific customer's requirements.

11 Chapter summary

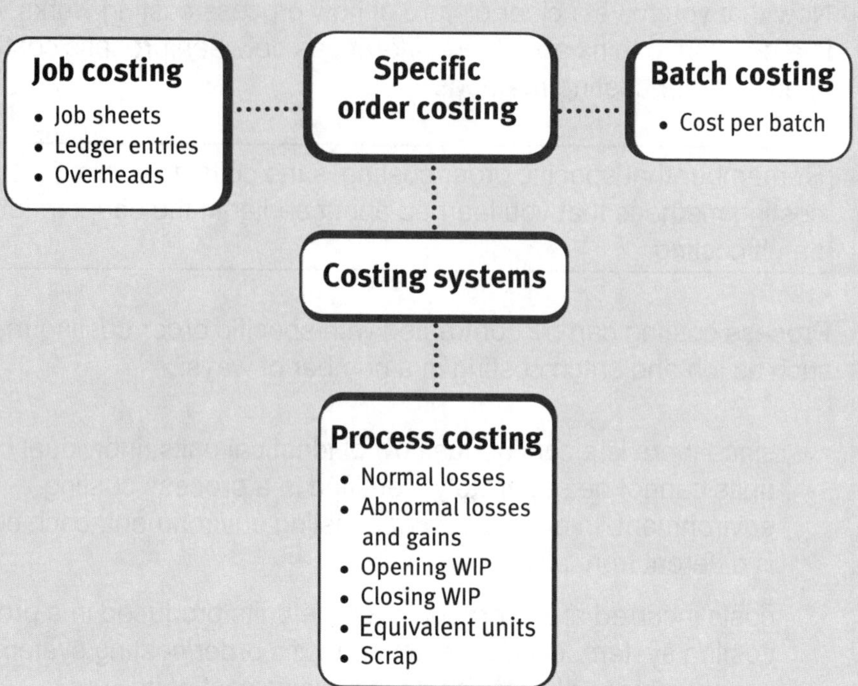

12 End of chapter questions

Question 1

Which of the following are characteristics of job costing?

(i) Customer-driven production.

(ii) Complete production possible within a single accounting period.

(iii) Homogeneous products.

A (i) and (ii) only

B (i) and (iii) only

C (ii) and (iii) only

D All of them

Question 2

The following items may be used in costing jobs:

(i) Actual material cost.

(ii) Actual manufacturing overheads.

(iii) Absorbed manufacturing overheads.

(iv) Actual labour cost.

Which of the above are contained in a typical job cost?

A (i), (ii) and (iv) only

B (i) and (iv) only

C (i), (iii) and (iv) only

D All of them

Question 3

Match the organisational activities below to the most appropriate costing method by writing (a) or (b) in the box provided.

Costing methods

(a) Job costing

(b) Batch costing

Organisational activities

- Accounting and taxation services
- Shoe manufacturing
- Plumbing and heating repairs
- Building maintenance and repairs

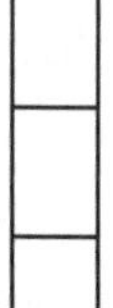

Question 4

A commercial decorating organisation budgets for 4% idle time on all its jobs.

The estimated number of active labour hours required to complete decorating job D47 is 120 hours. The hourly labour rate is $11.

The estimated labour cost of job D47 is (to the nearest $) $_______.

Question 5

Process B had no opening WIP. 13,500 units of raw material were transferred in from process A at $4.50 per unit. Additional material at $1.25 per unit was added during the process. Labour and overheads were $6.25 per completed unit and $2.50 per unit incomplete. If 11,750 completed units were transferred out, what was the closing WIP in process B?

A $77,625.00

B $14,437.50

C $141,000.00

D $21,000.00

Question 6

In a process account, abnormal losses are valued:

A at their scrap value

B at the same rate as good production

C at the cost of raw materials

D at good production cost less scrap value

Question 7

A chemical process has a normal wastage of 10% of input. In a period, 2,500 kg of material was input and there was an abnormal loss of 75 kg.

What quantity of good production was achieved?

A 2,175 kg

B 2,250 kg

C 2,325 kg

D 2,475 kg

Question 8

In process costing, where losses have a positive scrap value, when an abnormal gain arises the abnormal gain account is:

A credited with the normal production cost of the abnormal gain units

B debited with the normal production cost of the abnormal gain units and credited with the scrap value of the abnormal gain units

C credited with the normal production cost of the abnormal gain units and debited with the scrap value of the abnormal gain units

D credited with the normal production cost of the abnormal gain units and credited with the scrap value of the abnormal gain units

Question 9

A product is manufactured as a result of two processes, A and B. Details of process B for the month of August were as follows:

Materials transferred from process A	10,000 kg valued at $40,500
Labour costs	1,000 hours @ $5.616 per hour
Overheads	50% of labour costs
Output transferred to finished goods	8,000 kg
Closing work in progress	900 kg

Normal loss is 10% of input and losses do not have a scrap value.

Closing work in progress is 100% complete for material, and 75% complete for both labour and overheads.

(a) What is the value of the abnormal loss (to the nearest $)?

A Nil

B $489

C $544

D $546

(b) What is the value of the output (to the nearest $)?

A $39,139

B $43,488

C $43,680

D $43,977

(c) What is the value of the closing work in progress (to the nearest $)?

A $4,403

B $4,698

C $4,892

D $4,947

Question 10

The following data relate to a process for the latest period:

Opening work in process	1,000 litres valued at $1,500
Input	30,000 litres costing $15,000
Conversion costs	$10,000
Output	24,000 litres
Closing work in process	3,500 litres

Losses in the process are expected to be 10% of period input. They are complete as to input material costs but are discovered after 60% conversion. Losses have a scrap value of $0.20 per litre.

Closing work in process is complete as to input materials and 80% complete as to conversion.

(a) The number of material-equivalent units was:

A 24,000

B 28,000

C 30,000

D 31,000

(b) The number of conversion-equivalent units was:

A 27,100

B 27,300

C 28,000

D 30,100

Question 11

A firm operates a process. The details for period 2 were as follows:

There was no opening work in progress.

During the period, 8,250 units were received from the previous process at a value of $453,750, labour and overheads were $350,060 and material introduced was $24,750.

At the end of the period, the closing work in progress was 1,600 units, which were 100% complete in respect of materials, and 60% complete in respect of labour and overheads.

The balance of units were transferred to finished goods.

Required:

(a) The number of equivalent units of labour and overheads produced during the period was ______

(b) In the process account for the period, the following values will be credited:

(i) finished goods value: $ ______

(ii) closing work in progress value: $ ______

Question 12

Chemical Processors manufacture Wonderchem using two processes – mixing and distillation. The following details relate to the distillation process for a period:

Input from mixing	36,000 kg at a cost of $166,000
Labour for period	$43,800
Overheads for period	$29,200

There was no opening work in progress.

Closing WIP of 8,000 kg, which was 100% complete for materials and 50% complete for labour and overheads.

The normal loss in distillation is 10% of fully complete production. Actual loss in the period was 3,600 kg, fully complete, which was scrapped.

Required:

(a) The abnormal loss for the period was _______ kg.

(b) The number of equivalent kg produced during the period was:

materials:__________ equivalent kg.

labour and overhead: _________equivalent kg.

(c) (i) The value of the abnormal loss is $ _______

(ii) (*Tick the correct box*): This value is entered in the process account as a:

debit □

credit □

(d) The values to be credited in the process account in respect of the following outputs for the period are:

finished goods $_________

normal loss $__________

closing work in progress $__________

Question 13

A company operates an expensive processing plant to produce a single product from one process. At the beginning of October, 3,400 completed units were still in the processing plant awaiting transfer to finished goods. They were valued as follows:

	$	
Direct material	25,500	
Direct wages	10,200	
Production overhead	20,400	(200% of direct wages)

During October, 37,000 further units were put into process and the following costs charged to the process:

	$
Direct materials	276,340
Direct wages	112,000
Production overhead	224,000

A total of 36,000 units was transferred to finished goods and 3,200 units remained in work in progress at the end of October, which were complete as to material and half complete as to labour and production overhead. The normal level of scrap (1,200 units) occurred during the process.

Required:

(a) The number of equivalent units produced during the period was:

materials:	
labour and overhead:	

(b) The value of the outputs from the process during the period was:

finished goods $ _______

closing work in progress $ _______

Question 14

Complete the following account for process 3. The work in progress was complete as to materials and 50% complete as to labour and overhead.

Process 3 account

	Units	$		*Units*	$
Process 2 input	2,000	8,000	Finished goods	1,800	
Labour and overhead		3,800	Closing WIP	200	
	2,000	11,800		2,000	11,800

Question 15

A company calculates the prices of jobs by adding overheads to the prime cost and adding 30% to total costs as a profit mark-up. Complete the following job cost summary information:

Job Y256	$
Prime cost	
Overheads	694
Total cost	
Profit mark up	
Selling price	1,690

Question 16

Jetprint Ltd specialises in printing advertising leaflets and is in the process of preparing its price list. The most popular requirement is for a folded leaflet made from a single sheet of A4 paper. From past records and budgeted figures, the following data have been estimated for a typical batch of 10,000 leaflets.

Artwork	$65
Machine setting	4 hours at $22 per hour
Paper	$12.50 per 1,000 sheets
Ink and consumables	$40
Printers' wages	4 hours at $8 per hour (**Note:** Printers' wages vary with volume.)

General fixed overheads are $15,000 per period, during which a total of 600 labour hours are expected to be worked.

The firm wishes to achieve 30% profit on sales.

Required:

(a) The selling prices (*to the nearest $*) per thousand leaflets for quantities of:

(i) 10,000 leaflets is $ ______.

(ii) 20,000 leaflets is $ ______.

(b) During the period, the firm printed and sold 64 batches of 10,000 leaflets and 36 batches of 20,000 leaflets. All costs were as expected.

(i) General fixed overhead for the period was (tick the correct box):

□ under-absorbed

□ over-absorbed

(ii) The value of the under-/over-absorption of general fixed overhead was $ ______.

Question 17

Amy Archer Ltd makes chemical ABC in a three stage manufacturing process. The details for process 3 are as follows:

Transferred from process 2	200 litres at a value of $510
Material	500 litres at $3.10/litre
Labour	300 hours at $6/hour
Overheads	absorbed at 133⅓% of direct labour cost
Normal loss	5% of input
	lost units have a scrap value of $2/unit
Output	590 litres

Required:

Show the process account, abnormal loss or gain account and the scrap account.

Question 18

A company producing a single product from one process has an opening work in progress of 3,200 units which were complete as to material but only 75% complete as to labour and overhead. These units at the end of September had been valued as follows:

Direct materials	$14,000
Direct wages	$6,500
Production overhead (200% on direct wages)	$13,000

During the month of October a further 24,800 units were put into the process and the following costs were incurred:

Direct materials	$97,000
Direct wages	$59,125
Production overhead (200% on direct wages)	$118,250

Normal loss was expected to be 500 units and all losses have a scrap value of $2 per unit. Units completed and transferred to finished goods inventory amounted to 24,000.

Work in progress at the end of October was 2,500 units which were complete as to material and 50% complete as to labour and overhead.

Required:

Prepare the process account, the abnormal gain or loss account and the scrap account for the month of October.

Question 19

The following details relate to the main process of X Ltd, a chemical manufacturer:

Opening work in progress 2,000 litres, fully complete as to materials and 40% complete as to conversion

Material input 24,000 litres

Normal loss is 10% of input

Output to process 2 is 19,500 litres

Closing work in progress 3,000 litres, fully complete as to materials and 45% complete as to conversion

Required:

The numbers of equivalent units to be included in X Ltd's calculation of the cost per equivalent units are:

	Materials	*Conversion*
A	21,400	19,750
B	21,400	20,850
C	22,500	21,950
D	23,600	21,950

Question 20

In job costing systems a separate work in progress account is maintained for each job, as well as a summary work in progress control account for all jobs worked on in the period.

The best way to see how this is done is to work carefully through the following example and ensure that you understand each entry that is made in every account. You will need to apply the principles of integrated accounts that you learned in Chapter 9.

Example

JC Ltd operates a job costing system. All jobs are carried out on JC's own premises and then delivered to customers as soon as they are completed.

Direct employees are paid $10 per hour and production overhead is absorbed into job costs using a predetermined absorption rate of $24 per labour hour. General overhead is charged to the statement of profit or loss on completed jobs using a rate of 12% of total production cost.

Details of work done during the latest period are as follows:

Work in progress at beginning of period

Job number 308 was in progress at the beginning of the period:

Cost incurred up to beginning of period:

	$
Direct material	1,790
Direct labour	960
Production overhead absorbed	2,304
Production cost incurred up to beginning of period	5,054

Activity during the period

Job numbers 309 and 310 commenced during the period.

The following details are available concerning all work done this period.

Job number:	*308*	*309*	*310*
Direct materials issued from stores	$169	$2,153	$452
Excess materials returned to stores	–	$23	–
Direct labour hours worked	82	53	28
Invoice value	$9,900	$6,870	–

Jobs 308 and 309 were completed in the period.

Further information:

Cost of material transferred from job 309 to job 310	$43
Production overhead cost incurred on credit	$4,590
General overhead cost incurred on credit	$1,312

Required:

(a) Prepare the ledger account for the period for each job, showing the production cost of sales transferred on completed jobs.

(b) Prepare the following accounts for the period:
- work in progress control
- production overhead control
- general overhead control
- overhead under- or over absorbed control
- statement of profit or loss

(c) Calculate the profit on each of the completed jobs.

Test your understanding answers

Test your understanding 1

D

Total direct labour cost = (12,500) + (23,000) + (4,500) = $40,000

$$\text{Overhead absorption rate} = \frac{\$140{,}000}{\$40{,}000} \times 100\% = 350\% \text{ of direct labour.}$$

Work in progress valuation	$	$
Costs given in question:		
Job 1	38,150	
Job 2	52,025	
		90,175
Overhead absorbed:		
Job 1 $12,500 × 350%	43,750	
Job 2 $23,000 × 350%	80,500	
		124,250
		214,425

Test your understanding 2

Job A: Selling price = $45 + 25% = **$56.25**

Job B: Selling price = $38 +10% = $41.80 total cost + 20% = **$50.16**

Job C: Selling price = ($75 × (100/85)) = **$88.24**

Note that for Job C the margin is expressed as a percentage of selling price.

Test your understanding 3

C

	$
Costs given in question	50,500
Overhead absorbed: $4,500 × 350%	15,750
Total production cost	66,250
Mark up 50%	33,125
Sales value of batch	99,375

Selling price per circuit board $\frac{99,375}{2,400}$ = **$41.41**

Test your understanding 4

Process 1

	kg	$		kg	$
Materials	500	6,000	Output	500	10,000
Labour		1,000			
Expenses		2,000			
Overheads		1,000			
	500	10,000		500	10,000

Process 2

	kg	$		kg	$
Process 1	500	10,000	Output	700	21,000
Materials	200	4,000			
Labour		2,000			
Expenses		3,000			
Overheads		2,000			
	700	21,000		700	21,000

Process 3

	kg	$		kg	$
Process 2	700	21,000	Output	1,000	40,000
Materials	300	9,000			
Labour		3,000			
Expenses		4,000			
Overheads		3,000			
	1,000	40,000		1,000	40,000

Unit cost calculations:

Process 1
10,000 / 500 = **$20**

Process 2
21,000 / 700 = **$30**

Process 3
40,000 / 1,000 = **$40**

Test your understanding 5

Process 1

	kg	$		kg	$
Material	1,000	4,300	Output	900	8,100
Labour		3,000	Normal loss	100	200
Overhead		1,000			
	1,000	8,300		1,000	8,300

Note: When balancing the quantity column, the output quantity was not given, but as losses were as expected, the output quantity must be 900.

$$\textbf{Unit Cost} = \frac{\textbf{Total input costs – scrap value of normal loss}}{\textbf{Expected output}}$$

= (8,300 – 200) / 900 = **$9.00**

Value of output = (900 × $9) = $8,100

Test your understanding 6

Process account

	kg	$		kg	$
Materials	1,200	8,500	Output	1,100	25,850
Labour		2,500	Normal loss	120	420
Expenses		7,000			
Overheads		7,800			
Abnormal gain	20	470			
	1,220	26,270		1,220	26,270

To balance the quantity column the abnormal gain must be 20 kg.

Calculate the cost per unit, then value the output and the abnormal gain:

$$\textbf{Unit Cost} = \frac{\textbf{Total input costs – scrap value of normal loss}}{\textbf{Expected output}}$$

$$\text{Unit Cost} = \frac{(8{,}500 + 2{,}500 + 2{,}000 + 7{,}000 + 7{,}800) - 420}{(1{,}200 - 120)}$$

Unit cost = **$23.50**

The value of output = $23.50 × 1,100 = **$25,850**

The value of abnormal gain = $23.50 × 20 = **$470**

Scrap account

	$		$
Process account	420	Abnormal gain	70
		Receivables/cash	350
	420		420

Abnormal gain account

	$		$
Scrap account (20 × \$3.50)	70	Process	470
Statement of profit or loss	400		
	470		470

Test your understanding 7

Process account

	kg	$		kg	$
Material	1,200	8,500	Output	1,000	23,500
Labour		2,500	Normal loss	120	420
Expenses		7,000	Ab loss	80	1,880
Overheads		7,800			
	1,200	25,800		1,200	25,800

To balance the quantity column the abnormal loss must be 80 kg.

Calculate the cost per unit, then value the output and the abnormal loss:

$$\textbf{Unit Cost} = \frac{\textbf{Total input costs – scrap value of normal loss}}{\textbf{Expected output}}$$

Remember the abnormal loss was unexpected, so the expected output is the input less the normal loss.

$$\text{Unit Cost} = \frac{(8{,}500 + 2{,}500 + 2{,}000 + 7{,}000 + 7{,}800) - 420}{(1{,}200 - 120)}$$

Unit cost = **$23.50**

The value of output = $23.50 × 1,000 = **$23,500**
The value of abnormal loss = $23.50 × 80 = **$1,880**

Scrap account

	$		$
Process – normal loss	420	Receivables/cash	700
Abnormal loss transfer	280		
	700		700

Abnormal loss account

	$		$
Process	1,880	Scrap account: (80 × $3.50)	280
		Statement of profit or loss	1,600
	1,880		1,880

Test your understanding 8

Input	Units	Output	Units		Equivalent units to absorb cost: Materials	Conversion costs
Materials	500	Output	400		(100%) 400	(100%) 400
		Closing WIP	100		(100%) 100	(70%) 70
	500		500		500	470
		Costs			$	$
		Input costs			1,500	14,570
				$	$	$
		Cost per unit			3.00	31.00
		Evaluation				
		Output		13,600	1,200	12,400
		Closing WIP		2,470	300	2,170

Process 2 account

	kg	$		kg	$
Materials	500	1,500	Output	400	13,600
Labour		6,500	Closing WIP	100	2,470
Overhead		8,070			
	500	16,070		500	16,070

Test your understanding 9

The first step is to prepare an input/output reconciliation to see if there was an abnormal loss or abnormal gain. This is found as a balancing figure in the output column.

				Equivalent units to absorb cost		
				Process 1	*Materials*	*Conversion*
Input	*Units*	*Output*	*Units*	*units*	*added*	*costs*
Opening WIP	600	To process 3	3,950	3,950	3,950	3,950
Process 1	4,000	Normal loss	200	–	–	–
		Abnormal loss	100	100	90	60
		Closing WIP	350	350	315	105
	4,600		4,600	4,400	4,355	4,115
		Costs		$	$	$
		Opening WIP		810	450	220
		Input costs		6,280	3,109	4,698
		Normal loss value		(200)		
				6,890	3,559	4,918
			$	$	$	$
		Cost per unit	3.578	1.566	0.817	1.195
		Evaluation				
		To process 3	14,133	6,186	3,227	4,720
		Abnormal loss	303	157	74	72
		Closing WIP	931	548	257	126

Process 2 account

	kg	$		kg	$
Opening WIP	600	1,480	Process 3	3,950	14,133
Process 1	4,000	6,280			
Materials		3,109	Normal loss	200	200
Conversion		4,698	Ab loss	100	303
			Closing WIP	350	931
	4,600	15,567		4,600	15,567

Abnormal loss account

	$		$
Process 2	303	Scrap account	100
		Statement of profit or loss	203
	303		303

Scrap account

	$		$
Process 2	200	Bank/receivables: (200 + 100) × $1	300
Abnormal loss account	100		
	300		300

Question 1

A

Job costing applies to situations where work is carried out to customer specifications, and each order is of relatively short duration. Each job is separately identifiable, therefore characteristic (iii) is incorrect.

Question 2

C

Actual material cost and actual labour cost will be contained in a typical job cost.

Actual manufacturing overheads will not be able to be identified for each job, therefore the absorbed manufacturing overheads will be included in the job cost.

Question 3

• Accounting and taxation services	**(a)**
• Shoe manufacturing	**(b)**
• Plumbing and heating repairs	**(a)**
• Building maintenance and repairs	**(a)**

Question 4

The estimated labour cost of job D47 is **$1,375**.

Workings:

The idle time would be stated as a percentage of the *paid* labour hours.

	Hours
Active labour hours required	120
Idle time (× 4/96)	5
Total paid hours required	125
Labour cost @ $11 per hour	**$1,375**

Question 5

B

Closing WIP in process B = (13,500 – 11,750) units = 1,750 units

Unit value = $4.50 + $1.25 + $2.50 = $8.25

Closing WIP value = $8.25 × 1,750 = **$14,437.50**

Question 6

B

Abnormal losses are valued at the same rate as good production, so that their occurrence does not affect the cost of good production.

Question 7

A

	kg
Input	2,500
Normal loss (10%)	(250)
Abnormal loss	(75)
Good production	**2,175**

Question 8

C

The abnormal gain account shows the net benefit of the abnormal gain. The scrap value must be debited to the abnormal gain account to allow for the 'forgone' scrap value of the normal loss units which did not arise.

Question 9

(a) **D**

Value of abnormal loss = 100 × ($4.50 + $0.96) = **$546**.

(b) **C**

Value of output = 8,000 × ($4.50 + $0.96) = **$43,680**.

(c) **B**

Closing work in progress:	$
900 × $4.50	4,050
675 × $0.96	648
	4,698

Workings:

Input	Units	Output	Units	Materials	Conversion
				Equivalent units produced	
Material	10,000	Output	8,000	8,000	8,000
		Normal loss	1,000	–	–
		Closing WIP	900	900	675
		Abnormal loss	100	100	100
	10,000		10,000	9,000	8,775
		Cost		$	$
		Period costs		40,500	8,424
		Cost per unit		4.50	0.96

Question 10

(a) **B**

(b) **A**

Input	Litres	Output	Litres	Input material		Conversion costs
				Equivalent litres		
Opening WIP	1,000	Finished output	24,000	24,000		24,000
Input	30,000	Normal loss	3,000	–		–
		Abnormal loss	500	500	(60%)	300
		Closing WIP	3,500	3,500	(80%)	2,800
	31,000		31,000	**28,000**		**27,100**

Question 11

(a) **7,610**

(b) (i) **$691,600**
(ii) **$136,960**

Workings:

				Equivalent units produced		
				Previous process	*Materials added*	*Labour and o/h*
Input	*Units*	*Output*	*Units*			
Previous process	8,250	Finished goods (1)	6,650	6,650	6,650	6,650
		Closing WIP	1,600	1,600	1,600	960 (60%)
	–––––		–––––	–––––	–––––	–––––
	8,250	Equiv. units produced	8,250	8,250	8,250	**7,610**
	–––––		–––––	–––––	–––––	–––––
		Costs	$	$	$	$
		Period costs		453,750	24,750	350,060
		Cost per equiv. unit	104	55	3	46
		Valuation				
		Finished goods	**691,600**			
		Closing WIP	**136,960**	88,000	4,800	44,160
				(1,600 × $55)	(1,600 × $3)	(960 × $46)

(1) The transfer to finished goods is calculated as follows: 8,250 units input, less 1,600 units in progress, equals 6,650 units to finished goods.

Question 12

(a) The abnormal loss for the period was **800 kg**.

(b) Materials: **33,200 equivalent kg**.
Labour and overhead: **29,200 equivalent kg**.

(c) (i) **$6,000**
(ii) **Credit**

(d) Finished goods: **$183,000**
Normal loss: **$0**
Closing work in progress: **$50,000**.

Workings:

	kg
Input	36,000
Less: Closing WIP	(8,000)
Production	28,000
Normal loss:	2,800
10% × 28,000 kg (1)	
Actual loss	3,600
Abnormal loss	**800**

Note (1): The normal loss calculation is based on the completed production rather than on the more usual basis of input to the process.

				Equivalent units		
			Total	*Material*	*Labour*	*Overhead*
Input	*kg*	*Output*	*kg*	*kg*	*kg*	*kg*
From mixing	36,000	Finished goods	24,400	24,400	24,400	24,400
		Abnormal loss	800	800	800	800
			25,200	25,200	25,200	25,200
		Normal loss	2,800	–	–	–
		Closing WIP:				
		Material (100%)	8,000	8,000		
		Labour (50%)			4,000	
		Overheads (50%)				4,000
			36,000	33,200	29,200	29,200
		Cost ($)	239,000	166,000	43,800	29,200
		Cost per unit ($)	*7.50*	*5.00*	*1.50*	*1.00*
		Evaluation ($)				
		Finished goods	183,000			
		Abnormal loss	6,000			
		Closing WIP	50,000	40,000	6,000	4,000

Scrap account

	$		$
Process 3	70	Bank/receivables	220
Abnormal loss account	150		
	——		——
	220		220
	——		——

Question 18

					Equivalent units to absorb cost	
						Conversion
Input	*Units*	*Output*	*Units*		*Materials*	*costs*
Opening WIP	3,200	Output	24,000		(100%) 24,000	(100%) 24,000
Materials	24,800	Normal loss	500		–	–
		Abnormal loss	1,000		(100%) 1,000	(100%) 1,000
		Closing WIP	2,500		(100%) 2,500	(50%) 1,250
	——		——		——	——
	28,000		28,000		27,500	26,250
	——		——		——	——
		Costs			$	$
		Opening WIP			14,000	19,500
		Input costs			97,000	177,375
		Scrap value			(1,000)	
					——	——
					110,000	196,875
					——	——
					$	$
		Cost per unit			4.00	7.50
		Evaluation				
		Output		276,000	96,000	180,000
		Abnormal loss		11,500	4,000	7,500
		Closing WIP		19,375	10,000	9,375

Process 1 account

	Units	$		Units	$
Opening WIP	3,200	33,500	Output	24,000	276,000
Materials	24,800	97,000	Normal loss	500	1,000
Labour		59,125	Ab loss	1,000	11,500
Overhead		118,250	Closing WIP	2,500	19,375
	28,000	307,875		28,000	307,875

Abnormal loss account

	$		$
Process 1	11,500	Scrap account (1,000 × $2)	2,000
		Statement of profit or loss	9,500
	11,500		11,500

Scrap account

	$		$
Process 1	1,000	Bank/receivables	3,000
Abnormal loss account	2,000		
	3,000		3,000

Question 19

D

Input	*Units*	*Output*	*Units*	*Equivalent units to absorb cost* Materials		*Conversion costs*	
Opening WIP	2,000	Output	19,500	(100%)	19,500	(100%)	19,500
Materials	24,000	Normal loss	2,400		–		–
		Abnormal loss	1,100	(100%)	1,100	(100%)	1,100
		Closing WIP	3,000	(100%)	3,000	(45%)	1,350
	26,000		26,000		23,600		21,950

Question 20

(a) The figures in brackets refer to the explanatory notes below the accounts.

Job 308

	$		$
Balance b/f (1)	5,054	Production cost of sales	8,011
Material stores	169		
Wages control (82 × $10)	820		
Production overhead (82 × $24)	1,968		
	8,011		8,011

Job 309

	$		$
Material stores	2,153	Material stores (2)	23
Wages control (53 × $10)	530	Job 310 (3)	43
Production overhead (53 × $24)	1,272	Production cost of sales	3,889
	3,955		3,955

Job 310

	$		$
Job 309 (3)	43	Balance c/f (4)	1,447
Material stores	452		
Wages control (28 × $10)	280		
Production overhead (28 × $24)	672		
	1,447		1,447

(b)

Work in progress control

	$		$
Balance b/f (1)	5,054	Material stores (2)	23
Material stores control (5)	2,774	Production cost of sales to statement of profit or loss (6)	11,900
Wages control (163 hours × $10)	1,630		
Production overhead (163 × $24)	3,912	Balance c/f (7)	1,447
	13,370		13,370

Production overhead control

	$		$
Payables control (8)	4,590	Work in progress control (9)	3,912
		Overhead under-/over-absorbed control (10)	678
	4,590		4,590

General overhead control

	$		$
Payables control (8)	1,312	General overhead cost to statement of profit or loss (11)	1,428
Overhead under-/over-absorbed control (10)	116		
	1,428		1,428

Overhead under-/over-absorbed control

	$		$
Production overhead control (10)	678	General overhead control (10)	116
		Statement of profit or loss	562
	678		678

Statement of profit or loss

	$		$
Production cost of sales (6)	11,900	Sales (9,900 + 6,870)	16,770
General overhead control (11)	1,428		
Under-absorbed overhead	562		
Profit for the period	2,880		
	16,770		16,770

Notes:

(1) The cost of the opening work in progress is shown as a brought forward balance in the individual job account and in the work in progress control account.

(2) The cost of materials returned to stores is credited in the individual job account and in the work in progress control account.

(3) The cost of materials transferred between jobs is credited to the job from which the material is transferred and debited to the job that actually uses the material.

(4) Job 310 is incomplete. The production cost incurred this period is carried down as an opening work in progress balance for next period.

(5) The total cost of all materials issued is debited to the work in progress control account.

(6) The production cost of both completed jobs ($3,889 + $8,011) is transferred to the statement of profit or loss.

(7) The balance carried forward to next period is the cost of the work in progress represented by job 310.

(8) The overhead cost incurred is debited in the control account.

(9) The production overhead absorbed into work in progress is credited to the overhead control account.

(10) Production overhead is under-absorbed and general overhead is over absorbed this period.

(11) The general overhead cost charged to the statement of profit or loss on completed jobs =12% × $(3,889 + 8,011) = $1,428.

(c)

	Job 308	*Job 309*
	$	$
Production cost	8,011.00	3,889.00
General overhead absorbed at 12%	961.32	466.68
	8,972.32	4,355.68
Invoice value	9,900.00	6,870.00
Profit	**927.68**	**2,514.32**

The total profit on the two jobs is $3,442. The difference of $562 between this total and the profit shown in the statement of profit or loss is the result of the under absorbed overhead of $562.

chapter

11

Presenting management information

Chapter learning objectives

After completing this chapter you should be able to:

- prepare financial statements that inform management;
- distinguish between managerial reports in a range of organisations, including commercial enterprises, charities and public sector undertakings.

1 Session content diagram

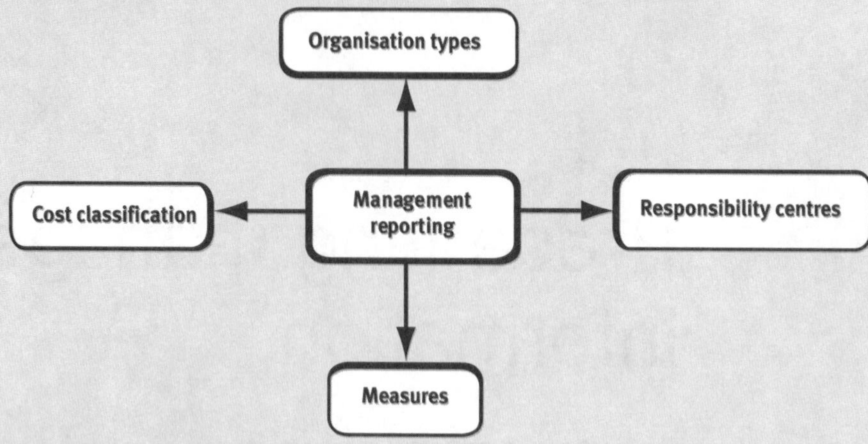

2 Management reporting

Management accounting reports are used by management for:

- planning
- controlling
- decision making.

It is essential that these reports are presented clearly and effectively.

These reports might be structured in different ways depending on their purpose and their recipient, and a range of different performance measures might be highlighted depending on the type of organisation.

In Chapter 1 we looked at the characteristics of good information and how information needs differed at different levels of the organisation. It is worth recapping on these areas before considering management reporting.

Responsibility centres

Responsibility centres were covered in Chapter 8. This is an important area when it comes to presenting management information. In responsibility reporting, costs and revenues are grouped according to which individual manager or management team is responsible for their control. It is worth recapping on the definitions of the types of responsibility centres and what the managers of each type of centre may require.

Profit centre managers might be interested in assessing the profitability of a particular product or service, in which case, costs might be classified by purpose so that they can be traced to individual products or services.

Investment centre managers will be interested in assessing the return being made by a product or service centre in relation to the capital outlay for that product or service.

Senior managers might be interested in assessing the costs incurred by a particular responsibility centre within the organisation. In this situation, it would be more useful to trace costs to individual responsibility centres rather than to particular products or services.

3 Preparing financial statements that inform management

The usefulness of a financial statement is greatly enhanced if it highlights subtotals, totals and performance measures that are relevant to the recipient.

This enables the manager who receives the information to focus on the most relevant information from the point of view of management action. The same information may be used in reports to different managers but it may be presented with different sub totals to highlight different points of interest.

A performance measure will be particularly relevant if it is **controllable** by the manager for whom the report is prepared, that is if the manager is able to take action to influence the measure, and if an improvement in the performance measure would improve the performance of the responsibility centre or the organisation overall.

Let us look now at a number of performance measures that you might see highlighted in management reports:

- gross revenue
- contribution
- gross margin
- value added
- expenses – marketing, general and administration
- return on capital

Gross revenue

The total sales achieved by a company is known as gross revenue. This is the total of all sales transactions made by the company. This is a useful figure for the sales director of a company who needs to know how many customers their products or services have reached.

However, for various reasons, not all sales are successful and companies can experience returns from customers or goods could be lost in transit. It is important that these deductions are made from the gross revenue figure to give another meaningful measure called **sales revenue**.

Contribution

Contribution is an important measure within management decision making. It is calculated as follows:

Contribution = sales revenue – variable costs

Contribution is often highlighted in management reports when it is important for managers to be able to see whether individual cost objects are generating sufficient revenue to cover the variable costs they incur.

Highlighting contribution can also help managers to see the potential effect on profit of an increase or decrease in activity.

Gross margin

Another measure which may be useful to manager is gross margin. Gross margin is calculated as follows:

Gross margin = sales revenue – direct production or purchasing costs incurred

This is a useful measure which shows how effective the company's trading activity is. It shows if the sales revenue is enough to cover the direct cost of the item sold.

Net profit can then be calculated by deducting indirect costs or overheads from the gross margin.

The **gross margin percentage** is also a useful measure in reporting. It is calculated as follows:

$$\text{Gross margin \%} = \frac{\text{Gross margin}}{\text{Sales revenue}}$$

This measure helps to highlight the relationship between sales revenues and production/purchasing costs. As it is a % measure, it can be used to compare the performance of different areas of the business or different products.

Value added

Value added is a performance measure which is sometimes used as an alternative to profit. Traditionally, value added is calculated as follows.

Value added = sales revenue – cost of materials and bought-in services

Since value added excludes all bought-in costs paid to people from outside the organisation, it effectively focuses on the additional revenue created by the organisation's own internal efforts. You might sometimes see value added calculated by 'working backwards' from the profit figure:

Value added = profit + interest + all conversion costs

You should remember from your process costing studies that conversion costs are the costs of converting raw material into the finished product.

If you have to calculate value added in an assessment question then you should use the traditional method of calculation, i.e. sales revenue – cost of materials and bought-in services.

Expenses – marketing, general and administration

In management reports it can be important to highlight areas of expenditure. Particular types of expenditure will be of interest to different managers. For example, marketing expense is often a large discretionary spend and, as such, companies need to see this figure highlighted in reports.

General and administration expenses can also be significant costs. Managers are generally concerned with controlling the level of these costs.

Return on capital

Capital is the investment in an entity, it is often referred to as capital employed.

Capital employed is calculated as total assets less current liabilities.

There are a number of measures which can be used to calculate the return on capital, the main one is return on capital employed (ROCE). It is calculated as follows:

$$\textbf{Return on capital employed (ROCE)} = \frac{\textbf{earnings before interest and tax}}{\textbf{capital employed}}$$

Earnings before interest and tax is often referred to as operating profit or net profit.

This measure helps to highlight the productivity of the capital employed.

You can see from the above that the information contained in a management report will depend on the needs of the manager using that report.

Test your understanding 1

An extract from the performance report of the GFD Company for the latest period is as follows:

	$	$
Sales revenue		654,500
Cost of goods sold		
Material costs	120,360	
Labour costs	89,400	
Production overhead	36,950	
		246,710
Gross margin		407,790
Marketing overhead	42,540	
General and administration overhead	59,600	
		102,140
Net profit		305,650

For the GFD Company for the latest period, the value added was $ _______.

Test your understanding 2

KJG Ltd has two production divisions, A and B which operate as investment centres. A report for July has been prepared for the two divisions and extracts are shown on the next page.

	A	B
	$000	$000
Sales revenue	300	550
Variable cost of production	160	230
Fixed cost of production	50	160
Non-production costs	25	32
Net profit	65	128
Capital employed	500	1,300

Calculate the return on capital employed for divisions A and B.

Illustration 1

A product contribution analysis

This example will demonstrate why it might be important to highlight the contribution earned by each product.

	Product A	Product B	Product C	Total
	$000	$000	$000	$000
Gross revenue	931	244	954	2,129
Variable costs:				
Direct material and labour	547	87	432	1,066
Variable production overhead	54	58	179	291
Variable marketing expense	9	3	7	19
Total variable cost	610	148	618	1,376
Contribution	321	96	336	753
Fixed production overhead	43	35	34	112
Fixed marketing expense	38	10	40	88
Fixed general expense	60	56	60	176
Profit/(loss)	180	(5)	202	377
Contribution to sales (PV) ratio	34.5%	39.3%	35.2%	

This product contribution analysis reveals the following:

- Product B appears to be incurring a loss. Its contribution is not sufficient to cover the fixed production, marketing, general and administration expenses attributed to it.
- However the product is earning a contribution. If the fixed costs attributed to product B are costs that would be incurred anyway, even if product B was discontinued, then it may be worth continuing production of product B since it does earn a contribution of $96,000 towards these fixed costs. If product B was discontinued then this $96,000 contribution would be forgone.
- Although product B is earning a contribution, it does not at present generate sufficient contribution to cover its fair share of support costs such as marketing and general overheads. The profitability of product B does require management attention.
- Product B earns the highest contribution to sales ratio. This means that if gross sales revenue of product B can be increased without affecting the fixed costs, the resulting increase in contribution will be higher than with the same sales increase on products A and C. Thus the key to product B's profitability might be to increase the volume sold.

Illustration 2

A gross margin analysis

The following extract is taken from the monthly managerial report of the DD Organisation.

	Month 1	*Month 2*	*Month 3*	*Month 4*
	$000	$000	$000	$000
Gross sales revenue	896	911	919	935
Direct cost of goods sold	699	713	722	737
	——	——	——	——
Gross margin	197	198	197	198
	——	——	——	——
Gross margin percentage	22.0%	21.7%	21.4%	21.2%
	——	——	——	——

This gross margin analysis focuses managers' attention on the relationship between the sales value and the direct cost of sales, before indirect costs or overheads are taken into account. This analysis reveals the following:

- Although the gross sales revenue is steadily increasing, the gross margin is relatively constant each month.
- The gross margin percentage is steadily decreasing each month. If the gross margin percentage could have been maintained at 22% the total gross margin earned would have been higher.
- Perhaps selling prices are being increased but the reduction in the gross margin percentage might be the result of a failure to increase selling prices sufficiently in line with increasing direct costs.
- Alternatively the sales volume might be increasing but direct costs are not being controlled as sales increase.

4 Management reports in a service organisation

There is a wide variety of service organisations, ranging from private sector organisations such as hotels and courier services, to public sector organisations such as hospitals and schools.

One aspect of service organisations that can present difficulties for the information provider is establishing a suitable cost unit.

Establishing a suitable cost unit

Many service organisations produce an intangible 'output', that is, their output has no physical substance and it cannot be physically seen and touched. In order to maintain effective cost control it is essential to establish a measurable cost unit for which we can ascertain and monitor the costs.

In Chapter 2 we saw how **composite cost units** are often used to monitor and control the costs in service operations. Any cost unit can be used as long as it can be objectively measured and its cost can be determined and compared from one period to another and if possible from one organisation to another.

Composite cost units that could be used in each of these service organisations:

- Hotel — bed-night or room-night.
- Hospital — in-patient day
- Haulage contractor — tonne-kilometre

Establishing the cost per unit

Once a suitable cost unit has been selected, the cost for each unit can be determined using an averaging method:

$$\textbf{Average cost per units of service} = \frac{\textbf{Total cost incurred in period}}{\textbf{Units of service supplied in the period}}$$

The nature of services

The instantaneous and perishable nature of services

Many services are provided instantaneously rather than for inventory; for example, a restaurant meal is cooked as it is ordered by the customer. This brings with it particular management problems of planning and control but it does mean that the incidence of work in progress is very low, that is, it is rarely necessary to value part-finished units of service at the end of an accounting period.

Many services also 'perish' immediately; for example, if a cinema seat is vacant when a film is showing it cannot be stored in inventory for a later sale. The opportunity to gain revenue from that seat at that particular showing of the film has been lost forever. Therefore, capacity utilisation becomes a very important issue for managers in many service organisations.

Example

Managerial reporting in a consultancy business

As you read through this example, notice that we are applying all of the principles of cost analysis that you have already learned about. The only difference is that the principles are being applied to determine the cost of intangible services, rather than of tangible products.

Mr G and Mrs H have recently formed a consultancy business and they wish to establish the following rates to charge clients:

- an hourly rate for productive client work;
- an hourly rate for time spent travelling to/from the clients' premises;
- a rate per mile for expenses incurred in travelling to/from the clients' premises.

Pricing policy

Mr G and Mrs H have decided that their pricing policy will be based on the cost per hour plus a 5% profit mark-up. Travelling time will be charged to clients at one-third of the normal hourly rate. Travelling expenses will be charged to clients at cost.

Activity estimates

Mr G and Mrs H each expect to work for 8 hours per day, 5 days per week, 45 weeks per year. They refer to this as 'available time'.

- 25% of the available time will be spent dealing with administrative matters relating to the general running of the business.
- In the first year, 22.5% of the available time will be idle, that is, no work will be done in this time.
- The remainder of the available time is expected to be chargeable to clients.
- Travelling time will amount to 25% of the chargeable time, during which a total of 18,000 miles will be travelled.

Cost estimates

- Mr G and Mrs H each wish to receive a salary of $25,000 in the first year of trading.
- Other costs to be incurred in the first year of trading:

	$
Electricity	1,200
Fuel for vehicles	1,800
Depreciation of vehicles	6,000
Insurance – professional liability and office	600
Vehicle insurance and road tax	1,080
Office rent and rates	8,400
Telephone expenses	3,000
General office expenses	8,900
Servicing and repair of vehicles	1,200

Required:

Calculate the three client charge rates that Mr G and Mrs H wish to establish.

Solution

Rate per mile for travelling expenses	$0.56
Hourly rate for productive client work	$48.07
Hourly rate for travelling time	$16.02

Workings:

We firstly need to classify the costs provided to determine the total cost associated with travelling, and that associated with providing consultancy services.

	Consultancy	*Travelling*
	$	$
Salaries	50,000	
Electricity	1,200	
Fuel		1,800
Depreciation		6,000
Insurance	600	
Vehicle insurance, etc.		1,080
Office rent and rates	8,400	
Telephone expenses	3,000	
General office expenses	8,900	
Servicing vehicles, etc.		1,200
	72,100	10,080

Now we need to determine the number of units of service by which each of these cost totals is to be divided.

The calculation of the rate per mile for travelling expenses is relatively straightforward:

$$\text{Rate per mile} = \frac{\text{Total travelling expenses}}{\text{Miles travelled}} = \frac{\$10{,}000}{18{,}000} = \mathbf{\$0.56\ per\ mile}$$

The calculation of the hourly rate for productive work and travelling time is a little more complicated. The first step is to determine the number of units of service supplied, that is, the chargeable hours. We need to look at the activity estimates provided in order to analyse the available time.

Total available hours for the first year:		*Hours*
(2 people × 8 hours × 5 days × 45 weeks)		3,600
Less: administration time	25.0%	
Less: idle time	22.5%	
	47.5% × 3,600	(1,710)
Time chargeable to clients		1,890
Productive time spent with clients (75%)		1,417.5
Travelling time (25%)		472.5

Travelling time will be charged at one-third of the normal hourly rate, therefore we need to calculate a 'weighted' figure for chargeable time.

Weighted chargeable hour $= 1{,}417.5 + \dfrac{472.5}{3} = 1{,}575$ hours

Now we can combine the consultancy services costs and the weighted chargeable time to determine an hourly rate for each type of work.

Cost per chargeable hour $= \dfrac{\$72{,}100}{1{,}575} = \$45.78$

Hourly rate for productive client work = $45.78 + 5% profit mark-up = **$48.07 per hour**

Hourly rate for travelling time $= \dfrac{\$48.07}{3} =$ **$16.02 per hour**

Test your understanding 3

Records for a passenger limousine company reveal the following data for last period:

No. of passengers	*Miles travelled*
80	4
40	5
90	6
100	7
140	8
180	9
150	10

The drivers' wages cost incurred was $1,100.

The drivers' wages cost per passenger mile was (to the nearest cent):

A $0.03

B $0.18

C $1.41

D $22.45

5 Not-for-profit organisations

Not-for-profit organisations such as local authorities and charities have their own rules and requirements in terms of accounting. Some of the measures we have looked at so far (gross margin, contribution, value added) will not always be appropriate in a not-for-profit organisation.

Local authorities and charities are normally more concerned about the output they are able to achieve for the funds they have available. They are usually constrained by the level of funding they have and will look at measures which allow them to assess their

- Effectiveness
- Efficiency
- Economy.

These are known as the 3Es.

Example of a managerial report for a charity

The TW Care Charity has just completed an overseas aid programme to assist homeless orphans. Cost and revenue data concerning the programme are as follows.

	$
Income from donations	157,750
Grants received from government and others	62,000
Fundraising costs	23,900
Direct staff costs, including travel and insurance	68,800
Medical supplies and temporary accommodation	78,120
Food, blankets and clothes	17,100
Transport costs	24,300
Other direct costs	9,800
Apportioned administrative support costs	13,200

Required:

Prepare a statement to enable managers to monitor the total net cost of the aid programme, highlighting any subtotals that you think may be useful to the managers.

Solution

TW Care Charity: Report on overseas aid programme

	$	$
Income from donations		157,750
Grants received from government and others		62,000
Gross revenue		219,750
Less fundraising costs		23,900
Net revenue		195,850
Direct staff costs, including travel and insurance	68,800	
Medical supplies and temporary accommodation	78,120	
Food, blankets, clothes	17,100	
Transport costs	24,300	
Other direct costs	9,800	
Total direct cost		198,120
Net direct cost of programme		(2,270)
Apportioned administrative support costs		13,200
Total net cost of programme		15,470

Points to note about the statement are as follows.

- The fundraising costs are netted off against the gross revenue. Managers can use the resulting net revenue to monitor the effectiveness of the fundraising activities undertaken.
- Direct costs of the programme are highlighted separately. Managers are able to see whether the net revenue from the fundraising efforts was sufficient to cover the directly identifiable costs of undertaking the programme. In this case, the direct costs exceeded the net fundraising revenue by $2,270.
- Administrative support costs are apportioned so that managers can see the final net impact of this programme on the charity's resources.

Test your understanding 4

The following data are available for the Central Hospital for the latest period.

Activity data	
Number of patients	1,040
Number of patient nights	4,750
Number of operating theatres	5
Number of days theatres in use during month	26
Number of hours theatres used per day	15

Cost data	$
Operating theatre costs in total	510,000
Updating patient records on admission	33,900
Bed scheduling costs	20,833
Nursing	1,077,000
Patient catering costs	244,200
Medical supplies	120,000
Patient laundry costs	100,000
Other patient care costs	60,900

Use this data to calculate the following cost control measures for the monthly management report, (to the nearest cent):

(a) Operating theatre cost per hour.

(b) Admission costs per patient.

(c) Patient care cost per night.

6 Chapter summary

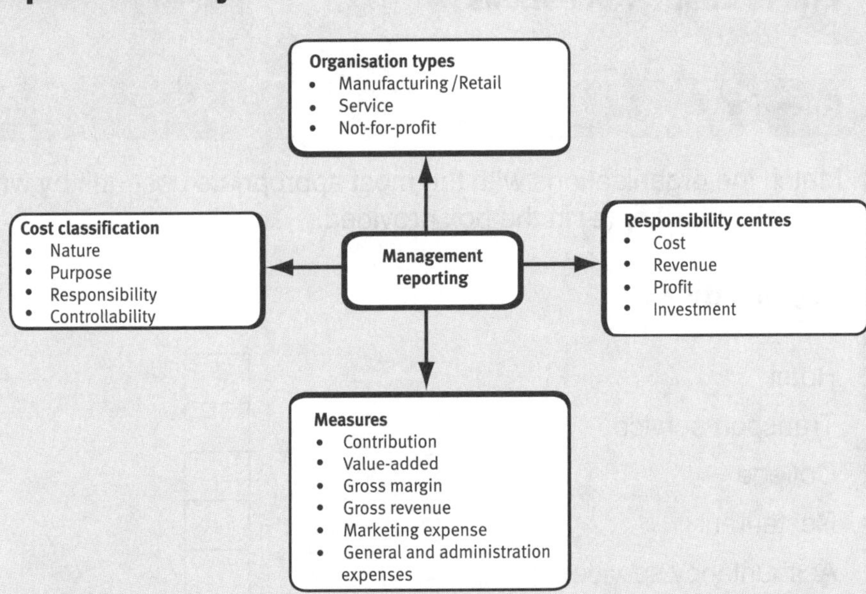
Organisation types
Manufacturing /Retail
Service
Not-for-profit
Cost classification
Nature
Purpose
Responsibility
Controllability
Management reporting
Responsibility centres
Cost
Revenue
Profit
Investment
Measures
Contribution
Value-added
Gross margin
Gross revenue
Marketing expense
General and administration expenses

7 End of chapter questions

Question 1

Match the organisations with the most appropriate cost unit by writing (a), (b), (c), (d) or (e) in the box provided.

Organisations

Hotel	
Transport service	
College	
Restaurant	
Accountancy service	

Cost units

(a) Enrolled student

(b) Meal served

(c) Chargeable hour

(d) Room night

(e) Tonne-kilometre

Question 2

Happy Stays hotel has 345 rooms. During the latest week, the following data were collected concerning unoccupied rooms.

Day	*Number of unoccupied rooms*
Monday	77
Tuesday	43
Wednesday	26
Thursday	31
Friday	17
Saturday	12
Sunday	88

(a) The number of occupied room nights during the week was ________.

(b) The overall percentage room occupancy rate during the week was % (to the nearest whole number) ________%

Question 3

State which of the following are characteristics of managerial reports prepared in a service organisation:

(i) a low incidence of work in progress at the end of a period

(ii) the use of composite cost units

(iii) the use of equivalent units

A (i) only

B (i) and (ii) only

C (ii) only

D (i), (ii) and (iii)

Question 4

An extract from the performance report of the HH Division for the latest period is as follows.

	$	$
Sales revenue		150,000
Cost of goods sold		
Material costs	25,600	
Labour costs	19,750	
Production overhead	23,400	
		68,750
Gross margin		81,250
Non-production overhead		39,700
Net profit		41,550

The following salary costs are included within the overhead costs:

	Salary cost included
Production overhead	$15,200
Non-production overhead	$ 7,950

For the HH Division for the latest period, the value added was $ ________.

Question 5

The Ludford Hotel and Conference Centre is used for conference bookings and private guest bookings. Conference bookings use some bedrooms each week, the balance being available for private guests.

Data have been collected relating to private guest bookings which are summarised below for a 10-week period.

Week	*Double rooms available for private guest bookings*	*Number of guests*	*Average stay (nights)*
1	55	198	2.1
2	60	170	2.6
3	72	462	1.4
4	80	381	3.2
5	44	83	5.6
6	62	164	3.4
7	80	348	2.6
8	54	205	1.7
9	80	442	1.8
10	24	84	3.2

Some of the costs for private guest bookings vary with the number of guests, regardless of the length of their stay, while others vary with the number of rooms available in any week.

Variable cost per guest	$17.50
Variable cost per week per room available	$56.00

The general fixed cost for private guest bookings per week is $8,100.

Required:

(a) To the nearest cent, the total costs for private guests' bookings for the 10-week period is $ ________.

(b) To the nearest whole number, the number of private guest-nights achieved in the 10-week period is ________.

(c) The number of private guest-nights available for the 10-week period is ________.

Question 6

LWL Ltd has two production divisions, Y and X which operate as investment centres. A report for April has been prepared for the two division, extracts are shown below:

	Y	X
	$000	$000
Sales revenue	3,000	4,100
Variable cost of production	1,560	2,430
Fixed cost of production	650	860
Marketing expenses	250	320
General and administration expenses	365	128
Capital employed	1,500	2,700

Calculate the return on capital employed for divisions Y and X.

Question 7

Which of the following is a correct calculation of value added?

A Sales revenue minus variable production costs

B Sales revenue minus direct labour costs

C Sales revenue minus all bought-in costs

D Sales revenue minus all variable costs

Question 8

Happy Returns Ltd operates a haulage business with three vehicles. The following estimated operating costs and performance data are available:

Petrol	$0.50 per km on average
Repairs	$0.30 per km
Depreciation	$1.00 per km, plus $50 per week per vehicle
Drivers' wages	$300.00 per week per vehicle
Supervision costs	$550.00 per week
Loading costs	$6.00 per tonne

During week 26 it is expected that all three vehicles will be used, 280 tonnes will be loaded and a total of 3,950 km travelled (including return journeys when empty) as shown in the following table:

Journey	*Tonnes carried (one way)*	*Kilometres (one way)*
1	34	180
2	28	265
3	40	390
4	32	115
5	26	220
6	40	480
7	29	90
8	26	100
9	25	135
	280	1,975

Required:

(a) The total variable operating cost incurred in week 26 was $ ________.

(b) The total fixed operating cost incurred in week 26 was $ ________.

(c) The total cost for week 26, including administration cost, amounted to $13,265. To the nearest cent, the average total cost per tonne-kilometre for week 26 was $ ________.

Test your understanding answers

Test your understanding 1

For the GFD Company for the latest period, the value added was **$395,050**:

Value added = sales revenue less materials costs and the cost of bought-in goods and services. Wages and salary costs are not bought-in costs and must be excluded when calculating the value added.

	$	$
Sales revenue		654,500
Less materials cost	120,360	
Less production overhead cost	36,950	
Less marketing overhead cost	42,540	
Less general and admin. overhead	59,600	
Total bought in goods and services		259,450
Value added		395,050

Test your understanding 2

ROCE (A) = **13%**

ROCE (B) = **9.8%**

$$\textbf{Return on capital employed (ROCE)} = \frac{\textbf{Earnings before interest and tax}}{\textbf{Capital employed}}$$

ROCE (A) = 65 ÷ 500 = 13%

ROCE (B) = 128 ÷ 1300 = 9.8%

Test your understanding 3

B

No. of passengers	*Miles travelled*	*Passenger miles*
80	4	320
40	5	200
90	6	540
100	7	700
140	8	1,120
180	9	1,620
150	10	1,500
	Total passenger miles	6,000

Drivers' wages cost per passenger mile = $1,100/6,000 = $0.18

Test your understanding 4

(a) Number of theatre hours = 5 theatres × 26 days × 15 hours = 1,950

Operating theatre cost per hour = $510,000/1,950 = **$261.54**

(b)

Admission costs	$
Updating patient records	33,900
Bed scheduling	20,833
Total admission costs	54,733

Admission costs per patient = $54,733/1,040 = **$52.63**

(c) *Patient care costs*

	$
Nursing	1,077,000
Patient catering costs	244,200
Medical supplies	120,000
Patient laundry costs	100,000
Other patient care costs	60,900
Total patient care costs	1,602,100

Patient care cost per patient night = $1,602,100/4,750 = **$337.28**

Question 1

Hotel	(d)
Transport service	(e)
College	(a)
Restaurant	(b)
Accountancy service	(c)

Question 2

(a) The number of occupied room nights during the week was **2,121**.

(b) The overall percentage room occupancy rate during the week was **88%**.

Workings:

Number of room nights available = 345 × 7 nights = 2,415 room nights
Total number of unoccupied room nights = 294
Number of occupied room nights = 2,415 – 294 = **2,121**

Percentage occupancy = 2,121/2,415 = **88%**

Question 3

B

Many services are consumed as soon as they are made available to the customer. They cannot be held in inventory for sale at a later date. Therefore there is a low incidence of work in progress at the end of a period.

Composite cost units are often used because they are more useful for control purposes, for example in a haulage company a cost per tonne mile might be more useful for planning and control purposes than a simple cost per tonne.

Equivalent units are more likely to be used in process costing.

Question 4

For the HH Division for the latest period, the value added was **$84,450**

Value added = sales revenue less materials costs and the cost of bought-in goods and services. Wages and salary costs are not bought-in costs and must be excluded from the overhead cost figures when calculating the value added.

	$	$	$
Sales revenue			150,000
Less materials cost		25,600	
Production overhead cost	23,400		
Less salaries included	15,200		
Bought-in production overhead cost		8,200	
Non-production overhead cost	39,700		
Less salaries included	7,950		
Bought-in non-production overhead cost		31,750	
Total bought in goods and services			65,550
Value added			84,450

Question 5

(a) **$159,613.50**

(b) **6,064 private guest nights achieved**

(c) **8,554 private guest nights available**

Workings:

You will be using a composite cost unit in this question: a guest night. The cost per guest night is the cost incurred by the hotel for one guest to stay for one night. In this example, the number of guest nights is calculated as:

Guest nights = number of guests × average number of nights stayed

Week	*Rooms*	*Guests*	*Average stay*	*Guest nights*
1	55	198	2.1	415.8
2	60	170	2.6	442.0
3	72	462	1.4	646.8
4	80	381	3.2	1,219.2
5	44	83	5.6	464.8
6	62	164	3.4	557.6
7	80	348	2.6	904.8
8	54	205	1.7	348.5
9	80	442	1.8	795.6
10	24	84	3.2	268.8
	611	2,537		6,063.9

(a) Total costs for private guests' bookings:

	$
Variable cost per room (611 × $56)	34,216.00
Variable cost per guest (2,537 × $17.50)	44,397.50
Fixed costs (10 × $8,100)	81,000.00
	159,613.50

(b) Guest nights achieved (from above table) = **6,064**.

(c) Guest nights available = 611 rooms × 7 nights × 2 guests = **8,554**

Question 6

ROCE (Y) = **11.7%**

ROCE (X) = **13.4%**

	Y	X
	$000	$000
Sales revenue	3,000	4,100
Variable cost of production	1,560	2,430
Fixed cost of production	650	860
Marketing expense	250	320
General and administration expenses	365	128
Net profit	175	362

Return on capital employed (ROCE) = $\dfrac{\textbf{Earnings before interest and tax}}{\textbf{Capital employed}}$

ROCE (Y) = 175 ÷ 1,500 = 11.7%

ROCE (X) = 362 ÷ 2,700 = 13.4%

Question 7

C

Direct labour is not a bought-in cost therefore options A, B and D are incorrect.

Question 8

(a) **$8,790**

(b) **$1,600**

(c) **$0.20**

Workings:

This question provides an example of the use of a composite cost unit. The cost per tonne-kilometre is the cost of transporting 1 tonne for 1 km.

Journey	*Tonnes carried*	*km*	*Tonne-km*
1	34	180	6,120
2	28	265	7,420
3	40	390	15,600
4	32	115	3,680
5	26	220	5,720
6	40	480	19,200
7	29	90	2,610
8	26	100	2,600
9	25	135	3,375
	280	1,975	66,325

Variable operating costs

			$
Loading: 280 × $6 =			1,680
		$ per km	
Running costs:	Petrol	0.50	
	Repairs	0.30	
	Depreciation	1.00	
		1.80 × 3,950	7,110
			8,790

Fixed operating costs

	$	
Depreciation (3 × $50)	150	
Supervision	550	
Drivers' wages (3 × $300)	900	
		1,600
Total operating cost		10,390

Average total cost per tonne-kilometre $= \dfrac{\$13{,}265}{66{,}325} =$ **$0.20**

chapter

12

Preparing for the Assessment

Chapter learning objectives

The next three chapters are intended for use when you are ready to start revising for your assessment. They contain:

- details of the format of the assessment;
- a summary of useful revision techniques;
- guidance on how to tackle the assessment;
- a bank of assessment-standard revision questions and suggested solutions;
- two mock assessments. These should be attempted when you consider yourself to be ready for the assessment, and you should simulate assessment conditions when you attempt them.

1 Format of the assessment

The assessment for *Fundamentals of Management Accounting* is a two hour computer-based assessment (CBA) comprising 50 objective test questions with one or more parts. There will be no choice of questions and all questions should be attempted if time permits. There is no penalty for incorrect answers.

Objective test questions are used. The most common type is multiple choice, where the candidate is required to select the correct answer from a list of possible options. Other types of objective test questions that may be used include true/false questions, matching pairs of text and graphic, sequencing and ranking, labelling diagrams and single and multiple numeric entry. Candidates answer the questions by pointing and clicking the mouse, moving objects around the screen, typing numbers, or a combination of these responses.

You are also advised to keep an eye on the articles in the 'Study Notes' section of *Financial Management* magazine which will forewarn of any changes in question styles. Students should also read the articles published in the student e-magazine *Velocity*.

Information about the CIMA Certificate level assessments can be found at: http://www.cimaglobal.com/cba2011

2 Revision technique

Planning

The first thing to say about revision is that it is an addition to your initial studies, not a substitute for them. In other words, don't coast along early in your course in the hope of catching up during the revision phase. On the contrary, you should be studying and revising concurrently from the outset. At the end of each week, and at the end of each month, get into the habit of summarising the material you have covered to refresh your memory of it.

As with your initial studies, planning is important to maximise the value of your revision work. You need to balance the demands for study, professional work, family life and other commitments. To make this work, you will need to think carefully about how to make best use of your time.

Begin by comparing the estimated hours you will need to devote to revision with the hours available to you in the weeks leading up to the assessment. Prepare a written schedule setting out the areas you intend to cover during particular weeks, and break that down further into topics for each day's revision. To help focus on the key areas try to establish which areas you are weakest on, so that you can concentrate on the topics where effort is particularly needed.

Do not forget the need for relaxation, and for family commitments. Sustained intellectual effort is only possible for limited periods, and must be broken up at intervals by lighter activities. Also, do not continue your revision timetable right up to the moment when you enter the assessment room; you should aim to stop work a day or even two days before the assessment. Beyond this point, the most you should attempt is an occasional brief look at your notes to refresh your memory.

Getting down to work

By the time you begin your revision you should already have settled into a fixed work pattern: a regular time of day for doing the work, a particular location where you sit, particular equipment that you assemble before you begin and so on. If this is not already a matter of routine for you, think carefully about it now in the last vital weeks before the assessment.

You should have notes summarising the main points of each topic you have covered. Begin each session by reading through the relevant notes and trying to commit the important points to memory.

Usually this will be just your starting point. Unless the area is one where you already feel very confident, you will need to track back from your notes to the relevant chapter(s). This will refresh your memory on points not covered by your notes and fill in the detail that inevitably gets lost in the process of summarisation.

When you think you have understood and memorised the main principles and techniques, attempt some assessment questions. At this stage of your studies, you should normally be expecting to complete the questions in something close to the actual time allocation allowed in the assessment. After completing your effort, check the solution provided and add to your notes any extra points it reveals.

Tips for the final revision phase

As the assessment looms closer, consider the following list of techniques and make use of those that work for you:

- Summarise your notes into a more concise form, perhaps on index cards that you can carry with you for revision on the way to work.
- Go through your notes with a highlighter pen, marking key concepts and definitions.
- Summarise the main points in a key area by producing a wordlist, mind map or other mnemonic device.
- On areas that you find difficult, rework questions that you have already attempted, and compare your answers with those provided.
- Rework questions you attempted earlier in your studies with a view to completing them within the time limits.

- In the week preceding the assessment, quickly go through any recent articles in the 'Study Notes' section of *Financial Management* magazine, paying particular attention to those relevant to your subject.
- Avoid late-night study, as your assessment is based on daytime performance, not night-time performance.
- Make sure that you cover the whole syllabus in your revision, as all questions in the assessment are compulsory.

3 How to tackle the assessment

Assessment day

- Before leaving for the assessment you should ensure that you know where you are going: plan your route and ensure that you have the necessary documentation with you.
- Arrive early and settle into your assessment environment. You will have enough nerves on the day without compounding them by arriving late.

The assessment

Multiple-choice questions

Multiple-choice questions (MCQs) are broken down into two parts; the problem or task to be solved, and the options you must choose from. There is only ever one correct answer: the other options are known as distractors.

Your approach to MCQs should be as follows:

- For numerical MCQs, in the majority of cases you will need to do some rough workings.
- Never rush to select your answer; some options might initially look plausible, but on closer scrutiny turn out to be distractors. Unless you are certain of the answer, look carefully at *all* the options before choosing.
- If you are finding the MCQ difficult and you are taking up too much time, move on to the next one.
- Time permitting, revisit those MCQs which you left unanswered and refer to your original workings.
- Remember: you must never omit to answer any question in the assessment as there is no penalty for an incorrect answer.

Other types of question

- Prepare neat workings where necessary *for your own benefit*. Only your final answers will be marked, not workings, methods or justifications. However, your workings will help you to achieve the necessary 100% accuracy.
- Check your answer carefully. If you have typed in your answer, check the figures are typed correctly.

4 Question bank

Test your understanding 1

Management accounting

Place each of the comments on the left in the correct box, depending on whether it relates to management or financial accounting.

	Management accounting	Financial accounting
Forward looking		
Statutory requirement		
Uses both financial and non-financial information		
Links closely with taxation and auditing		
Used in performance measurement		
Used in internal decision making		

Test your understanding 2

Management accounting

Which one of the following is used for control purposes within organisations?

A Process costing

B Breakeven analysis

C Limiting factor analysis

D Standard costing

Test your understanding 3

Management information

Place each of the characteristics of information shown on the left in the correct box on the right, depending on whether it relates to strategic **or** operational levels.

	Strategic level	Operational level
Detailed		
Historical		
Accurate		
Subjective		
Summarised		

Test your understanding 4

Management accounting

Which one of the following shows the three main purposes of management accounting?

A Planning, Reporting and Controlling

B Reporting, Auditing and Controlling

C Decision making, Planning and Reporting

D Planning, Controlling and Decision Making

Test your understanding 5

CIMA

Are the following statements about CIMA *true* or *false*?

A CIMA was established 50 years ago

B Members of CIMA are known as Chartered Certified Accountants

C CIMA is a worldwide organisation

D CIMA may discipline students or members who bring the profession into disrepute

Test your understanding 6

High–low method

The following data relate to the overhead expenditure of a contract cleaner at two activity levels:

Square metres cleaned	12,750	15,100
Overheads	$73,950	$83,585

What is the estimate of the overheads if 16,200 square metres are to be cleaned?

A $88,095

B $89,674

C $93,960

D $98,095

Test your understanding 7

Cost behaviour patterns

AG Ltd rents an office photocopier for $300 per month. In addition, the cost incurred per copy taken is $0.02.

If $ y = total photocopying cost for the month and x = the number of photocopies taken, which of the following would express the total photocopying cost for a month:

A y = 300 + 2x

B y = 300x + 2

C y = 300 + 0.02x

D y = 300x + 0.02

Test your understanding 8

Cost object

Which of the following could be used as a cost object in an organisation's costing system? (*tick all that apply).*

(i)	Customer number 879	□
(ii)	Department A	□
(iii)	The finishing process in department A	□
(iv)	Product H	□
(v)	Employee number 776	□
(vi)	Order processing activity	□

Test your understanding 9

Direct cost and indirect cost

Which of the following costs would a local council classify as a direct cost of providing a door-to-door refuse collection service? *Tick all that apply.*

(i)	Depreciation of the refuse collection vehicle	□
(ii)	Wages paid to refuse collectors	□
(iii)	Cost of leaflets sent to customers to advertise refuse collection times and dates	□
(iv)	Employer's liability insurance premium to cover all council employees	□

Test your understanding 10

Full cost

'The only cost that is really useful in setting a selling price for a particular service to be provided is the full cost'.

Is the above statement true or false?

Test your understanding 11

Direct cost

Wages paid to which of the following would be classified as direct labour costs of the organisation's product or service. *Tick all that apply.*

A driver in a taxi company	☐
A carpenter in a construction company	☐
An assistant in a factory canteen	☐
A hair stylist in a beauty salon.	☐

Test your understanding 12

Cost attribution

A method of accounting for overheads involves attributing them to cost units using predetermined rates. This is known as:

A overhead allocation

B overhead apportionment

C overhead absorption

D overhead analysis

Test your understanding 13

Overhead absorption

A company absorbs overheads on standard machine hours which were budgeted at 11,250 with overheads of $258,750. Actual results were 10,980 standard machine hours with overheads of $254,692. Overheads were:

A under-absorbed by $2,152

B over-absorbed by $4,058

C under-absorbed by $4,058

D over-absorbed by $2,152

Test your understanding 14

Overhead absorption rates

XX Ltd absorbs overheads based on units produced. In one period, 23,000 units were produced, actual overheads were $276,000 and overheads were under absorbed by $46,000.

The budgeted overhead absorption rate per unit was:

A $10

B $12

C $13

D $14

Test your understanding 15

Overhead absorption

XY operates a standard absorption costing system. Data for last period are as follows:

Budgeted labour hours	48,500
Actual standard labour hours	49,775
Budgeted overheads	$691,125
Actual overheads	$746,625

To the nearest whole number, the overhead for the period was (*tick the box to indicate whether the overhead was over- or under-absorbed, and insert the value of the under- or over-absorption).*

$ _______.

under-absorbed □

over-absorbed □

The following data is required for Questions 16 and 17.

TRI-D Ltd has three production departments – Assembly, Machining and Finishing – and a service department known as Production Services which works for the production departments in the ratio of 3:2:1.

The following data, which represent normal activity levels, have been budgeted for the period ending 31 December 20X6:

	Assembly	*Machining*	*Finishing*	*Production Services*	*Total*
Direct labour hours	7,250	9,000	15,000		31,250
Machine hours	15,500	20,000	2,500	2,000	40,000
Floor area (m^2)	800	1,200	1,000	1,400	4,400
Equipment value	$160,000	$140,000	$30,000	$70,000	$400,000
Employees	40	56	94	50	240

Test your understanding 16

Overhead analysis

The template being used by the management accountant to analyse the overheads for the period is shown below:

		Extrusion	*Machining*	*Finishing*	*Production Services*	*Total*
Cost allocated	*Basis*	$	$	$	$	$
Indirect wages	Allocated					102,000
Apportioned						
Depreciation	Equipment value		**A**			84,000
Rates	Floor area	**B**				22,000
Power				**C**		180,000
Personnel					**D**	60,000
Other						48,000
					109,600	
Production services		**E**			(109,600)	
					–	496,000

The values that would be entered on the overhead analysis sheet at A to E are:

A	
B	
C	
D	
E	

Test your understanding 17

Overhead analysis

After completion of the allocation, apportionment and reapportionment exercise, the total departmental overheads are:

Assembly	*Machining*	*Finishing*
$206,350	$213,730	$75,920

Calculate appropriate overhead absorption rates (to two decimal places) for the period ending 31 December 20X6 and tick the box to indicate in each case whether labour hours or machine hours are to be used as the absorption basis:

(i) Assembly:	$	per labour hour	□
		per machine hour	□
(ii) Machining:	$	per labour hour	□
		per machine hour	□
(iii) Finishing:	$	per labour hour	□
		per machine hour	□

Test your understanding 18

Overhead analysis

X Ltd has two production cost centres (Machining and Assembly) and two service departments (Stores and Maintenance). The management accountant has just completed the allocation and apportionment of overheads to the four departments. The analysis showed:

	Machining	*Assembly*	*Stores*	*Maintenance*	*Total*
	$	$	$	$	$
Total	2,250,000	1,900,000	250,000	800,000	5,200,000

The management accountant has now established the workloads of the service departments. The service departments provide services to each other as well as to the production departments as shown below:

	Machining	*Assembly*	*Stores*	*Maintenance*
Stores	30%	30%	–	40%
Maintenance	45%	30%	25%	–

After the apportionment of the service department overheads to the production departments (and acknowledging the reciprocal servicing), the total overhead for the machining department will be $ _______ (to the nearest $000).

Test your understanding 19

Elements of cost

Data concerning one unit of product B produced last period are as follows.

Direct material 3 kg @ $9 per kg

Direct labour:	department A	4 hours @ $14 per hour
	department B	6 hours @ $11 per hour

Machine hours:	department A	3 hours
	department B	2 hours

Production overhead is absorbed at a rate of $7 per direct labour hour in department A and $6 per machine hour in department B.

(a) The direct cost per unit of product B is $ _______

(b) The full production cost per unit of product B is $ _______

Data for Questions 20 and 21.

JJ Ltd manufactures a product which has a selling price of $14, a variable cost of $6 per unit. The company incurs annual fixed costs of $24,400. Annual sales demand is 8,000 units.

New production methods are under consideration, which would cause a 30% increase in fixed costs and a reduction in variable cost to $5 per unit. The new production methods would result in a superior product and would enable sales to be increased to 8,500 units per annum at a price of $15 each.

Test your understanding 20

Breakeven analysis

If the change in production methods were to take place, the breakeven output level would be:

A 122 units higher

B 372 units higher

C 610 units lower

D 915 units higher

Test your understanding 21

Breakeven analysis

If the organisation implements the new production methods and wishes to achieve the same profit as that under the existing method, how many units would need to be produced and sold annually to achieve this?

A 7,132 units

B 8,000 units

C 8,500 units

D 9,710 units

Test your understanding 22

Breakeven analysis

X Ltd produces and sells a single product, which has a contribution to sales ratio of 30%. Fixed costs amount to $120,000 each year.

The number of units of sale required each year to break even:

A is 156,000

B is 171,428

C is 400,000

D cannot be calculated from the data supplied

The following graph relates to Questions 23 and 24.

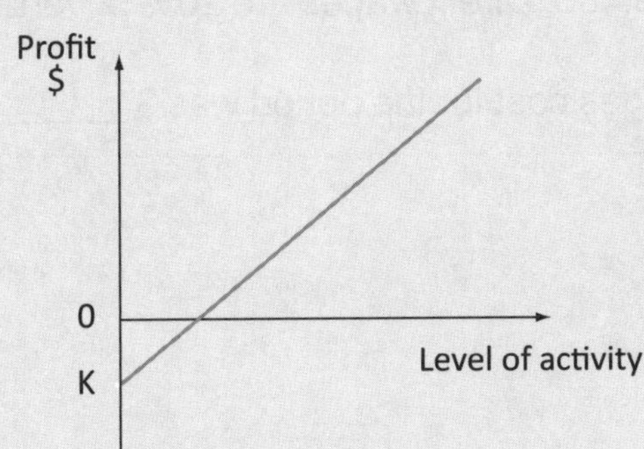

Test your understanding 23

Breakeven graph

Point K on the graph indicates the value of:

A semi-variable cost

B total cost

C variable cost

D fixed cost

Test your understanding 24

C-V-P analysis

This graph is known as a:

A conventional breakeven chart

B contribution breakeven chart

C semi-variable cost chart

D profit–volume chart

Test your understanding 25

Cost analysis

A company makes a single product which generates a contribution to sales ratio of 30%. In a period when fixed costs were $30,000 the net profit was $56,400. Direct wages are 20% of variable costs.

The direct wages cost for the period was $ _______.

Test your understanding 26

Breakeven analysis

A company makes and sells a single product. If the fixed costs incurred in making and selling the product decrease:

(tick the correct boxes)

	Increase	*Decrease*	*Stay the same*
(a) the breakeven point will	□	□	□
(b) the contribution to sales ratio will	□	□	□
(c) the margin of safety will	□	□	□

Test your understanding 27

Cost behaviour/breakeven chart

Z plc operates a single retail outlet selling direct to the public. Profit statements for August and September are as follows:

	August	*September*
	$	$
Sales	80,000	90,000
Cost of sales	50,000	55,000
Gross profit	30,000	35,000
Less:		
Selling and distribution	8,000	9,000
Administration	15,000	15,000
Net profit	7,000	11,000

The data for August has been used to draw the following breakeven chart:

Contribution breakeven chart

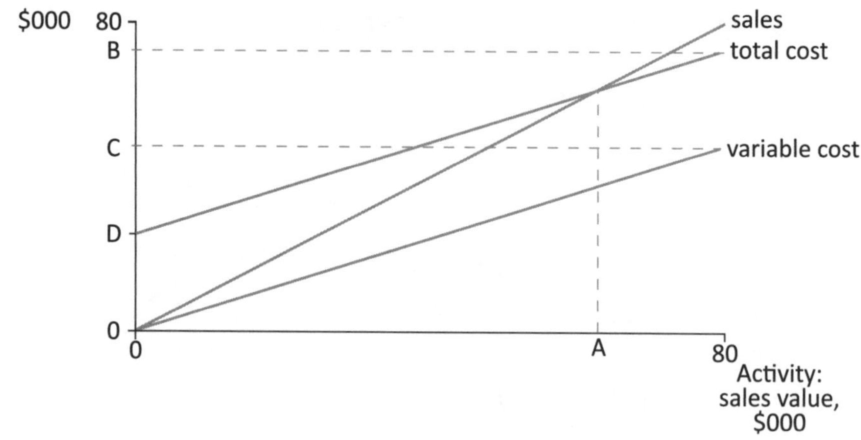

Required:

The values of A–D read from the chart would be:

A	
B	
C	
D	

Test your understanding 28

Limiting factor

The following budgeted information is available for a company that manufactures four types of specialist paints:

	Product W per batch	*Product X per batch*	*Product Y per batch*	*Product Z per batch*
	$	$	$	$
Selling price	20.00	15.00	15.00	17.50
Variable overhead	9.60	6.00	9.60	8.50
Fixed overhead	3.60	3.00	2.10	2.10
Profit	6.80	6.00	3.30	6.90
Machine hours per batch	12	9	6	11

All four products use the same machine.

In a period when machine hours are in short supply, the product that makes the most profitable use of machine hours is:

A Product W

B Product X

C Product Y

D Product Z

Test your understanding 29

Limiting factor decision-making

Triproduct Ltd makes and sells three types of electronic security systems for which the following information is available:

Standard cost and selling prices per unit

	Day scan	*Night scan*	*Omni scan*
	$	$	$
Materials	70	110	155
Manufacturing labour	40	55	70
Installation labour	24	32	44
Variable overheads	16	20	28
Selling price	250	320	460

Fixed costs for the period are $450,000 and the installation labour is available for 25,000 hours only in a period and is paid $8 per hour.

Both manufacturing and installation labour are variable costs.

The maximum demand for the products is:

Day scan	2,000 units
Night scan	3,000 units
Omni scan	1,800 units

Required:

(a) The shortfall in hours of installation labour each period is ________ hours.

(b) In order to maximise profits for the next period, the optimum production plan is:

Day scan		units
Night scan		units
Omni scan		units

Test your understanding 30

Make or buy decision

P Limited is considering whether to continue making a component or buy it from an outside supplier.

The internal manufacturing cost comprises:

	$/unit
Direct materials	3.00
Direct labour	5.00
Variable overhead	1.50
Specific fixed cost	3.00
Apportioned fixed costs	2.50
	15.00

The maximum price per component at which buying is preferable to internal manufacture is $ _______.

Test your understanding 31

Relevant cost

A company is evaluating a project that requires 4,000 kg of a material that is used regularly in normal production. 2,500 kg of the material, purchased last month at a total cost of $20,000, are in inventory. Since last month the price of the material has increased by 2.5 %.

What is the total relevant cost of the material for the project?

A $12,300

B $20,500

C $32,300

D $32,800

Test your understanding 32

Relevant cost

A company has just secured a new contract that requires 1,000 hours of labour.

There are 600 hours of spare labour capacity. The remaining hours could be worked as overtime at double time or labour could be diverted from the production of product X. Product X currently earns a contribution of $8 in four labour hours and direct labour is currently paid at a rate of $10 per normal hour.

What is the relevant cost of labour for the contract?

A $7,200

B $8,000

C $4,800

D $10,000

Test your understanding 33

Standard costing

Which of the following are not provided by a system of standard costing and variance analysis?

A Unit standard costs as a benchmark for comparison

B Variances to direct managers' attention where control action will be most worthwhile

C Actual unit costs to be incurred in the future

D Unit standard costs for budgetary planning

Test your understanding 34

Standard cost

JR Limited produces product H. The standard cost card indicates that each unit of H requires 4 kg of material W and 2 kg of material X at a standard price of $1 and $5 per kg, respectively.

Standard direct labour hours required per unit are 14 at a standard rate of $8 per hour. Variable production overheads are absorbed at a rate of $4 per direct labour hour.

The standard variable production cost of one unit of product H is $ ______.

Test your understanding 35

Materials variances

In a period, 11,280 kg of material were used at a total standard cost of $46,248. The material usage variance was $492 adverse. What was the standard allowed weight of material for the period?

A 11,520 kg

B 11,280 kg

C 11,394 kg

D 11,160 kg

Test your understanding 36

Variance analysis

During a period, 25,600 labour hours were worked at a standard rate of $7.50 per hour. The direct labour efficiency variance was $8,250 adverse.

The number of standard hours produced was ______.

Test your understanding 37

Labour variances

Direct labour cost data relating to last month is as follows:

Actual hours worked	28,000
Total direct labour cost	$117,600
Direct labour rate variance	$8,400 Adverse
Direct labour efficiency variance	$3,900 Favourable

To the nearest thousand hours, the number of standard labour hours produced last month was

A 31,000 hrs

B 29,000 hrs

C 27,000 hrs

D 25,000 hrs

Test your understanding 38

Labour variances

In a period, 6,500 units were made and there was an adverse labour efficiency variance of $26,000. Workers were paid $8 per hour, total wages were $182,000 and there was a nil rate variance.

How many standard labour hours were allowed per unit?

A 3 hours

B 3.5 hours

C 4 hours

D They cannot be calculated without more information.

Test your understanding 39

Sales variances

Budgeted sales of product V are 4,800 units per month. The standard selling price and variable cost of product V are $45 per unit and $25 per unit respectively.

During June the sales revenue achieved from actual sales of 4,600 units of product V amounted to $249,700.

(a) The sales price variance for product V for June was $ _______ adverse/favourable (*delete as appropriate*).

(b) The sales volume contribution variance for product V for June was $ _______ adverse/favourable (*delete as appropriate*).

Test your understanding 40

Contribution reconciliation

The following variances have been calculated for the latest period:

	$
Sales volume contribution variance	13,420(F)
Material usage variance	5,400 (F)
Labour rate variance	310 (A)
Variable overhead expenditure variance	6,250 (A)

All other variances were zero. The budgeted contribution for the period was $37,200.

The actual contribution reported for the period was $ _______.

Test your understanding 41

Variance interpretation

The direct labour efficiency variance for the latest period was adverse. Which of the following reasons could have contributed to this variance? (*tick all that apply*).

(a) Output was higher than budgeted ☐

(b) The purchasing department bought poor quality material which was difficult to process ☐

(c) The original standard time for the output was set too low ☐

(d) The hourly labour rate was higher than had been expected when the standard was set ☐

(e) Employees were more skilled than specified in the standard ☐

Test your understanding 42

Variance interpretation

The sales volume contribution variance for the latest period was favourable. Which of the following reasons could have contributed to this variance? (*tick all that apply*).

(a) A lower selling price was charged than standard ☐

(b) The variable cost per unit was lower than standard, which led to a higher actual contribution per unit than standard ☐

(c) Demand for the product was greater than had been expected ☐

Test your understanding 43

Integrated accounts

A company operates an integrated cost and financial accounting system. The accounting entries for the return to stores of unused direct materials from production would be:

	Debit	*Credit*
A	Work in progress account	Stores control account
B	Stores control account	Work in progress account
C	Stores control account	Finished goods account
D	Cost of sales account	Work in progress account

Test your understanding 44

Integrated accounts

ABC Ltd operates an integrated cost accounting system. The y/e production overhead control account was as follows:

Production overhead control account

	$		$
Trade payables	50,000	Work in progress	120,000
Bank	20,000	?	5,000
Depreciation	5,000		
Salaries	40,000		
Materials	10,000		
	125,000		125,000

The $5,000 credit entry represents the value of the transfer to:

A the statement of profit or loss for the under-recovery of production overheads.

B the statement of profit or loss for the over-recovery of production overheads.

C the work in progress account for the under-recovery of production overheads.

D the following period.

Test your understanding 45

Integrated accounts

Wages incurred last period amounted to \$33,400, of which \$27,400 were direct wages and \$6,000 were indirect production wages. Wages paid in cash were \$31,700.

Which of the following entries would arise as a result of these transactions? (*tick all that are correct).*

			\$	
(a)	Debit	Wages control account	33,400	□
(b)	Debit	Wages control account	31,700	□
(c)	Debit	Work in progress account	27,400	□
(d)	Debit	Production overhead control account	6,000	□
(e)	Credit	Wages control account	33,400	□
(f)	Credit	Wages control account	31,700	□
(g)	Credit	Work in progress account	27,400	□
(h)	Credit	Production overhead control account	6,000	□

The following data relates to Questions 46 and 47.

WYZ Limited operates an integrated accounting system.

The following information was available for period 7:

	\$
Cost of finished goods produced	1,241,500
Direct wages	173,400
Direct material issues	598,050
Indirect material issues	32,800
Direct material purchases on credit	617,300
Production overheads (actual expenditure)	359,725
Depreciation of production machinery	35,000

At the beginning of the period, the relevant account balances were:

Account	$
Work in progress control	125,750
Direct material stores control	48,250

Production overheads are absorbed on the basis of 280% of direct wages cost. Any production overheads under- or over-absorbed for the period are transferred to the statement of profit or loss at the end of the period.

Test your understanding 46

Integrated accounting systems

Direct material stores control account (extract)

	$		$
Balance b/f	**A**	Work in progress	**B**
Payables	**C**	Production overhead control	**D**

The values that would be entered as A–D in the above account extract are:

A $	
B $	
C $	
D $	

Test your understanding 47

Integrated accounting systems

(i) The production overheads for the period were:

under-absorbed □

over-absorbed □

(ii) The value of the under-/over-absorption was $ _______

(iii) In the statement of profit or loss at the end of the period, this amount will be transferred as a:

credit □

debit □

Test your understanding 48

Standard cost bookkeeping

A company uses standard costing and an integrated accounting system. The double entry to record a favourable labour rate variance is:

	Debit	*Credit*
A	Work in progress account	Labour rate variance account
B	Labour rate variance account	Work in progress account
C	Wages control account	Labour rate variance account
D	Labour rate variance account	Wages control account

Test your understanding 49

Standard cost bookkeeping

STD Ltd operates an integrated standard costing system for its single product. All inventories are valued at standard price.

During a period the following variances were recorded:

	Favourable	*Adverse*
	$	$
Material price		3,950
Material usage	1,925	
Labour rate		1,325
Labour efficiency	1,750	

Tick the correct boxes to show the entries that will be made to record the material price variance.

	Debit	*Credit*	*No entry in this account*
Materials control account	□	□	□
Material price variance account	□	□	□
Work in progress account	□	□	□

Tick the correct boxes to show the entries that will be made to record the material usage variance.

	Debit	*Credit*	*No entry in this account*
Materials control account	□	□	□
Material usage variance account	□	□	□
Work in progress account	□	□	□

The labour force was paid at a:

higher hourly rate than standard	□
lower hourly rate than standard	□

Tick the correct boxes to show the entries that will be made to record the labour efficiency variance.

	Debit	*Credit*	*No entry in this account*
Wages control account	☐	☐	☐
Labour efficiency variance account	☐	☐	☐
Work in progress account	☐	☐	☐

Test your understanding 50

Pricing to achieve a specified return on investment

Data for product Q are as follows.

Direct material cost per unit	$54
Direct labour cost per unit	$87
Direct labour hours per unit	11hours
Production overhead absorption rate	$7 per direct labour hour
Mark-up for non-production overhead costs	3%

10,000 units of product Q are budgeted to be sold each year. Product Q requires an investment of $220,000 and the target rate of return on investment is 14% per annum.

The selling price for one unit of product Q, to the nearest cent is $ _______.

Test your understanding 51

Job costing

An accountant is to set up in private practice. She anticipates working a 35-hour week and taking four weeks' holiday per year. General expenses of the practice are expected to be $20,000 per year, and she has set herself a target of $40,000 a year salary.

Assuming that only 75% of her time worked will be chargeable to clients, what should she quote (to the nearest $) for a job anticipated to take 50 hours?

A $1,587

B $1,786

C $2,381

D $2,976

Test your understanding 52

Job costing

A company has been asked to quote for a job. The company aims to make a net profit of 30% on sales. The estimated cost for the job is as follows:

Direct materials	10 kg @ $10 per kg
Direct labour	10 hours @ $10 per hour

Variable production overheads are recovered at the rate of $4 per labour hour.

Fixed production overheads for the company are budgeted to be $200,000 each year and are recovered on the basis of labour hours. There are 10,000 budgeted labour hours each year.

Other costs in relation to selling, distribution and administration are recovered at the rate of $50 per job.

The company quote for the job should be:

A $572

B $637

C $700

D $833

Test your understanding 53

Job/batch costing

Acme Electronics Ltd makes specialist electronic equipment to order. There are three main departments: Preparation, Etching and Assembly. Preparation and Etching are departments which use a considerable amount of machinery while Assembly is mainly a manual operation using simple hand tools.

For period 7, the following budgets have been prepared:

	Production overheads	
Department	$	*Activity*
Preparation	165,000	3,000 machine hours
Etching	98,000	1,400 machine hours
Assembly	48,600	1,800 labour hours

During the period, an enquiry is received for a batch of 200 control units for which the following estimates have been made:

Total direct materials	$26,500
Preparation	260 machine hours
	90 labour hours at $8 per hour
Etching	84 machine hours
	130 labour hours at $7 per hour
Assembly	180 labour hours at $6 per hour

Required:

(a) (i) The prime cost of the batch of 200 control units is $ _______

(ii) The production overhead cost of the batch of 200 control units is:

Preparation Department overheads:	$	
Etching Department overheads:	$	
Assembly Department overheads:	$	

(b) After an addition has been made to the batch cost to cover administrative overheads, the total cost of the batch of 200 control units is $65,100.

If the company wishes to achieve a 30% profit margin on sales, the price per control unit which should be quoted is $ _______.

Data for Questions 54 to 56.

A company produces a single product that passes through two processes. The details for process 1 are as follows:

Materials input	20,000 kg at $2.50 per kg
Direct labour	$15,000
Production overheads	150% of direct labour

Normal losses are 15% of input in process 1 and without further processing any losses can be sold as scrap for $1 per kg.

The output for the period was 18,500 kg from process 1.

There was no work in progress at the beginning or at the end of the period.

Test your understanding 54

Process costing

What value (to the nearest $) will be credited to the process 1 account in respect of the normal loss?

A Nil

B $3,000

C $4,070

D $5,250

Test your understanding 55

Process costing

What is the value (to the nearest $) of the abnormal loss/gain for the period in process 1?

A $6,104

B $6,563

C $7,257

D $7,456

Test your understanding 56

Process costing

What is the value (to the nearest $) of the output to process 2?

A $88,813

B $90,604

C $91,956

D $94,063

Test your understanding 57

Process costing

A cleansing detergent is manufactured by passing raw material through two processes. The details of the process costs for Process 1 for April were as follows:

Opening work in progress	5,000 litres valued as follows:	
	Material cost	$2,925
	Conversion costs	$6,600
Raw material input	50,000 litres valued at a cost of	$37,500
Conversion costs		$62,385

Normal loss is 3% of the input during the period and has a scrap value of $0.20 per litre. It is company policy to deduct the income from the sale of normal loss from that period's materials cost.

Actual output to Process 2	49,000 litres
Closing work in progress	4,000 litres, which were 100% complete for materials and 40% complete for conversion costs.

The cost per equivalent unit has been calculated as:

Materials: $0.75

Conversion: $1.35

(a) The total value of the transfers to process 2 is $ ________.

(b) The value of the abnormal loss is $ ________.

(c) The value of the closing work in progress is $ ________.

Test your understanding 58

Process costing

Industrial Solvents Ltd mixes together three chemicals – A, B and C – in the ratio 3:2:1 to produce Allklean, a specialised anti-static fluid. The chemicals cost $8, $6 and $3.90 per litre, respectively.

In a period, 12,000 litres in total were input to the mixing process. The normal process loss is 5% of input and in the period there was an abnormal loss of 100 litres, while the completed production was 9,500 litres. There was no opening work in progress (WIP) and the closing WIP was 100% complete for materials and 40% complete for labour and overheads. Labour and overheads were $41,280 in total for the period. Materials lost in production are scrapped.

Required:

(a) The number of equivalent litres of labour and overhead produced during the period was ________ equivalent litres.

(b) The cost per equivalent litre of materials produced was $ ________.

Test your understanding 59

Process costing

A company manufactures a variety of liquids which pass through a number of processes. One of these products, P, passes through processes 1, 2 and 3 before being transferred to the finished goods warehouse.

The following process 3 data are available for October:

	$
Work in process at 1 October is 6,000 units, valued as:	
Transfer from process 2	14,400
Materials added	2,160
Wages and overhead	2,880
	19,440
Transfer from process 2 during October:	
48,000 units	110,400
Transferred to finished goods: 46,500 units	
Costs incurred:	
Materials added	27,180
Wages and overhead	54,720
Work in process at 31 October: 4,000 units	
Degree of completion:	
Materials added: 50%	
Wages and overhead: 30%	

Normal loss in process: 6% × (units in opening WIP *plus* transfers from process 2 *less* closing WIP)

At a certain stage in the process, it is convenient for the quality control inspector to examine the product and, where necessary, to reject it. Rejected products are sold for $0.80 per unit. During October an actual loss of 7% was incurred, with product P having reached the following stage of production:

Direct materials added: 80%

Wages and overhead: 60%

Required:

The cost per equivalent unit produced was:

(a) process 2 input:	$		per equivalent unit
(b) material added:	$		per equivalent unit
(c) wages and overhead:	$		per equivalent unit.

Test your understanding 60

The role of budgets

Which of the following is not a main role of a budget?

A A budget gives authority to budget managers to incur expenditure in their area of responsibility

B A budget provides a means for an organisation to expand its activities

C A budget coordinates the activities of various parts of the organisation

D A budget acts as a comparator for current performance

Test your understanding 61

Principal budget factor

A principal budget factor is:

A the highest value item of cost

B a factor which limits the activities of an undertaking

C a factor common to all budget centres

D a factor controllable by the manager of the budget centre

Test your understanding 62

IT in the budget process

Which of the following are benefits of using a computerised budget system as opposed to a manual one? *(tick all that are correct.)*

(a) □ data used in drawing up the budget can be processed more quickly.

(b) □ budget targets will be more acceptable to the managers responsible for their achievement.

(c) □ changes in variables can be incorporated into the budget more quickly.

(d) □ the principal budget factor can be identified before budget preparation begins.

(e) □ continuous budgeting is only possible using a computerised system.

Test your understanding 63

Production budget

AB Ltd is currently preparing its production budget for product Z for the forthcoming year. The sales director has confirmed that he requires 120,000 units of product Z. Opening inventory is estimated to be 13,000 units and the company wishes to reduce inventory at the end of the year by 50%. How many units of product Z will need to be produced?

A 113,500 units

B 120,000 units

C 126,500 units

D 133,000 units

Test your understanding 64

Material budget

A company is currently preparing a material usage budget for the forthcoming year for material Z that will be used in product XX. The production director has confirmed that the production budget for product XX will be 10,000 units.

Each unit of product XX requires 4 kg of material Z. Opening inventory of material Z is budgeted to be 3,000 kg and the company wishes to reduce inventory at the end of the year by 25%.

What is the usage budget for material Z for the forthcoming year?

A 34,750 kg

B 39,250 kg

C 40,000 kg

D 40,750 kg

Test your understanding 65

Functional budgets

Budgeted sales of product P for next month are 4,000 units. Each unit of P requires 2 kg of raw material. Other budget information for next month is as follows:

Raw materials	
Opening inventories	3,000 kg
Closing inventories	4,500 kg
Finished product P	
Opening inventories	2,400 units
Closing inventories	1,800 units

The budgeted purchases of raw material for next month should be:

A 8,000 kg

B 8,300 kg

C 9,500 kg

D 12,500 kg

Test your understanding 66

Cash budget

The following details have been extracted from the receivables collection records of X Ltd:

Invoices paid in the month after sale	60%
Invoices paid in the second month after sale	20%
Invoices paid in the third month after sale	15%
Bad debts	5%

Credit sales for June to August are budgeted as follows:

June	$100,000
July	$150,000
August	$130,000

Customers paying in the month after sale are entitled to deduct a 2% settlement discount. Invoices are issued on the last day of the month. The amount budgeted to be received in September from credit sales is

A $115,190

B $116,750

C $121,440

D $123,000

Test your understanding 67

Budgetary control

Tick the correct box.

A budget which is designed to show the allowed expenditure for the actual level of activity achieved is known as

a rolling budget □

a flexible budget □

a fixed budget □

Test your understanding 68

Functional budgets

RD Ltd is in the process of preparing its budgets for 20X2. The company produces and sells a single product, Z, which currently has a selling price of $100 for each unit.

The budgeted sales units for 20X2 are expected to be as follows:

J	*F*	*M*	*A*	*M*	*J*	*J*	*A*	*S*	*O*	*N*	*D*
5,000	5,500	6,000	6,000	6,250	6,500	6,250	7,000	7,500	7,750	8,000	7,500

The company expects to sell 7,000 units in January 20X3.

The selling price for each unit will be increased by 15% with effect from 1 March 20X2.

A total of 1,000 units of finished goods are expected to be in inventory at the end of 20X1. It is company policy to hold a closing inventory balance of finished goods equal to 20 per cent of the following month's sales.

Each unit of Z produced requires 3 kg of material X, which currently costs $5 per kg. This price is expected to increase by 10 per cent on 1 June 20X2.

Inventory of raw material at the end of 20X1 is expected to be 3,750 kg. The company requires the closing inventory of raw materials to be set at 20 per cent of the following month's production requirements.

The production of each unit of Z requires 4 hours of skilled labour and 2 hours of unskilled labour..

Required:

(a) The sales budget for quarter 1 is $ ________.

(b) The production budget for quarter 4 is ________ units.

(c) The material usage budget for quarter 2 is ________ kg.

(d) The material purchase budget for quarter 1 is $ ________.

(e) The direct labour budget for quarter 3 is ________ hours.

Test your understanding 69

Cash budget

The following data and estimates are available for ABC Limited for June, July and August:

	June	*July*	*August*
	$	$	$
Sales	45,000	50,000	60,000
Wages	12,000	13,000	14,500
Overheads	8,500	9,500	9,000

The following information is available regarding direct materials:

	June	*July*	*August*	*September*
	$	$	$	$
Opening inventory	5,000	3,500	6,000	4,000
Material usage	8,000	9,000	10,000	

Notes:

(1) 10% of sales are for cash: the balance is received the following month.

(2) Wages are paid in the month in which they are incurred.

(3) Overheads include $1,500 per month for depreciation. Overheads are settled in the month following.

(4) Purchases of direct materials are paid for in the month purchased.

Required:

(a) The budget value of direct materials purchases is:

June:	$	
July:	$	
August:	$	

(b) The budgeted cash receivable from customers in August is $ ________.

(c) The budgeted cash payable for wages and overhead in July is $ ________.

Test your understanding 70

Flexible budgets

S Ltd makes a single product for which the budgeted costs and activity for a typical month are as follows:

Budgeted production and sales	15,000 units
Budgeted unit costs	$
Direct labour	46
Direct materials	30
Variable overheads	24
Fixed overheads	80
	180

The standard selling price of the product is $220 per unit.

Required:

(a) During October, only 13,600 units were produced. The total budget cost allowance contained in the flexed budget for October is $ ________.

(b) During November, 14,500 units were produced and sold at the standard selling price, and the following actual costs were incurred:

	$
Direct labour	658,000
Direct materials	481,400
Variable overheads	334,600
Fixed overheads	1,340,000
	2,814,000

(i) The sales volume contribution variance for November was $ ________.

adverse ☐

favourable ☐

(ii) The total expenditure variance for November was $ ________.

adverse ☐

favourable ☐

Test your understanding 71

Interpreting cash budgets

CB Ltd's cash budget forewarns of a short-term cash deficit. Which of the following would be appropriate actions to take in this situation? (*tick all that apply*).

(a) Arrange a bank overdraft ☐

(b) Reduce receivables ☐

(c) Increase inventories ☐

(d) Sell more shares in the company ☐

Test your understanding 72

Managerial reporting in a service organisation

Speedee Ltd has three main divisions – a motor-cycle courier service, a domestic parcel delivery service, and a bulk parcel service for industry.

The following information is available for a period:

	Courier service	*Domestic parcels*	*Bulk parcels*
Sales ($000)	205	316	262
Distance travelled (000km)	168	82	54

Variable costs vary both with the distance travelled and also the type of vehicle used, and are $307,800 for the company as a whole. A technical estimate shows that the various vehicles used for the three services incur variable costs per kilometre in the ratio of 1:3:5, respectively, for the courier service, domestic parcels and bulk parcels.

Required:

The contribution for each service for the period is:

(a) courier service:	$	
(b) domestic parcels:	$	
(c) bulk parcels:	$	

Test your understanding 73

Value added

An extract from the performance report of the F Division for the latest period is as follows.

	$	$
Sales revenue		289,500
Cost of goods sold		
Material costs	89,790	
Labour costs	72,340	
Production overhead	54,030	
		216,160
Gross margin		73,340
Marketing overhead	21,890	
General and administration overhead	38,120	
		60,000
Net profit		13,330

The following salary costs are included within the overhead costs.

	Salary cost included
Production overhead	$10,710
Marketing overhead	$14,560
General and administration overhead	$21,330

Required:

For the F Division for the latest period, the value added was $ ________.

Test your understanding 74

Managerial reporting in a charity

As part of its fundraising and awareness-raising activities a charity operates a number of retail shops, selling new and donated second-hand goods.

Data for the latest period for the Southmere shop are as follows.

	$
Sales income	
New goods	6,790
Donated goods sold to customers	4,880
Purchase cost of new goods	3,332
Cost of laundering and cleaning selected donated goods	120
Delivery cost paid for new goods	290
Other income: low-quality donated goods sold for recycling	88
Salary costs	810
Amount paid to valuer to assess selected donated items	30
General overhead costs	1,220

Required:

(a) The gross margin generated by second-hand donated goods sold was $ ________.

(b) The gross margin generated by new goods sold was $ ________.

Test your understanding 75

Payback

An investment of $10 million is expected to generate net cash inflows of $3.5 million each year for the next 5 years.

Calculate the payback period for the project (to the nearest month).

Test your understanding 76

Discounting

What would be the discount factor for an interest rate of 8.6%, for 8 years. Give your answer to 3 decimal places.

Test your understanding 77

Payback

Which of the following are advantages of the payback appraisal method. (*tick all that apply).*

(a) Easy to understand □

(b) Takes account of the time value of money □

(c) Provides a simple measure of risk □

(d) Uses cash flows □

(e) Ensures maximisation of shareholder wealth □

Test your understanding 78

IRR

A project requires an initial investment of $190,000. The company has a cost of capital of 10%. The following cash flows have been estimated for the life of the project:

Year	*Cash flow*
1	$ 40,000
2	$ 80,000
3	$ 70,000
4	$ 50,000

Required:

Calculate the IRR of the project to one decimal place.

Test your understanding answers

Test your understanding 1

Management accounting	Financial accounting
Forward looking	
	Statutory requirement
Uses both financial and non-financial information	
	Links closely with taxation and auditing
Used in performance measurement	
Used in internal decision making	

Test your understanding 2

D

Standard costing is used for control. It allows actual results to be compared to the pre-set standards and variances can be calculated and investigated by management.

Test your understanding 3

Strategic level	Operational level
	Detailed
	Historical
	Accurate
Subjective	
Summarised	

Test your understanding 4

D

Reporting and auditing relate more to financial accounting.

Test your understanding 5

A CIMA was established 50 years ago – **FALSE**: CIMA was established over 90 years ago.

B Members of CIMA are known as Chartered Certified Accountants – **FALSE**: they are known as Chartered Management Accountants, Chartered Certified Accountants belong to ACCA.

C CIMA is a worldwide organisation – **TRUE**.

D CIMA may discipline students or members who bring the profession into disrepute – **TRUE**.

Test your understanding 6

A

(1) Find the variable overhead per square metre:

Extra m^2 cleaned = 15,100 – 12,750 = 2,350

Extra overhead cost = \$83,585 – \$73,950 = \$9,635

Variable overhead per m^2 = \$9,635/2,350 = \$4.10

(2) Find the fixed overhead:

		$
Total overheads of cleaning 12,750 m^2	=	73,950
Variable overheads = 12,750 × \$4.10	=	52,275
Fixed overhead	=	21,675

(3) Total overheads for 16,200 m^2

		$
Variable overhead = 16,200 × \$4.10	=	66,420
Fixed overhead	=	21,675
		88,095

Test your understanding 7

C

Do not be confused by the use of the y and x notation. You simply need to think through how to calculate the total cost of a semi-variable cost.

Total semi-variable cost = fixed cost + (variable cost per unit × no. of units)

So, the total photocopying cost for a month can be shown as: **y = 300 + 0.02x**

Test your understanding 8

All of the items described could be used as a cost object.

The *CIMA Terminology* provides the following description of a cost object: 'for example a product, service, centre, activity, customer or distribution channel in relation to which costs are ascertained'.

Test your understanding 9

Costs (i), (ii) and (iii) are direct costs of the service because they can be specifically attributed to the service provided.

Cost (iv) is an indirect cost of the service because it applies to all council employees, not only to those who are providing the refuse collection service.

Remember: A direct cost is a cost which can be specifically attributed to a single cost object without the need for any potentially arbitrary apportionments.

Test your understanding 10

The statement is false.

- Think carefully before you answer a true/false question like this. For a statement to be true it must apply in all circumstances.

Although the full cost, which includes absorbed overhead, shows the long run average cost that will be incurred per unit of service provided, it might be necessary to consider the marginal or incremental cost when making a special, one-off pricing decision.

Test your understanding 11

The wages paid to the driver, carpenter and hair stylist are all direct labour costs.

The wages paid to the canteen assistant are indirect wages because the assistant is not working directly on the organisation's output.

- Direct wages are those paid to employees working directly on the organisation's output. Their wages can be traced to specific cost units.

Test your understanding 12

C

- Take your time and read all the options. This is a straightforward question but it would be easy to rush and select the wrong answer.

Overhead allocation is the allotment of whole items of cost to cost units or cost centres. Overhead apportionment is the sharing out of costs over a number of cost centres according to the benefit used. Overhead analysis refers to the whole process of recording and accounting for overheads.

Test your understanding 13

A

- First you need to calculate the overhead absorption rate per standard machine hour. Remember that this is always based on the budgeted data.
- Next you must use the absorption rate to calculate the overhead absorbed, and then compare this with the overhead incurred to determine the over- or under-absorption.

$$\text{Overhead absorption rate} = \frac{\$258,750}{11,250} = \$23 \text{ per standard machine hour}$$

	$
Overhead absorbed = 10,980 std. hours × $23	252,540
Overhead incurred	254,692
Under absorption	**2,152**

Test your understanding 14

A

- Use the under-absorption to adjust the actual overhead incurred, to determine the overhead absorbed. Since there was an under absorption, the actual overhead incurred must be greater than the overhead absorbed.
- Lastly, divide the overhead absorbed by the number of units produced.

	$000
Actual incurred	276
Under absorption	46
Absorbed	230
No. of units	23,000

Rate per unit = $230,000/23,000 = **$10**.

Test your understanding 15

The overhead was under-absorbed by $37,331

- Remember that the overhead absorption rate (OAR) is based on the budgeted data.
- Overheads absorbed for the period = OAR × actual standard labour hours achieved.

$$\text{OAR} = \frac{\$691,125}{48,500} = \$14.25$$

	$	
Overhead absorbed during period		
49,775 × $14.25	709,293.75	
Overhead incurred	746,625.00	
Under-absorbed	**37,331**	(to nearest whole number).

Test your understanding 16

A: ($140,000/$400,000)	× $84,000	= **$29,400**
B: (800/4,400)	× $22,000	= **$4,000**
C: (2,500/40,000)	× $180,000	= **$11,250**
D: (50/240)	× $60,000	= **$12,500**
E: (3/(3 + 2 + 1))	× $109,600	= **$54,800**

Test your understanding 17

Overhead absorption rates:

Assembly $\frac{\$206,350}{15,500 \text{ machine hours}}$ = **$13.31 per machine hour**

Machining $\frac{\$213,730}{20,000 \text{ machine hours}}$ = **$10.69 per machine hour**

Finishing $\frac{\$75,920}{15,000 \text{ machine hours}}$ = **$5.06 per machine hour**

The basic data on labour and machine hours seem to indicate that the Assembly and Machining departments are machine-intensive, so a machine hour rate would be most appropriate. The Finishing department appears to be labour-intensive, so a labour hour rate would be more suitable.

Test your understanding 18

The total overhead for the machining department will be **$2,850,000** (to the nearest $000).

Workings:

	Machining	*Assembly*	*Stores*	*Maintenance*
	$	$	$	$
Initial allocation	2,250,000	1,900,000	250,000	800,000
Apportion stores	75,000	75,000	(250,000)	100,000
Apportion maintenance	405,000	270,000	225,000	(900,000)
Apportion stores	67,500	67,500	(225,000)	90,000
Apportion maintenance	40,500	27,000	22,500	(90,000)
Apportion stores	6,750	6,750	(22,500)	9,000
Apportion maintenance	4,050	2,700	2,250	(9,000)
Apportion stores	675	675	(2,250)	900
Apportion maintenance	405	270	225	(900)
Apportion stores	68	67	(225)	90
Apportion maintenance	40	27	23	(90)
Total apportioned	**2,849,988**			

Test your understanding 19

(a) The direct cost per unit of product B is **$149**

(b) The full production cost per unit of product B is **$189**

- The full production cost includes production overheads absorbed using the predetermined rates provided in the question.

Working:

	$	$
Direct material (3 kg × $9)		27
Direct labour		
Department A (4 hours × $14)	56	
Department B (6 hours × $11)	66	
	—	
		122
		—
Total direct cost		149
Production overhead		
Department A (4 labour hours × $7)	28	
Department B (2 machine hours × $6)	12	
	—	
		40
		—
Full production cost		189
		—

Test your understanding 20

A

- Calculate the breakeven point before and after the change in production methods, using the formula:

$$\text{Breakeven point in units} = \frac{\text{Fixed costs}}{\text{Contribution per unit}}$$

Existing situation:

$$\text{Breakeven point} = \frac{\$24{,}400}{\$8} = \mathbf{3{,}050\ units}$$

Working:

Contribution per unit	$
Selling price	14
Variable cost	(6)
	—
Contribution	8
	—

New production methods:

$$\text{Breakeven point} = \frac{\$24{,}400 \times 1.3}{\$10} = \mathbf{3{,}172\ units}$$

Working:

Contribution per unit	$
Selling price	15
Variable cost	(5)
	—
Contribution	10
	—

Increase in number of units: 3,172 – 3,050 = **122.**

Test your understanding 21

A

- First calculate the existing profit level.
- Using the new cost and selling price, calculate the required sales volume using the formula:

$$\text{Required sales volume} = \frac{\text{(Fixed costs + required profit)}}{\text{Contribution per unit}}$$

$$\frac{\$31,720 + \$39,600}{\$15 - \$5} = \textbf{7,132 units}$$

(Working for existing profit: 8,000 units × $8 = $64,000 contribution less fixed costs $24,400 = $39,600.)

Test your understanding 22

D

- Do not rush this question. You can probably easily calculate the breakeven point in terms of sales value, but then you will need to stop and think carefully.

$$\text{Breakeven point in terms of sales value} = \frac{\$120,000}{0.3} = \$400,000$$

This must now be divided by the selling price.

The breakeven point in terms of units cannot be derived because we do not know the unit selling price.

Test your understanding 23

D

- The single line drawn on the graph represents profits or losses earned for a range of activity levels.

Point K indicates the loss incurred at zero activity. At this point, the loss incurred is equal to the fixed cost.

Test your understanding 24

D

- Profit-volume chart is the name given to a graph which indicates the profits or losses earned for a range of activity levels.

Charts A and B would include lines for costs and revenues. Chart C would be depicted by a single line, starting at a point above the origin on the vertical axis. This point represents the total fixed cost incurred at zero activity.

Test your understanding 25

The direct wage cost for the period was = **$40,320**.

- Remember that contribution for a period is equal to the fixed costs plus the profit for the period.
- Once you have calculated the contribution you can use the C/S ratio to derive the sales value, and that will lead you to the variable costs and thus the direct wages for the period.

Contribution = $30,000 + $56,400 = $86,400

$$\frac{\text{Contribution}}{\text{Sales}} = 0.3$$

$$\text{Sales} = \frac{\$86{,}400}{0.3} = \$288{,}000$$

Variable costs = sales value – contribution = $288,000 – $86,400 = $201,600

Direct wages = 20% × $201,600 = **$40,320**.

Test your understanding 26

(a) The breakeven point will **decrease**.

(b) The contribution to sales ratio will **stay the same**.

(c) The margin of safety will **increase**.

- For a given level of sales, the margin of safety and the breakeven point will always move in the 'opposite direction' to each other. If one increases then the other decreases.
- The contribution to sales ratio is not affected by the level of fixed costs incurred.

Test your understanding 27

A	**$62,500**
B	**$73,000**
C	**$48,000**
D	**$25,000**

- You will need to use the contribution to sales (C/S) ratio in this question, in calculating the breakeven sales value. Once you have calculated the variable costs as a percentage of sales value you should be able to use this to determine the C/S ratio.
- The contribution breakeven chart that has been drawn shows the variable cost line instead of the fixed cost line. This means that contribution can be read directly from the chart.

Workings:

	August	*September*	*Change*
	$	$	$
Sales	80,000	90,000	10,000
Cost of sales	50,000	55,000	5,000
Selling and distribution	8,000	9,000	1,000
Administration	15,000	15,000	nil

(i) Cost of sales:

Variable $5,000/$10,000 = 50c/$1 of sales (50% of sales)

Fixed $50,000 – (50% × $80,000) = $10,000

(ii) Selling and distribution:

Fixed nil

Variable $1,000/$10,000 =10c/$1 of sales (10% of sales)

(iii) Administration:

Fixed	$15,000
Variable	nil

$$\text{Breakeven sales value} = \frac{\text{Fixed costs}}{\text{C/S ratio *}} = \frac{\$25,000}{0.4} = \mathbf{\$62,500}$$

*Variable costs have been calculated to be 60% of sales. Therefore, C/S ratio is 40%.

Total cost of $80,000 sales value = **$73,000** (from original data).

Total variable cost for $80,000 sales value = $80,000 × 0.6 = **$48,000**.

Total fixed cost = cost of sales $10,000 + administration $15,000 = **$25,000**.

Test your understanding 28

B

- The products must be ranked in order of their contribution per machine hour used.

	Product W	*Product X*	*Product Y*	*Product Z*
	$	$	$	$
Contribution per batch	10.40	9.00	5.40	9.00
Contribution per machine hour	10.40/12	9.00/9	5.40/6	9.00/11
=	0.8667	1.0000	0.9000	0.8182
Ranking	3rd	1st	2nd	4th

Test your understanding 29

(a) **2,900 hours**.

Workings:

Hours of installation labour required to satisfy maximum demand:

	Hours
Day scan*: 2,000 units × 3 hours/unit	6,000
Night scan: 3,000 units × 4 hours/unit	12,000
Omni scan: 1,800 units × 5.5 hours/unit	9,900
	27,900
Available hours	25,000
Shortfall	2,900

* Hours of installation labour for Day scan $= \frac{\$24}{\$8} = 3$ hours.

(b) Day scan **2,000 units**
Night scan **2,275 units**
Omni scan **1,800 units**

The best production plan in part (b) is that which will maximise the contribution from the installation labour. The products must therefore be ranked in order of their contribution per hour.

Workings:

	Day scan	*Night scan*	*Omni scan*
	$	$	$
Selling price	250	320	460
Variable costs			
Material	(70)	(110)	(155)
Manufacturing labour	(40)	(55)	(70)
Installation labour	(24)	(32)	(44)
Variable overheads	(16)	(20)	(28)
Contribution per unit	100	103	163
Installation hours required	3	4	5.5
Contribution per installation hour	$33.33	$25.75	$29.64
Production priority	1st	3rd	2nd

Best production plan

	Units		Hours used
Day scan to maximum demand	2,000	(× 3.0)	6,000
Omni scan to maximum demand	1,800	(× 5.5)	9,900

This leaves (25,000 26,000 29,900) 5 9,100 installation labour hours for Night scan.

$$\text{Therefore, production of Night scan} = \frac{9{,}100}{4} = 2{,}275$$

Test your understanding 30

The maximum price at which buying is preferable to internal manufacture is **$12.50.**

The relevant internal manufacturing cost in this make versus buy decision comprises two elements:

	$
Variable manufacturing cost (3 + 5 + 1.5)	9.50
Specific fixed cost	3.00
	12.50

The specific fixed cost is included because it is specific to the component.

Test your understanding 31

D

4,000 × [$20,000 ÷ 2,500 × 1.025] = **$32,800**

Test your understanding 32

C

The relevant cost of labour is the lower cost of:

(1) the cost of working overtime and

(2) the cost of diverting labour from other work.

	$
Incremental cost of working overtime:	
Incremental cost of using 600 hours spare capacity	0
Incremental cost of overtime:400 hours × $10 × 200%	8,000
	8,000
Incremental cost of diverting labour from other work:	
Labour cost: 400 hours × $10	4,000
Contribution forgone: 400 hours × ($8/4)	800
	4,800

It would be cheaper to divert labour from other work, and the relevant cost is **$4,800.**

Test your understanding 33

C

Although standard costs are based on estimates of what might happen in the future, a standard costing system does not provide actual future costs.

Test your understanding 34

The standard variable production cost of one unit of product H is **$182**

- This is a straightforward exercise in accumulating costs using the data provided.

		$ *per unit*
Direct material W	(4 kg × $1)	4
Direct material X	(2 kg × $5)	10
Direct labour	(14 × $8)	112
Variable production overhead	(14 × $4)	56
		——
Total variable production cost		182
		——

Test your understanding 35

D

- The usage must have been higher than standard because the usage variance is adverse.
- Remember that the usage variance is equal to the excess usage multiplied by the standard price per kg of material.

Standard price per kilogram of material: $\frac{\$46,248}{11,280} = \$4.10$

Number of kilograms excess usage: $\frac{\$492}{\$4.10} = 120$ kg.

Standard usage: 11,280 kg – 120 kg = **11,160 kg**.

Test your understanding 36

The number of standard hours produced was **24,500**.

- Backwards variance questions are a good way of testing whether you really understand the logic of the variance calculations.
- If you got this question wrong, go back and study variance analysis again to ensure that you can calculate all the required variances quickly and accurately.

Actual labour hours worked		25,600
Adverse efficiency variance in hours	$\frac{\$8,250}{\$7.50}$	1,100
		———
Standard hours expected for production achieved		**24,500**
		———

Test your understanding 37

B

The number of standard labour hours produced last month was **29,000 hours.**

	$
Actual labour cost	117,600
Rate variance (adverse - therefore deduct from actual cost)	8,400
	———
Standard cost of hours worked	109,200
Hours worked	28,000
Standard rate per hour (109,200/28,000)	$3.90
Efficiency variance = $3,900 (F) In hours = $3,900/$3.90 per hour =	1,000
Actual hours worked	28,000
	———
Standard hours produced (actual hours + fav efficiency variance)	29,000
	———

Test your understanding 38

A

- The adverse efficiency variance means that the actual time taken was higher than the standard allowance.
- Notice that there was a nil rate variance. This means that the actual rate per hour was the same as the standard rate per hour.
- There are a number of ways of calculating the correct solution. You might have used a different method – it does not matter as long as you arrive at the correct answer!

Excess hours above standard time	=	efficiency variance / standard rate per hour
	=	$26,000/$8 = 3,250 hours
Actual hours worked	=	$182,000/$8= 22,750 hours
Standard hours for actual output	=	22,750 – 3,250 = 19,500 hours
Standard hours for one unit	=	19,500/6,500 = **3 hours**

Test your understanding 39

(a) The sales price variance for product V for June was **$42,700 favourable**

(b) The sales volume contribution variance for product V for June was **$4,000 adverse**

- Remember that the sales volume contribution variance is evaluated using the standard contribution per unit.

	$	
4,600 units should sell for (× $45)	207,000	
But did sell for	249,700	
Sales price variance	42,700	favourable
Actual sales volume	4,600	units
Budget sales volume	4,800	units
Sales volume variance in units	200	adverse
× standard contribution per unit $(45 – 25)	× $20	
Sales volume contribution variance	$4,000	adverse

Test your understanding 40

The actual contribution reported for the period was **$49,460**.

- Adverse variances are deducted from the budgeted contribution to derive the actual contribution. Favourable variances are added because they would increase the contribution above the budgeted level.

$37,200 + $(13,420 + 5,400 – 310 – 6,250) = $49,460.

Test your understanding 41

Only **(b)** and **(c)** could have contributed to an adverse direct labour efficiency variance.

(a) Higher output would not in itself cause an adverse efficiency variance. In calculating the efficiency variance the expected labour hours would be flexed according to the actual output achieved.

(b) If material was difficult to process the number of labour hours taken might have been higher than standard. This would result in an adverse labour efficiency variance.

(c) If the original standard time was set too low then actual times are likely to be higher than standard, thus resulting in an adverse labour efficiency variance.

(d) A higher hourly labour rate would cause an adverse labour rate variance, not an adverse efficiency variance.

(e) Using employees who are more skilled than specified in the standard is more likely to result in a favourable direct labour efficiency variance.

Test your understanding 42

Reasons **(a)** and **(c)** could have contributed to a favourable sales volume contribution variance.

A lower sales price might encourage more customers to buy which, as with (c), might increase sales volumes above budget and a favourable sales volume contribution variance would result.

A higher actual contribution than the standard per unit (reason (b)) would not result in a favourable sales volume contribution variance, since the variance is evaluated at the standard contribution per unit.

Test your understanding 43

B

- Remember: if you are reduced to guessing, then eliminate first the options that are obviously incorrect. For example, option D must be incorrect because direct materials returned to stores unused cannot yet have become part of cost of sales.

This is the reverse of the entries that would have been made when the direct materials were first issued to production.

Test your understanding 44

A

- Ensure that you read the introduction to the question carefully. We need to know that this is the company's year-end, in order to be able to select the correct entry.

Since this is the year-end, the balance on the overhead control account would be transferred to the statement of profit or loss, rather than carried forward to the following period.

The debit side of the account (the overhead incurred) is greater than the credit side of the account (the overhead absorbed into work in progress). Therefore, the overhead is under-recovered or under-absorbed.

Test your understanding 45

The correct choices are **(b), (c), (d)** and **(e)**.

- You might find it easiest to quickly sketch the T-accounts from the data provided, then you can simply pick out the correct journal entries and tick them.
- Wages incurred are higher than the wages paid, so there must be an accrual for the period, but you are not asked about the accounting entries for this element of the transactions.

The correct choices are:

(b) Debit Wages control account: $31,700

Wages actually paid are debited to the wages control account and credited to the bank or cash account.

(c) Debit Work in progress account: $27,400

(d) Debit Production overhead control account: $6,000

(e) Credit Wages control account: $33,400

Direct wages incurred are credited to the wages control account and debited to work in progress. Indirect wages incurred are credited to the wages control account and debited to the production overhead control account, pending their later absorption into work in progress

Test your understanding 46

A **$48,250**

B **$598,050** (direct materials issued to work in progress)

C **$617,300**

D **$32,800** (indirect materials issued).

Test your understanding 47

The production overheads for the period were **over-absorbed by $57,995**. This amount will be transferred as a **credit** in the statement of profit or loss at the end of the period.

- You might like to draw up your own production overhead control account. Although you would not earn marks for this, it might help you to collect together all the information you need to calculate the under- or over-absorption.

Working:

Production overhead control account

	$		$
Payables	359,725	Work in progress (280% × $173,400)	485,520
Provision for depreciation	35,000		
Indirect materials	32,800		
Over-absorption	57,995		
	485,520		485,520

Test your understanding 48

C

- A favourable variance is always credited to the relevant variance account, so you can easily eliminate options (B) and (D) as incorrect.

As a general rule, all variances are entered in the accounts at the point at which they arise. The labour rate variance is therefore recorded in the wages control account.

Test your understanding 49

(a)

	Debit	Credit	No entry in this account
Materials control account		✓	
Material price variance account			
Work in progress account	✓		✓

(b)

	Debit	Credit	No entry in this account
Materials control account			✓
Material usage variance account		✓	
Work in progress account	✓		

(c) The labour force was paid at a **higher hourly rate than standard**. (Because the labour rate variance is adverse.)

(d)

	Debit	Credit	No entry in this account
Wages control account			✓
Labour efficiency variance account		✓	
Work in progress account	✓		

- Remember that adverse variances are always debited in the relevant variance account, and favourable variances are always credited in the variance account.

Test your understanding 50

The selling price for one unit of product Q, to the nearest cent, is **$227.62**

- Remember to add on the target return for one unit of Q and not the total required return from all 10,000 units.

	$ per unit
Direct material cost	54.00
Direct labour cost	87.00
Total direct cost	141.00
Production overhead absorbed = 11 hours × $7	77.00
Total production cost	218.00
Mark-up for non-production costs = 3% × $218.00	6.54
Full cost	224.54
Profit mark-up (see working)	3.08
Selling price	227.62

Working:

Target return on investment in product Q = $220,000 × 14% = $30,800

Target return per unit of product Q = $30,800/10,000 units = $3.08.

Test your understanding 51

C

Chargeable hours each year will be (52 – 4 weeks =) 48 weeks × 35 hours per week = 1,680 hours × 75% = 1,260 hours.

In these 1,260 hours, she must make $60,000 to cover her salary and general expenses. Therefore, her charge rate should be

$$\frac{\$60,000}{1,260} = \$47.62 \text{ per hours}$$

Thus, the quote for a 50-hour job should be $47.62 per hour × 50 = **$2,381**.

- Use the information provided to determine the number of chargeable hours each year.
- Calculate the hourly rate that the accountant needs to charge to cover her expenses and salary, based on the number of chargeable hours.
- Apply the hourly rate to the job in question.

Test your understanding 52

C

- Read the question carefully. Profit is calculated as a percentage of sales, not as a percentage of cost.

	$	
Direct materials 10 × $10	100	
Direct labour 10 × $10	100	
	——	
Prime cost	200	
Variable production overheads 10 × $4	40	
Fixed production overheads 10 × $20*	200	
	——	
Total production cost	440	
Other costs	50	
	——	
Total cost	490	70%
Profit	210	30%
	——	
Quote for the job	**700**	100%
	——	

*$200,000 overheads/10,000 hours = $20 per hour.

Test your understanding 53

(a) (i) **$29,210**

Workings:

	$	$
Direct materials		26,500
Labour		
Preparation: 90 × $8	720	
Etching: 130 × $7	910	
Assembly: 180 × $6	1,080	
		2,710
		29,210

(ii) Preparation Department overheads **$14,300**

Etching Department overheads **$5,880**

Assembly Department overheads **$4,860**

Workings:

Overhead absorption rates:

Preparation: $\frac{\$165,000}{3,000}$ = $55 per machine hour

Etching: $\frac{\$98,000}{1,400}$ = $70 per machine hour

Assembly: $\frac{\$48,600}{1,800}$ = $27 per machine hour

Overheads charged to batch

Preparation: 260 × $55	$14,300
Etching: 84 × $70	$5,880
Assembly: 180 × $27	$4,860

(b) **$465**

Workings:

	$
Batch cost	65,100
Profit (×30/70)	27,900
Sales value of batch	93,000
Selling price per unit (93,000/200)	$465

- Be careful when you are adding the profit percentage to the total cost in part (b). The question states that the company wishes to achieve 30% profit margin on sales. Do not make the common mistake of simply adding 30% to cost. This will not produce 30% profit margin on sales.

Test your understanding 54

B

20,000 kg input × 15% = 3,000 kg normal loss × $1 = **$3,000**

Test your understanding 55

D

Input	*Kg*	*Output*	*Kg*	*Kg to absorb cost*
Materials	20,000	To process 2	18,500	18,500
		Normal loss	3,000	–
		Abnormal gain	(1,500)	(1,500)
	20,000		20,000	17,000

Costs	$
Materials input	50,000
Direct labour	15,000
Production overheads	22,500
Scrap value normal loss	(3,000)
	84,500
Cost per kg $84,500/17,000	4.9706

Value of abnormal gain = 1,500 kg × $4.9706 = **$7,456**.

Test your understanding 56

C

Value of output = 18,500 kg × $4.9706 = **$91,956**.

Test your understanding 57

(a) **$102,900**

Working:

Value of transfer to process 2 = 49,000 litres × ($0.75 + $1.35) = $102,900.

(b) **$1,050**

Working:

Value of abnormal loss = 500 litres × $(0.75 + 1.35) = $1,050.

(c) **$5,160**

Working:

Value of closing work in progress = (4,000 litres × $0.75)
+ [(4,000 × 40%) litres × $1.35]
= $3,000 + $2,160
= 5,160

Test your understanding 58

(a) **10,320 equivalent litres**

(b) **$7.00 per equivalent litre**

The materials lost in production are scrapped. Therefore, no value is allocated to the normal loss. A common error would be to attempt to allocate a monetary value to the normal loss.

Workings:

Material cost:		$
A	3/6 × 12,000 × $8.00	48,000
B	2/6 × 12,000 × $6.00	24,000
C	1/6 × 12,000 × $3.90	7,800
		79,800

Statement of equivalent litres

	Total	*Materials*	*Labour and overheads*
Completed production	9,500	9,500	9,500
Abnormal loss	100	100	100
Normal loss	600	–	–
Closing WIP:			
Material	1,800	1,800	–
Labour and overheads (40% × 1,800)		–	720
Equivalent litres	12,000	11,400	10,320
Cost		$79,800	$41,280
Cost per equivalent litre	$11.00	$7.00	$4.00

Test your understanding 59

The cost per equivalent unit produced was:

(a) process 2 input: **$2.40 per equivalent unit**

(b) material added: **$0.60 per equivalent unit**

(c) wages and overhead: **$1.20 per equivalent unit**

You will find process costing questions much quicker and easier to answer if you learn a pro-forma layout for your working papers, but remember that you will earn no marks for your workings.

When you are carrying out your equivalent units calculation, remember that any units that are now in process 3 must be complete as regards process 2 input.

Workings:

Input	*Units*	*Output*	*Units*	*Process 2 input*	*Material added*	*Wages and overhead*
Opening WIP	6,000	Finished goods	46,500	46,500	46,500	46,500
Process 2	48,000	Normal loss	3000[1]	–	–	–
		Abnormal loss	500[2]	500	400	300
		Closing WIP	4,000	4,000	2,000	1,200
	54,000		54,000	51,000	48,900	48,000
		Costs	$	$	$	$
		Opening WIP		14,400	2,160	2,880
		Input costs		110,400	27,180	54,720
		Normal loss value		(2,400)	–	–
				122,400	29,340	57,600
		Cost per unit	4.20	2.40	0.60	1.20

Notes:

(1) Normal loss = 6% × (6,000 + 48,000 – 4,000) = 3,000 units.

(2) The abnormal loss is found as a balancing figure in the input/output reconciliation.

Test your understanding 60

B

- Only three of the budget roles are correct here, but there are others that are not mentioned including communication, planning, resource allocation and motivation.

A budget does not provide a means for expansion. In fact, an organisation can budget to reduce its level of activity.

Test your understanding 61

B

- If you remember that the principal budget factor is sometimes referred to as the limiting factor, then you should not have too many problems in selecting the correct answer!

The principal budget factor is important because it must be identified at the start of the budgeting process. Once the budget for the limiting factor has been prepared, all other budgets must be coordinated with it.

Test your understanding 62

Options (a) and (c) are correct.

- Although continuous budgeting is quicker and easier using a computerised system it can be accomplished with a manual system.

Test your understanding 63

A

- Remember the formula to calculate budgeted production:

  Budgeted sales + Budgeted closing inventory – Budgeted opening inventory

	Units
Required by sales	120,000
Required closing inventory	6,500
Less opening inventory anticipated	(13,000)
Production level	**113,500**

Test your understanding 64

C

Did you read the question carefully and note that the material usage budget was required, not the material purchases budget?

10,000 units × 4 kg = **40,000 kg**

Test your understanding 65

B

- The first step is to calculate the required production volume, taking account of the budgeted change in finished goods inventories.
- Convert the production volume into material usage requirements, then adjust for the budgeted change in raw materials inventories to determine the budgeted purchases.

	Units
Budgeted sales of product P	4,000
Required decrease in finished goods inventory	600
Required production	3,400
	Kg
Raw materials usage budget (× 2 kg)	6,800
Increase in raw materials inventories	1,500
Budgeted purchases of raw material	**8,300**

Test your understanding 66

C

- Note that the 5% bad debts will never be received in cash.
- Do not forget to allow for the 2% settlement discount for those customers paying in September for August sales.

	$
Receipts in September from:	
June sales $100,000 × 15%	15,000
July sales $150,000 × 20%	30,000
August sales $130,000 × 60% less 2% settlement discount	76,440
Total receipts in September	**121,440**

Test your understanding 67

A budget which is designed to show the allowed expenditure for the actual level of activity achieved is known as a **flexible budget**. A fixed budget is prepared for a single level of activity and a rolling budget is a continuously updated budget.

Test your understanding 68

(a) **$1,740,000**

Quarter 1 ***Sales Budget***

	January	*February*	*March*	*Total*
Sales (units)	5,000	5,500	6,000	
Selling price for each unit	$100	$100	$115	
Sales ($)	$500,000	$550,000	$690,000	$1,740,000

(b) **23,100 units**

Quarter 4 Production Budget	*Units*	
Required sales units	23,250	(7,750 + 8,000 + 7,500)
Add:		
Required closing inventory	1,400	(20% × 7,000 – January 20X3 sales units)
Less:		
Opening inventory	(1,550)	(20% × 7,750 – October sales units)
Production budget	23,100	

(c) **56,400 kg**

Quarter 2 Material Usage Budget

Quarter 2 production units	18,800*
Material usage for each unit	3 kg
Total quarter 2 material usage	56,400 kg

* It is calculated below as a result of the production budget.

Quarter 2 Production Budget	*Units*	
Required sales units	18,750	(6,000 + 6,250 + 6,500)
Add:		
Required closing inventory	1,250	(20% × 6,250 – July sales units)
Less:		
Opening inventory	(1,200)	(20% × 6,000 – April sales units)
Production budget	18,800*	

(d) **$249,900**

Quarter 1 Material Purchases Budget

Quarter 1 material usage	50,100 kg	(16,700* × 3 kg)
Add:		
Required closing inventory	3,630 kg	(6,050* × 3 kg × 20%)
Less:		
Opening inventory	(3,750)kg	
Purchases	49,980 kg	
Price of each kg	$5.00	
Total material purchases budget	$249,900	

Quarter 1 Production Budget	*Units*	
Required sales units	16,500	(5,000 + 5,500 + 6,000)
Add:		
Required closing inventory	1,200	(20% × 6,000 – April sales units)
Less:		
Opening inventory	(1,000)	
Production budget	16,700*	

April Production Budget	*Units*	
Required sales units	6,000	
Add:		
Required closing inventory	1,250	(20% × 6,250 – May sales units)
Less:		
Opening inventory	(1,200)	(20% × 6,000 – April sales units)
Production budget	6,050*	

(e) **126,300 hours**

Quarter 3 Production Budget	*Units*	
Required sales units	20,750	
Add:		
Required closing inventory	1,550	(20% × 7,750 – October sales units)
Less:		
Opening inventory	(1,250)	(20% × 6,250 – July sales units)
Production budget	21,050	

Total skilled labour hours required	84,200 hours	(21,050 × 4 hours)
Total unskilled labour hours required	42,100 hours	(21,050 × 2 hours)
Total hours required	126,300 hours	

Test your understanding 69

(a) June: **$6,500**
July: **$11,500**
August: **$8,000**

Workings:

	June	*July*	*August*
	$	$	$
Closing inventory	3,500	6,000	4,000
Material usage	8,000	9,000	10,000
	11,500	15,000	14,000
Less: opening inventory	5,000	3,500	6,000
Direct material purchases	6,500	11,500	8,000

(b) $51,000

(c) $20,000

Workings:

		$
(b)		
	Sales receipts in August:	
	Cash sales (10% × $60,000)	6,000
	Credit sales from July (90% × $50,000)	45,000
(c)		51,000
	Cash payments in July:	
	Wages	12,000
	Overheads (June $8,500 less depreciation)	7,000
		20,000

Remember to exclude depreciation from your calculations of overhead cash payments. It is not a cash flow.

Test your understanding 70

(a) **$2,560,000**

Workings:

	$
Direct labour: $46 × 13,600 units	625,600
Direct material: $30 × 13,600 units	408,000
Variable overheads: $24 × 13,600 units	326,400
Fixed overheads: original budget ($80 × 15,000 units)	1,200,000
	2,560,000

(b) (i) **$60,000** adverse
(ii) **$164,000** adverse

Workings:

	$	$
Actual cost		2,814,000
Budget cost allowance:		
Labour, materials and variable o/h		
$(46 + 30 + 24) × 14,500	1,450,000	
Fixed overhead – original budget	1,200,000	
		2,650,000
Expenditure variance		164,000 (A)

Sales volume contribution variance = volume shortfall × standard contribution per unit
= 500 units × $(220 – 100)
= $60,000 adverse

- The flexed budgets are reasonably straightforward to produce: all variable costs are multiplied by a factor of 13,600 and 14,500, respectively, and fixed overheads remain unaltered by the change in activity.

Test your understanding 71

Actions (a) and (b) would be appropriate actions.

Action (c) would not be appropriate because increasing receivables would drain the cash balance still further. Action (d) is more suited to a long-term deficit, since share capital is a long term source of finance.

- Be careful to select actions that are appropriate both for a deficit and for the short term.

Test your understanding 72

(a) Courier service	**$129,400**
(b) Domestic parcels	**$205,300**
(c) Bulk parcels	**$140,500**

Workings:

Weighted total kilometres travelled

Weight	Distance km	Weighted km
1	168,000	168,000
3	82,000	246,000
5	54,000	270,000
		684,000

Total variable costs = $307,800

Variable costs per weighted km =

$$\frac{\$307,800}{684,000} = \$0.45 \text{ per weighted km}$$

Variable cost per service is therefore:

	$
Courier service: 168,000 × 0.45	75,600
Domestic parcels: 246,000 × 0.45	110,700
Bulk parcels: 270,000 × 0.45	121,500
	307,800

Thus, contribution per service is:

	Courier	Domestic	Bulk
	$	$	$
Sales	205,000	316,000	262,000
Variable costs	(75,600)	(110,700)	(121,500)
Contribution	129,400	205,300	140,500

- We are told that the various vehicles incur variable costs per kilometre in the ratio 1:3:5. Therefore, we need to calculate a weighted total number of kilometres travelled, in order to fairly share out the total variable costs incurred. We cannot simply calculate the variable cost per kilometre as (costs incurred ÷ kilometres travelled), because a kilometre travelled by a motor-cycle costs less than a kilometre travelled by a bulk parcel van or lorry.

Test your understanding 73

For the F Division for the latest period, the value added was **$132,270**

	$	$	$
Sales revenue			289,500
Less materials cost		89,790	
Production overhead cost	54,030		
Less salaries included	10,710		
Bought-in production overhead cost		43,320	
Marketing overhead cost	21,890		
Less salaries included	14,560		
		7,330	
General and admin. overhead	38,120		
Less salaries included	21,330		
		16,790	
Total bought in goods and services			157,230
Value added			132,270

- Value added = sales revenue less materials costs and the cost of bought-in goods and services. Wages and salary costs are not bought-in costs and must be excluded from the overhead cost figures when calculating the value added.

Test your understanding 74

(a) The gross margin generated by second-hand donated goods sold was **$4,818**

(b) The gross margin generated by new goods sold was **$3,168**

Second-hand donated goods	$	$
Sales income		
Sold to customers	4,880	
Sold for recycling	88	
		4,968
Cost of laundering, etc.	120	
Valuation costs	30	
		150
Gross margin		4,818

New goods	$	$
Sales income		6,790
Less: purchase cost	3,332	
delivery cost	290	
		3,622
Gross margin		3,168

- The salary costs and general overhead costs cannot be specifically attributed to either type of goods therefore these costs should not be included in the calculation of gross margin.

Test your understanding 75

The payback period is **2 years 11 months**.

Payback period = $\frac{\textbf{Initial investment}}{\textbf{Annual cash flow}}$

= 10,000,000/3,500,000 = 2.857

The payback period is 2 years + (0.857 × 12) months = 2 years 11 months.

Test your understanding 76

Discount factor = $(1 + r)^{-n}$

= $(1 + 0.86)^{-8}$ = **0.517** (to 3 decimal places)

Test your understanding 77

(a), **(c)** and **(d)** are advantages of the payback method.

(a) Easy to understand
(c) Provides a simple measure of risk
(d) Uses cash flows

Test your understanding 78

IRR = 9.8%.

		Discount factor 10%		*Discount factor 5%*	
Year	*Cash flow* $	*DF (10%)*	*Present value* $	*DF(5%)*	*Present value* $000
0	(190,000)	1	(190,000)	1	(190,000)
1	40,000	0.909	36,360	0.962	38,480
2	80,000	0.826	66,080	0.907	72,560
3	70,000	0.751	52,570	0.864	60,480
4	50,000	0.683	34,150	0.823	41,150
		NPV =	**(840)**	**NPV =**	**22,670**

so:

L = 5%, H = 10%

N_L = \$22,670, N_H = (\$840)

$$IRR \approx L + \frac{N_L}{N_L - N_H}(H - L)$$

$$IRR = 5 + \frac{22{,}670}{22{,}670 - (840)} \times (10 - 5)$$

= 9.8%

chapter

13

Mock Assessment 1

Certificate in Business Accounting Fundamentals of Management Accounting

You are allowed two hours to complete this assessment.

The assessment contains 50 questions.

All questions are compulsory.

Do not turn the page until you are ready to attempt the assessment under timed conditions.

Mock Assessment Questions

Test your understanding 1

Decide whether the following statements are true or false:

	True	*False*
Management accounting information is internally focused		
Financial accounting is concerned with the production of statutory accounts		
Management accounting information is used for internal decision making		
Management accounting information is used by company shareholders		

Test your understanding 2

Which ONE of the following would be classified as direct labour?

- □ Personnel manager in a company servicing cars.
- □ Bricklayer in a construction company.
- □ General manager in a DIY shop.
- □ Maintenance manager in a company producing cameras.

Test your understanding 3

The principal budget factor is the

- ☐ factor which limits the activities of the organisation and is often the starting point in budget preparation.
- ☐ budgeted revenue expected in a forthcoming period.
- ☐ main budget into which all subsidiary budgets are consolidated.
- ☐ overestimation of revenue budgets and underestimation of cost budgets, which operates as a safety factor against risk.

Test your understanding 4

R Ltd absorbs overheads based on units produced. In one period, 110,000 units were produced and the actual overheads were $500,000. Overheads were $50,000 over-absorbed in the period.

The overhead absorption rate was $ _______ per unit.

Test your understanding 5

X operates an integrated cost accounting system. The Work-in-Progress Account at the end of the period showed the following information:

Work-in-Progress Account

	$		$
Stores ledger a/c	100,000	?	200,000
Wage control a/c	75,000		
Factory overhead a/c	50,000	Balance c/d	25,000
	225,000		225,000

The $200,000 credit entry represents the value of the transfer to which account?

A Cost of sales account

B Material control account

C Sales account

D Finished goods inventory account

Test your understanding 6

X Ltd absorbs overheads on the basis of machine hours. Details of budgeted and actual figures are as follows:

	Budget	*Actual*
Overheads	$1,250,000	$1,005,000
Machine hours	250,000 hours	220,000 hours

(a) Overheads for the period were:

under-absorbed □

over-absorbed □

(b) The value of the under/over absorption for the period was $ ________.

Test your understanding 7

In an integrated bookkeeping system, when the actual production overheads exceed the absorbed production overheads, the accounting entries to close off the production overhead account at the end of the period would be:

	Debit	*Credit*	*No entry in this account*
Production overhead account	□	□	□
Work in progress account	□	□	□
Statement of profit or loss	□	□	□

Test your understanding 8

A Limited has completed the initial allocation and apportionment of its overhead costs to cost centres as follows.

Cost centre	*Initial allocation*
	$000
Machining	190
Finishing	175
Stores	30
Maintenance	25
	420

The stores and maintenance costs must now be reapportioned taking account of the service they provide to each other as follows.

	Machining	*Finishing*	*Stores*	*Maintenance*
Stores to be apportioned	60%	30%	–	10%
Maintenance to be apportioned	75%	20%	5%	

After the apportionment of the service department costs, the total overhead cost of the production departments will be (to the nearest $000):

Machining $ ________

Finishing $ ________

Test your understanding 9

A project requires an initial investment of $2.4million. The following cash flows have been estimated for the life of the project:

Year	*Cash flow*
1	$ 500,000
2	$ 700,000
3	$ 900,000
4	$ 450,000
5	$ 200,000

Using a discount rate of 10%, calculate the NPV of the project (to the nearest $1,000)

Test your understanding 10

The budgeted contribution for R Limited last month was $32,000. The following variances were reported.

Variance	$
Sales volume contribution	800 adverse
Material price	880 adverse
Material usage	822 favourable
Labour efficiency	129 favourable
Variable overhead efficiency	89 favourable

No other variances were reported for the month.

The actual contribution earned by R Limited last month was $ ________.

Test your understanding 11

The following scattergraph has been prepared for the costs incurred by an organisation that delivers hot meals to the elderly in their homes.

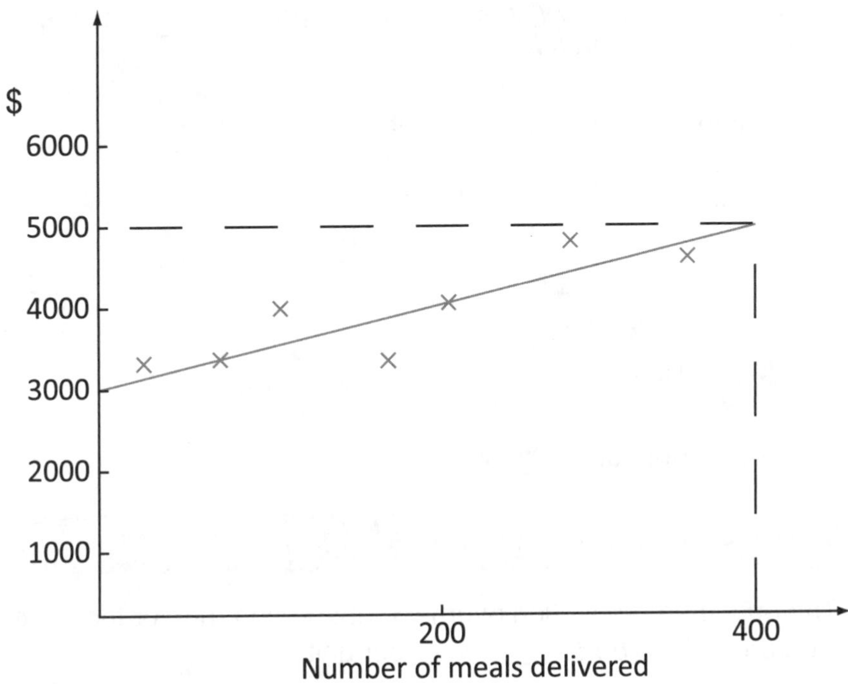

Based on the scattergraph:

(a) the period fixed cost is $ ________

(b) the variable cost per meal delivered is $ ________.

Test your understanding 12

Which one of the following is the definition of overtime premium?

A the additional amount paid for hours worked in excess of the basic working week

B the additional amount paid over and above the normal hourly rate for hours worked in excess of the basic working week

C the additional amount paid over and above the overtime rate for hours worked in excess of the basic working week

D the overtime rate

The following information is required for Questions 13 and 14.

X Ltd has two production departments, Assembly and Finishing, and one service department, Stores.

Stores provide the following service to the production departments: 60% to Assembly and 40% to Finishing.

The budgeted information for the year is as follows:

Budgeted production overheads:

Assembly	$100,000
Finishing	$150,000
Stores	$50,000

Budgeted output 100,000 units

Test your understanding 13

The budgeted production overhead absorption rate for the Assembly Department will be $ _________ per unit.

Test your understanding 14

At the end of the year, the total of all of the production overheads debited to the Finishing Department Production Overhead Control Account was $130,000, and the actual output achieved was 100,000 units.

The overheads for the Finishing Department were:

under-absorbed ☐
over-absorbed ☐

The value of the under/over absorption was $ ________.

Test your understanding 15

R Ltd has been asked to quote for a job. The company aims to make a profit margin of 20% on sales. The estimated total variable production cost for the job is $125.

Fixed production overheads for the company are budgeted to be $250,000 and are recovered on the basis of labour hours. There are 12,500 budgeted labour hours and this job is expected to take 3 labour hours.

Other costs in relation to selling, distribution and administration are recovered at the rate of $15 per job.

The company quote for the job should be $ ________.

Test your understanding 16

Which of the following would NOT be included in a cash budget? Tick all that would NOT be included.

- ☐ Depreciation
- ☐ Provisions for doubtful debts
- ☐ Wages and salaries

Test your understanding 17

(1) Information used by strategic management tends to be detailed.

(2) Information used by strategic management tends to be historical.

(3) Information used by operational management tends to be objective.

(4) Information used by operational management tends to be provided frequently.

Which of the above statements are true?

A (1), (2) and (4) only

B (1), (3) and (4) only

C (2) and (3) only

D (3) and (4) only

The following information is required for Questions 18 and 19.

X is preparing its budgets for the forthcoming year.

The estimated sales for the first 4 months of the forthcoming year are as follows:

Month 1	6,000 units
Month 2	7,000 units
Month 3	5,500 units
Month 4	6,000 units

40% of each month's sales units are to be produced in the month of sale and the balance is to be produced in the previous month.

50% of the direct materials required for each month's production will be purchased in the previous month and the balance in the month of production.

The direct material cost is budgeted to be $5 per unit.

Test your understanding 18

The production budget for Month 1 will be __________ units.

Test your understanding 19

The material cost budget for Month 2 will be $ ________.

Test your understanding 20

When calculating the material purchases budget, the quantity to be purchased equals

A material usage + materials closing inventory – materials opening inventory

B material usage – materials closing inventory + materials opening inventory

C material usage – materials closing inventory – materials opening inventory

D material usage + materials closing inventory + materials opening inventory

Test your understanding 21

The following extract is taken from the overhead budget of X Ltd:

	50%	75%
Budgeted activity	50%	75%
Budgeted overhead	$100,000	$112,500

The overhead budget for an activity level of 80% would be $ ________.

Test your understanding 22

Which of the following would be included in the cash budget, but would not be included in the budgeted statement of profit or loss? Tick all that are correct.

- ☐ Repayment of a bank loan.
- ☐ Proceeds from the sale of a non-current asset.
- ☐ Bad debts write off.

Test your understanding 23

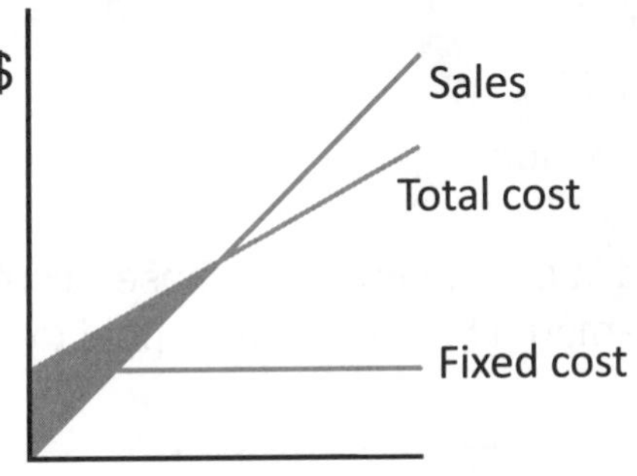

(a) This graph is known as a

- ☐ semi-variable cost chart.
- ☐ conventional breakeven chart.
- ☐ contribution breakeven chart.
- ☐ profit volume chart.

(b) The shaded area on the graph represents:

- ☐ loss
- ☐ fixed cost
- ☐ variable cost
- ☐ profit

Test your understanding 24

Fred is due to receive $50,000 in 5 years time. Using a discount rate of 7.3%, how much will this be worth in today's value? (to the nearest $10)

Test your understanding 25

The following details have been extracted from the payables records of X:

Invoices paid in the month of purchase	25%
Invoices paid in the first month after purchase	70%
Invoices paid in the second month after purchase	5%

Purchases for July to September are budgeted as follows:

July	$250,000
August	$300,000
September	$280,000

For suppliers paid in the month of purchase, a settlement discount of 5% is received. The amount budgeted to be paid to suppliers in September is $ ________.

Test your understanding 26

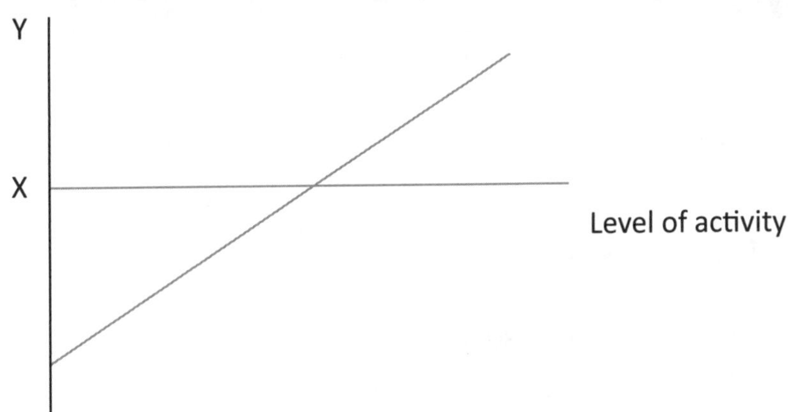

The difference in the values ($) between point X and point Y on the profit volume chart shown above represents:

A contribution

B profit

C breakeven

D loss

Test your understanding 27

In a standard cost bookkeeping system, when the actual material usage has been greater than the standard material usage, the entries to record this is in the accounts are:

	Debit	*Credit*	*No entry in this account*
Material usage variance account	☐	☐	☐
Raw material control account	☐	☐	☐
Work in progress account	☐	☐	☐

Test your understanding 28

R Ltd makes one product, which passes through a single process.

Details of the process for period 1 were as follows:

	$
Material cost – 20,000 kg	26,000
Labour cost	12,000
Production overhead cost	5,700
Output	18,800 kg
Normal losses	5% of input

There was no work-in-progress at the beginning or end of the period. Process losses have no value.

The cost of the abnormal loss (to the nearest $) is $ _______.

The following information is required for Questions 29 to 33.

X Ltd operates a standard costing system. The following budgeted and standard cost information is available:

Budgeted production and sales	10,000 units
	$ per unit
Selling price	250
Direct material cost – 3 kg × $10	30
Direct labour cost – 5 hours × $8	40
Variable production overheads – 5 hours × $4	20

Actual results for the period were as follows:

Production and sales	11,500 units
	$
Sales value	2,817,500
Direct material – 36,000 kg	342,000
Direct labour – 52,000 hours	468,000
Variable production overheads	195,000

Test your understanding 29

The direct material variances are:

	Material Price	*Material Usage*
A	$3,000 F	$15,000 F
B	$18,000 F	$15,000 A
C	$42,000 A	$15,000 A
D	$18,000 F	$60,000 A

Test your understanding 30

The direct labour variances are:

	Labour Rate	*Labour Efficiency*
A	$52,000 A	$16,000 A
B	$8,000 A	$44,000 F
C	$12,000 F	$16,000 F
D	$52,000 A	$44,000 F

Test your understanding 31

The variable production overhead variances are:

	Expenditure	*Efficiency*
A	$13,000 F	$22,000 F
B	$5,000 A	$22,000 F
C	$13,000 F	$8,000 A
D	$5,000 F	$22,000 A

Test your understanding 32

The sales variances are:

	Sales Price	*Sales Volume Contribution*
A	$57,500 F	$240,000 F
B	$57,500 A	$240,000 F
C	$317,500 A	$375,000 F
D	$57,500 A	$240,000 A

Test your understanding 33

The budgeted contribution for the period was $ ________.

Test your understanding 34

X Ltd manufactures a product called the 'ZT'. The budget for next year was:

Annual sales	10,000 units
	$ per unit
Selling price	20
Variable cost	14
Fixed costs	3
Profit	3

If the selling price of the ZT were reduced by 10%, the sales revenue that would be needed to generate the original budgeted profit would be $ ________.

Test your understanding 35

A company is faced with a shortage of skilled labour next period.

When determining the production plan that will maximise the company's profit next period, the company's products should be ranked according to their:

- ☐ profit per hour of skilled labour
- ☐ profit per unit of product sold
- ☐ contribution per hour of skilled labour
- ☐ contribution per unit of product sold

Test your understanding 36

Which of the following would contribute towards a favourable sales price variance (tick all that apply)?

(a) The standard sales price per unit was set too high ☐

(b) Price competition in the market was not as fierce as expected ☐

(c) Sales volume was higher than budgeted and therefore sales revenue was higher than budgeted ☐

Test your understanding 37

The following data relate to a process for the latest period.

Opening work in progress	300 kg valued as follows
	Input material $1,000
	Conversion cost $200
Input during period	8,000 kg at a cost of $29,475
Conversion costs	$11,977
Output	7,000 kg
Closing work in progress	400 kg

Closing work in progress is complete as to input materials and 70% complete as to conversion costs.

Losses are expected to be 10% of input during the period and they occur at the end of the process. Losses have a scrap value of $2 per kg.

The value of the completed output (to the nearest $) is $ ________.

Data for Questions 38 and 39.

A company makes a single product T and budgets to produce and sell 7,200 units each period. Cost and revenue data for the product at this level of activity are as follows.

	$ *per unit*
Selling price	53
Direct material cost	24
Direct labour cost	8
Other variable cost	3
Fixed cost	7
	—
Profit	11
	—

Test your understanding 38

The contribution to sales ratio (P/V ratio) of product T (to the nearest whole number) is __________ %.

Test your understanding 39

The margin of safety of product T (to the nearest whole number) is __________ % of budgeted sales volume.

Test your understanding 40

In management accounting, the format of reports is governed by statute.

Is the above statement *True* or *False*?

Data for Questions 41 and 42.

The total figures from TY Division's budgetary control report are as follows.

	Fixed budget	*Flexed budget allowances*	*Actual results*
	$	$	$
Total sales revenue	520,000	447,000	466,500
Total variable cost	389,000	348,000	329,400
Total contribution	131,000	99,000	137,100

Test your understanding 41

(a) The sales price variance for the period is
$ ________ *adverse/favourable*

(b) The sales volume contribution variance for the period is
$ ________ *adverse/ favourable*

Test your understanding 42

(a) The total expenditure variance for the period is
$ ________ **adverse/favourable**

(b) The total budget variance for the period is
$ ________ **adverse/favourable**

Test your understanding 43

In an integrated bookkeeping system, the correct entries to record the depreciation of production machinery are:

	Debit	*Credit*	*No entry in this account*
Depreciation of production machinery	☐	☐	☐
Work in progress account	☐	☐	☐
Production overhead control account	☐	☐	☐

Test your understanding 44

In an integrated bookkeeping system, the correct entries to record the issue of indirect materials for production purposes are:

	Debit	*Credit*	*No entry in this account*
Materials control account	□	□	□
Work in progress account	□	□	□
Production overhead control account	□	□	□

Test your understanding 45

H Limited budgets to produce and sell 4,000 units of product H next year. The amount of capital investment required to support product H will be $290,000 and H Limited requires a rate of return of 14% on all capital invested.

The full cost per unit of product H is $45.90.

To the nearest cent, the selling price per unit of product H that will achieve the specified return on investment is $ ________.

Test your understanding 46

The Drop In Café sells specialist coffees to customers to drink on the premises or to take away.

The proprietors have established that the cost of ingredients is a wholly variable cost in relation to the number of cups of coffee sold whereas staff costs are semi-variable and rent costs are fixed.

Within the relevant range, as the number of cups of coffee sold increases (*tick the correct box*):

	increase	*decrease*	*stay the same*
(a) The ingredients cost per cup sold will	□	□	□
(b) The staff cost per cup sold will	□	□	□
(c) The rent cost per cup sold will	□	□	□

Test your understanding 47

The use of Shared Services Centres (SSCs) can ensure consistency of reporting throughout the organisation.

Is this statement True or False?

The following information relates to Questions 48 and 49.

Wakehurst is about to tender for a one-off contract.

Requirements for this contract have been established as follows:

	$
Labour: Skilled workers (100 hours at $9/hour)	900
Semi-skilled workers (200 hours at $5/hour)	1,000
Management (20 hours at $20/hour)	400
Materials: N (100 litres at $4.50/litre)	450
T (300kg at $7/kg)	2,100
	4,850

The skilled workers will be diverted from production of product P with resulting loss of sales. Each unit of P generates a contribution of $7 and takes two skilled labour hours to make. Semi-skilled workers will be hired as required. The management cost represents an allocated amount for hours expected to be spent. At the moment the management team has spare capacity.

Current stocks of material N are 200 litres and it is in continuous use by the business. It cost $4.50/litre originally but new supplies now cost $4.00/litre due to improved negotiating by the purchasing department. It could be sold as scrap for $2/litre.

The current stocks of material T are 200kg, which cost $7/kg some years ago but has not been used by the business for some time. If not used for the contract it would be scrapped for $4/kg. The current purchase price is $8/kg.

Test your understanding 48

The relevant cost of labour for the contract is $ _______.

Test your understanding 49

The relevant cost of materials for the contract is $ ______.

Test your understanding 50

P Limited is considering whether to continue making a component or buy it from an outside supplier. It uses 12,000 of the components each year.

The internal manufacturing cost comprises:	$/unit
Direct materials	3.00
Direct labour	4.00
Variable overhead	1.00
Specific fixed cost	2.50
Other fixed costs	2.00
	12.50

If the direct labour were not used to manufacture the component, it would be used to increase the production of another item for which there is unlimited demand. This other item has a contribution of $10.00 per unit but requires $8.00 of labour per unit.

The maximum price per component at which buying is preferable to internal manufacture is $ _______.

Test your understanding answers

Test your understanding 1

	True	False
Management accounting is internal focused	X	
Financial accounting is concerned with the production of statutory accounts	X	
Management accounting is used for internal decision making	X	
Management accounting is used by company shareholders		X

Test your understanding 2

Bricklayer in a construction company.

The bricklayer's wages can be identified with a specific cost unit therefore this is a direct cost. The wages paid to the other three people cannot be identified with specific cost units. Therefore they would be indirect costs.

Test your understanding 3

The principal budget factor is **the factor which limits the activities of the organisation and is often the starting point in budget preparation**.

Test your understanding 4

The overhead absorption rate was **$5 per unit**.

Workings:

	$
Actual overheads	500,000
Over-absorption	50,000
Overhead absorbed	550,000

Overhead absorption rate = $550,000/110,000 units = $5.

Test your understanding 5

D

Finished goods inventory account.

Test your understanding 6

Overheads for the period were **over-absorbed by $95,000**.

Workings:

Overhead absorption rate = $1,250,000/250,000 = $5 per hour

	$
Absorbed overhead = 220,000 hours × $5	1,100,000
Actual overhead incurred	1,005,000
Over-absorbed overhead	95,000

Test your understanding 7

	Debit	*Credit*	*No entry in this account*
Production overhead account		✓	
Work in progress account			✓
Statement of profit or loss	✓		

Test your understanding 8

After the apportionment of the service department costs, the total overhead cost of the production departments will be:

Machining	**$230,000**
Finishing	**$190,000**

Workings:

	Machining	*Finishing*	*Stores*	*Maintenance*
	$000	$000	$000	$000
Apportioned costs	190.00	175.00	30.0	25.0
Stores apportionment	18.00	9.00	(30.0)	3.0
Maintenance apportionment	21.00	5.60	1.4	(28.0)
Stores apportionment	0.84	0.42	(1.4)	0.14
Maintenance apportionment	0.11	0.03	–	(0.14)
Total	229.95	190.05		

Test your understanding 9

NPV = **$260,000**

Year	*Cash flow ($)*	*Discount factor (10%)*	*Present value (future value × discount factor)*
0	(2,400,000)	1	(2,400,000)
1	500,000	0.909	454,500
2	700,000	0.826	578,200
3	900,000	0.751	675,900
4	450,000	0.683	307,350
5	200,000	0.621	124,200
		NPV =	**(259,850)**

Test your understanding 10

The actual contribution earned by R Limited last month was **$31,360**.

$(32,000 – 800 – 880 + 822 + 129 + 89) = $31,360.

Test your understanding 11

(a) The period fixed cost is **$3,000**

(b) The variable cost per meal delivered is **$5**

Workings:

$$\text{Variable cost per meal} = \frac{\$5{,}000 - \$3{,}000}{400 \text{ meals}} = \$5$$

Test your understanding 12

B

Overtime premium is the additional amount paid over and above the normal hourly rate for hours worked in excess of the basic working week.

Test your understanding 13

The budgeted production overhead absorption rate for the Assembly Department will be **$1.30 per unit**.

Workings:

	Assembly
	$
Budgeted overheads	100,000
Reapportioned stores overhead 60% × $50,000	30,000
Total budgeted overhead	130,000

OAR = $\frac{\$130,000}{100,000}$ = $1.30 per unit

Test your understanding 14

The overheads for the Finishing Department were **over-absorbed by $40,000**.

Workings:

	Finishing
	$
Budgeted overheads	150,000
Reapportioned stores overhead 40% × $50,000	20,000
Total budgeted overhead	170,000

OAR = $\frac{\$170,000}{100,000}$ = $1.70 per unit

	$
Absorbed overhead $1.70 × 100,000	170,000
Actual overhead incurred	130,000
Over-absorption	40,000

Test your understanding 15

The company quote for the job should be **$250**.

Workings:

	Job quote
	$
Variable production costs	125
Fixed production overheads (20[1] × 3)	60
Selling, distribution and administration	15
Total cost	200
Profit margin 20%	50
Quote	250

Note [1]: Fixed production overhead absorption rate = (250,000 ÷ 12,500) = $20

Test your understanding 16

Depreciation and **provisions for doubtful debts** are not cash flows and would not be included in a cash budget.

Test your understanding 17

D

Information used by operational management tends to be objective and provided frequently.

Test your understanding 18

The production budget for month 1 will be **6,600 units**.

Workings:

	Month 1	*Month 2*	*Month 3*	*Month 4*
	Units	*Units*	*Units*	*Units*
Sales	6,000	7,000	5,500	6,000
Production				
40% in the month	2,400	2,800	2,200	2,400
60% in the previous month	4,200	3,300	3,600	
Production	6,600	6,100	5,800	

Test your understanding 19

The material cost budget for Month 2 will be **$30,500**.

Workings:

Month 2 6,100 units produced @ $5 per unit = $30,500.

Test your understanding 20

A

The quantity to be purchased equals material usage + materials closing inventory – materials opening inventory.

Test your understanding 21

The overhead budget for an activity level of 80% would be **$115,000**.

Workings:

Using the high/low method

		$	
High	75%	112,500	
Low	50%	100,000	
Change	25%	12,500	– variable cost of 25%
	1%	500	– variable cost of 1%

	$
Substitute into 75% activity	
Total overhead	112,500
Variable cost element 75 × $500	37,500
Fixed cost element	75,000
Total overhead for 80% activity	
Variable cost element 80 × $500	40,000
Fixed cost element	75,000
Total overhead	115,000

Test your understanding 22

Repayment of a bank loan and **proceeds from the sale of a non-current asset** would be included in a cash budget.

Both these items result in a cash flow and would therefore be included in the cash budget. However, they would not be included in the statement of profit or loss. The bad debts write off would be included in the statement of profit or loss, but not in the cash budget.

Test your understanding 23

(a) The graph is known as a **conventional breakeven chart**.

(b) The shaded area on the breakeven chart represents **loss**.

Test your understanding 24

Present value = $50,000 × 0.703 = **$35,150**

The discount factor = $(1 + r)^{-n} = (1 + 0.73)^{-5} = 0.703$

Test your understanding 25

The amount budgeted to be paid to suppliers in September is **$289,000**.

Workings:

	July	*August*	*September*
	$	$	$
Purchases	250,000	300,000	280,000
25% paid in the month of purchase	62,500	75,000	70,000
5% discount allowed	(3,125)	(3,750)	(3,500)
70% paid in the first month		175,000	210,000
5% paid in the second month			12,500
Budgeted payment			289,000

Test your understanding 26

B

The difference in the values ($) between point X and point Y on the profit volume chart represents *profit*.

Test your understanding 27

	Debit	*Credit*	*No entry in this account*
Material usage variance account	✓		
Raw material control account			✓
Work in progress account		✓	

Test your understanding 28

The cost of the abnormal loss is **$460**.

Workings:

	$
Direct material cost	26,000
Labour cost	12,000
Production overhead cost	5,700
	43,700

	Kg
Input	20,000
Normal loss	1,000
Expected output	19,000
Actual output	18,800
Abnormal loss	200

Cost per kg = $43,700/19,000 = $2.30

Cost of abnormal loss = $2.30 × 200 kg = $460.

Test your understanding 29

B

The direct material price variance is **$18,000 favourable**.

Workings:

	$	
36,000 kg should cost (× $10)	360,000	
but did cost	342,000	
Variance	18,000	F

The direct material usage variance is **$15,000 adverse**.

Workings:

11,500 units should use (× 3 kg)	34,500 kg
but did use	36,000 kg
Difference	1,500 kg
× std price per kg	× $10
Variance	$15,000 A

Test your understanding 30

D

The direct labour rate variance is **$52,000 adverse**.

Workings:

	$
52,000 hours should cost (× $8)	416,000
but did cost	468,000
Variance	52,000 A

The direct labour efficiency variance is **$44,000 favourable**.

Workings:

11,500 units should take (× 5 hours)	57,500 hours
but did take	52,000 hours
Difference	5,500 hours
× std rate per hour	× $8
Variance	$44,000 F

Test your understanding 31

A

The variable production overhead expenditure variance is **$13,000 favourable**.

Workings:

	$	
52,000 hours should have cost (× $4)	208,000	
but did cost	195,000	
Variance	13,000	F

The variable production overhead efficiency variance is **$22,000 favourable**.

Workings:

Variance in hours from labour efficiency variance	= 5,500	hours
× standard variable production overhead per hour	× $4	
Variance	$22,000	F

Test your understanding 32

B

The sales price variance is **$57,500 adverse**.

Workings:

	$
11,500 units should sell for (× $250)	2,875,000
But did sell for	2,817,500
Sales price variance	57,500 adverse

The sales volume contribution variance is **$240,000 favourable**.

Workings:

Actual sales volume	11,500	units
Budget sales volume	10,000	units
Variance in units	1,500	favourable
× standard contribution per unit[1]	× $160	
Sales volume contribution variance	$240,000	favourable

Note [1]: Standard contribution per unit = $(250 – 30 – 40 – 20) = $160

Test your understanding 33

Budgeted contribution = (250 – 30 – 40 – 20) × 10,000 = **$1,600,000**

Test your understanding 34

The sales revenue that would be needed to generate the original budgeted profit would be **$270,000**.

Workings:

Fixed costs are not relevant because they will remain unaltered.

Original budgeted contribution = 10,000 units × $(20 – 14) = $60,000

Revised contribution per unit = $(18 – 14) = $4

Required number of units to achieve same contribution = $60,000/$4 = 15,000 units

Required sales revenue = 15,000 units × $18 revised price = $270,000

Test your understanding 35

When determining the production plan that will maximise the company's profit next period, the company's products should be ranked according to their **contribution per hour of skilled labour**.

Test your understanding 36

Only reason **(b)** would contribute to a favourable sales price variance.

Reason (a) would result in an adverse variance. Reason (c) would not necessarily result in any sales price variance because all the units could have been sold at standard price.

Test your understanding 37

The value of the completed output is **$38,500**

Workings:

				Equivalent kg		
				Input material		*Conversion costs*
Input	*kg*	*Output*	*kg*			
Opening WIP	300	Finished output	7,000	7,000		7,000
Input	8,000	Normal loss	800	–		–
		Abnormal loss	100	100		100
		Closing WIP	400	400	70%	280
	8,300		8,300	7,500		7,380
		Costs	$	$		$
		Opening WIP	1,200	1,000		200
		Period costs	41,452	29,475		11,977
		Normal loss	(1,600)	(1,600)		–
			41,052	28,875		12,177
		Cost per equivalent kg	5.50	3.85		1.65

The value of the completed output is $5.50 × 7,000 kg = $38,500

Test your understanding 38

The contribution to sales ratio (P/V ratio) of product T is **34%**.

Workings:

Contribution per unit of product T = $(53 – 24 – 8 – 3) = $18
Contribution to sales ratio = 18/53 = 34%

Test your understanding 39

The margin of safety of product T is **61%** of budgeted sales volume.

Workings:

Period fixed costs = 7,200 × $7 = $50,400

$$\text{Breakeven point} = \frac{\$50,400}{\$18} = 2,800 \text{ units}$$

Margin of safety = (7,200 – 2,800) units = 4,400 units

Margin of safety as percentage of budgeted sales = 4,400/7,200 = 61%

Test your understanding 40

The statement is **false**. The format of financial accounting reports is governed by statute, but in management accounting the format is dictated by the needs of the user.

Test your understanding 41

(a) The sales price variance is $(466,500 – 447,000) = **$19,500 favourable**

(b) The sales volume contribution variance is $(99,000 – 131,000) = **$32,000 adverse**

Test your understanding 42

The total expenditure variance is $(329,400 – 348,000) = **$18,600 favourable**

The total budget variance is $(137,100 – 131,000) = **$6,100 favourable**

Test your understanding 43

	Debit	*Credit*	*No entry in this account*
Depreciation of production machinery		✓	
Work in progress account			✓
Production overhead control account	✓		

Test your understanding 44

	Debit	*Credit*	*No entry in this account*
Materials control account		✓	
Work in progress account			✓
Production overhead control account	✓		

Test your understanding 45

The selling price per unit of product H that will achieve the specified return on investment is **$56.05**

Workings:

Required return from capital invested to support product H	= $290,000 × 14%
	= $40,600
Required return per unit of product H sold = $40,600/4,000	= $10.15
Required selling price = 45.90 full cost + $10.15 = $56.05	

Test your understanding 46

Within the relevant range, as the number of cups of coffee sold increases:

(a) the ingredients cost per cup sold will **stay the same**.

(b) the staff cost per cup sold will **decrease**.

(c) the rent cost per cup sold will **decrease**.

Test your understanding 47

The statement is **true.**

Test your understanding 48

The relevant cost of labour is **$2,250**

Relevant costs	$
Skilled workers:	
Basic pay	900
Opportunity cost of lost contribution (100 × $7/2 per hour)	350
Semi-skilled: basic pay	1,000
Management cost (zero, as there is spare capacity)	0
Total relevant cost of labour	2,250

Test your understanding 49

The relevant cost of materials is **$2,000.**

The historical cost of N is irrelevant. The relevant cost of N is its replacement cost, because if units of N are used, they will be replaced.

Relevant costs	$
N: 100 litres × $4 (replacement cost)	400
T: New stocks of T to be purchased: 100 kg × $8	800
T: Lost scrap proceeds: 200 kg × $4	800
Total relevant cost of material	2,000

Test your understanding 50

The maximum price at which buying is preferable to internal manufacture is **$15.50.**

The relevant internal manufacturing cost in this make versus buy decision comprises three elements:

	$
Variable manufacturing cost	8.00
Unitised specific fixed cost (W1)	2.50
Opportunity cost of the labour (W2)	5.00
	15.50

Workings:

(W1) The unitised specific fixed cost is included because it is specific to the component.

(W2) The opportunity cost is the alternative contribution from the same amount of labour.

$10/$8 = $1.25 per $1 of labour cost.

The component has a labour cost of $4.00 so the alternative contribution is

$1.25 × 4 = $5.00

chapter

14

Mock Assessment 2

Certificate in Business Accounting Fundamentals of Management Accounting

You are allowed two hours to complete this assessment.

The assessment contains 50 questions.

All questions are compulsory.

Do not turn the page until you are ready to attempt the assessment under timed conditions.

Mock Assessment Questions

Test your understanding 1

In an integrated accounting system, the accounting entries to complete the production overhead control account at the end of the period, when the production overheads absorbed exceed the actual production overhead incurred are:

	Debit	*Credit*	*No entry in this account*
Production overhead control account	☐	☐	☐
Work in progress account	☐	☐	☐
Finished goods account	☐	☐	☐
Statement of profit or loss	☐	☐	☐

Test your understanding 2

A company expects to sell h units in the next accounting period, and has prepared the following breakeven chart.

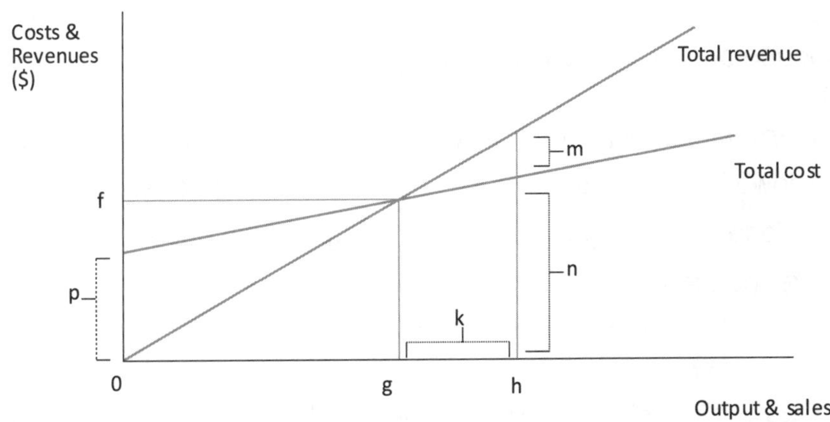

(a) The margin of safety is shown on the diagram by (insert correct letter).

(b) The effect of an increase in fixed costs, with all other costs and revenues remaining the same, will be

	increase	*decrease*	*stay the same*
m will	□	□	□
k will	□	□	□
f will	□	□	□
p will	□	□	□

Test your understanding 3

A company uses the repeated distribution method to reapportion service department costs. The use of this method suggests

A the company's overhead rates are based on estimates of cost and activity levels, rather than actual amounts

B there are more service departments than production cost centres

C the company wishes to avoid under- or over-absorption of overheads in its production cost centres

D the service departments carry out work for each other

Test your understanding 4

The management accountant's report shows that fixed production overheads were over-absorbed in the last accounting period. The combination that is certain to lead to this situation is

(tick one option from each column):

	Production activity	*and*		*Fixed overhead expenditure*
□	lower than budget		□	lower than budget
□	higher than budget		□	higher than budget
□	as budgeted		□	as budgeted

Test your understanding 5

Which of the following costs would be classified as production overhead cost in a food processing company (*tick all that apply*)?

- □ The cost of renting the factory building.
- □ The salary of the factory manager.
- □ The depreciation of equipment located in the materials store.
- □ The cost of ingredients.

Test your understanding 6

A company has just secured a new contract that requires 500 hours of labour.

There are 400 hours of spare labour capacity. The remaining hours could be worked as overtime at time-and-a-half or labour could be diverted from the production of product X. Product X currently earns a contribution of $4 in two labour hours and direct labour is currently paid at a rate of $12 per normal hour.

What is the relevant cost of labour for the contract?

A $200

B $1,200

C $1,400

D $1,800

Test your understanding 7

Which of the following are roles of management accounting as defined by CIMA:

(1) Plan long, medium and short-run operations

(2) Design reward strategies for executives and shareholders

(3) Prepare statutory accounts consisting of statements of profit or loss, statements of financial position and cash flow statements

(4) Control operations and ensure the efficient use of resources

A (1) and (2) only

B all of them

C (2) and (4) only

D (1), (2) and (4) only

Test your understanding 8

The normal loss in process 2 is valued at its scrap value. Extracts from the process account and the abnormal gain account for the latest period are shown below.

Process 2 account

	Units	$		*Units*	$
Opening WIP		1,847	Output	5,100	22,695
Materials		6,490	Normal loss	100	120
Conversion		14,555			
Abnormal gain	220				

Abnormal gain account

	$		$
Statement of profit or loss	A	Process 2	B

The values to be entered in the abnormal gain account for the period are:

A = $ ________

B = $ ________

The following information is required for Questions 9 and 10.

The incomplete process account relating to period 4 for a company which manufactures paper is shown below:

Process account

	Units	$		*Units*	$
Material	4,000	16,000	Finished goods	2,750	
Labour		8,125	Normal loss	400	700
Production overhead		3,498	Work in progress	700	

There was no opening work in process (WIP). Closing WIP, consisting of 700 units, was complete as shown:

Materials	100%
Labour	50%
Production overhead	40%

Losses are recognised at the end of the production process and are sold for $1.75 per unit.

Test your understanding 9

Given the outcome of the process, which ONE of the following accounting entries is needed in each account to complete the double entry for the abnormal loss or gain?

	Debit	*Credit*	*No entry in this account*
Process account	□	□	□
Abnormal gain account	□	□	□
Abnormal loss account	□	□	□

Test your understanding 10

The value of the closing WIP was $ _______.

Test your understanding 11

A machine operator is paid $10.20 per hour and has a normal working week of 35 hours. Overtime is paid at the basic rate plus 50%. If, in week 7, the machine operator worked 42 hours, the overtime premium paid to the operator would be $ _______.

Test your understanding 12

An engineering firm operates a job costing system. Production overhead is absorbed at the rate of $8.50 per machine hour. In order to allow for non-production overhead costs and profit, a mark up of 60% of prime cost is added to the production cost when preparing price estimates.

The estimated requirements of job number 808 are as follows:

Direct materials	$10,650
Direct labour	$3,260
Machine hours	140

The estimated price notified to the customer for job number 808 will be $ _______.

Test your understanding 13

Two NPVs have been calculated for a project using the following discount rates:

10% = $(173,500)
5% = $15,150

Calculate the IRR for the project.

Test your understanding 14

The diagram represents the behaviour of a cost item as the level of output changes:

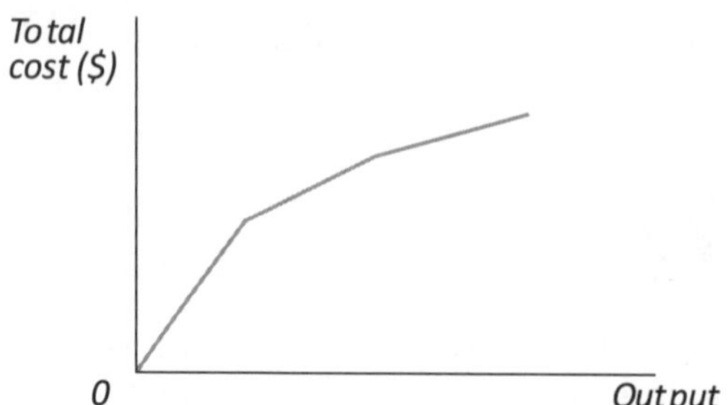

Which ONE of the following situations is depicted by the graph?

A Discounts are received on additional purchases of material when certain quantities are purchased

B Employees are paid a guaranteed weekly wage, together with bonuses for higher levels of production

C A licence is purchased from the government which allows unlimited production

D Additional space is rented to cope with the need to increase production

Test your understanding 15

A hospital's records show that the cost of carrying out health checks in the last five accounting periods have been as follows:

Period	*Number of patients seen*	*Total cost*
		$
1	650	17,125
2	940	17,800
3	1,260	18,650
4	990	17,980
5	1,150	18,360

Using the high–low method and ignoring inflation, the estimated cost of carrying out health checks on 850 patients in period 6 is $ ________.

Test your understanding 16

The principal budget factor for a footwear retailer is

- □ the cost item taking the largest share of total expenditure.
- □ the product line contributing the largest amount to sales revenue.
- □ the product line contributing the largest amount to business profits.
- □ the constraint that is expected to limit the retailer's activities during the budget period.

The following information is required for Questions 17 and 18.

Extracts from the budget of H, a retailer of office furniture, for the six months to 31 December show the following information:

	$
Sales	55,800
Purchases	38,000
Closing inventory finished goods	7,500
Opening inventory finished goods	5,500
Opening receivables	8,500
Opening payables	6,500

Receivables and payables are expected to rise by 10% and 5%, respectively, by the end of the budget period.

Test your understanding 17

The estimated cash receipts from customers during the budget period are $ ________.

Test your understanding 18

The profit mark-up, as a percentage of the cost of sales (to the nearest whole number) is ________ %.

Test your understanding 19

Which of the following actions are appropriate if a company anticipates a temporary cash shortage (*tick all that apply*)?

(i) issue additional shares;
(ii) request additional bank overdraft facilities;
(iii) sell machinery currently working at half capacity;
(iv) postpone the purchase of plant and machinery.

The following information is required for Questions 20 and 21.

A company manufactures three products, X, Y and Z. The sales demand and the standard unit selling prices and costs for period 1, are estimated as follows:

	X	*Y*	*Z*
Maximum demand (000 units)	4.0	5.5	7.0
	$ per unit	*$ per unit*	*$ per unit*
Selling price	28	22	30
Variable costs:			
Raw material ($1 per kg)	5	4	6
Direct labour ($12 per hour)	12	9	18

Test your understanding 20

If supplies in period 1 are restricted to 90,000 kg of raw material and 18,000 hours of direct labour, the limiting factor would be

- ☐ direct labour.
- ☐ raw material.
- ☐ neither direct labour nor raw material.

Test your understanding 21

In period 2, the company will have a shortage of raw materials, but no other resources will be restricted. The standard selling prices and costs and the level of demand will remain unchanged.

In what order should the materials be allocated to the products if the company wants to maximise profit?

First: product □
Second: product □
Third: product □

The following information is required for Questions 22 and 23.

W makes leather purses. It has drawn up the following budget for its next financial period:

Selling price per unit	$11.60
Variable production cost per unit	$3.40
Sales commission	5% of selling price
Fixed production costs	$430,500
Fixed selling and administration costs	$198,150
Sales	90,000 units

Test your understanding 22

The margin of safety represents _______ % of budgeted sales.

Test your understanding 23

The marketing manager has indicated that an increase in the selling price to $12.25 per unit would not affect the number of units sold, provided that the sales commission is increased to 8% of the selling price.

These changes will cause the breakeven point (*to the nearest whole number*) to be _________ units.

Test your understanding 24

A performance standard which assumes efficient levels of operation, but which includes allowances for factors such as waste and machine downtime is known as:

- ☐ an allowable standard
- ☐ an attainable standard
- ☐ an ideal standard
- ☐ a current standard

Test your understanding 25

Over long time periods of several years, supervisory labour costs will tend to behave as:

- ☐ linear variable costs
- ☐ step fixed costs
- ☐ fixed costs
- ☐ semi-variable costs

Test your understanding 26

Which of the following are characteristics of good information? (*tick all that apply*)

(a) Concise

(b) Understandable

(c) Accurate

(d) Complete

(e) Responsible

(f) Easy to use

(g) Accountable

Test your understanding 27

A firm calculates the material price variance when material is purchased. The accounting entries necessary to record a favourable material price variance in the ledger are:

	Debit	*Credit*	*No entry in this account*
Material control account	☐	☐	☐
Work-in-progress control account	☐	☐	☐
Material price variance account	☐	☐	☐

Test your understanding 28

When data is processed, organised, structured or presented in a given context so as to make it useful, it is called Information.

Is the above statement *true* or *false*?

Test your understanding 29

The accounting entries necessary to record an adverse labour efficiency variance in the ledger accounts are:

	Debit	*Credit*	*No entry in this account*
Wages control account	☐	☐	☐
Labour variance account	☐	☐	☐
Work-in-progress control account	☐	☐	☐

Test your understanding 30

J absorbs production overheads on the basis of machine hours. The following budgeted and actual information applied in its last accounting period:

	Budget	*Actual*
Production overhead	$180,000	$178,080
Machine hours	40,000	38,760

(a) At the end of the period, production overhead will be reported as:

- □ under-absorbed
- □ over-absorbed.

(b) The amount of the under/over-absorption will be $ ________.

Test your understanding 31

An advertising agency uses a job costing system to calculate the cost of client contracts. Contract A42 is one of several contracts undertaken in the last accounting period. Costs associated with the contract consist of:

Direct materials	$5,500
Direct expenses	$14,500

Design staff worked 1,020 hours on contract A42, of which 120 hours were overtime. One-third of these overtime hours were worked at the request of the client who wanted the contract to be completed quickly. Overtime is paid at a premium of 25% of the basic rate of $24.00 per hour.

The prime cost of contract A42 is $ ________.

Data for Questions 32 and 33.

Sales of product G are budgeted as follows.

	Month 1	*Month 2*	*Month 3*	*Month 4*	*Month 5*
Budgeted sales units	340	420	290	230	210

Company policy is to hold in inventory at the end of each month sufficient units of product G to satisfy budgeted sales demand for the forthcoming 2 months.

Test your understanding 32

The budgeted production of product G in month 2 is ______ units.

Test your understanding 33

Each unit of product G uses 2 litres of liquid K. Company policy is to hold in inventory at the end of each month sufficient liquid K for the production requirements of the forthcoming month.

The budgeted purchases of liquid K in month 2 are _______ litres.

Test your understanding 34

The following data have been extracted from the budget working papers of GY Limited.

Production volume (units)	2,000	3,000
	$ per unit	$ per unit
Direct materials	6.00	6.00
Direct labour	7.50	7.50
Production overhead – department A	13.50	9.00
Production overhead – department B	7.80	5.80

(a) The total budgeted variable cost per unit is $ ________.

(b) The total budgeted fixed cost per period is $ ________.

Test your understanding 35

Data for product W are as follows.

Direct material cost per unit	$22
Direct labour cost per unit	$65
Direct labour hours per unit	5 hours
Production overhead absorption rate	$3 per direct labour hour
Mark-up for non-production overhead costs	8% of total production cost

The company requires a 15% return on sales revenue from all products.

The selling price per unit of product W, to the nearest cent, is $ ________.

Test your understanding 36

M plc makes two products – M1 and M2 – budgeted details of which are as follows:

	M1	*M2*
	$	$
Selling price	10.00	8.00
Costs per unit:		
Direct materials	2.50	3.00
Direct labour	1.50	1.00
Variable overhead	0.60	0.40
Fixed overhead	1.20	1.00
Profit per unit	4.20	2.60
Budgeted production and sales for the year are:	10,000 units	12,500 units

The fixed overhead shown above comprises both general and specific fixed overhead costs. The general fixed overhead cost has been attributed to units of M1 and M2 on the basis of direct labour cost. The specific fixed cost totals $2,500 per annum and relates to product M2 only.

Both products are available from an external supplier. If M plc could purchase only one of them, the maximum price which should be paid per unit of M1 or M2 instead of internal manufacture would be:

	M1	*M2*
A	$4.60	$4.40
B	$4.20	$2.60
C	$4.60	$4.60
D	$5.40	$3.60

Test your understanding 37

G repairs electronic calculators. The wages budget for the last period was based on a standard repair time of 24 minutes per calculator and a standard wage rate of $10.60 per hour.

Following the end of the budget period, it was reported that:

Number of repairs	31,000
Labour rate variance	$3,100 (A)
Labour efficiency variance	Nil

Based on the above information, the actual wage rate per hour during the period was $ _______.

Test your understanding 38

Which ONE of the following factors could explain a favourable direct material usage variance?

A More staff were recruited to inspect for quality, resulting in a higher rejection rate

B When estimating the standard product cost, usage of material had been set using ideal standards

C The company had reduced training of production workers as part of a cost reduction exercise

D The material price variance was adverse

Test your understanding 39

A company produces a single product B. The company budgets to sell 2,200 units of product B during period 4 and sales are budgeted to be 10% higher in period 5. It is company policy to hold inventories of finished goods equal to 20% of the following period's sales.

The budgeted production of product B for period 4 is _______ units.

Test your understanding 40

The following extract is taken from the delivery cost budget of D Limited:

Miles travelled	4,000	5,500
Delivery cost	$9,800	$10,475

The flexible budget cost allowance for 6,200 miles travelled is $ _______.

Data for Questions 41 to 45.

Extracts from the standard cost card for product C are as given:

	$ per unit
Selling price	90.50
Direct labour 3 hours at $14 per hour	42.00
Direct Material 4 kg at $8.10 per kg	32.40

Budgeted sales and production for June were 47,200 units. However a machine breakdown occurred and as a result labour were idle for 150 hours and actual sales and production were 45,600 units.

Actual data for June are as follows.

	$
Sales revenue	4,058,400
Direct labour cost for 134,100 hours, including 150 idle hours	1,850,580
Direct material cost for 184,000 kg	1,490,400

Test your understanding 41

The sales price variance for June is $ _______.

adverse ☐

favourable ☐

Test your understanding 42

The sales volume contribution variance for June is $ _______.

adverse ☐
favourable ☐

Test your understanding 43

The idle time variance for June is $ _______.

adverse ☐
favourable ☐

Test your understanding 44

The labour rate variance for June is $ _______.

adverse ☐
favourable ☐

Test Your Understanding 45

The labour efficiency variance for June is $ _______.

adverse ☐
favourable ☐

Test your understanding 46

A company provides a shirt laundering service. The standard cost and revenue for laundering one batch of shirts is as follows.

	$ per batch
Selling price	23
Materials cost (detergent, starch, etc.)	3
Labour cost	14
Variable overhead cost	1

Fixed costs incurred each month amount to $15,900.

The number of batches of shirts to be laundered to earn a profit of $4,300 per month is ________ batches.

Test your understanding 47

The following information relates to M Company's April production of product K:

	Budget
Units	600
Material per unit (2.5 kg × $51/kg)	$127.50

	Actual
Units	580
Total cost of material purchased and input (1,566kg)	$77,517

The direct material variances are:

	Material Price	*Material Usage*
A	$2,349 F	$5,916 A
B	$2,349 A	$5,916 A
C	$2,349 F	$3,366 A
D	$1,017 A	$3,366 A

Test your understanding 48

Is the following statement *true* or *false?*

Professional behaviour and Confidentiality are two of the fundamental principles from the CIMA code of ethics.

Test your understanding 49

A project requires an initial investment of $2.4million. The following cash flows have been estimated for the life of the project:

Year	*Cash flow*
1	$500,000
2	$700,000
3	$900,000
4	$450,000
5	$200,000

Calculate the payback period in years (*to one decimal place*).

Test your understanding 50

A company purchased a machine four years ago at a cost of $25,000. It is to be depreciated on a straight line basis over five years.

It is no longer used on normal production work and has a scrap value of $2,000.

A one-off contract is being considered which would make use of this machine for six months. The contract would require adjustments to be made to the machine costing $800. At the end of the contract it is estimated that the scrap value would be $1,500.

What is the relevant cost of the machine to the contract?

A $1,300

B $3,300

C $4,300

D $23,500

Test your understanding answers

Test your understanding 1

	Debit	*Credit*	*No entry in this account*
Production overhead control account	✓		
Work in progress account			✓
Finished goods account			✓
Statement of profit or loss		✓	

Test your understanding 2

(a) The margin of safety is shown on the diagram by **k**. This is the difference between the expected sales level and the breakeven point.

(b) m will **decrease** (extra fixed cost = lower profit)
k will **decrease** (extra fixed cost = higher breakeven point = smaller margin of safety)
f will **increase** (extra fixed cost = higher breakeven point)
p will **increase** (p = fixed costs, which have increased)

Test your understanding 3

D

The use of this method suggests the service departments carry out work for each other.

Test your understanding 4

The combination that is certain to lead to over-absorption is **production activity higher than budget** *and* **fixed overhead expenditure lower than budget**.

Test your understanding 5

The costs are all production overheads with the exception of the cost of ingredients, which is a direct cost.

Test your understanding 6

C

The relevant cost of labour is the lower cost of:

(1) the cost of working overtime and

(2) the cost of diverting labour from other work.

Incremental cost of working overtime:	$
Incremental cost of using 400 hours spare capacity	0
Incremental cost of overtime: 100 hours × $12 × 150%	1,800
	1,800

Incremental cost of diverting labour from other work:	
Labour cost: 100 hours × $12	1,200
Contribution forgone: 100 hours × $2	200
	1,400

It would be cheaper to divert labour from other work, and the relevant cost is **$1,400.**

Test your understanding 7

D

(3) is NOT a role of management accounting. It is a financial accounting role.

Test your understanding 8

A = **$715**

B = **$979**

Workings:

Cost per complete unit in process 2 = $22,695/5,100 = $4.45

Cost of abnormal gain units= $4.45 × 220 = $979

Scrap value of normal loss per unit = $120/100 = $1.20

Forgone scrap value of abnormal gain = $1.20 × 220 units = $264

Transfer to statement of profit or loss in respect of abnormal gain = $979 – $264 = $715

Test your understanding 9

Process account = **credit**

Abnormal gain account = **no entry in this account**

Abnormal loss account = **debit**

Test your understanding 10

The value of the closing WIP was **$4,158**.

Abnormal loss = (4,000 – 2,750 – 400 – 700) units = 150 units

Statement of equivalent units

	Total	*Material*	*Labour*	*Overhead*
Finished goods	2,750	2,750	2,750	2,750
Normal loss	400	–	–	–
Abnormal loss	150	150	150	150
WIP c/fwd	700	700	350	280
		3,600	3,250	3,180

	$	$	$
Costs	16,000	8,125	3,498
Scrap value normal loss	(700)		
	15,300		
Cost per equivalent unit	$4.25	$2.50	$1.10

Statement of evaluation of WIP

	$
WIP c/fwd – material (700 × $4.25)	2,975
labour (350 × $2.50)	875
production overhead (280 × $1.10)	308
	4,158

Test your understanding 11

The overtime premium paid to the operator would be **$35.70**.

Overtime = 7 hours
Overtime premium per hour = $5.10
Overtime premium = (7 hours × $5.10) = $35.70

Test your understanding 12

The estimated price notified to the customer for job number 808 will be **$23,446**.

	$
Direct material	10,650
Direct labour	3,260
Prime cost	**13,910**
Production overhead (140 × $8.50)	1,190
Mark up on prime cost (60%)	8,346
	23,446

Test your understanding 13

IRR = 5.4%

H = 10%

L = 5%

N_H = $(173,500)

N_L = $15,150

$$IRR \approx L + \frac{N_L}{N_L - N_H}(H - L)$$

$$IRR = 5 + \frac{15,150}{15,150 - (173,500)} \times (10 - 5)$$

= 5.4%

Test your understanding 14

A

Discounts are received on additional purchases of material when certain quantities are purchased. The graph depicts a variable cost where unit costs decease at certain levels of production.

Test your understanding 15

The estimated cost of carrying out health checks on 850 patients is **$17,625**.

	Patients	*Total cost*
		$
High	1,260	18,650
Low	650	17,125
	610	1,525

Variable cost per patient $= \dfrac{\$1,525}{610} = \$2.50$

At 650 patients:	$
Total cost	17,125
Total variable cost (650 × $2.50)	1,625
Total fixed cost	15,500

Total cost of 850 patients:	$
Fixed cost	15,500
Variable cost (850 × $2.50)	2,125
	17,625

Test your understanding 16

The principal budget factor for a footwear retailer is the **constraint that is expected to limit the retailer's activities during the budget period**.

Test your understanding 17

The estimated cash receipts from customers during the budget period are **$54,950**.

Cash received = Sales + opening receivables – closing receivables
= $(55,800 + 8,500 – 9,350)
= $54,950.

Test your understanding 18

The profit mark-up is **55%**.

cost of sales = Opening inventory + purchases – closing inventory
= $(5,500 + 38,000 – 7,500)
= $36,000.

$36,000 + Mark up = $55,800
Mark Up = $19,800

$$\text{Mark Up\%} = \frac{19{,}800}{36{,}000} \times 100\% = 55\%$$

Test your understanding 19

The appropriate actions are **(ii)** and **(iv)**. These are short term actions to cover a temporary cash shortage. Actions (i) and (iii) would be more appropriate for a longer term cash shortage.

Test your understanding 20

The limiting factor would be **direct labour**.

	X	*Y*	*Z*	*Total*
Material (kg)	20,000	22,000	42,000	84,000
Direct labour (hours)	4,000	4,125	10,500	18,625

Test your understanding 21

First: **product Y**

Second: **product X**

Third: **product Z**

	X	Y	Z
	$	$	$
Selling price	28	22	30
Variable cost	17	13	24
Contribution	11	9	6
Kg	5	4	6
Contribution per kg	$2.20	$2.25	$1.00
Ranking	2	1	3

Test your understanding 22

The margin of safety represents **8.3%** of budgeted sales.

$$\text{BEP} = \frac{\$(430{,}500 + 198{,}150)}{\$11.60 - \$(3.40 + 0.58)} = 82{,}500 \text{ units}$$

$$\text{Margin of safety} = \frac{90{,}000 - 82{,}500}{90{,}000} \times 100\% = 8.3\%$$

Test your understanding 23

These changes will cause the breakeven point to be **79,879 units**.

$$\text{New BEP} = \frac{\$628{,}650}{\$12.25 - \$(3.40 + 0.98)} = 79{,}879 \text{ units.}$$

Test your understanding 24

A performance standard which assumes efficient levels of operation, but which includes allowances for factors such as waste and machine downtime is known as **an attainable standard**.

Test your understanding 25

Over long time periods of several years, supervisory labour costs will tend to behave as **step fixed costs**.

Test your understanding 26

(b), (c), (d) and **(f)** are characteristics of good information.

(b) Understandable
(c) Accurate
(d) Complete
(f) Easy to use

Test your understanding 27

Material control account = **debit**

Work in progress = **no entry in this account**

Material price variance account = **credit**

The price variance is calculated at the point of purchase, therefore, the work in progress account is not affected. The favourable variance is credited to the variance account and debited in the material control account.

Test your understanding 28

The statement is **true**.

Test your understanding 29

Wages control account = **no entry in this account**

Labour variance account = **debit**

Work in progress control account = **credit**

The efficiency variance is recorded at the point at which it arises, i.e. in the work in progress account rather than in the wages control account. The adverse variance is debited to the variance account.

Test your understanding 30

Production overhead will be reported as **$3,660 under absorbed**.

Machine hour rate = $180,000/40,000 = $4.50 per machine hour

	$
Overheads incurred	178,080
Overheads absorbed (38,760 × $4.50)	174,420
Under absorbed	3,660

Test your understanding 31

The prime cost of contract A42 is **$44,720**.

	$
Direct materials	5,500
Direct expenses	14,500
Basic staff hours 1,020 hrs × $24	24,480
Overtime premium 40 hrs × $6	240
	44,720

Test your understanding 32

The budgeted production of product G in month 2 is **230 units**.

Workings:

	Units	
Closing inventory month 2 (290 + 230)	520	
Month 2 sales requirements	420	
	940	
Less opening inventory month 2 (420 + 290)	(710)	
Budgeted production month 2	230	(month 4 sales volume)

Test your understanding 33

The budgeted purchases of liquid K in month 2 are **420 litres**.

Workings:

Purchases each month will be the quantity required for production the following month.

Production in month 3 = 210 units (month 5 sales), therefore, purchases in month 2 will be 210 × 2 litres = 420 litres.

Test your understanding 34

(a) The total budgeted variable cost per unit is **$15.30**

(b) The total budgeted fixed cost per period is **$39,000**

Workings:

Department A production overhead	= fixed cost
	= 2,000 units × $13.50 or 3,000 units × $9.00
	= $27,000
Department B production overhead	= semi-variable cost

Using the high-low method:

Units	*Total cost*
	$
3,000	17,400
2,000	15,600
1,000	1,800

Variable cost per unit = $1,800/1,000 = $1.80

Fixed cost = $17,400 – $(1.80 × 3,000) = $12,000

Total budgeted variable cost = $(6.00 + 7.50 + 1.80) = $15.30

Total budgeted fixed cost = $(27,000 + 12,000) = $39,000

Test your understanding 35

The selling price per unit of product W, to the nearest cent is **$129.60**

Workings:

	$ per unit
Direct material cost	22.00
Direct labour cost	65.00
Production overhead absorbed = 5 hours × $3	15.00
Total production cost	102.00
Mark-up for non-production costs = 8% × $102.00	8.16
Full cost	110.16
Profit mark-up = 15/85 × $110.16	19.44
Selling price	129.60

Test your understanding 36

C

Relevant production costs are those which are variable or, if fixed, are product specific. The relevant costs are therefore:

	M1	*M2*
	$/unit	$/unit
Variable costs	4.60	4.40
Fixed cost: $2,500/12,500 units		0.20
	4.60	4.60

Test your understanding 37

Actual wage rate per hour = **$10.85**

Labour efficiency variance = zero, therefore hours worked = standard hours for 31,000 repairs.

Hours worked = 31,000 × 24/60 = 12,400 hours

Adverse rate variance per hour = 3,100/12,400 = $0.25

Therefore, actual wage rate per hour = $10.60 + $0.25 = $10.85

Test your understanding 38

D

Option D is the only factor that could explain a favourable direct material usage variance. Higher priced material may be of a higher quality than standard with the result that scrap and rejections were lower than standard.

Options A to C are all likely to result in an adverse direct material usage variance.

Test your understanding 39

The budgeted production of product B for period 4 is **2,244 units**.

	Units
Period 4 sales	2,200
Period 4 closing inventory (2,200 × 1.10 × 0.20)	484
Period 4 opening inventory (2,200 × 0.20)	(440)
Period 4 budgeted production	2,244

Test your understanding 40

The flexible budget cost allowance for 6,200 miles travelled is **$10,790**.

	Miles	$
High	5,500	10,475
Low	4,000	9,800
	1,500	675

Variable cost per mile = $675/1,500 = $0.45

Fixed cost = $10,475 – $(0.45 × 5,500) = $8,000

Total cost for 6,200 miles = $8,000 + $(0.45 × 6,200) = $10,790

Test your understanding 41

The sales price variance for June is **$68,400 adverse**.

Workings:

	$	
45,600 units should sell for (×$90.50)	4,126,800	
But did sell for	4,058,400	
	68,400	adverse

Test your understanding 42

The sales volume contribution variance for June is **$25,760 adverse**

Workings:

Actual sales volume	45,600	units
Budget sales volume	47,200	units
Sales volume variance in units	1,600	units adverse
× standard contribution per unit	×$16.10	
	$25,760	adverse

Test your understanding 43

The idle time variance for June is **$2,100 adverse**

Workings:

Idle time variance = 150 hours idle × $14 standard labour cost per hour = $2,100 adverse

Test your understanding 44

The labour rate variance for June is **$26,820 favourable**.

Workings:

	$	
134,100 hours should cost (×$14)	1,877,400	
but did cost	1,850,580	
	26,820	favourable

Test Your Understanding 45

The labour efficiency variance for June is **$39,900 favourable**

Workings:

45,600 units produced should take (×3 hours)	136,800	hours
But did take (active hours)	133,950	hours
Variance in hours	2,850	hours favourable
× standard rate per hour	×$14	
	$39,900	favourable

Test your understanding 46

The number of batches of shirts to be laundered to earn a profit of $4,300 per month is **4,040 batches**.

Workings:

Contribution per batch of shirts = $(23 – 3 – 14 – 1) = $5

Number of batches to achieve required profit = $(15,900 + 4,300)/$5 = 4,040 batches.

Test your understanding 47

A

The materials usage variance is **$5,916 adverse.**

	kg
580 units should use (x2.5)	1,450
Did use	1,566
Usage variance in kg	116 (A)
× standard price per kg	$51
Usage variance in $	$5,916 (A)

The materials price variance is **$2,349 favourable.**

	$
1,566 kg should cost (× $51)	79,866
Did cost	77,517
Materials price variance	2,349 (F)

Test your understanding 48

True. Both are fundamental principles of the code of ethics.

Test your understanding 49

Payback period = **3.7 years**

Year	*Cash flow ($000)*	*Cumulative cash flow*
0	(2,400)	(2,400)
1	500	(1,900)
2	700	(1,200)
3	900	(300)
4	450	150
5	200	350

Payback period = 3 years + (300/450) = 3.7 years

Test your understanding 50

A

Fall in scrap value	$500
Cost of adjustments	$800
Relevant cost	$1,300

Index

Index

Index

Index

W

Z